Contents

Preface

This book is for the amateur videographer who wants to make great looking video productions using home video equipment (probably a camcorder).

You will learn how to:

1. Select, connect, and get the most out of home video equipment.
2. Plan, script, and produce your own shows in a professional manner.
3. Record crisp sound and mix in musical backgrounds.
4. Master creative lighting and color.
5. Rivet viewers with graphics which come alive.
6. Dazzle your friends with special effects from your TV camera.
7. Maintain your own VCR (saving high repair charges).
8. Select and care for videotape.
9. Choose video equipment which is exactly right for *you,* while getting the best price.
10. Prop up wobbly tables and sofas (sometimes two books are needed so buy an extra).

Here are some things this book won't do:

1. Razzle-dazzle you with technical terms and endless details about unimportant things. (I hate it when books tell me *everything* when all I wanted to know was how to get started having fun).

2. Bore you. (Just when I think you're nodding off, I'll crack a joke.)
3. Sound like it was written for doctors or mechanical engineering (The language in this book will be easy to understand, probably because I don't know any big words).

This book gives you a gentle first step into the fascinating world of home video production, with simple straight talk about what you can do and how to do it. You will need no prior electronic or photographic knowledge to read this book. You won't have to be mechanically minded or familiar with any video language. You'll learn the lingo as you go along. All important video terms will be explained, first appearing in SMALL CAPITALS to help you remember them. There will be plenty of pictures and diagrams to clarify and reinforce new ideas. When you finish this book, you will know how to produce your own video shows using many of the techniques that the professionals use.

Biography

Dr. Peter Utz has operated a television studio for eight years, during which time he has produced more than 500 instructional TV programs for the City University of New York. He has published more than 150 articles for journals such as *AV Video, Videomaker,* and *Popular Photography,* and is the author of *Video User's Handbook,* 2nd ed. (Prentice Hall, 1982), *The Complete Home Video Book,* (Prentice Hall, 1983), *Do-It-Yourself Video: A Beginner's Guide* (Prentice Hall, 1984), and *Today's Video: Equipment, Setup, and Production* (Prentice Hall, 1987). He currently supervises the Instructional Media Department at the County College of Morris in Randolph, NJ.

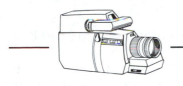

1

How TV works

In the Preface, I promised not to razzle-dazzle you with unimportant technical details. This chapter keeps that promise. It is easy to read and will prepare you with the language and general science background necessary to understand how this electronic chain of machinery all fits together. *Knowing how* things work will help you make sense of all the knobs and meters and cables you will be introduced to later on. It also will satisfy your curiosity about how TV works.

TV SETS

A TV set is a box of electronics and a big, empty glass bottle called a PICTURE TUBE. Some people call this a CATHODE RAY TUBE or CRT. The flat part of the bottle, you've come to know as the TV screen. The neck of the bottle is hidden beneath that bump you see in the middle of the back of every TV set. Inside the neck of the bottle is an electronic gun—sort of a machine gun that shoots electricity. This gun shoots a beam of electrons at the inside face of the TV screen which is covered with phosphor dust. Where the electrons hit the phosphor, it glows. To make a picture, this gun sweeps across the screen from side to side, much as your eyes sweep across each line of this page and eventually cover the entire page. Special SYNC circuits tell the gun how fast to sweep and when to sweep as well as when to stop shooting at the end of a line (just as you stop reading at the end of a line and zip your eyes back to the beginning of the next line). SYNC also tells the gun to stop shooting when it reaches the bottom of a TV screen, then reaims it at the top and starts it shooting again. As the beam zigzags across the screen, another signal (VIDEO) tells the gun to shoot harder or weaker depending on whether it is tracing a lighter or darker part of the picture. By turning up the BRIGHTNESS control on your TV, you tell the gun to shoot harder at the screen thus lighting up the phosphor brighter. By adjusting the VERTICAL hold or the HORIZONTAL controls on your TV set, you adjust the electronics which tells the gun when to sweep and how fast to sweep.

This gun zips its beam across the screen about 15,750 times each second and it starts at the top of the screen 60 times each second. The phosphors keep glowing until the next time the beam comes around and zaps them again. Thus the screen appears smooth and flicker free. European TVs, incidently, retrace themselves only 50 times per second rather than 60 and as a result, European TV flickers more noticeably than American TV. If you look very closely at your TV screen, especially at the light part of the picture, you will be able to see all those tiny horizontal sweep lines that make up the picture. Figure 1–1 diagrams the process.

Actually, when the electron gun sweeps its lines across the screen, it doesn't do all the lines at once. First it does the odd-numbered lines leaving empty spaces for the even-numbered lines. Then it goes back and fills in the even-numbered lines. In the first sixtieth of a second, it will sweep lines one, three, five, seven, and so

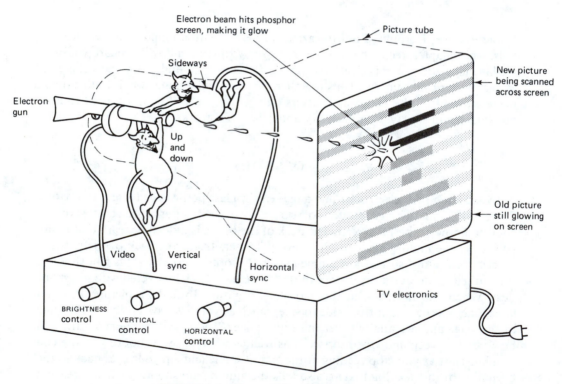

FIGURE 1–1   How a TV set makes a picture.

on, making a total of 262 1/2 lines on the screen. This is called the ODD FIELD. In the next sixtieth of a second, it draws lines two, four, six, eight, and so on, making another 262 1/2 lines on the screen. This is called the EVEN FIELD. Therefore, it really takes a thirtieth of a second to draw each *complete* picture. The complete picture is called a FRAME. Each of these frames are still, but because they go by so quickly, (30 per second) they make the picture appear to be moving. The process is much like what a movie projector does.

TV CAMERAS

A TV camera works like a TV set in reverse. Instead of making light, it senses light.

The camera lens focuses the image of a scene onto a light sensitive PICKUP TUBE in the TV camera. This tube is shaped like a miniature TV picture tube and works in a similar way. The inside surface of the tube is electronically sprayed with electrons which stick to the place where the lens image is projected. Wherever light strikes the tube, the electrons get "bumped off"; thus the light and dark parts of a scene create "bare and full" places on the PICKUP TUBE's surface. If you could see electrons, you would see a tiny picture painted with electrons sitting on the face of the tube. Inside the camera tube, an electron gun zigzags in the same pattern as the TV's electron gun did, only this gun knocks off the remaining electrons as it scans back and forth. As they are shot off, the electrons are collected, counted, and turned into electric vibrations—a VIDEO signal.

So following the whole process from camera to TV: light and dark parts of a scene get projected onto the TV camera tube, the light areas dislodge electrons from the surface creating an image made of electrons. The electron gun in the camera tube sweeps across the surface knocking off the remaining electrons which get measured and turned into a VIDEO signal. This signal goes to your TV set and tells *its* electron gun to "shoot, don't shoot." Thus the light and dark parts of the original scene become "shoot, don't shoot" commands for the TV's electron gun, which creates a light and dark image on the TV screen. SYNC circuits in the camera make a signal (which becomes part of the VIDEO signal) that starts the camera tube's electron gun at the top of the picture and sweeps it back and forth. When the TV set receives the signal, it uses the SYNC signal to start the TV tube's electron gun at the top of its picture at the same moment and makes it zigzag back and forth coinciding with the camera's electron gun. Thus the zigging and zagging of both are SYNChronized and the TV set can create a picture similar to what the camera saw. Figure 1-2 diagrams the process.

Inexpensive older TV cameras use *vidicon tubes* to sense the pictures. More expensive cameras use *saticon, plumbicon,* or *newvicon* tubes for higher quality pictures. Most of today's cameras don't use any tubes at all to sense the picture. Instead, they use an integrated circuit chip about the size of a postage stamp.

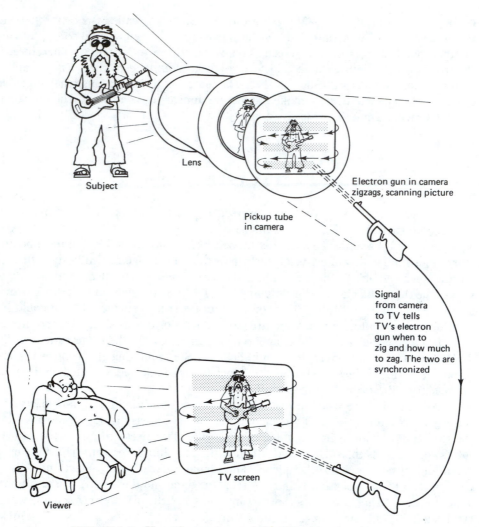

FIGURE 1–2   How the camera and the TV make the picture.

COLOR

In a darkened room, aim a red flashlight at a white wall and you'll see red; turn it off and you'll see black. Shine a blue light on the wall and you'll see blue. Shine green and you'll see green. Shine red and blue together and the colors will mix to create a new color, magenta. Shine red and green and you'll see yellow. Shine all three and you'll get white, as illustrated in Figure 1–3. All the other colors can be made from shining various proportions of these three PRIMARY COLORS.

Circuit chip replaces pickup tubes in newer color cameras. (Courtesy of RCA Broadcast Systems)

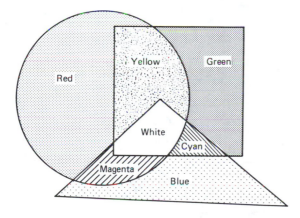

When you shine colors on a wall or light up color phosphors near each other, their colors add, making new colors.

The red circle + the green box = yellow.

The green box + the blue triangle = cyan.

The blue triangle + the red circle = magenta.

Red + green + blue = white. Different proportions of red, green, and blue make up all the other colors.

When mixing paint (rather than projecting light), the colors *subtract*, resulting in colors completely different from the above when they mix (usually various shades of brown).

FIGURE 1-3 Additive color mixing.

A monochrone (black-and-white) TV set makes its picture by electronically projecting black (which is really just the absence of white) and white onto a screen in various proportions. A colored TV makes its color picture by creating three pictures on its screen: one red and black, another green and black, and the third blue and black. Where only red is projected, you see only red. Where red and green pictures overlap on the screen, you see yellow. Where all three pictures are black, you see black. Where all three colors converge with equal strength, you see white.

The picture tubes in color TV sets have three electron machine guns, one for each color. The face of the color TV screen is made of dots or bars of phosphor which shine red, blue, or green when hit by electrons. Look really closely at your TV screen while it's displaying a white picture and you'll be able to see the tiny colored dots or stripes which make up the whole colored picture. As shown in Figure 1–4, the electron gun for the blue color is arranged so that it can only hit the blue phosphors on the screen. The red gun can only hit red, and the green gun, only green. The three guns independently scan a picture onto the screen, and the three pictures overlap to create dazzling views of sea rescues and loose dentures alike.

In the back of some colored TV sets, there are adjustments for these three electron guns. They are used by TV repairmen to weaken or strengthen a certain color, balancing all three so that one doesn't overpower the others and tint all your pictures.

Color TV cameras work much like color TV sets in reverse. Somehow the camera has to make a red, a green, and a blue picture, and combine them into a single VIDEO signal.

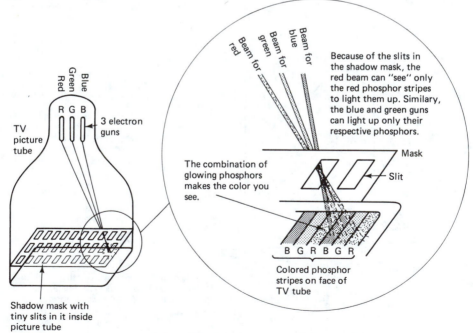

FIGURE 1-4 How TV sets make a color picture.

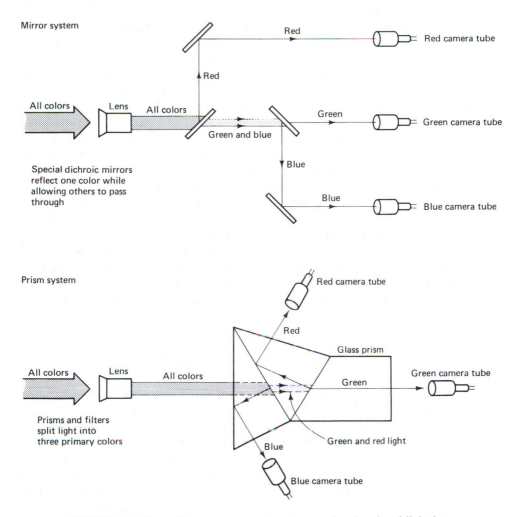

FIGURE 1–5 Three-tube color camera systems to break colored light into its primary colors.

One way to do this would be to have three black-and-white TV cameras, side by side, all taking a picture of the same subject. One camera would look through a red lens and see only the red parts of the picture. Another camera would look through a blue lens and would see only the blue parts of the picture. The third camera, looking through a green lens, would see only green. Thus the three black-and-white cameras could give you a red, a blue, and a green VIDEO signal. To simplify matters, manufacturers have put the three cameras into the same box where they can share some of the same electronics. They also share the same lens and are called THREE TUBE or THREE CHIP cameras. So that each PICKUP CHIP can "see" a particular color, the lens image is split into three images using either two-way mirrors or glass prisms (Figure 1–5). Each image passes through a colored filter so that one PICKUP CHIP sees red, another blue, and another green. These "pure" VIDEO signals are called RGB (red, green, blue) VIDEO and are used by computers, TV projectors, and other devices where super-sharp colored pictures are necessary. But RGB VIDEO requires three wires to carry the three colored signals. To make things simpler, most cameras have a circuit which combines the three colors into a single VIDEO signal which requires only wire. In the U.S., this VIDEO signal is called NTSC (National Television Standards Committee) VIDEO. The TV set at the other end of the wire separates this signal back out into its red, green, and blue components which it sends to the red, green, and blue guns in its picture tube. Because the three picture signals had to be combined to run down a single wire and then had to be separated again, some of the picture sharpness was lost in the process. For this reason, NTSC colored pictures are not as sharp as RGB or black-and-white TV pictures.

Less expensive TV color cameras use only one PICKUP TUBE or CHIP to "see" all three colors. The tube has colored stripes on it much like the stripes on a color TV screen. Red parts of a picture would activate the red stripes on the camera tube. Blue parts would activate the blue stripes, and green parts would activate the green stripes. The electronics in the camera then sense which stripes were activated and turn this information into a color VIDEO signal. Because of the space taken up by the stripes on the face of the PICKUP TUBE or CHIP, SINGLE CHIP color cameras don't give as sharp a picture as THREE CHIP color cameras.

AUDIO, VIDEO, SYNC, AND RF

When a television program is produced, whether "live" or by videotape recording, a camera takes the picture, changing it into an electrical signal called VIDEO. A microphone takes the sound and makes another electrical signal called AUDIO. And a special device called a SYNC GENERATOR creates a third electrical signal called SYNC that keeps the picture stable. When SYNC and VIDEO are electronically combined into an electrical pulse, the signal is called *composite VIDEO*, but most TV people refer to this simply as "VIDEO." The TV broadcaster then combines the AUDIO,

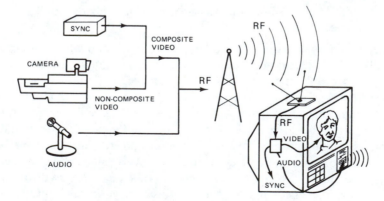

FIGURE 1–6 AUDIO, VIDEO, SYNC, and RF.

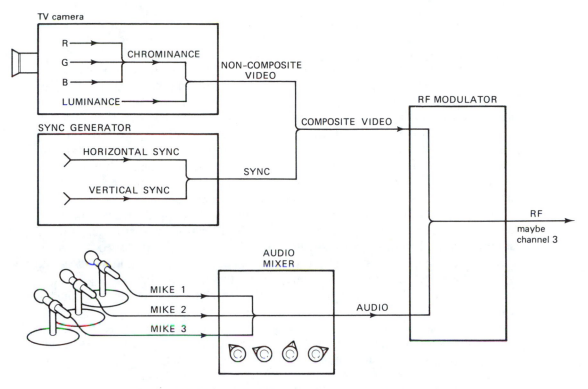

FIGURE 1-7 Combining TV signals onto a single wire.

VIDEO, and SYNC using a device called a MODULATOR, which codes the three into another signal called RF (which stands for radio frequency). The signal is now a channel number, like channel 4. The RF is transmitted, travels through the air, gets picked up by your TV antenna, and goes into your TV receiver. By tuning your TV receiver to a particular channel (the same one that was broadcast), the tuner circuit in the TV set decodes the RF signal and separates it back into VIDEO, AUDIO, and SYNC as shown in Figure 1-6. The VIDEO goes to the TV screen, the AUDIO goes to the speaker, and the SYNC goes to special circuits which hold the picture steady. By adjusting your TV's BRIGHTNESS, CONTRAST, HUE, and COLOR INTENSITY knobs, you adjust the TV's VIDEO circuits. By manipulating the VOLUME control, you adjust the AUDIO circuits. By turning the VERTICAL or HORIZONTAL controls, you adjust the SYNC circuits in your TV.

Television signals may sound confusing until you realize that all you have is just a few basic signals and the rest are merely combinations of these basic signals. Figure 1-7 diagrams how these signals are combined.

The color camera's signal, you'll remember, was really three signals: one red, one green, and one blue. To make them fit on one wire, they were combined to make one VIDEO signal. Coded into that one signal are two kinds of information. The color information is called CHROMINANCE. The black-and-white part of the information is called LUMINANCE. The CHROMINANCE part of the signal tells your TV set what colors to paint on its screen. The LUMINANCE part of the signal actually creates the light and dark parts of the picture.

Just as the color VIDEO signal has two components, the television SYNC signal has two main parts: VERTICAL SYNC which aims the electron gun in your TV set up and down, and HORIZONTAL SYNC which zigzags the gun from side to side. If you misadjust the VERTICAL control on your TV set, you'll see the VERTICAL SYNC signal as a black bar rolling through the picture. Misadjust the HORIZONTAL SYNC control on your TV set and you'll see a vertical bar or diagonal lines going across your picture. Those are the HORIZONTAL SYNC signals. The combination of these two signals holds the TV picture steady on your screen. If either signal becomes weak or is missing, your picture will roll up or down or will tear sideways.

SYNC is made by an electronic clock circuit called a SYNC GENERATOR. SYNC GENERATORS can be built into cameras or can be a separate box wired into the TV studio circuits. Professional ones make not only VERTICAL and HORIZONTAL SYNC signals, but some other SYNC signals with bizarre names like BURST, BLANKING, and SUBCARRIER. Relax; these last three are beyond the scope of this text.

As mentioned before, the VIDEO and the SYNC signals are usually combined to form what we commonly call VIDEO. All this can fit on just one wire.

Compared to VIDEO, AUDIO sounds simple. A microphone or some other audio device makes an electrical signal which can pass down a wire and perhaps be tape recorded. When several microphones are used at once, their signals can be mixed together (using an AUDIO MIXER, naturally) to travel down a single wire.

The next trick is to find a way to combine the AUDIO and VIDEO signals so that the sound and picture can share the same wire. This is where RF comes in. An RF GENERATOR or MODULATOR can combine the AUDIO and VIDEO signals and change them into a TV channel number. All home videotape recorders have a MODULATOR built in and generally change the VIDEO and AUDIO signals into a channel 3 signal which now can be fed to the antenna terminals of any TV set and tuned in by switching the set to channel 3.

One of the great features of RF is that more than one channel can be transmitted on a wire at the same time. You're already familiar with how one antenna wire going to your TV set at home can give you channels 2, 4, 5, 7, and so on with no problem.

The bad thing about RF is that in the process of MODULATING and AUDIO and VIDEO signals together, a little of the picture sharpness is lost. When your TV tuner separates an RF signal back into VIDEO and AUDIO again, the picture sharpness decreases further still. About 10% of your picture sharpness is lost by MODULATING and DEMODULATING it. Figure 1–8 shows an example.

Now that you know a little about how TV works and what the TV signals do, we will focus on particular items of TV equipment. As we study each item, we may examine in further detail how each machine goes about the magic of making television.

(a) RF signal.

(b) VIDEO signal.

FIGURE 1-8 Comparing an RF signal with a direct VIDEO signal.

If this chapter sounds a bit complicated, perhaps you can now appreciate how hard it was to build the first TV. Television wasn't invented all at once; it was the result of one man making something *like* television, and others improving upon the idea until it became TV as we know it today. The invention of television probably started in 1843 when a Scottish watchmaker, Alexander Bain, received a patent for an ''automatic telegraph'' which was able to print out pictures of letters over a telegraph wire. In 1883 a German science student, Paul Nipkow proposed a method of creating images using a spinning disc with holes in it. It was 1925 before John Logie Baird of Great Britain demonstrated a spinning disc system for mechanically transmitting pictures. The same year, C. Francis Jankins was independently doing the same thing in Washington, DC. But these were awkward mechanical devices, able to recreate only fuzzy silhouettes and basic shapes. Meanwhile, Vladimir K.

Plugs, cables, and connections.

Zworykin, in 1923 was busy developing the first TV camera tube (called an icono-scope). Philo T. Farnsworth used a form of one in 1927 when he demonstrated the first *electronic* (as opposed to a mechanical spinning disc) picture transmission system. So who invented TV? Baird and Farnsworth get most of the credit, but both gentlemen were using combinations of machines invented by somebody else.

PLUGS, CABLES, AND CONNECTIONS

There is no way to become a videographer without becoming familiar with the plugs, cables, and other contraptions which carry your signals from place to place. As you play around with video more and more, you will learn how handy it is to have the right cables, the right connections, and to know how to properly name them so your friends can share their video signals with you.

RF Connectors

The most common (but not necessarily the best) way to send signals from your camcorder or VCR to another VCR or TV is via RF (Radio Frequency). As you saw before, a MODULATOR in your VCR will combine your video and audio signals, and change them into a channel number (usually channel 3) and send this signal out

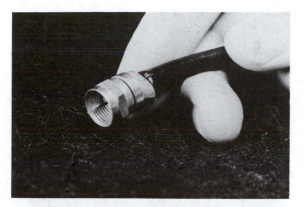

F PLUG

F SOCKET on the back of a TV set

FIGURE 1-9 F CONNECTORS for RF (antenna) signals.

of the VCR through a socket called RF OUT or ANT (antenna) OUT. Usually this signal will travel over a wire called COAX (short for coaxial) which is stiff and round and about the size of a pencil. The connector on the end is called an F PLUG. The F PLUG screws into the F SOCKET on the back of the TV set (or on another VCR) as shown in Figure 1-9.

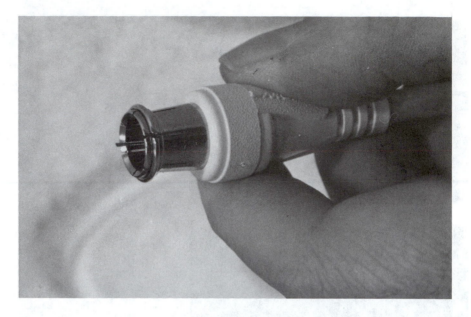

Simple PUSH-ON plug.

Whenever using this wire to connect your VCR to your TV, you will be playing your VCR (which turns your video and audio signals from the tape into channel 3) and sending the signal into your TV's antenna input. You will need to tune your TV to channel 3 for your TV to decode the RF back into its original video and audio signals for you to see and hear. Incidentally, when your VCR is not playing a tape, it is probably receiving antenna TV signals and passing *them* onto your TV which allows your TV to tune in other TV channels. Thus this one wire carries all the TV channels including the VCR's TV channel.

Some older TVs and VCRs don't have F CONNECTORS, but instead use a flat, ribbon-like wire called TWIN LEAD. Just as before, you would run the wire from the VCR's ANT OUT or RF OUT to the TV's ANT IN or VHF IN, placing the wires under the little screw terminals in the back of the machine and tightening the terminals.

Often the wire comes with little SPADE LUGS on the end to make it easy for you to connect the wire to the screw terminals, but sometimes the lugs break off. Or maybe you bought a scrap of TWIN LEAD from your local radio store and it doesn't have SPADE LUGS. In these cases, you make your own connector by shaving the plastic off the ends of the wire. Then you twist the wire a few times and then bend it into a U shape, slide it under the screw terminals on your TV or VCR, and tighten them down. Figure 1–10 shows the process.

VHF and UHF   Notice that you run these wires to the VHF (very high frequency) terminals in the back of your TV set. VHF represents channels 2 through 13. There is another RF signal called UHF (ultra high frequency) represented by

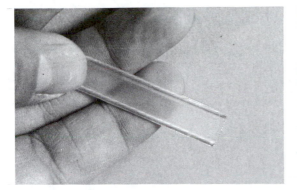

Sometimes the wire ends have no metal showing . . .

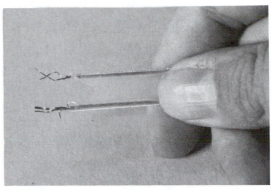

. . . or most of the strands have broken off.

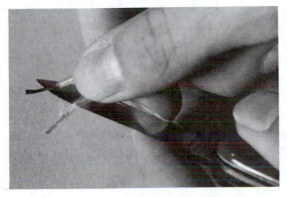

Shave off the insulation revealing bare wires.

Wind wire around antenna screw terminals and tighten.

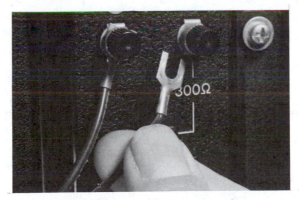

300 Ω TWIN LEAD with SPADE LUGS for easy connecting.

FIGURE 1-10 Connecting TWIN LEAD antenna wires.

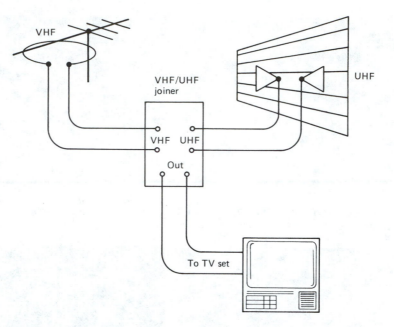

FIGURE 1-11 ANTENNA JOINER combines UHF and VHF signals onto one wire.

channels 14 through 83. Your UHF antenna would connect to the UHF terminals on your VCR or TV, while your VHF antenna would connect to the VHF terminals.

Sometimes, instead of using two wires, TV antenna installers will combine the UHF and VHF TV signals and send them down one wire as shown in Figure 1-11. The device which does this job is called an ANTENNA JOINER, and Figure 1-12 shows two of them. The model on the left uses TWIN LEAD, while the model on the right uses COAX wire.

At the other end of the line, the UHF and VHF signals may need to be separated again so that they may go to the proper terminals on the TV set. You can do this with a VHF/UHF SIGNAL SPLITTER. Figure 1-13 shows how it may be connected up.

Impedance You cannot connect COAX antenna wire directly to the VHF screw terminals on the back of a TV set; nor can you run TWIN LEAD directly to your TV's F CONNECTOR; nor can you directly connect COAX to TWIN LEAD wires. Although both kinds of wire carry the same signals, they have different electrical properties called IMPEDANCE. COAX wires have 75 ohms (75 Ω) IMPEDANCE, and TWIN LEAD has 300 ohms (300 Ω) IMPEDANCE. Seventy-five-ohm antennas, connectors, cables, and inputs are designed to work together; and 300-ohm antennas, connectors, wires, and inputs are designed to work together. So what do you do if you have 75-ohm COAX wire leading up to your VCR or TV which only has a 300-ohm antenna input? You can convert from one IMPEDANCE to another by using an

75 Ω

BAND JOINER
(Courtesy of
Winegard Company)

300 Ω

BAND JOINER
(Courtesy of
Blonder Tongue)

FIGURE 1–12 ANTENNA JOINERS.

adapter called an IMPEDANCE MATCHING TRANSFORMER. A BALUN is another name for this gadget the size of your little finger. Figure 1–14 shows one. You would connect your COAX wire to one end and your TV to the other. Sometimes IMPEDANCE MATCHING TRANSFORMERS are combined with SIGNAL SPLITTERS so that 75-ohm COAX carrying UHF and VHF channels can be converted into separate UHF and VHF signals which can be sent to your TV's antenna terminals as shown in Figure 1–15.

Sending RF to two places at once Sometimes you would like to send your antenna signal (or the signal from your VCR) to two places at once. You can do

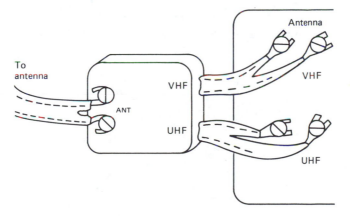

FIGURE 1–13 VHF/UHF SIGNAL SPLITTER.

75 Ω COAX
cable connect
here

300 Ω TWIN LEAD
to TV set

FIGURE 1–14   IMPEDANCE MATCHING TRANSFORMER or BALUN. (Courtesy of Winegard Co.)

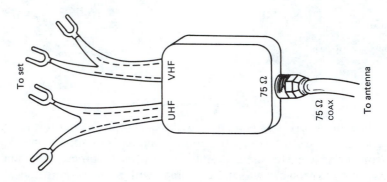

FIGURE 1–15   MATCHING TRANSFORMER which converts 75Ω COAX to 300Ω TWIN LEAD while separating UHF from VHF.

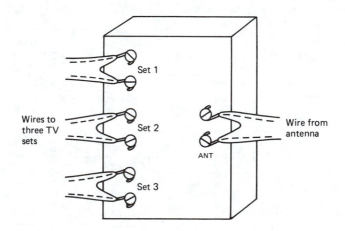

FIGURE 1–16   Connecting a TV COUPLER.

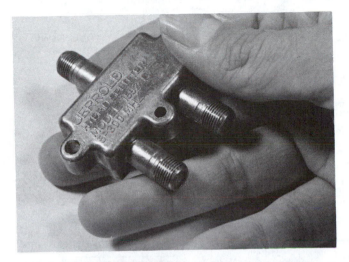

FIGURE 1–17 COAX TV COUPLER.

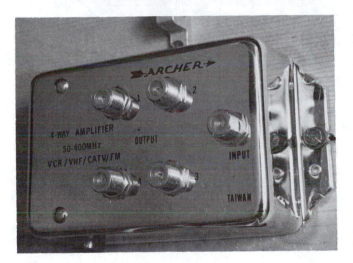

FIGURE 1–18 AMPLIFIED TV COUPLER.

this by using a TV COUPLER (sometimes also called a SPLITTER). One antenna wire comes into the TV COUPLER while several antenna wires come out of it, traveling to other TVs or VCRs. Figure 1–16 shows how to connect up a TV COUPLER and Figure 1–17 shows a common two-TV COUPLER used with COAX wire. You never get something for nothing in this world, and when you divide your signal between two TVs, the signal is only half as strong for each. Sometimes weak antenna signals cannot stand to be divided too many times before the picture gets grainy or snowy, so there are special TV COUPLERS designed to boost the signal while dividing it. Figure 1–18 shows an AMPLIFIED TV COUPLER which uses AC power from your wall outlet to power a small amplifier inside the box, boosting the signal before sending it to the

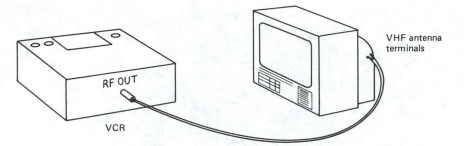

FIGURE 1-19 Playing a tape into a regular TV set.

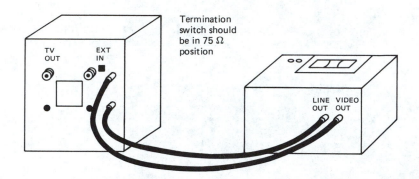

FIGURE 1-20 Wiring separate AUDIO and VIDEO to your MONITOR or MONITOR/RECEIVER.

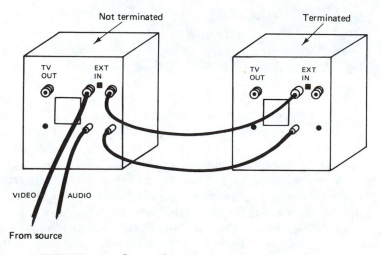

FIGURE 1-21 Connecting two TV MONITOR/RECEIVERS.

four outputs. Using one of these, you can send your cable TV signal, antenna signal, or VCR signal to TV sets in several rooms at once without weakening the signal.

Video Connectors

As mentioned earlier, you can send the VCR's RF signal to the TV receiver's VHF antenna terminals as shown in Figure 1-19 or you can use the better method of sending the audio and video signals separately to a TV monitor/receiver (as in Figure 1-20), if you have one.

Connecting video to two TV monitors at once   Many TV monitors have two video inputs side by side. You may use either. The second input is used when you wish to connect two monitors together to show the same picture. You might do this if you were displaying your TV program to a group of 40 people. Since only 20 people can comfortably view a single 21″ TV set at a time, you would want to use two TVs. Anyway, the process of chaining two or more TVs together is called LOOP-ING or BRIDGING, and the wires are connected up as follows: Feed your VCR's video to the first TV's VIDEO IN, then run another video wire from the first TV's twin VIDEO IN socket to the second TV VIDEO IN. I know it sounds strange to take a signal *out* of a socket called *in,* but that's okay. The first set takes in the signal, uses a tiny bit, and passes the rest along to the next set. The audio connects up the same way.

If you ever choose to LOOP sets together, note that there is one little switch to throw on the back of your TV monitor/receivers. It is called the TERMINATION SWITCH or 75 Ω/HI Z switch. When you are running your audio and video signals directly into *one monitor only,* this switch should be in the 75 Ω position. If, on the other hand, you are running wires to a second TV set from the first, the first TV should *not* be TERMINATED and its switch should be in the HI Z position (away from 75 Ω). All this switch does is allow the signal to easily travel to the next set. If, however, there is no next set, or this is the last set in the chain, then its TERMINATOR should be *on* or in the 75 Ω position. Figure 1-21 diagrams this situation.

Monitors and receivers   Notice that sometimes I have used the term TV RE-CEIVER, and other times I have used the term MONITOR or MONITOR/RECEIVER? Technically there is a difference between these TV sets. A TV RECEIVER is a television set with a tuner. It can pick up channel numbers, but it cannot pick up direct video signals. A TV MONITOR is a TV set *without* a tuner. It can pick up direct video (and sometimes audio) signals, but it has no tuner. You cannot connect a TV antenna wire to a TV MONITOR and expect to get anything. Industrial televisions and more recently some of the better home TVs are MONITOR/RECEIVERS which means that they do both jobs. They can accept antenna signals or audio and video signals. Some TVs have a TV/VTR switch on them which tells the TV which input it is supposed to listen to. Throw the switch in the TV position and the set will listen to its antenna input and you may change TV channels. Switch to the VTR (or sometimes VIDEO)

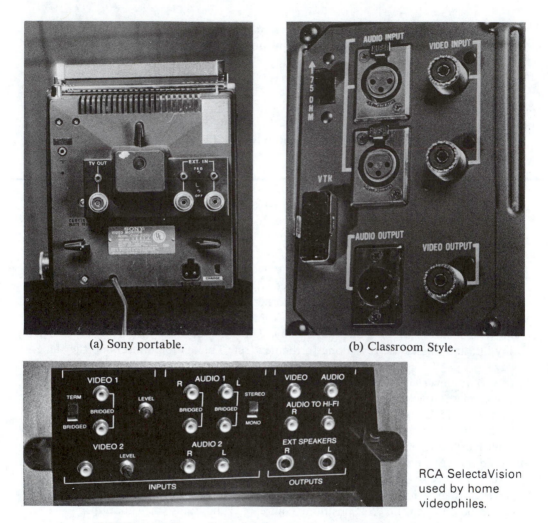

(a) Sony portable.

(b) Classroom Style.

RCA SelectaVision used by home videophiles.

FIGURE 1-22 Rear view of some popular TV MONITOR/RECEIVERS.

position and the TV becomes a MONITOR and listens only to its audio and video inputs.

Some home TVs switch on their audio and video inputs by using a special channel number. For instance, you would punch in channel 13 to watch channel 13, and punch in channel 91 to select the direct audio and video inputs.

Plugs and sockets Figures 1-22 and 1-23 show the rear of some popular TV MONITOR/RECEIVERS. You can see that there are a lot of ways to get a video signal into a TV MONITOR/RECEIVER. The first two examples in Figure 1-22 show

TVs with the older style UHF or SO239 video sockets. The last example in Figure 1–22 shows a homestyle TV MONITOR/RECEIVER which uses RCA or PHONO sockets for its video connections. Figure 1–23 shows a TV monitor with BNC video connectors as well as an 8-PIN connector which carries both audio and video through separate wires in an umbilical cable. Figures 1–24 through 1–26 show close-ups of these common video plugs. The RCA is most commonly found on home video equipment, while the BNC plug is most commonly found on industrial video equipment.

You may notice that the RCA looks the same as the plugs you may have been using in your home hi-fi equipment. Yes indeed, the RCA plugs and sockets are used for home audio gear, too. If you had a few extra video cables hanging around with these RCA plugs on them, you could use the cables to carry video signals from your audio cassette deck to your hi-fi amplifier, if you wanted. You *cannot,* however, use your hi-fi audio cables to carry video signals. The plugs would fit and the signals would travel through the wire, but the signals would be degraded. Your pictures would look grainy and would probably show ghosts and other interference. That is because the video signals need to travel through the special COAX wire to be efficiently transmitted from place to place. Only properly made COAX video cables can do this job right. You may notice from Figure 1–24 the label on the COAX cable,

FIGURE 1–23 Industrial TV with 8-PIN plug.

FIGURE 1-24 PHONO (or RCA) plug and socket. Normally used for AUDIO, most home videocassette recorders use these connectors for VIDEO.

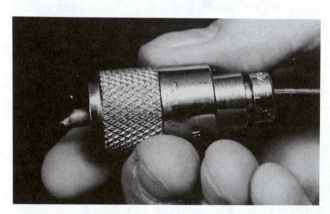

FIGURE 1-25 PL239 or UHF connector used in professional video.

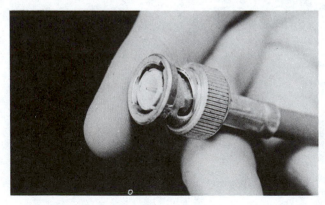

FIGURE 1-26 BNC plug used in professional video.

BNC female
to PL259 male

BNC male
to PL259 female

PL259 female to
PL259 female or
"barrel" connector
used to connect
two cables that have
male PL259s on them

T connector

FIGURE 1-27   VIDEO adapters.

"RG-59/U." RG-59/U is a type of COAX cable. If you see this printed on a COAX cable, you can be sure that it can carry video signals (and RF as well).

Naturally, you will run into situations where one piece of equipment uses RCA connectors while another uses BNC connectors. What do you do? You buy some video adapters which will convert from one kind of connector to another. Figure 1-27 shows some.

I could go on to describe audio cables and plugs, but it's about time to do something more interesting, so I'll save the audio connectors for the audio chapter.

2

How to buy home video equipment at the best prices

What's the best camcorder to buy? Where can I get the best price? I am asked these questions at least once a week. Unfortunately, I cannot spit out a model number and the name of a store to help my friends in their quest for video equipment. Instead I go into a long song and dance which lasts about the length of one chapter of this book.

The reason this question is so hard to answer becomes obvious if I ask you, "What is the best house to buy? Where can I get the best price?" or "What is the best car to buy? Who gives the best deal?" If I asked you these questions, you would naturally come back with more questions, such as "How big a house do you want?" "Do you want a sports car or a pickup truck?"

The best video equipment is the equipment that matches *your* needs. There are very few "dogs" out there; most video equipment works pretty well and is made by reputable manufacturers. The "best" equipment for you, however, is the equipment that does the things *you* want. So first you have to sit down and decide what you want your VCR to do for you. Quality and features, however, don't come free and you will have to balance your desires against the amount you're willing to spend. This process of deciding what you want may take you an hour or so. You may even have to read other parts of this book or read some current video magazines to get a feel for what is available. After that, you may spend another hour searching out the best models and prices (I'll show you a method shortly).

For your two hours' work, you will end up with the *right* equipment for *you,* purchased at the best price you can get.

The process of buying home video equipment has five easy steps:

1. Decide which features you want.
2. Narrow down the search to four or five models which have those features.
3. Get the best price.
4. Avoid sales pressure in the store.
5. Check everything out when you get it home.

Let's go through these steps one by one.

STEP 1 — DECIDING ON FEATURES

All video equipment has features, "bells and whistles" which make one model stand out above competing brands. This is true for TV sets, cameras, and all sorts of video gadgets. For this chapter we are going to concentrate on camcorders, but the techniques described can be used for all other video equipment.

Deciding on features.

It's now time to ask yourself the big question: Are you sure you want a camcorder at all? If you plan to spend 99% of your time watching rental tapes and programs recorded off the air, then maybe what you really want to do is *rent* a camcorder for the few rare occasions when you wish to record your kid's birthday party or to capture that gala two-week vacation trip to Secaucus, NJ.

If you already own a VCR, perhaps you could borrow, rent, or buy a camera for those occasions when you wish to record baby's first steps. All of these options are cheaper than buying a thousand-dollar camcorder and having this expensive investment sit on the shelf. You might even consider buying a used camera and portable VCR combination for your once-in-a-while recordings. Because separate camera-VCR combinations are no longer very popular, and also because used video equipment depreciates rapidly, you will probably be able to buy a good used camera and VCR at a fraction of its original cost. Just make sure you try it out before you take it home.

Select a Format

Once you have decided that you want a camcorder, (or any kind of VCR, for that matter) you have to choose a VCR format. Chapter 3 will tell you more about VCRs, but here is a taste to get you started.

The popular VCR formats today are

Super VHS
VHS HQ
VHS
ED Beta
Beta
8mm (millimeter)
Hi8mm
3/4U
3/4U-SP
Betacam
M2

There will probably be three other formats coming out before this page leaves the typewriter, but at least this is a good start.

Different format VCRs cannot play each other's tapes. You can't play a beta tape on a VHS VCR. Some of the subformats are partially compatible or totally compatible. For instance, you can play a VHS HQ on a regular VHS machine. You can also play a VHS tape on a Super VHS tape machine, but not vice versa: A Super VHS recording won't play on a VHS machine. Two things which are always compatible, fortunately, are the audio and video signals. You can always play a beta

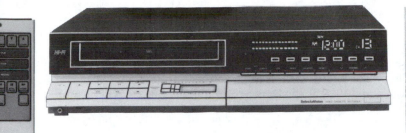

VHS (Courtesy of RCA Consumer Electronics)

VHS cassette

¾U cassette

¾U (Courtesy of Sony Corp. of America)

8mm (Courtesy of Sony Corp. of America)

8mm cassette

Different format VCRs and tape.

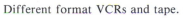

tape and send the video and audio signals to a VHS VCR and rerecord them. Thus, if you have a beta machine and your friends have VHS machines, you can get together and copy your tapes onto their equipment. All of these processes will be described in detail later, but the point here is that you need to select a format for your VCR and this is the most important selection you will probably make.

Let's briefly look at some VCR formats and compare them (there will be more detail in Chapter 3).

VHS   VHS is the most popular video format. Nearly 90% of home VCR owners have VHS machines. That means it will be easy to trade tapes with your friends and the video rental stores will stock plenty of VHS movies. The cassette is somewhat bulky and makes a camcorder somewhat large and heavy. Also, VHS creates a fairly poor picture compared to the other formats. A VHS camcorder will generally record up to two hours onto a tape, but home decks can record six to even eight hours on a single T-120 videocassette, so VHS allows long recordings.

VHS HQ (VHS high quality)   This is an improved version of VHS which is totally compatible with it. HQ stands for high quality and represents improved circuits which make the picture appear sharper. VHS HQ machines cost just a little bit more than regular VHS machines and, unless price is paramount, VHS HQ machines are a better buy than their regular VHS brothers.

VHS-C (VHS compact)   This is a subformat of VHS. It uses a tiny videocassette about the size of a deck of cards which records one-third to one hour per tape. Although the tiny cassette cannot be played directly in a regular VHS machine (and also a large VHS cassette won't fit into the tiny mouth of the VHS-C machine), you can place the miniature VHS-C cassette in an adapter which looks like a regular VHS cassette. Once in the adapter, the cassette will play on any VHS machine. The benefit here is that the VHS-C camcorder can be much smaller and lighter than its regular VHS brothers. The disadvantage is that you always have to mess with this adapter whenever you want to play this compact tape on a regular VHS machine.

S-VHS (super VHS)   Super VHS is another format entirely. The cassette *looks* the same as a regular VHS cassette but the tape in it is special. When the special tape is recorded in an S-VHS recorder, *and then* played back on a S-VHS machine, the results are stunning. You will see an extremely sharp picture and will hear high fidelity sound. S-VHS is the way to go if picture quality is most important. The picture is so good that you can copy an S-VHS tape and then copy the copy and still have a picture that looks better than an original VHS tape. Further, your S-VHS machine will play regular VHS tapes (but without improved picture), and also your S-VHS machine can be switched to the normal mode and can record regular VHS signals on regular VHS tape (to trade with your friends who have VHS VCRs). The only thing you cannot do is play a Super VHS recording on a regular VHS machine. S-VHS machines presently cost more than regular VHS machines.

All in all, S-VHS is the way to go if you plan to copy, edit, or use your tapes professionally. S-VHS camcorders are also available which can record on the miniature VHS-C cassettes. Thus you can get miniaturization plus high quality.

Beta   Beta was Sony's home VCR format. Its picture is about 10% sharper than VHS but beta is no longer sold in the US. Less than 10% of VCR owners have a beta machine. Like VHS, beta can be recorded at several speeds ranging from one to four-and-a-half hours on a tape. Although beta tapes are smaller than VHS tapes, they are still large enough to make the camcorder bulky and cumbersome.

ED Beta (extended definition beta)   ED beta is the only beta format still sold in the US. A special tape recorded on an ED beta machine and played back on an ED beta machine will result in a super sharp picture. An ED beta recording, however, cannot be played on a beta or Superbeta machine. The ED beta machines can play regular beta tapes and can also be switched to a NORMAL mode where they record regular beta tapes.

8mm   Eight millimeter videocassettes are about the size of an audiocassette. The tape inside is eight millimeters wide and can hold two to four hours of recording. Picture quality is about the same as VHS; its big advantage is its size. Because the tape is so small, the camcorder can also be very small. This format competes mostly with regular VHS-C and VHS-C with HQ.

HI8   Just as S-VHS is an improved version of VHS, Hi8 is an improved version of 8mm. The cassette is the same size as its 8mm brother, but contains an improved tape formulation. Hi8 camcorders can record or play regular 8mm or Hi8 tapes, but regular 8mm machines cannot play the Hi8 recordings. Hi8's picture sharpness is similar to S-VHS's.

3/4U (or U-matic)   These industrial VCRs are heavy and popular in business, industry, and schools. Their pictures are a little sharper than regular VHS and their cassettes larger. Recordings can last up to one hour. U-matic (another name for 3/4U) is not a camcorder format, but is the format used by industrial professionals everywhere. 3/4U machines cost $2,000 and up.

3/4U-SP   This is an improved version of the 3/4U industrial format that yields a substantially sharper picture—about as good as S-VHS. Because it is bulky it is not used in camcorders but is becoming popular among industrial 3/4U users because its picture is sharper and the SP tapes are compatible with the regular 3/4U equipment.

Betacam   This is the most popular professional video format. These camcorders make commercial quality pictures, but cost about $40,000.

Features galore.

M2 Less popular than Betacam, this professional video format also makes outstanding pictures appropriate for commercial use. The machines cost $16,000 and up.

D2 This is a recent professional video format whereby the video signal is recorded digitally and capable of repeated copying without degradation. Cost: $75 kilobucks.

From the preceding, you can see that how you plan to use your VCR determines which format to buy. Must the VCR be lightweight, cheap, and compatible with most of your friend's equipment, or should it give you the best picture at any cost? Only you can decide.

Select Important Features

The bells and whistles on camcorders are proliferating faster than anyone can ring or blow them. The trick here is to select those features which are important and useful to you. Here are some camcorder features with a brief description of how these features may be useful.

Minimum illumination   This is the minimum amount of light that it takes to make a picture with a camera. It can be measured in either lux or footcandles (10 lux equals about 1 footcandle). Cameras range in sensitivity from about 7 to 20 lux. A 7-lux camera will work in dim light and is therefore better than a 20-lux camera which requires more light to make a picture. I know it seems backward, but the lower the number of lux describing the camera, the better the camera. Incidentally, these are *minimums*. Using the minimum amount of light will create a grainy picture with poor color, but at least you will see a picture. You often need 20 times as much light to get a decent picture out of most cameras. The more sensitive a camera, the more expensive it will be. You may wish to consider spending $50 on extra lights rather than $200 on a more sensitive camera.

Auto focus   Most cameras have this feature which allows the camera to automatically focus the lens wherever it is aimed. This feature is very handy, especially for nonphotographers, children, and Aunt Martha who needs all the help she can get making sharp pictures. All autofocus cameras can be fooled (although some are better than others) and need a manual override for those special situations where you *want* to focus on one object while making another one blurry, or perhaps wish to defocus your whole shot just for effect.

Lens opening   The larger the lens opening, the more light the lens allows into the camera, and the more sensitive the camera will be in dim light. Camcorder lenses generally range from f1.2 to f1.6 where f1.2 is the better (larger opening) lens. I know the numbers seem backwards, but the smaller the f number, the better.

A lens with a low f-stop number is better.

6:1 zoom ratio.

8:1 zoom ratio.

Zoom ratio   Most cameras have a zoom lens (although a few do not). The zoom lens allows you to go smoothly from a wide angle shot (where everything looks small) to a close-up shot (where you see less but it looks big). The broader this zoom range, the more versatile (and expensive) the lens. Camcorder lenses generally vary from 6:1 to 8:1 in range, where 8:1 is better. The number 8:1 means that the lens can make something look eight times closer when you zoom it in.

Image sensor or pickup   The "eye" of the camera could be a light sensitive tube or a photosensitive circuit chip. Most cameras use the solid state MOS (metal oxide semiconductor) or CCD (charged couple device) chips. Professional tube-type cameras generally give sharper pictures than chip-type cameras. They also generally work in dimmer light. Thus, if you are doing a lot of indoor shooting, you may want a tube-type camera. All tube-type cameras will be damaged if aimed at the sun and will leave temporary streaks on the screen if panned across very bright objects.

Saticon tubes are less prone to this problem than the other types. CCDs and MOS chips, however, are very burn resistant and exhibit almost no streaking. Thus the chip cameras are very durable, making them appropriate for use by children or by your clumsy brother-in-law, Harold, who is likely to aim the camera just about anywhere. The chip cameras are not as sensitive in dim light, however, making them more appropriate for outdoor use.

Chips are smaller than tubes and also use much less power, thus making your camera smaller, lighter, and longer lasting on a battery.

Tubes and chips come in various sizes, one-half inch and two-thirds inch being the most common. The larger the surface of the pickup area, the sharper your picture is likely to be, making the two-thirds inch image sensors the better buy.

Auto iris   Just as you squint when you step out into the sun, your camera has to close its lens opening to reduce the amount of light that enters the camera. The iris (the part with the f numbers) handles this job. Most cameras today have an automatic iris which senses the amount of light and adjusts the camera for it so that the light is never too bright or too dim. Although this is a very handy feature, it is nice to have a manual override which can shut this feature off when you wish to create a special effect or to see something in the shadows which normally would be too dark. Put another way, if you can manually override the automatic iris, you can make the picture as bright as you want it.

Viewfinder size   A few cameras don't have any viewfinders. These cameras are cheap and very lightweight, but when looking through the little telescopic viewfinder, you cannot tell exactly what your *video* picture looks like. Electronic viewfinders, on the other hand, take the camera's electronic image and turn it into a tiny black-and-white TV picture for you to view. Thus you can tell exactly what the contrast and brightness is of your recorded picture, as well as its sharpness. Camcorder viewfinders range in size from about one-half inch to one inch. The bigger viewfinders are bulkier and heavier and more expensive, but yield a sharper picture.

Auto white balance   If you stood in a pink room and placed a piece of white paper on the floor, you could tell that the paper was white. A TV camera, on the other hand, cannot. A TV camera will see a pink piece of paper because of the light bouncing from the walls. All TV cameras have to be taught what the color "white" is in a process called WHITE BALANCE. Older cameras required you to make this adjustment manually, but nearly all camcorders today have AUTOMATIC WHITE BALANCE whereby you press a button and hold it for a moment while aiming your camera at your subject. The camera will automatically make the appropriate adjustments so that white things look white. Some cameras have another feature called CONTINUOUS WHITE BALANCE whereby the white balance is adjusted while the camera is in use. If you were to aim the camera from the reddish interior of your house to the bluish outdoors, this camera would automatically adjust its WHITE BALANCE as you went.

Play in camera   Nearly every camcorder with an electronic viewfinder will allow you to play back your tape and view the results in your camera's viewfinder. This is handy when you wish to review your work as you go along to see if you have to take any shots over.

Scan   This feature allows you to play a tape at several times the normal speed while viewing the picture. Nearly all camcorders have this feature and it is handy for quickly locating events on a tape.

Freeze frame   When the tape is playing, you may press a pause button and hold the picture still. This feature is found on most camcorders today. It is mostly useful when you are playing back tapes to people, and wish to stop the motion in order to study the action.

Maximum recording length   You can generally record from 20 minutes to 6 hours on a tape depending upon the format of the VCR and the tape speed. VCRs with tiny cassettes, such as 8mm and VHS-C models are likely to record the least amount of time. VCRs with full-size VHS tapes can record longer times. VCRs which can record at the slower tape speeds (often called the EP for extra play speed) will record longer but will give poorer picture quality in the process. It is more convenient to have a camcorder which can record a long time. However, you pay for this convenience with bulkiness (larger tape sizes) or poor quality (slower speed used). The best camcorders will work at two speeds allowing you to use the faster speed when the quality is most important and use the slower speed when length of recording is most important.

Dimensions   Naturally, the smaller the camcorder the easier it is to carry. The smaller the mechanism is, however, the more expensive it may be to build, so you pay for this convenience.

Weight   Camcorders weigh between 2 1/2 pounds and 7 1/2 pounds. Naturally, the lighter the camcorder, the easier it is to carry around. If you plan to use the camcorder on a tripod to record weddings, then the weight probably doesn't matter much. In fact, a heavier weight camera is likely to be less expensive and easier to handle; the extra weight makes it more stable. If, however, you plan to trudge into the broiling canyons of Bryce National Park with your camcorder, the apparent weight of this monster will seem to double with every mile you walk. Even 2 1/2 pounds will seem like a lot after a few hours. Incidentally, for comparison sake, a 4-pound camcorder weighs about the same as a half-gallon of milk. How far would you like to carry a half-gallon of milk?

When comparing camcorder weights, make sure that you compare them with the tape and batteries included. It's not fair to compare one model *with* the battery and tape (whose weight adds substantially) with another model not including these things.

The farther you carry it, the more important a camcorder's weight is.

Auto fade   Sometimes it would be nice to fade the picture to black at the end of a scene. Cameras with AUTO FADE can do this at the press of a button. They can also fade up from black to begin a new scene.

Backlight   Sometimes the background behind your performer is lighter than your performer. This will make your performer look dark. If your performer is important and your background is not, it is better to have your background *too* bright and your performer look just right. Some cameras which can manually override their automatic iris will allow you to brighten the whole scene by opening the lens and letting more light in. Other cameras do this with the press of a button, opening the lens just a certain amount to make up for the bright background. Although a manual override to the automatic iris gives you more flexibility in this matter, a BACKLIGHT control is very easy to use and may be preferable.

Date/time/character generator   Some camcorders will allow you to insert the date and/or time over your pictures while you are recording them (or if you made a recording of black, you would just see the date and time). This is handy when you wish to document when a recording was being made. Fancier (and more expensive) cameras and camcorders have character generators which allow you to spell out messages and electronically record them (Figure 2–1). It is much handier to type your TV titles onto an electronic keyboard than it is to mess with papers, magic markers, or stencils to make your titles.

Keyboard with a button for each letter

Image in camera viewfinder

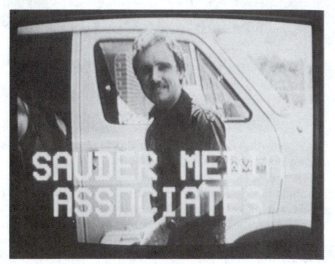

TV screen image

FIGURE 2–1   In-camera titler.

Edit, backspace, or preview   By whatever name you call it, this feature will back up your tape a little ways when you stop recording. When you wish to start recording again, it will play you a piece of your last scene, and when it comes to the end of the scene, will switch into the record mode making a ''clean'' edit. Thus your scenes flow seamlessly together. Also you get a chance to look at the tail end of your last scene, which helps you organize your camera placement for the next scene.

Macro lens   Common TV camera lenses allow you to focus up to four feet from your object. If the subject comes closer than that, it goes out of focus no matter what you do. Cameras with a macro lens can focus on objects up to one inch away, allowing you to take close-up pictures of flowers, postage stamps, slides, postcards, photographs, printed text, and other small things. Although a macro lens is very handy, you can buy lens attachments which screw onto your lens and allow it to do the same thing. Note that while the macro lens is in the MACRO mode, your lens will not zoom. Your zoom function only works in the NON MACRO mode.

External inputs and outputs   The more inputs and outputs your camcorder has, the more versatile it is. If it has an earphone output, you may then listen to the sound as you record your picture. Thus if your mike is picking up wind or other noises, you can solve the problem before going on with your recording. The earphone output also allows you to play back your recordings and check the sound and picture together.

An external microphone input is also very handy. Instead of using the microphone built onto the camera, which generally ends up eight feet away from your performer and picks up your breathing plus all the echoes in the room, you could plug in an external microphone with a long microphone cord and hang the microphone around your performer's neck, getting much better sound.

An audio output would be handy if you wish to play your camcorder sound directly into a TV monitor or amplifier and listen to the sound over loudspeakers.

An auxiliary audio input is handy if you wish to play music from an audiocassette deck, record player, hi-fi, tuner, mic mixer, or some other fancy audio device and record it directly onto the videotape. Although you can sometimes send these audio signals into the camera's external mike input, you get better fidelity if you can send them into a less sensitive auxiliary input. You'll read more about this later.

An external video input (or LINE INPUT) will allow your camcorder to record images from another VCR, from another camera, or from the video output of the TV monitor/receiver.

An external video output will allow your camcorder to play its image into a TV monitor or maybe send its signal to another VCR for copying.

You can see that the foregoing inputs and outputs make your camcorder more like a regular home VCR, capable of taking audio/video signals in as well as sending them out. Camcorders which don't have these features can only record what they "see" through their cameras and can only send their signals out their RF outputs.

The camera's RF output allows it to modulate the audio and video together and change it into a channel number (probably channel 3) which can now be sent to the antenna terminals of a TV for viewing or sent to another VCR for rerecording.

Boom mike   There are lots of ways to attach a microphone to a camera. Since many camcorders nowadays are capable of excellent hi-fi recordings, it is a shame for the microphones to have poor quality. The better microphones are a little larger and stick out on a telescopic boom placing them farther in front of the camera and away from the sounds of the zoom motors and the sniffing and snorting of the camera operator.

Fast shutter speed   When you take a picture of a fast moving object, it generally looks blurry. Some of the more recent chip cameras have adjustable shutter speeds which take quicker pictures, making moving objects appear sharper. This is very handy if you wish to study motion (like a golf swing) in detail.

Resolution   Resolution is the sharpness of your TV picture. It is measured in LINES. The greater the number of LINES OF RESOLUTION, the sharper your picture. Common VHS VCRs can record up to 240 LINES OF RESOLUTION, while Super VHS VCRs can record up to 400 LINES OF RESOLUTION—a much sharper picture.

Image stabilization   Some camcorders have electronically controlled lenses which stabilize your picture as you shoot. They make up for your little wiggles and jiggles.

Digital electronic effects   Some camcorders can produce still frames, wipes, and other video effects digitally within the camera by storing a picture and manipulating it electronically.

Price   Money used to talk. Now it just whispers. Camcorders range from $700 to $2,000 in price, depending upon the brand name, features, and whether the unit is on sale. When you read prices in magazines and charts, they generally list the manufacturer's suggested retail (or list) price. This is the price you expect to pay when a new model just comes out, or if you are buying the unit in a fancy store which gives you lots of tender loving service. If you shop around, you can generally buy your camcorder for a third less than the list price. Still, it is good to use the retail price as a comparative guide between the more expensive and less expensive camcorders. In other words, if one camcorder's retail price is a third less than another's, its sale price will be about a third less than the other's.

Brand name   There are over 35 manufacturers making over 150 different models of VCRs. Although nearly all of them are good, it is sometimes safer to stick with a well-known brand machine because

- More stores will carry the machine, making the price competitive.
- The machine has more reputation behind it.
- Spare parts will be easier to get.
- You are more likely to read reviews about the more popular models in magazines.

Handling   The feel and comfort of using your camcorder is not something that can be listed in a chart or specification sheet. This is a very important feature which you can only experience by picking up the camcorder and using it for a while. Does it feel comfortable in your hand? Does it feel tippy or stable? Is it easy to see the viewfinder? Are the important buttons easy to reach? Are the buttons touchy—

do they activate when you simply brush up against them? The feel of a camcorder is much like the feel of a house or a car. It is definitely a very important feature but one which cannot be put into words.

Now that you understand the more popular camcorder features, it is time to go to the next step, narrowing down your search to a few models which satisfy your needs.

STEP 2—NARROW DOWN THE SEARCH

Now that you know what you want, the next task is to find out who is manufacturing the model that is best for you. This can best be done by looking in one of the popular video magazines such as *Video* or *Video Review* or *Videomaker* or in a consumer digest such as *Consumer Reports*. Each of these journals will periodically print detailed buyer's guides listing the current models and features. Table 2–1 gives an example of what one of these charts might look like, but the data here are old. Only a magazine or booklet is likely to give you up-to-date information on models and prices. The table here is just provided for demonstration purposes to show how to compare features and narrow down the selection.

Note that not every buying guide will list all of the attributes important to you. If the guide happens to be missing crucial features, then hunt for another guide which is more complete. Table 2–2 lists the addresses of *Video, Videomaker, Video Review,* and several consumer magazines should you wish to subscribe.

Sometimes the buying guides include all of the camcorder formats, and sometimes there are separate guides for each format. Use the guides with the formats that appeal to you, or cross out the camcorder models with undesirable formats.

Next you would look through the buying guide and, paying special attention to the features *you absolutely couldn't live without,* cross out any models that don't have those features. For instance, the Sony CCD M7U doesn't have an electronic viewfinder and cannot play your tapes inside the camcorder. If this feature is absolutely necessary for you, then veto the Sony CCD M7U by crossing it out.

Thus we have eliminated the unwanted formats and the models which fail to have a feature that we absolutely must have.

Now, armed with your camcorder buying guide, give a point value to each of the features that are important to you. Write these "importance numbers" at the top of the corresponding feature column in the guide. For instance, if it is crucial that the camera works in low light, then assign three points to the column marked "minimum illumination." If it would be nice, but not awfully important, for the camera to have a manual override to its automatic focus, you might assign one point to the column marked "focus." If a macro lens is pretty important to you, you might give two points to that column, and if low price is extremely important to you, you may give four points to that column.

TABLE 2-1 CAMCORDER BUYING GUIDE

Importance

Manufacturer	Model number	Format	Minimum illumination (lux)	Focus	Aperture	Zoom ratio	Power zoom	Macro lens	Pickup device	Continuous white balance	Backlight	Auto fade	Date/time generator	Viewfinder (size in.)	Tape speeds	Max. record length (min.)	Playback in camera	Scan	Freeze frame	Dimensions (H, W, D, in.)	Weight (lbs.)	Price	Total score
Canon	VM-E2	8MM	8	A/M	f/1.2	6:1	Y	Y	1/2" CCD	Y	N	N	N	E/.7	SP	120	Y	Y	Y	6×6×12	4	1699	
Hitachi	VM5000A	VHS HQ	7	A	f/1.2	6:1	Y	N	2/3" MOS	Y	N	Y	N	E/.7	SP	160	Y	Y	Y	7×6×14	6.4	1695	
Magnavox	VR8297	VHS-C HQ	7	A	f/1.2	6:1	Y	N	1/2" CCD	Y	N	N	N	E/.7	SP/EP	60	Y	Y	Y	6×5×10	3.1*	1899	
Minolta	CR8000AF	8MM	7	A/M	f/1.2	6:1	Y	N	2/3" MOS	Y	N	N	Y	E/.7	SP	120	Y	Y	Y	5×5×13	3.2*	2165	
Panasonic	PV 300	VHS HQ	7	A	f/1.2	8:1	Y	Y	1/2" CCD	Y	N	N	N	E/.7	SP	160	Y	Y	Y	9×15×5	6.9	2000	
RCA	CPR 100	VHS-C HQ	10	A/M	f/1.4	6:1	N	N	2/3" MOS	Y	N	Y	Y	E/.7	SP/EP	60	Y	Y	N	6×5×9	4	1399	
Sony	CCD-V110	8MM	15	A	f/1.4	6:1	N	Y	1/2" CCD	N	N	N	N	E/1	SP/EP	120	Y	Y	N	8×4×15	5.8	1995	
Zenith	VM 6200	VHS-C HQ	15	A	f/1.6	6:1	Y	Y	1/2" CCD	Y	Y	N	N	E/.6	SP/EP	60	Y	Y	N	7×5×9	3.5	1500	
Zenith	VM 7100	VHS HQ	8	A	f/1.6	6:1	Y	N	1/2" CCD	Y	N	N	N	E/.7	SP/EP	480	Y	Y	N	9×6×14	5.3*	1795	
JVC	GR-C7U	VHS-C HQ	15	A	f/1.4	6:1	N	N	1/2" CCD	Y	N	N	N	E/.7	SP/LP	60	Y	Y	Y	7×5×9	2.9	1495	
Sony	CCD M7U	8MM	10	M	f/1.6	1:1	N	N	1/2" CCD	Y	N	N	N	Optic	SP	120	N	N	N	4×4×9	2.1	1450	

*without battery   Focus - A (auto) M (manual)   E - electronic viewfinder

TABLE 2-2 BUYING GUIDES LISTED IN THESE MAGAZINES

Video
P.O. Box 56293
Boulder, CO 80322-6293

Video Review
P.O. Box 57751
Boulder, CO 80322-7751

Videomaker
PO Box 3727
Escondido, CA 92025

Consumer Reports
Subscription Department
Box 53009
Boulder, Co 80321-3009

Consumer's Digest
Box 3074
Harlan, Iowa 51593-4138

Consumer's Research
Box 642
Homles, PA 19043

Once you have finished assigning points to each of the columns, then go through each model and determine how many points it has earned for each of its features. For instance, the Hitachi VM5000A camcorder might earn one point for being an HQ machine, may earn three points for working in a low 7 lux, and may earn no points for failing to have a manual override for its automatic focus. You may have given the Hitachi one point for having a wide aperture f/1.2 lens, and given it one point for having a 6:1 zoom ratio which you wanted. You could give it a one for having a power zoom lens, but would give it no points for lacking a macro lens. Perhaps you didn't care what kind of pickup device it had or the pickup device's size, and perhaps you didn't care if the camera had continuous white balance, backlight control, or auto fade. So, you wouldn't give any scores for these items. Perhaps you would give an extra point to a camcorder having two speeds and since the Hitachi has only one, it gets no points. Since the camcorder's weight is in the middle, it gets no points there, but maybe you give the camcorder two points for being the middle price (rather than very expensive). When this whole process is done, you can add up the points across the row and come to perhaps nine points for the Hitachi VM5000A. Write down the total score for the row.

You would repeat this process for all of the models.

When all the scores are listed, pick the top four or five scores. These are the brands and models you want most. With these top four or five contenders in mind, we progress to the next step, getting the best price for these particular models.

STEP 3—GET THE BEST PRICE

The retail prices you see listed in articles or buying guides are typically 33% higher than bargain basement prices. One notable exception is the "new model" with the hot new feature. These first-of-a-kind machines will command top dollar for several months, depending on the market.

If you shop at the fashionable video boutiques and respectable department stores, you're likely to pay the retail price for your video gear.

It's not always a bad deal to buy retail. Because of their greater profit margin, some retail stores can afford to hire more expert salespeople who can assist the novice in selecting the best equipment. If service, attention, and tender loving care are what you are after, then the malls and classy retail stores are the place for you.

If, on the other hand, you want the down-and-dirty best price in the country, read on 'cause here's how to get it. The process will take about 45 minutes. It's not for the timid! It goes like this:

1. Phone about 10 discount houses and get price quotes.
2. Contact your local discount houses (the ones that advertise in your area that they'll beat any price) and see if they have any of the models you want.
3. Get the discount houses to bid against each other.

Let's look at this process in more detail.

Phone Discount Houses

Any issue of *Video Review, Videomaker,* or *Video* magazine will be filled with ads for camcorder and VCR discount houses. Some of these ads will even list prices of models you will want, but most will tell you to phone for a quote. Before phoning them, get yourself organized by making a chart like the one shown in Table 2–3. (Incidentally, don't try to use the chart here since it is way out of date; make your own.)

For your convenience, Table 2–4 shows a list of telephone numbers of mail order discount houses which advertise low prices. Because some of these companies appear and disappear faster than soap bubbles in a laundry tub, you may wish to refer to an up-to-date video magazine to assemble your own current list of companies and telephone numbers.

While paging through the ads in your video magazine, call each of the telephone numbers (many of them are toll free) and ask them if they carry one of the models you want. You might start with, for instance, the RCA CPR100. If they say no, then go on to your next desired model. If they don't carry that one, go on to the next. Assuming you pick brands and models which are popular (one reason for avoiding off brands), the company may give you a quote on one or two of the models on your list. Take this information down on your chart, then go on to the next discounter. *Do not offer to buy a VCR at this time.*

TABLE 2-3 COMPARISON SHOPPING

	RCA CPR 100	Panasonic PV 300	JVC GR-C7U	Zenith VM6200
Retail	1399	2000	1495	1500
Grand Central	998	1098	998	×
Video Direct	950	×	×	×
Empire State	949	1119	889	×
Photron	×	1150	1040	989
Reliable	×	1299	920	949
Electronic Wholesalers	×	×	919	×
NY Camera	989	1139	×	×
Nationwide	×	1159	1139	×
Garden Camera	999	1249	1099	×
Camera World	×	1239	×	×
Olden	998	1088	988	1029
Smile Photo	×	1225	1190	949
Crazy Eddie	998 Jim	1189	998	×
Dirty Harry	×	1219 Joe	989	1029
Videorama	989 Mary	1199	1019	999

TABLE 2-4 MAIL ORDER DISCOUNT HOUSES

B & H Photo	NY 1 212 807 7474 info 1 800 221 5662 orders
Camera World	OR 1 503 227 6008 info 1 800 222 1557 orders
Competitive Camera	NY 1 212 868 9175 info 1 800 544 5442 orders
Consumer's Discount Warehouse	NY 1 800 882 4460
Direct Camera Warehouse	NY 1 212 391 0313 1 800 283 6633
Electronic Mailbox	NY 1 516 759 1943 1 800 323 2325
Electronic Wholesalers	NJ 1 800 444 6300 1 800 247 4654 orders 1 201 696 6531
Foto Cell Inc	NY 1 212 924 7474 info 1 800 847 4092 orders
High Voltage	NY 1 212 564 4410 info 1 800 654 7787 orders
J & R Music World	NY 1 800 221 8180
Le Baron	FL 1 305 577 4469
Mibro	NY 1 212 695 7133 info 1 800 223 0322 orders

(*continued*)

TABLE 2–4   CONTINUED

New York Camera	NY 1 212 695 0697 info
	1 800 777 0499 orders
Olden	NY 1 212 725 1234 info
	1 800 221 3160 orders
Photron	NY 1 212 221 1011
	1 800 444 7283
Planet Video	MI 1 313 467 2235
	1 800 247 4663
Pro Video Distributors	NY 1 516 741 5440 info
	1 800 541 4055 orders
Reliable	NY 1 718 462 9500 info
	1 800 525 9922 orders
Smile Photo	NY 1 212 967 5900
	1 800 372 3700
Super Video (Panasonic only)	NJ 1 800 524 1596
United Video	NY 1 212 397 1081
	1 800 448 3738
Video Depot	WA 1 800 843 3687
Video Direct	VA 1 804 595 2572
	1 800 368 5020
Video Distribution Center	NY 1 212 465 8475 info
	1 800 283 3438 orders
Videoland	TX 1 713 777 5533
	1 800 877 2900
Vidicomp	TX 1 713 440 0040 info
	1 800 622 6599 orders
Wisconsin Discount Stereo	WI 1 608 271 6889

When these dealers quote you a price, ask them if it includes tax and shipping. If it doesn't, find out how much this is (the amount varies considerably from dealer to dealer) and add this on to the machine price before jotting it down. Also you might want to ask if their price includes all factory options in the package. Dealers are supposed to include everything, but some sneaky ones will separate out the batteries, carrying cases, and so on and try to charge you extra for them.

After calling six to ten discount houses, you will have a bunch of numbers to compare. Incidentally, some discount houses may not quote you a price but will ask you what price you got from someone else. It's okay to tell them the price that another discounter offered; this discounter may bid against it on the spot, offering you a lower price. If this happens, take that number down on your chart. Get the name of whoever offers you a price.

When you are finished, now look down your chart to see what the lowest price is for each model you want. Circle that price. That is the base price you are going to start bidding from.

Armed with this information, you are now ready to call your local "cutthroat" dealers, the ones you see on television advertising "We will beat anybody's price."

Contact Local Discount Houses

You may be wondering, why not buy from one of the mail order distributors you just telephoned? You could do that—in fact some will bid against each other (in a process you'll see shortly), driving their prices down even further. One advantage of buying a VCR from outside your state is that you can avoid paying your state sales tax (although technically you are still obligated to pay it to your state when you pay your income tax at the end of the year). The disadvantage of buying from a mail order house is that they sometimes don't have the equipment in stock, (although they always say they do) and you may end up waiting a long time for them to order it, receive it, and transship it to you. During this time they may be holding your money (or may have processed your credit card number) and when you run out of patience, it is sometimes hard to get them to return the money to you so that you can shop elsewhere.

Mail order houses also have the problem of charging you freight. It costs a bit to mail a camcorder clear across the country. Furthermore, if the machine arrives damaged or it doesn't work, it is a big hassle trying to send it back. I personally find it much nicer working with a real human being around the corner—one whom you can talk to, one whose store you can walk into, and one whose boss you can speak to.

For these reasons, I like to deal with someone within an hour's drive from home. Those of us who live in metropolitan areas have a number of "discount" stores to choose from. You can find out where they are by watching the loudest, noisiest, most obnoxious commercials on TV, by viewing their enormous ads in the newspapers, or by checking your Yellow Pages under "Video recorders and players—dealers."

Starting with the first of these dealers, call them up and ask them the following questions in precisely this order:

1. Do they carry the RCA CPR-100 (or whatever the first model is on your list)? If the answer is no, immediately go on to the next model and ask this question again. If the answer is yes, then proceed to step 2.

2. Ask if they have this model *in stock*. If the answer is no, don't bother bargaining with them as the company will have no inclination to order a machine for you if you are bargaining them down to a paper thin profit margin. Simply go on to your next model and start over. That's why you narrowed yourself down to four or five models. If the answer is yes, proceed to step 3.

3. Say, "You advertise that you will beat any price. I have a price of $950 from Video Direct Company (or whatever the amount and company may be). Will you beat that price?" The answer is invariably "yes." If it were no, the false

advertising would be a great embarrassment to the company, so you might even wish to speak to the manager. Generally, however, this is not worth your trouble because there are plenty of companies who are willing to bid against each other without giving you a runaround. (Note, the runaround may come later, as you'll see.)

4. Note their price quote on your chart, and also note the salesperson's name.

5. It takes some guts to do this, but when this round is over and there are still models you haven't asked about, you may wish to start this process again by asking if they carry another model on your list and work your way towards getting a price on that model. The salesperson won't want to talk to you very long, so you should start out with a model you want most and follow with a model you want second most. You may never get to the third or fourth models, even if the stores carry them.

IMPORTANT NOTE: All this telephoning and wheeling and dealing is best done *long* before the Christmas selling season or other holidays. During these holidays the phones are usually busy and so are the salespeople. You will spend a lot of time waiting and get almost no attention. So pick your time carefully.

Get Discount Houses to Bid against Each Other

Once you have your price quotes from your first local dealer, thank the person kindly and *go on to the next. Do not buy anything at this time.* So far, you've probably gotten price quotes $30 to $40 below what you had previously.

Repeat this process from the beginning with the next dealer. Quote the person the prices that the previous dealer gave you and the second dealer will probably beat them by $20 or $30. Remember to deal only in models that the company has in stock. And don't get sidetracked with alternate models or package deals. You can't bid one brand or model against another over the phone; it's like comparing apples and oranges over the phone. Forge ahead unswervingly.

Go on to a third local dealer. When that person tells you that the company will beat any price, he or she now must beat the lowest price you have gotten so far which is, incidentally, a legitimate price that you can back up with a name and telephone number (if you have to).

This process can go on and on, but you will soon discover that each time they beat the previous price they will beat it by a smaller and smaller amount—maybe $5. You have the option of going back to the first dealer and having that person now beat the lowest price you have gotten so far. There is no end to how many rounds you can do, but it is wise to stop before the salespeople get surly. Besides, it only takes three or four quotes to get to the rock bottom price that no one will beat by more than a dollar or two anyway. Plan it so that your last quote is from the discount house nearest you, or the one you like dealing with the best, because that is where you are going to go next—in person, while that salesperson is still in the store and remembers you. Bring your wallet and take a deep breath because the real tension is yet to come. (Great fun, huh?)

STEP 4—AVOIDING TRAPS

No man's credit is as good as his money. When you go off to the store, bring with you your checkbook or cash *as well as* your charge card. It is possible that when bargaining down to the last dollar, a store may be reluctant to accept your charge card (which costs them money to process). Besides, offering to cut a cash or check deal instead of using your charge card may even get you a few more dollars off in some places.

Also, bring with you all of your data: your buying guide charts, your telephone log with the names and prices from the different stores, and any other notes you may have taken. You'll see why in a moment.

By now, you have narrowed down your search to one or two models and probably know which of those you want the most. Walk into the store and find the salesperson you spoke with on the phone. Tell him or her who you are and that you wish to purchase the RCA CPR100 for $989 (or whatever).

In most stores, the sales staff is honorable and will write up your order and hand you your merchandise in a sealed carton. When this happens, do two things: Check the cardboard box before accepting it or leaving the store. Make sure that it doesn't have any big dents or holes, or has not been opened and resealed. Here are the reasons: Some equipment gets damaged in shipping. Usually a dented box is evidence of rough handling. If the box is in good condition, the contents are probably in good condition, but if the box is dented, that's your cue to ask to examine the contents before leaving to make sure that the contents are not physically damaged. You are not checking to see if the equipment works; you are just making sure the machine is not dented, cracked, or damaged in some physical way. The reason for making this inspection *inside* the store is that the paperwork of bringing a damaged item back (and almost every store will take a damaged unit back) is time consuming. Also, the store may have the option of fixing the damaged machine and giving it back to you which is not as desirable as having a perfect machine from the start. If you haven't accepted the machine, you can merely say, "No thank you, I would rather have another one" and avoid all of the hassles.

Here's another reason for checking the cardboard box: Every reputable store will allow you to bring a machine back for repair or replacement within five to seven days after purchase. This is good protection for you if the machine should be defective. But sometimes other people return a machine, getting another, while the store repairs the broken one, repackages it, and sells it to you. The problem with repackaged equipment is:

1. It may not be in as good condition as a totally "virgin" machine.
2. The person who brought the machine back may have lost one or two of the thirty-one little doodads like adapters, wires, free blank tape, carrying straps, and so on, which originally came with the equipment. If you took this repackaged equipment home, opened it up and checked the contents against the instruction manual's list of parts (usually the included accessories are listed on the last page), you may discover some of the parts missing and have a hard time getting the store to replace them for you.
3. If the machine comes without a box or the box has been opened, this may indicate that the machine is a "demonstrator" used for display purposes. Such machines are not desirable either because they may have parts missing or have been tossed around by 183 little kids over the last three months. Unless the machine has been sitting safely on the shelf, it may have been *used,* in demonstrating how it works. The machine, therefore, is "used" equipment, and not "new" and you can argue with the salesperson that the advertising slogan "We will beat any price" does not say that the company is selling only used equipment for lower prices. The advertisement *means* "We will beat any price . . . on new equipment." So hold out for a new machine (unless the salesperson wants to dicker the price down further for the used one and you are willing to take a chance on its condition).

Bait-and-Switch

The most common trick used by cutthroat salespeople is "bait-and-switch" where a company will advertise (in an ad or verbally over the phone) one machine for a fantastic price and then when you get to the store they will tell you that they are out of the item or that the machine is really no good, and try to talk you into buying another brand or model. In most states, the bait-and-switch scheme is illegal, but you can avoid most of the hassles by simply sticking to your guns.

Connie Consumer: "I would like to buy your RCA CPR 100 for the $940 you quoted me over the phone."

Slippery Sam the salesperson: "We've been having a lot of trouble with that model recently. Customers keep bringing them back saying that they are no good. How would you like to try a General Obscurity Model 300 camcorder over here. It costs just $95 more than the one you wanted and is much better."

Connie: "No, I only want the RCA CPR 100, and nothing else, thank you."

Slippery Sam: "No, I really don't think you'll be happy with it. Besides, I'm not sure the RCA is in stock right now."

Connie: "I already checked with you over the phone; it is in stock, and that's the one I want."

Sam: "I tell you what; I'll sell you the General Obscurity for the *same* price as your RCA model. How's that for a deal?"

Connie: "No, I only want the RCA."

Buy only the features you want.

Sam: "I think that, for cash, I can even beat the price of the RCA by $25. And the General Obscurity has many more features than the RCA model."

At this point, the consumer is welcome to open her folder of consumer guides and look up the General Obscurity model which the salesman is pushing. It should take but a moment to see what score was given to this machine and to identify the reason why it wasn't chosen as a major contender. *Possibly,* the General Obscurity has an excellent score (maybe losing by a point or two) and wasn't chosen because of some unimportant reason, making it now a viable candidate against the model that you originally wanted. Now you see why it is important to bring the buying guide with you to the store. You can look up the machine on the spot and compare it feature for feature against the desired machine and immediately pinpoint where it is lacking. And if it isn't lacking anything, maybe it *is* a good deal—one worth taking. Often a store will make a special deal with a manufacturer and buy a large quantity of a good machine to sell at rock bottom prices, beating most of the competition. Much of the time, however, the salesman is trying to push the model which has the greatest profit margin, or the model that the store has the most of (and wants to get rid of), or is pushing a model which comes with an "incentive plan" where the salesperson gets a higher commission on the sales of these units. In these cases, a change has no advantage for you, so you should stick to your guns: "No thank you, I really only want the RCA. Will you sell it to me?"

At this point the salesperson had better say yes or else you can now get a little louder and start reminding the salesperson that the store advertises that it will beat any price. You have a legitimate price that the store agreed to beat, and you now want them to make good on their advertising claims.

Roadblocks

At this point the cutthroat salesperson may dance a few fancy steps. One may be the statement, "But that offer is out of town (or out of state). We can't deal against faraway prices." At this point you may remind the salesperson that the advertisement says, "We will beat any price," and does not say "We will beat any price within five blocks, within five miles, or within the state."

The tricky salesperson may sail another tack by saying, "You have to bring me a written advertisement for that price. It is so low that I don't believe it." Indeed some ads do say "We will beat any published price," in which case you have to show a magazine or newspaper ad to prove your point. If, however, the store advertises that it will beat *any* price, you can simply show the salesperson your telephone log (he or she will be most impressed) and the prices that the various stores were offering. You may encourage the salesperson to call the store (the telephone number is listed right there along with the name of the salesperson you spoke with) to verify the prices you are quoting. This usually convinces the salesperson that you are serious and legitimate (assuming that you are not lying about your data) and it is also likely that the salesperson will know that this price is just a shade above the store's cost.

But there is still one more rabbit in the salesperson's tophat. The person may say, "Listen, if you can go to that other store and buy the RCA machine for that ridiculously low price, then go do so and bring me back the sales slip. When you show me the sales slip, I'll sell the RCA to you cheaper." At this point you should respond, "If I have to leave and go to another store to buy this machine, I'm not coming back, but I'm surely going to let everybody know," raising your voice, "that *you say you will beat anybody's price, and you aren't doing it. This is false advertising,* and I want to see the manager." This is hardball dealing. In reputable stores the runarounds never go this far. The salesperson simply will not let you go out the door without your machine, assuming you have dealt fairly and squarely and have all of your evidence to back up your claims.

The last gasp from the sinking salesperson may be, "But I can't sell the RCA to you at this price; I won't make any money. You're skinning me alive." Well? Do you believe this story? Do you hear violins in the background? Do you expect the dealer to immediately pull the store's "beat any price" ad campaign because of you? No way, because 95% of the consumers fall for one ploy or another before they reach this point. But not you! You read this book. And you did your homework. You're familiar with this game plan. Just hang in there, heart of steel. You're winning.

Warranties

At this point, the exasperated salesperson will sell the machine of your choice at the price you've negotiated, and will be seeing little or no profit. But you are not out the door yet and there is still one way to scoop little extra money from the unwary consumer, the SERVICE CONTRACT.

Virtually all video equipment sold legitimately in the U.S. comes with some form of warranty, a guarantee that if the machine should break down within a limited time, the manufacturer will repair or replace it. The SERVICE CONTRACT or EXTENDED WARRANTY is an *additional* warranty that you can buy for an extra $150 or so which will extend the original warranty up to two years. Generally the *store* sells the warranty and does the maintenance. The wily salesperson will try to talk you into buying this SERVICE CONTRACT, warning you that VCR repairs are very expensive, that the store's service department is excellent, and that you cannot afford to own a camcorder without one.

The truth of the matter is that the stores make a good profit on SERVICE CONTRACTS because new video equipment doesn't break down very often. Generally, new video equipment is likely to fail within the first few days of use (because of a manufacturing defect) and will be covered under the store's "return policy." A few equipment bugs may show up a little later, but still be within the 30- to 90-day manufacturer's warranty. After that period, it is very unlikely that something will go wrong with your equipment unless you bang it around (in which case the abuse is probably not covered by the EXTENDED WARRANTY anyway). EXTENDED WARRANTIES usually only cover two years, a period before the equipment starts to wear out. It is *after* two years that problems start to occur and a SERVICE CONTRACT would become a wise investment.

In short, video equipment is most likely to break down in its first few days of life or in its later years. The manufacturer's warranty already offers the first month (or several months), so an EXTENDED WARRANTY is protecting you during a time when you least need it. There are few people who end up ahead with such a deal, but the salesperson who talks fast enough might be able to scare you into buying the warranty anyway.

One more thought about warranty service: A common sales pitch maintains that *this* store has a better repair department than any other, so you should buy here (for more). But how do you measure "better"? If you can't, should you believe the claim? What salesperson would ever tell you that the store had a terrible repair department? Ask in five stores and they all will tell you their repair department is tops; that the others are slugs. A good repair department *might* be an important factor—if you could only measure it. If you or your friends have had some direct experience with the company, then consider that aspect. Otherwise, plug your ears while the sales pitch drones on. Incidentally, camcorders, if treated kindly, seldom need repairs.

Gray Market

The GRAY MARKET consists of video equipment which doesn't come into the country through normal channels. Perhaps it is meant to be sold in a foreign country and a large stock of machines are purchased there and shipped here for resale. The machines may not have instructions, or the instructions may be in a foreign language. Often the machines have no warranty. Occasionally, they may be incompatible with U.S. video standards or TV channels. Unless you really know what you are doing, you should avoid gray market equipment, even at its reduced prices, because you are buying without much protection from the manufacturer.

This buying process may sound tedious and hardnosed. Indeed it is to some degree; it's business. You shouldn't be frightened, however, by all the negotiations or arguments you *might* encounter. In most cases, the process goes smoothly and the salespeople are friendly. This chapter aims to warn you against the less savory salespeople who may try to intimidate you. If you are ready for them, it is no contest. It is a game in which you know the rules, know the plays, and thoroughly know your options. If you've done your research, know what you want, and know the value of the machine you are buying, the good stores and good salespeople will enjoy doing business with you (at least it will be quick if not profitable). And the trickier stores and salespeople will be up against a formidable customer: you, the educated consumer.

Tricky ads. What brand? What model?

Regular price is $1099.00 Sale price is $999.95, but you have to buy the $99.95 case. You add them up.

What are your chances of scooping up the *only one* in the store?

STEP 5—WHEN YOU GET IT HOME

As soon as you get your machine home, take it out of the box, read the instructions (*really* read them, lazybones)! and try out your machine right away. This is a shake down cruise where you want to try every feature, every button, every accessory, every plug and wire to see if there are *any* defects in the machine. For the next couple of days, use the heck out of it so that if anything *can* go wrong, it will. Also, by becoming familiar with the machine immediately, you become more aware of its "personality" and will be able to detect defects quickly because of your knowledge of the machine. This exercise must occur within the first few days after receiving the machine so that if you *do* find something wrong with it, you can bring it back to the store under their "returns policy" rather than trucking it to an authorized service center or mailing it back to the manufacturer. It's usually easier dealing with the store than it is shipping your machine to faraway places. The store may swap the machine for another on the spot, putting you back in business right away. The manufacturer, on the other hand, may take weeks deciding what to do with your monster.

Incidentally, the store's service department is not likely to know what you paid for the machine and will probably give you the same service that it gives to the rest of its customers (which may be wonderful or terrible depending upon the store). Even after the first week is up, it is wise to use the equipment as much as possible during the manufacturer's warranty period. Again, this is to give the machine an opportunity to fail while somebody else is paying the repair bills.

READING ADS

Newspaper and magazine ads sometimes make things look too good to be true. If you have been diligently studying the features and prices of various models of VCRs, you get a "feel" for what is available. Then, when you look in a newspaper or magazine and see this fantastic offer, your first inclination might be to jump headlong into a purchase. Slow down. Read everything carefully. Here are some of the tricks you may find in published ads. (In fact, read some just for the fun of it. Bet you'll find these tricks everywhere.)

No Brand or Model

These ads say, "Famous brand camcorder. $895. Zoom lens. Electronic viewfinder. Auto white balance." The price looks good, but you still don't know what you are buying. Almost every camcorder has these features. It's the features you are *not* getting that makes the price so low. Sometimes the ad may indicate the brand but not the model. Manufacturers may sell stripped down models of camcorders that easily cost $500 less than the deluxe models.

Package Deals

The ad offers a camcorder and "10 free tapes" for $1,300. Check carefully the prices of the individual items from other stores or from other pages of the store's catalog. Add up the prices and see what you are really saving. Those "10 free tapes" may be counterbalanced by a camcorder selling at list price or $200 above popular "sale" prices.

Unbundling

The manufacturer ships the camcorder and the appropriate accessories all in one box. The instruction manual generally lists what accessories come with the VCR. Some stores will open the box and separate the camcorder from its accessories to sell you the accessories separately. Thus they can offer you an appealing price for the camcorder, but when you add up the cost of all the other parts that make it work (such as batteries, charger, adapters, cables, carrying case) the total cost may be higher than the legitimate sale price of the camcorder in other stores.

Tricky Descriptions

"New" is better, right? Not if "new" is a cheaper, less sophistocated model lacking the bells and whistles of an "older" model.

"Eight-hour VHS" sounds like a better VCR than the standard "six-hour VHS." Actually, all VHSs which use standard sized tapes and operate in the EP (extended play) mode will record for six or eight hours depending upon the thickness of the tape. If ultra thin tape is used (a practice which is not recommended) you can squeeze an extra two hours out of the recording; but this is no virtue of the machine—it only has to do with the tape.

Some camcorders come with accessory tuners allowing the camcorders to record shows off the air. The tuners may be "programmable" but you should check to see if "programmable" means that you can record several shows on several channels over several nights unattended. In some ads the word "programmable" means that the timer will turn your VCR on and off once, period. You'll get one event, one channel, that's it.

"Cable ready" and "cable capable" are two other terms bandied about when talking tuners. Cable ready technically means that the tuner has a screw-on F terminal in the back which can connect directly with a coax cable, such as the type used by cable companies. It does not guarantee that the tuner can pick up cable stations directly without a converter box. It simply means that a *direct* connection between the coax cable and the tuner is possible and that you don't need to use an adapter to change the connection to TWIN LEAD before attaching the wire to the tuner's terminals. Cable capable means that the tuner can actually pick up cable stations directly. Not only will the tuner connect directly to coax wire, but the tuner will tune in the strange frequencies used by cable TV companies when they broadcast their various channels. Nevertheless, the words "cable ready" and "cable capable" are used quite interchangeably and you have to read the fine print to know what they mean.

Incidentally, some tuners are more "capable" than others. One tuner may pick up the regular UHF and VHF channels plus a few cable channels, while another tuner may pick up twice as many cable channels. If the tuner picks up only 68 or 82 channels, then it is *not* "cable capable." You will need a converter box to change the cable signals into something the tuner can understand. If the tuner can receive 95 channels, then it will pick up many of the important cable channels available today. If the tuner can pick up 105 channels (listed somewhere in the fine print), then it picks up most of the important channels and will serve almost anyone's needs. Some tuners are capable of picking up 135 channels. For most cable systems this is overkill, but it may come in handy if the cable companies expand in the future.

"Stereo" doesn't mean hi-fi. Stereo means that you have two channels of sound, one for the left ear and one for the right ear. The sound itself, however, may be low fidelity similar to what you get from a portable radio. The words "hi-fi stereo" mean you get two channels of sound and the sound will be exquisite.

BUYING USED EQUIPMENT

When buying *new* equipment, make sure that you are not receiving used equipment or demonstrators which have been repackaged by the salespeople. Check for dust, fingerprints, or other signs of use.

When buying someone's used equipment, try it out before taking it away. Bring a tape, an AC cord, or whatever is needed to make the item testable.

Be aware of obsolescence. The machine for sale may not have the features you've come to expect from today's models. Also, parts and service may be hard to get. On the other hand, obsolete equipment may be irresistibly cheap and may serve your purposes well especially if you don't plan to swap tapes with your friends.

When buying or selling used video equipment, you can get an idea of the machine's present worth by looking it up in the classified ads in your newspaper or in one of those weekly "Want Ad Press" tabloids. Or you could buy *Video Reference Guide,* Orion Publishing, 1012 Pacific Street, Suite A1, San Luis Obispo, CA 93401, telephone 805-544-3851. It's like a video dealer's "blue book" covering new list prices and used equipment in various conditions.

3

All about VCRs

If this is a book primarily about camcorders, why should you want to know all about VCRs? Here are five reasons:

1. A camcorder *is* a VCR, so the more you know about VCRs, the more you know about camcorders.
2. A lot of the scenes you shoot on your camcorder will eventually be edited on a VCR or distributed for playback on other people's VCRs. By understanding VCRs, you can understand the entire chain of equipment involved in displaying your program.
3. According to statistics, most people who have camcorders already own a home VCR. The more you know about that VCR, the better you can marry its capabilities to your new camcording hobby.
4. Some of you may be buying this book because you hope to go into business with your camcorder. This chapter will give you a little taste of professionalism and increase your understanding of the machinery that makes your pictures.
5. The name of this book is *Making Great Video*. At the heart of this process is your VCR. Successful videomaking requires you to know your VCR backwards and forwards, inside and output.

If you already have a videotape machine, this chapter will repeat a lot of things you should have read in your instruction manual, plus add some tips the instruction manual probably missed. Once you've mastered the videotape recorder, you'll have taken the biggest, most important step toward becoming video literate. Furthermore, the VCR is not a simple machine. That explains why this book has a fat chapter devoted just to the VCR alone.

KINDS OF VIDEOTAPE RECORDERS

Like critters in the ocean, videotape recorders come in all sizes. There are over 35 manufacturers making over 150 different videotape recorders. Professional models cost more than a home while some home models cost just a little more than dinner for four at a swanky restaurant.

VCRs and VTRs

A VTR is a videotape recorder. It can both record and play back a videotape. Technically, "VTR" means only reel-to-reel recorders as opposed to cassette. But people commonly use this term to mean any video recorder, even videocassette recorders.

A VCR is a videocassette recorder. It can record a videocassette or play it back. A cassette (or videocassette) is a small case that holds a full reel of videotape and an empty takeup reel. After the cassette has been inserted into the VCR, the machine automatically draws the tape from the cassette, threads it, plays it, and winds it back onto the takeup reel. You can remove the cassette in the middle of a program (the machine automatically unthreads the tape before it ejects the cassette to you) and come back later to pick up where you left off. Rewinding is not required unless you want the tape to start at the beginning again.

For people who only need to play back tapes and never record them, there are videotape players, VTPs. They don't record, just play. They are handy for libraries and learning centers where tapes are to be played and not accidentally recorded over and erased.

In the early days, all videotape machines were reel-to-reel. Now, everyone uses videocassette recorders. Broadcasters and other professionals are about the only ones using reel-to-reel VTRs nowadays.

Format and Compatibility

When one videotape machine can play tapes made on another tape machine, the two are said to be compatible. Two VCRs which are the same make and model are almost always compatible; they can play each other's recordings. The only time they *wouldn't* be able to play each other's tapes would be when one of them was malfunctioning. It is possible for you to record a tape and play it back on a malfunctioning machine. Like a crazy person who can understand what he's talking about although no one else can, the VCR can record a weird signal and be able to play it back, but another VCR can't. Thus you can never be 100% sure that the recordings you made and played on your machine will work on anybody else's; you can only be 99% sure.

Other than the preceding exception for malfunctioning machines, you should be able to play your friend's tapes back on your machine if the following criteria are met:

1. Both machines must be the same FORMAT.
2. Both must use compatible reels or cassettes.
3. Both the machine and the tape must be playing at the same speed.
4. The recording must be color and the TV monitor must be color for the VCR to display color. Both must be "hi-fi" to provide high fidelity sound.
5. Both must use the same television standard (one can't be a foreign country's standard).

Let's examine these criteria more closely.

Format Tape comes in different widths to fit various videotape machines. Every tape machine can work with only one width of tape. Generally, (but not always) the wider tapes give you a better picture quality and the videotape and tape equipment will be more expensive. There are 1/4-, 1/2-, 3/4-, 1-, and 2-inch tapes. But there is more to FORMAT than just the size. There are tape speed and other electronic differences which make not all 1/2-inch tapes playable on all 1/2-inch machines.

To simplify matters, various manufacturers and video associations have agreed to standardize on several FORMATS. *So, if a tape is recorded on a certain FORMAT machine, it should play back on the same FORMAT machine,* regardless of manufacturer (with a couple of minor exceptions to be discussed shortly).

Table 3–1 describes some of the more popular VCR FORMATS. You will notice from the table that there are expensive high quality professional formats (Betacam, M2, and Type C). There are also medium-priced industrial quality VCR formats (3/4U, 3/4U-SP, S-VHS, ED beta). Then there are the inexpensive home video formats (VHS, VHS-HQ, VHS-C, Beta, Superbeta, 8mm). Even among each format the VCRs vary widely in capability and cost. You can buy a $200 VHS VCR for your home as well as a $2,500 VHS editing VCR for a small studio.

You'll also notice from the table that there are main formats and subformats. The main home formats, for instance, are VHS, beta, and 8mm. These three formats are totally incompatible with each other; you can't play an 8mm tape on a VHS machine. Each format is broken into subformats where partial compatibility exists. You can play a VHS-C videocassette on a VHS machine if you have an adapter cassette; and you can play a VHS-HQ tape on a standard VHS machine, but you won't see the improved picture quality; and you can make a regular VHS tape on a Super VHS VCR, if you throw the switch turning off the Super circuits.

Various formats come in various sizes. Professional Type C VTRs are too large and heavy to be portable. 3/4U VCRs are too large to be used in camcorders, but still can be used portably with a separate camera. The rest of the formats are small

TABLE 3–1 POPULAR VIDEO RECORDER FORMATS

Format	Tape Size	Notes
C	1-inch reel-to-reel	Used by professionals. VTRs cost about $40,000. Tapes can play up to one and a half hours. Very high quality.
Betacam	1/2-inch cassette	Professional camcorder using 1/2-inch videocassettes similar to home beta videocassettes. The recordings, however, are not compatible with home tapes because they are recorded at six times the normal speed, and the signal recorded on them is COMPONENT (the colors are recorded separate from the black-and-white parts of the picture), making the picture extremely sharp. VCRs cost about $40,000. Recordings can be about 15 minutes in length.
M2	1/2-inch cassette	Professional camcorder format using VHS cassettes with a special tape formulation. Although these cassettes look like regular VHS cassettes, they are recorded at six times the normal speed using COMPONENT video and are thus incompatible with home VHS equipment. The picture quality is excellent and the machines cost $14,000 and up. The tapes can record up to 20 minutes each.
3/4U	3/4-inch U-Matic cassette	Industrial and semiprofessional videocassette recorders costing $2,000 to $8,000. Tapes can record up to one hour. Widely used in schools and industry.
3/4U portable	3/4-inch minicassette	Same as 3/4U except a smaller cassette is used lasting about 20 minutes. Although too bulky for camcording, 3/4U VCRs are used portably with separate cameras. The small 3/4U videocassette can be played in standard 3/4U players but a normal 3/4U videocassette cannot fit in the portable VCR's tiny mouth; the portable can only use the miniature 3/4U videocassette.
3/4U-SP	3/4-inch	Superior performance, improved version of 3/4U format making a picture 30% sharper *if* special tape is used and the tape is recorded and played back on an SP machine. Totally compatible with normal 3/4U machines and tape, but when used that way, the picture is no longer improved.
VHS	1/2-inch cassette	Comprising almost 90% of the home VCR market, VHS (video home system) is also popular among industry and schools, not as a mastering medium (where quality is very important), but as a distribution medium where inexpensive duplicates are important. VHS is actually three formats: SP (standard play), LP (long play), and EP (extra-

(continued)

TABLE 3–1 CONTINUED

Format	Tape Size	Notes
		long play), representing the three speeds yielding two, four, or six hours of playing time on a standard T-120 videocassette. A tape recorded at the six-hour speed must be played at the six-hour speed. Not all machines play all the speeds. Most VHS recorders will work at the two-, four-, and six-hour speeds and thus can play all three kinds of tapes. Some industrial editing VHS VCRs will only operate at the two-hour speed (SP); and thus you can't play back a six-hour tape on them. The LP (four-hour) speed is becoming unpopular and there are few tapes recorded this way. When making a recording, you select the VCR's speed (if it works at several speeds) by throwing a switch. When playing back a videocassette, the *machine* determines what speed the tape was recorded at and switches itself to the correct speed to play the tape (if it can). Home VHS VCRs cost $200 to $800. VHS camcorders cost about $1,000 and record up to two hours (SP speed) on a tape.
VHS HQ	1/2-inch cassette	HQ stands for high quality. Because of special circuitry, the VHS recorder makes a picture which *looks* sharper (it isn't *really* sharper, but because it is less grainy, it *looks* sharper). A tape recorded on a regular VHS machine is playable on a VHS HQ machine. A VHS HQ-recorded tape will also play back on a regular VHS machine. In neither case, however, do you get the benefits of the higher quality. An HQ-recorded tape must be played back on an HQ machine for you to see the improved picture. HQ machines cost just a little more than regular VHS machines.
VHS-C	1/2-inch minicassette	Stands for VHS compact, used in smaller camcorders. Tape lasts 20 minutes (SP speed) or one-hour (EP speed). The mouth of a VHS-C machine is too small to hold a normal VHS tape, but a VHS-C cassette can be played on a normal-sized VHS player if you first fit the tiny cassette into a special adapter. In short, a VHS-C videocassette can be played on a normal VHS machine with the help of an adapter which makes the minicassette look like a regular-sized VHS videocassette. VHS-C camcorders cost about $1000.
VHS-hi-fi	1/2-inch cassette	This is a regular VHS format in every way except one; the sound is recorded in excellent high fidelity and coded invisibly into the picture. The

(continued)

TABLE 3-1 CONTINUED

Format	Tape Size	Notes
		sound is simultaneously recorded on the VCR's linear audio tracks. To get the benefit of hi-fi, a VHS hi-fi recorded tape must be played back on a VHS-hi-fi machine. Regular VHS tapes may also be played back on a hi-fi VHS VCR and similarly, hi-fi tapes can be played back on a regular VHS VCR. In both cases, however, you no longer hear hi-fi sound, but the regular low fidelity sound.
S-VHS	1/2-inch special cassette	Super VHS requires a special VHS tape and can record pictures which are 70% sharper than regular VHS. To enjoy the improvement, the S-VHS tape must be used, the recording must be made on an S-VHS recorder, and played back on an S-VHS recorder. An S-VHS recording cannot be played back on a regular VHS machine. An S-VHS machine is capable of making regular VHS recordings (so that you may trade tapes with your regular VHS friends). Also, an S-VHS recorder can play back regular VHS tapes. In both cases, however, you do not see the benefit of S-VHS, but just see a regular VHS picture. S-VHS blank tapes can be used on regular VHS or S-VHS VCRs. Once the tape is recorded, however, an S-VHS tape has pictures viewable only on an S-VHS machine. S-VHS VCRs have a special "S" output which allows the VCRs to be connected to special "S" TV monitors. With the help of this special connection, the monitors will show sharper colors. S-VHS machines can also be used with regular TV monitors and monitor/receivers. TS-120 tapes last two-hours (SP speed) or 6-hours (EP speed). S-VHS VCRs cost about $1,100.
Beta	1/2-inch cassette	Beta comprises about 5% of the home VCR market. Actually three formats, Beta-1, Beta-2, Beta-3, (or X1, X2, and X3, as some call them), represent three speeds yielding playing times of one, two, and three hours (on a common L-500 casssette). A tape recorded at the three-hour speed must be played at the three-hour speed. Most home beta VCRs will play all three speeds, but some industrial beta models will only play the Beta-1 or Beta-2 speed. Beta VCRs are no longer sold in the U.S. Beta cassettes are totally incompatible with VHS cassettes.

(continued)

TABLE 3-1 CONTINUED

Format	Tape Size	Notes
Superbeta	1/2-inch cassette	This was an improved version of beta. The picture is 37% sharper than regular beta if a tape is recorded on a Superbeta machine and played back on a Superbeta machine. Superbeta machines can play regular beta tapes and regular beta machines can play Superbeta tapes, but in both situations, you see a regular rather than an improved picture.
Beta hi-fi	1/2-inch cassette	Similar to VHS hi-fi, the high quality sound is integrated invisibly into the picture. When a hi-fi beta recording is played back on a hi-fi beta machine, you may hear sound with excellent fidelity. Beta hi-fi is totally compatible with regular beta. Thus a regular beta tape can be played on a hi-fi machine and a hi-fi tape can be played on a regular beta machine; however, the sound will no longer be high fidelity.
ED beta	1/2-inch cassette	Extended definition beta is a different format than regular beta. It requires special tape (in a beta type cassette), and if the tape is recorded on an ED beta VCR and played back on an ED beta VCR, you will see super sharp pictures. ED beta tapes, either recorded or blank, are unusable on standard beta machines. ED beta machines, however, can record and play back standard beta tapes. Like S-VHS, ED beta machines have a special output which may connect to a special TV monitor, allowing sharper colors to be displayed. ED beta machines also make sharper pictures on regular video monitors. ED beta camcorders cost about $7,000.
8mm	8 millimeter	Used in ultra miniature camcorders. Standard P-120 tape records two hours (SP or standard play) or four hours (LP or long play speed) and looks like a fat audiocassette. Camcorders cost about $1,000 and can record hi-fi monaural sound. On console model VCRs it is also possible to dub in hi-fi sound after you have finished making your video recording. Certain models also allow you to forgo the picture entirely, replacing it with six simultaneous programs of stereo sound.
Hi8	8 millimeter high band	Recent new format yielding 400–500 lines of resolution in picture sharpness. Hi8 recorded tapes will not play on regular 8mm VCRs; however, Hi8 camcorders can record and play back regular 8mm videocassettes.

enough to be used in camcorders, but some are smaller than others. Full-sized Beta-cam, M2, VHS, and beta formats make fairly bulky camcorders because of the size of the tape cassette. The miniature VHS-C and 8mm cassettes allow these camcorders to be much smaller.

It is possible to combine several subformat features. For instance, you can have a full-sized S-VHS camcorder or you could have an S-VHS-C camcorder with HQ and hi-fi sound.

Foreign standards   A tape recorded in Europe on a VHS recorder will not play on a VHS VCR here in the United States; the electricity is different, and European TVs make their picture in a slightly different fashion. Even though the format is the same, tapes made using different *TV standards* are not interchangeable.

The United States, Canada, Mexico, and Japan use the NTSC (National Television Systems Committee) standard which broadcasts 525 lines of picture every thirtieth of a second and encodes the color in a certain way.

In most of Europe, Australia, Italy, and Singapore the PAL (Phase Alternate Line) system is used, with 625 scanning lines repeated every twenty-fifth of a second along with other changes. There are other variations of PAL like PAL-M in Brazil.

Russia, France, Iran, Poland, Saudi Arabia, and Issas use SECAM (Sequential Color and Memory), which scans 625 lines (except for France which uses 819 lines) every twenty-fifth of a second plus further variations from PAL.

All this boils down to one fact: You can't play most foreign tapes on your VCR even if they are both the same FORMAT.

You can buy TRI-STANDARD videocassette recorders which will record and play back in the three main standards. But just because the recorder can play the foreign signals, it doesn't mean that your TV can display the foreign signals. You also have to use a TRI-STANDARD TV.

There are machines called STANDARDS CONVERTERS which will change one country's standard of TV signal to another country's standard. Because STANDARDS CONVERTERS are so expensive, there are companies who will convert your tapes for you (for about $200).

A company called Instant Replay in Miami, Florida makes modified VCRs which can play back tapes made in foreign standards and the pictures are viewable on standard U.S. TV sets. These modified VCRs cost just a few hundred dollars more than regular VCRs and are very convenient for people who travel a lot or trade tapes with foreign friends.

Video and audio signals compatible   While it is true that a beta tape cannot be played on a VHS VCR, that doesn't mean you can't play a beta VCR's signals into a VHS VCR, recording a VHS tape. It doesn't matter what the FORMAT of the VCR is, the standard audio and video outputs of these VCRs can be fed to any TV monitor or VCR. For instance, if a friend of yours took a miniature 8mm Sony Handicam mountain climbing and you had a VHS VCR, he wouldn't be able to play his 8mm tape on your machine. He could, however, play his tape on *his* machine and you could copy the tape (described in Chapter 9) onto your VHS machine. Now you have a VHS copy which you can share with all your VHS friends.

PLAYING A TAPE

Your boss says, "I have an important client coming over in five minutes. Play him this tape. The equipment is set up. I'll be back in half an hour."

You could read the tape machine's instructions, but they are probably lost. Besides, almost all VCRs work the same. Here's what you do:

1. *Turn on the TV* you will use to watch this presentation. While it is warming up, *turn on the power for the tape player.* A little pilot light will probably

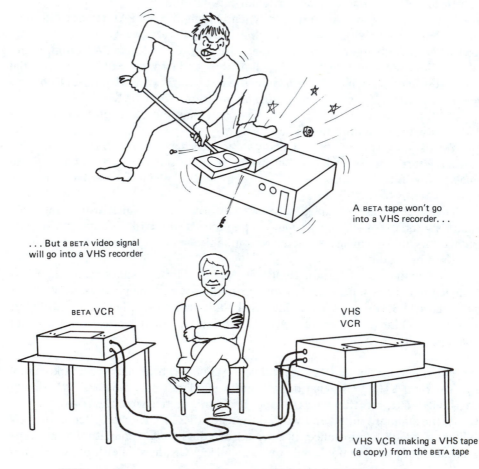

A BETA tape won't go into a VHS recorder...

... But a BETA video signal will go into a VHS recorder

BETA VCR

VHS VCR

VHS VCR making a VHS tape (a copy) from the BETA tape

Different format tapes may not be compatible but their video signals are.

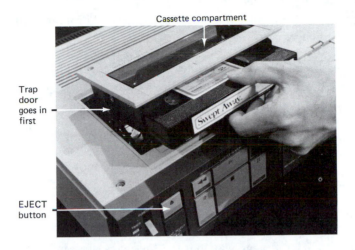

Cassette compartment

Trap
door
goes in
first

EJECT
button

FIGURE 3-1   Inserting videocassette.

come on to tell you the machine is getting power. If it isn't, look for a TIMER SWITCH and flip it off. (When the TIMER is on, the TIMER is in control of the VCR. When it is off, *you* are in control of the VCR.)

2. *Put the tape in the VCR.* First, press the machine's EJECT button and its mouth will open. If a cassette was already in the VCR, it will now be sticking out so that you may withdraw it. Remove the new videocassette from its cardboard box. Holding the cassette so that its label is right side up (readable), *insert the cassette* into the machine's mouth. The little trap door on the cassette goes in first as shown in Figure 3-1. Some VCRs are FRONT LOADING. Instead of a trap door opening, you simply push the cassette into a hole in the front of the machine. A little gate will flip up and out of the way. Then the VCR will "swallow" the cassette and lick its lips.

3. *Press down the cassette compartment* (closing its mouth) until it clicks, locking it into place (chomp!).

4. *Tune in the TV set.* If the VCR is sending its signal to the *antenna* input of the TV set, then tune the set to channel 3 or 4. If the VCR is sending *video* and *audio* to the TV set, make sure the set is switched to LINE or VTR (*not* AIR) or tuned to channel 91 or whatever number activates its direct audio and video inputs. Thus the TV is now "listening" to the VCR.

5. *Rewind the tape to the beginning if necessary.* Do this by pressing the REWIND button. You do not have to hold the button down.

6. *Play the tape.* Press the PLAY (or FORWARD or FWD) button on the VCR to set things in motion.

7. *Adjust the TV.* Loudness, brightness, color, and so forth are adjustments only made on the TV receiver. Stopping, playing, rewinding, and fast forwarding (winding ahead) are all functions of the VCR.

If while the tape is playing, you don't see the desired program on the TV, here are some things to check:

1. Maybe you are on the wrong channel. Try another.
2. Maybe the antenna signal instead of the VCR's signal is going to your TV. Look on the VCR for an OUTPUT SELECT (or TV/VIDEO, TV/CASSETTE, or TV/VTR switch and flip it to VCR—*away from* TV).

Assuming everything is working, rewind the tape to the beginning again so that it is ready for the important client (who invariably shows up four hours later and two minutes before you are ready to go home).

Working the Tape Player's Controls

Not all machines work the same way, but the following are some generalizations.

Most modern VCRs have feather touch buttons connected to the VCR's "brain." You can push any button in any order without fouling up the tape. If the machine is on rewind and you wish to now play the tape, simply push PLAY and the machine does the rest. If the machine does not obey your order, press STOP, wait for the tape to stop, and then press PLAY. The machine will either obey instantly or make you press STOP first and wait until *it* is ready for each command.

On many VCRs, if you press FORWARD or REWIND when the tape is stopped, the tape will move very quickly forward or backward and you will see nothing on the screen. If, however, you are in the play mode, when you press FORWARD the tape will probably scan forward at perhaps six times the normal speed, allowing you to view the tape as you go. If the tape is playing and you press REWIND, the tape will probably scan backwards, allowing you to view the show at six times the normal speed backwards.

PAUSE or STILL makes the tape stop moving but the picture on the TV screen holds still. The image is called a STILL FRAME or FREEZE FRAME. *Do not* stay in this mode for over two minutes. There is a spinning "head" in the VCR that reads the picture off the tape while rubbing against the tape. Too much rubbing in one place

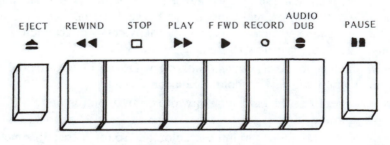

Tape player controls

*FINDING THINGS
QUICKLY ON A TAPE*

wears out the tape. Most VCRs will shut themselves off if you forget and leave them in PAUSE for too long.

Finding Things Quickly on a Tape

As the boss ran out the door, he told you to show the client the part of the tape on "Folding Bathtubs," a new product the company has just perfected. Here's how you'd find that section of the tape: You could play the tape straight through until you came to that part, but that could take you all afternoon.

You could switch the player to FAST FORWARD, let it wind for a minute and then switch it to PLAY to see where you were. If you were lucky enough to catch the middle of the folding bathtub exposition, you might then switch the machine to REWIND for a few seconds and then turn to PLAY again. You could repeat this process until you were at the beginning of the bathtub segment. In most cases, however, trying to find something on a tape this way is very haphazard. You could skip past something in FAST FORWARD and not even know it.

Another way to approximate how far you are into a tape is to look through the window of the cassette. If you know that the folding bathtub segment is near the middle of the tape, then the cassette takeup reel should be about half full.

Most videotape players have FAST SCAN or PICTURE SEARCH capabilities. It's like a FAST FORWARD or REWIND *with the picture showing.* If you FAST FORWARD *near* to where you think the segment starts, you can switch to PLAY and then press the FORWARD SEARCH button to watch the tape at three, six, or ten times the normal speed until you get to the point you want. Note that FAST FORWARD and REWIND are faster than the SEARCH speeds, so that it is best to get *close* to your target using FAST FORWARD or REWIND.

Footage	Contents
000	Violin tuning machine
225	Water hardener
340	Dandruff vacuum
405	Folding bathtub
560	Underwater bicycle
780	Shag carpet shears
900	Spider web remover
950	Infant repellant
1070	Scratch-and-sniff tee shirts
1250	End

All these methods are cumbersome. The best way to find something on a tape is to use the INDEX COUNTER.

Index counter   Nearly all tape machines have an INDEX COUNTER. Working like the odometer of your car, it keeps track of how much tape you have used. The more expensive machines count minutes or feet of tape and are quite accurate. Inexpensive home machines count turns of the takeup reel. Such counters are not very accurate, but at least give you a general idea of where you are on the tape.

Had your boss INDEXED his tape, he would have written something like this on a sheet of paper and put it with the tape or in the tape box:

To use this index, you would do the following:

1. REWIND the tape to the beginning.
2. Locate the INDEX COUNTER or TAPE FOOTAGE COUNTER. By pressing a button or turning a dial nearby, RESET the numbers on the counter to 0000.
3. To view the segment on folding bathtubs, FAST FORWARD the machine to about 400 and then press STOP. Next, press PLAY and watch for the dandruff vacuum section to finish and the folding bathtub section to begin. You may even scan forward to speed up this process.

The index allows you to jump ahead to 900 and examine the spider web remover and then zip back to 225 to view the presentation on water hardeners.

The counters on most inexpensive videotape equipment aren't too accurate and may err by 10%. And if you are using a JVC machine and the tape was recorded on a Panasonic machine, the difference may be as much as 30%. So don't put *too much* trust in the counter.

Most INDEXES do not measure time, making it hard for you to correlate the machine's index numbers with the length of programs on a tape. If you do a lot of searching for things on a tape, you may want to make a little table showing elapsed time versus INDEX COUNTER numbers.

There is an easy way to make such a chart. Start by drawing up a chart that looks like Figure 3–2. Next, aim a TV camera at a clock and hook it up to the video recorder. Walk away and let the VCR record for two hours at the SP mode. Then rewind the tape, RESET the COUNTER to 0000. FAST FORWARD the tape to 100. Play a little and see what time the clock shows. Write down the elapsed time next to the COUNTER number on your chart. Then move ahead to 200 and repeat the process. Do this until you've filled the chart with COUNTER numbers and elapsed times. Now whenever you want to find where the half-hour show ended and the next one began, you would look for the 30-minute mark on the chart and forward the machine to the corresponding COUNTER number. Note that if your cassette player works at three speeds, the one-hour mark at the fast speed will be the same as the two-hour mark at the middle speed and will be the same as the three-hour mark at the slow speed.

Professional and editing videotape recorders often have more accurate INDEX COUNTERS which can count accurately to a thirtieth of a second.

SETTING UP A VIDEOTAPE PLAYER

Suppose your boss didn't have time to set up the videotape player for you before he fled the office, but it's still your job to play his tape for the client.

Before getting into specifics, here are five general steps to setting up *any* video tape player and TV:

1. Check to see that you have a tape player that is compatible with your tape.
2. Somehow you have to get the picture and sound from the tape player to the TV set.

Counter Number	Elapsed Time
000	
100	
200	
300	
400	
500	
.	
.	
.	
.	

FIGURE 3–2   INDEX COUNTER vs. time.

3. Plug the tape player and TV set into a wall outlet and switch their POWER on.
4. You have to get the TV to "listen" to the tape player.
5. Load the tape and play it. A home VCR will automatically determine the right speed to play the tape and will play it if it can. If the tape plays at the wrong speed, that means that the machine *can't* play that speed and you will have to find another VCR.

You may find it handy, whenever you load a cassette, to rewind it to the beginning and RESET your INDEX COUNTER to 0000.

The rest of this ordeal involves quirks in the machinery you are using and is a matter of connecting the right cables and finding the right buttons.

Using a TV Receiver

A TV receiver, you remember, is a TV set which can only accept antenna signals and can't accept straight audio and video. Thus, the only way to get a signal into a TV receiver is through its antenna input. Find an output on the tape player labeled RF OUT, VHF OUT, ANT OUT, or TO TV. Connect the appropriate wire between the tape player's output and the TV's VHF antenna input as was shown in Figure 1–19. If using coax, one F connector will plug into the tape player while the other F connector plugs into the TV. Other systems may use flat twin lead wire between the two. In an emergency, use any kind of spare wire you can find to connect the two. It won't hurt anything and may get you by (without winning any prizes for picture quality, however).

Nearly all home VCRs have built-in RF GENERATORS that send out their signals on channels 3 or 4. The channel number is probably marked on the back or bottom of the video player. For best result, find out what TV channels are received in your area, find the RF switch (it's probably marked CH or CHANNEL) and switch it to a channel which is *unused* in your area. For instance, if your neighbor receives channel 3 and if your RF GENERATOR is also on channel 3, when you use the unit, the two signals will interfere with each other. But by using a vacant channel (channel 4), there is no competition between the signal from your RF GENERATOR and the one from the broadcasting transmitter.

The next step is getting your TV to "listen" to the tape player. Tune the TV set to the proper channel, the one the RF GENERATOR is switched to. Play the tape. Sound and picture should appear on the TV receiver, perhaps after some adjustment of the TV's fine tuning.

Home VCRs often have a switch on them which tells them to send their signal from the tape to the TV. Switch this OUTPUT SELECT or PROGRAM SELECT button to the VTR or VCR mode (*away* from TV). This will tell the VCR to send the signal from the tape to your TV rather than sending the antenna signal (all the other TV channels in your area) to the TV.

Using a Monitor/Receiver

You will recall that a TV monitor accepts direct video (and sometimes audio) signals on separate wires and does not accept antenna signals. It has no tuner. It is in vogue nowadays among video buffs to buy TV monitors because of their high quality picture. Most home videophiles, however, upgrade to a monitor/receiver which can receive both video/audio and RF. Incidentally, if you found yourself stuck with a straight TV monitor for playing back a tape, and the TV monitor had no speaker (some don't), you might manage by wearing headphones or an earphone connected directly to the VCR. Most VCRs have a PHONE or EAR output. (If you have two or three friends trying to watch at the same time, it can get a bit cozy trying to squeeze three pairs of ears under one headphone).

A monitor/receiver can be connected just like a TV receiver by sending RF from the tape player to the monitor/receiver's antenna terminals and switching the receiver to channel 3 or 4. But this does not give as sharp a picture as sending direct audio and video from the tape player to the monitor/receiver. Besides, some of the more professional 3/4U tape players don't have RF GENERATORS built in.

Figure 1–20 showed how to connect separate audio and video cables from a tape player to a monitor/receiver (or monitor with sound). If that didn't entirely confuse you, then we'll complete the process here. Essentially you connect a coax video cable from the tape player's VIDEO OUT or LINE OUT to the monitor/receiver's VIDEO IN or EXT IN. Similarly, you connect an audio cable from the tape player's LINE OUT or AUDIO OUT to the monitor/receiver's AUDIO IN or EXT IN. As before, the monitor/receiver has to be told to listen to those inputs. If the TV has a selector marked TV/VTR/LINE, switch it to LINE. If that doesn't work, try VTR. Other TVs activate their video inputs by switching to a special channel number. You might switch to channel 91 to activate video input 1. You might switch to channel 92 to activate video input 2. Figure 3–3 reviews this process.

MAKING A VIDEOTAPE RECORDING

Unlike industrial VCRs which are designed to do primarily one job—record from a camera or video input—home VCRs are designed to do several jobs:

1. Record audio and video signals from its video and audio inputs.
2. Record TV programs off the air from its antenna input.
3. Allow antenna signals to *pass through it* (as if it weren't there) on the way to a TV set.
4. Tune in a particular channel off its antenna and send that channel signal out its antenna output (or video and audio outputs) to a TV set.

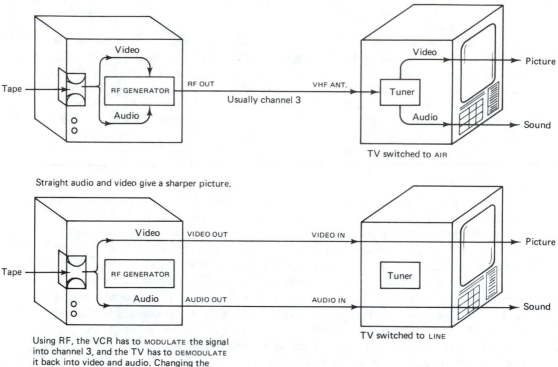

Straight audio and video give a sharper picture.

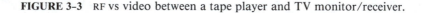

Using RF, the VCR has to MODULATE the signal into channel 3, and the TV has to DEMODULATE it back into video and audio. Changing the signal sacrifices some sharpness.

FIGURE 3-3 RF VS video between a tape player and TV monitor/receiver.

To do these extra jobs, home VCRs have extra buttons. To make sense of all the wiring and switches, we'll study the home VCR in detail for a moment.

Normal TV Viewing

VCRs, with the exception of some portables and camcorders, are designed to connect *between* your TV antenna and your TV set as shown in Figure 3-4. While watching normal TV, the antenna signals travel from the antenna, pass *through the VCR untouched* (the VCR could even be switched OFF), and then travel to your TV which you can watch normally. Just tune your TV to any channel you want.

To watch a tape played back on your VCR, you flip a switch which electrically disconnects the antenna and substitutes the VCR's signal on channel 3 or 4. Turn your TV channel to 3 to watch the tape. Some machines make the substitution automatically (flipping their own switch when you play a tape).

Reviewing, here are the steps you take to watch normal TV with a VCR hooked up:

1. *Turn on the TV set.*
2. *Switch the OUTPUT SELECTOR to TV.* The VCR does *not* have to be turned on.
3. *Select the desired TV channel* on your TV set.

That's all.

Playing a tape

To play a tape, switch the VCR's OUTPUT SELECTOR to VTR (away from TV). This feeds the cassette program to your TV and inhibits the antenna signal. Turn the TV to channel 3 (or 4). Again, some machines flip their own OUTPUT SELECTOR switches when you press PLAY. Figure 3–5 illustrates the process. Press PLAY.

Recording Programs Off the Air

Say your boss just got nabbed by the police. You want to record the event as it unfolds on the Six o'Clock News.

Let's assume that the VCR has been properly hooked up to the antenna and TV (you'll see how to do this later). Essentially you have to tell the VCR what source to listen to (camera, another VCR, or the TV antenna) and what OUTPUT to send to your TV (the show *it's* recording or *some other* show coming in on the antenna).

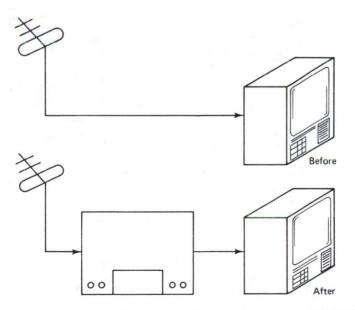

FIGURE 3-4 Home VCRs connect up between the antenna and the TV set.

Playing a tape:

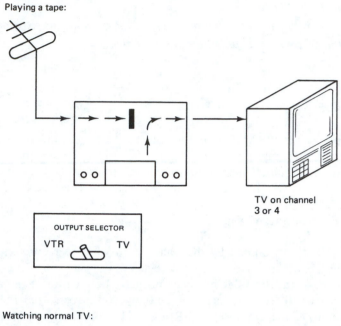

TV on channel
3 or 4

OUTPUT SELECTOR

VTR   TV

Watching normal TV:

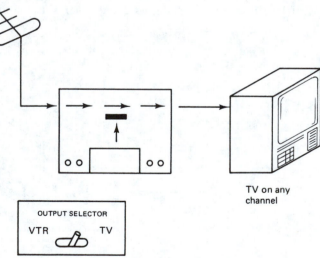

TV on any
channel

OUTPUT SELECTOR

VTR   TV

FIGURE 3-5 Playing a tape vs. watching TV.

You also have to tell the VCR which channel to record and at what speed to record it.

One thing all recorders *will* do by themselves is ERASE the tape automatically as they record.

Warning: If you have something on a tape you wish to keep and you accidentally record a new program over it, your old program will be erased and gone forever. Say you recorded the two-hour movie "A Room with a View" last week and this week you start the tape from the beginning with a new recording of the series "Bronx Zoo." You may get something like "Bronx Zoo . . . with a View". So be sure to label your recordings so that you don't accidentally record over them, erasing them.

Here are the steps to follow to record shows off the air:

1. *Turn on the VCR and TV set.* Tune the TV to the VCR's channel, usually 3. Deactivate the VCR's timer by pressing the button marked TIMER. The timer light should now go off. (With the timer engaged, the VCR won't listen to your commands; it will just sit there like a lump waiting for the *timer* to tell it when to go on.)

2. *Load a blank cassette into the VCR* as described earlier. Make sure that you have the proper length tape for the desired recording time.

3. *Tell the VCR which source to listen to.* The INPUT SELECTOR should be turned to TV.

4. *Tell your VCR what signal to send to your TV.* It's best to monitor the beginning of your recording to make sure that everything is okay. So you will want your TV to receive the VCR's signal that's being recorded. Switch the OUTPUT SELECTOR to VTR.

5. *Set the recorder's speed.* For highest quality picture and sound, use the fastest speed (shortest play time). On VHS machines, this may be labeled SP (standard play—two hours on a standard T-120 tape). If the program is too long to fit on the tape at that speed or if you are a cheapskate who likes to cram as much on a tape as possible regardless of picture quality, switch to a lower speed. On VHS machines, this may be labeled EP (extra play) or ELP (extra long play) or SLP (super long play) depending upon the manufacturers. This will give you six hours of recording on a T-120 tape.

6. *Switch the VCR's tuner to the channel you want to record.* Tuning a VCR is like tuning a TV. Just punch in the channel number, press the right button or turn the dial to the right number.

   (Note: If your antenna signal was poor or your VCR was mistuned, your recording will look bad. Once you have recorded a show poorly, it will remain that way—forever, or until you erase the tape and record something new.)

   If your TV set isn't perfectly tuned to start with, you will have difficulty knowing when you have properly tuned your VCR. You may think your signal is bad when it really isn't. Here is how to avoid this problem.

   First play a tape that you know is good. Tune your TV to channel 3 (or 4) to view the tape. FINE TUNE the TV until the picture comes in best. Now your TV is *calibrated.* Remove that tape and insert the tape you want to record. Press RECORD, if necessary, to get a picture from the VCR's tuner. As you fine tune the VCR, you will see the TV's picture get worse or better. Make it better. From here on do all your FINE TUNING adjustments on the VCR. Incidentally, the tuning of the TV set *will not* affect your recording. The TV could even be turned off. Your TV is just a monitor showing the results. Your VCR's tuner makes the results.

Incidentally, many VCRs and TVs nowadays have automatic fine tuning circuits in them; you can't FINE TUNE them as they FINE TUNE themselves.

7. *Reset the* TAPE INDEX COUNTER *to 000* by pressing the button next to it. Later this can help you find things on your tape.

8. *Start recording* if the TV says your picture and sound are okay. Press the record and play buttons simultaneously (unless your VCR has a single button that does this job).

9. *Check your recording* if you have time. Would you rather know that something was wrong right away or after two hours of recording *nothing?* Before the show starts, follow steps one through eight, recording just 15 seconds of any show. Then play it back. If it is okay, rewind and get ready to record for real. This precaution may sound silly now, but I guarantee it won't after you've lost a few shows.

10. *Rewind the tape* to the beginning when you've finished the recording. Label it.

Recording from Cable

All of the foregoing instructions work out nicely if you are recording from a TV antenna, or if your TV set and VCR are both CABLE COMPATIBLE. If they are not and you are receiving cable TV stations, you may have to use a CONVERTER BOX to convert the cable signals to a channel that your TV and VCR can accept. There are dozens of different ways to connect cable TV converters with several TVs and several VCRs, but they are all beyond the scope of this book. You will find the various techniques described in other Prentice Hall books such as *Do-It-Yourself Video* or *Today's Video.*

Meanwhile, Figure 3–6 shows one way to connect a VCR, TV, and cable CON-VERTER BOX. The CONVERTER BOX goes between the wire from the cable company and your VCR. The signal goes into the CONVERTER BOX and by pressing a button

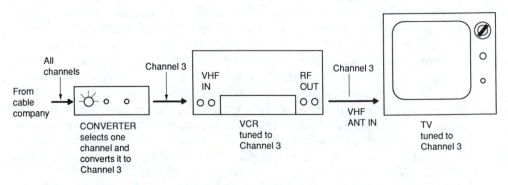

FIGURE 3–6   Recording cable TV through a CONVERTER BOX

CABLE COMPATIBLE TV takes signal straight from cable TV company.

or turning a dial, you select a station. (The cable company generally sends you a guide telling you which TV station goes with which button.) The CONVERTER pumps your selected station out its output as a channel 3 (or 4 or whatever the cable company selected). No matter what station you select on the CONVERTER BOX, channel 3 is the only signal that comes out of the box. You would connect the box's output to your VCR's VHF input and tune your VCR to channel 3 *forever.* You would connect the VCR's RF out to your TV's VHF antenna terminals and tune your TV to channel 3 *forever.* No longer will there be any point in tuning your TV or VCR to other channels. There is only one channel that comes out of the CONVERTER BOX and that's channel 3. You'll just get snow on the other channels if you tune to them.

Notice that your automatic timer on your VCR and the remote control on your VCR and TV are of no longer any use; changing channels on your TV and VCR do you no good because there is only one station in town—channel 3, the channel coming out of the CONVERTER.

For these reasons, it is nice to have CABLE COMPATIBLE VCRs and TVs. They can go about their business without being hampered by the cable company's CONVERTER.

Recording One Program while Viewing Another

Your children want you to record an important political debate for review in class, but you'd rather watch "Win, Lose, or Draw" on another channel. With home VCRs, it is possible to do both *if* your equipment is CABLE COMPATIBLE. If you are using cable TV and a CONVERTER as described earlier, you can only pick up one station at a time, the one the CONVERTER is tuned to. However, if you are using a TV antenna or are one of those lucky souls with CABLE COMPATIBLE equipment, read on:

1. *Carry out steps one through nine from the previous section, "Recording TV Programs Off the Air."*
2. *Once satisfied that your recording is successfully underway, send your antenna signals straight to your TV* by switching the VCR's OUTPUT SELECTOR to the TV position.
3. *Select your desired broadcast TV channel on your TV.* This will not affect your recording. The VCR is recording the channel *it* is tuned to while the TV is showing the channel *it* is tuned to.

If you want to check on your recording from time to time, simply flip that OUTPUT SELECT switch to VTR and tune your TV to channel 3. This will not affect your recording. Figure 3–7 diagrams the process.

Recording with an Automatic Timer

Automatic timers all work a little differently. Some are so complicated that you need a doctorate in electrical engineering just to program them. The simplest timers, called ONE EVENT timers, will record one event in one day. This means the recorder will tune in *one* channel and record it sometime within the next 24 hours. These timers are as easy to operate as an alarm clock.

1. *Prepare the VCR to make the recording.*
   a. Is it listening to the right input? The INPUT SELECT should be switched to TV.
   b. Have you tuned in the channel you want to record?
   c. Have you selected the recording speed?
   d. Did you put a long enough (or any) tape in the machine to record the *whole* show?
2. *Tell the VCR when to start and when to stop.* Setting the start and stop times is much like setting a digital electric clock. Somehow you need to press a START or ON button and set the clock for the time the recording is to begin. Next press an OFF or STOP button to set the clock again for the time the recording is to finish.
3. *Give control of the VCR over to the timer.* Often you do this by switching the timer ON. At this point the other VCR controls stop working and the timer is in command. Switching the timer OFF returns the control back to you.

More expensive VCRs have programmable timers which can record several events over several days. They can record one channel at one time, stop, switch

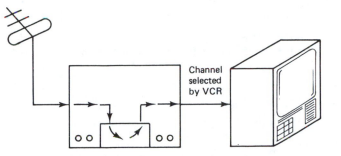

To see what your VCR is recording off-the-air:

1. The VCR must be listening to the right source. Switch its INPUT SELECT to TUNER or TV.

2. Your TV must be listening to the VCR. Switch the VCR's OUTPUT SELECT (or VTR/TV SELECT or ANTENNA switch or whatever) to VTR (or VCR or CASSETTE or VIDEO, or whatever). Tune the TV to channel 3 or 4.

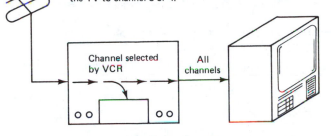

To watch other TV broadcasts while your VCR records one of them:

1. The VCR must *still* listen to the antenna. Switch its INPUT SELECT to TV.

2. Your TV must listen directly to the antenna. Switch the VCR's OUTPUT SELECT to TV. Tune the TV to the regular channels.

FIGURE 3-7 Watching your recording while you record vs. watching normal TV.

channels, and record another channel at another time. Some will record 14 different programs (which could be on 14 different channels) over a two-week period. Telling these timers exactly what you want them to do is fairly complicated. That's why the instruction manuals look so hairy. Programmable timers do what you *tell* them to do, not what you *want* them to do.

To record a show, your programmable timer needs to know six things (all those instructions in the manual are showing you how to *tell* the timer these six things):

1. Which of its eight (or so) memories you wish to store the instructions in. Each memory is like a pocket in which you place a message. When the right time comes, the message pops out of the pocket and the machine reads it to find out what to do next.

2. What week (this week or next week) the recording will start.

3. What day (Monday through Sunday) the recording will start. Some machines will permit you to select *all* days so that you can record the same show at the same time each day.

4. What time (hour, minute, A.M., or P.M.) the recorder will start.

5. What channel is to be recorded.

6. What week, day, and time the recording will stop.

Most timers will guide you by flashing on and off some part of their display to tell you what it is they want to know next. Others may display a menu of choices on your TV screen.

In short, somehow you have to tell the timer these six things *for each show* you want to record.

Remember, when you finish programming the timer, switch it ON. *(press the* TIMER *button) to give the timer control over the VCR.*

Recording from the Audio and Video Inputs

Most home VCRs are designed to accept straight video and audio signals as well as RF. Connect the audio and video wires to the VCR's audio and video inputs. Throw the INPUT SELECT switch to CAMERA, AUX, or VCR (away from TV) so that it listens to those inputs. Everything else is the same.

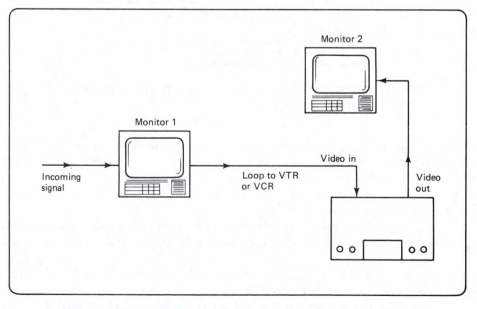

FIGURE 3-8 Setup showing the first monitor displaying the incoming signal and the second monitor displaying the VCR output.

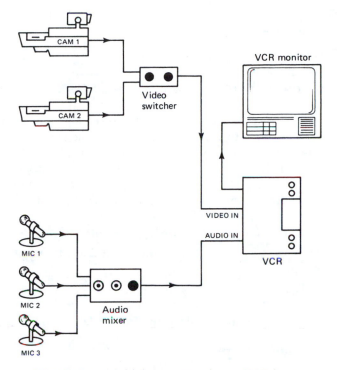

FIGURE 3-9   Multiple sources going to VCR inputs.

The following setup will apply to home and most industrial video recorders. The techniques are appropriate if you are trying to set up a mini TV studio in your home. Here is the step-by-step process to connect up and check out each piece of equipment in the video chain:

1. *Identify your signal sources (camera, microphone, or whatever) and run video and audio cables from them to your VCR.* If possible, run the video sources through a monitor first so you can confirm for yourself that there is indeed satisfactory video coming over those cables (as in Figure 3–8). The signals, whether connected directly to the VCR or connected indirectly by looping through the monitor, must go to the VCR inputs.

2. *Plug the sources into the VCR inputs.* A VCR can handle only one video and only one audio source at a time (except for two-channel or stereo VCRs which can record two audio tracks at once). If you're using two cameras or several microphones, they must be connected into some intermediate device that can select or mix the signals and send out only one video signal and only one audio signal. Figure 3–9 shows such a setup.

Audio   Most VCRs have a socket labeled MICROPHONE where an appropriate mike can be plugged in. An adapter may be necessary if the plug doesn't fit the socket. This socket is for weak signals such as

Microphones
Most record turntables
Telephone pickup coils
Electric guitar pickups
The MICROPHONE OUTPUT of an audio mixer.

In general, if your audio source has no power supply of its own, doesn't use batteries, and doesn't need to be plugged into the wall to work, it should be plugged into the MICROPHONE INPUT or MIC IN of the VCR.

VCRs are likely to have another audio input labeled AUX (for AUXiliary), LINE, LINE IN, HI LEVEL IN, or AUDIO IN. These inputs are not so sensitive and can take the stronger audio signals such as you would get from:

AM or FM tuner	Movie projector
Audio tape deck	Turntable with built-in preamplifiers
Audiocassette player	VCR
Monitor/receiver	Mike mixer

You can expect a strong audio signal from a device if its output is labeled as follows:

• LINE OUT	• AUDIO OUT
• HI LEVEL OUT	• PHONE
• PROGRAM OUT	• EAR
• AUX OUT	• MONITOR OUT
• PREAMP OUT	

LO LEVEL AND HI LEVEL EXPLAINED

A microphone turns sound into a tiny electrical signal. A preamplifier changes the tiny signal into a medium-sized electrical signal. An amplifier turns a medium-sized signal into a big electrical signal. A speaker changes a big signal into sound. Medium-sized signals are easiest for electronic equipment to handle, so most audio devices have PREAMP or HI-LEVEL outputs for sending medium-strength signals to other devices. They also have LINE, HI-LEVEL, or AUX inputs to receive medium-strength signals from other devices.

Some audio devices have earphone, headphone, or speaker outputs. In some cases, signals from these outputs are too loud even for the AUX IN of a VTR: The recorded sound may come out raspy and distorted. The cure for this is to connect an AUDIO ATTENUATOR between the source and the input. The ATTENUATOR cuts down the strength of the signal. If you don't have an ATTENUATOR, and the source's signal is too strong; try turning its volume control down very low.

LO LEVEL, HI LEVEL, explained.

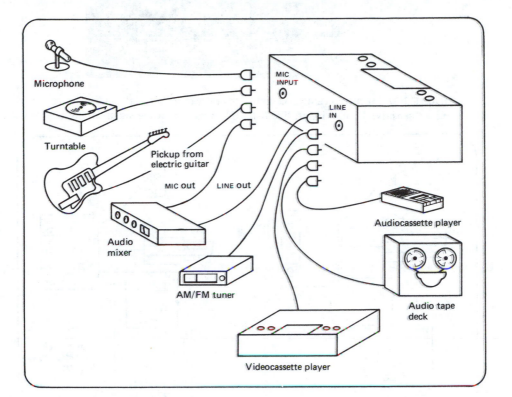

FIGURE 3–10 HIGH LEVEL and LOW LEVEL audio sources.

In most cases, if the audio source needs electricity to operate, the audio signal should go to the AUX IN or LINE IN of the VTR as shown in Figure 3–10.

Some home VCRs lack AUDIO INPUTS and have just the supersensitive MICROPHONE or MIC inputs. So how do you get HI LEVEL signals into the machine without overdriving the input? Use an AUDIO ANTENUATOR (Figure 3–11).

Video   Connect your video source to the VIDEO IN of the VCR. Some industrial VCRs have several video inputs and you may have to throw a switch to tell the VCR to "listen" to the right one.

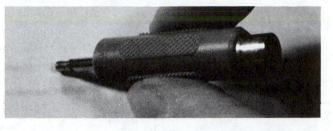

FIGURE 3-11 AUDIO ATTENUATOR connects between a "strong" audio source and a "sensitive" audio input, like MIC IN to cut down the signal strength.

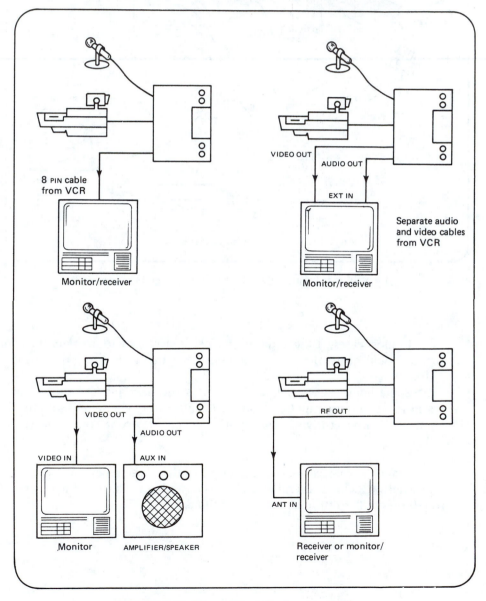

8 PIN cable from VCR

Monitor/receiver

VIDEO OUT
AUDIO OUT
EXT IN

Separate audio and video cables from VCR

Monitor/receiver

VIDEO OUT
AUDIO OUT
VIDEO IN
AUX IN

Monitor   AMPLIFIER/SPEAKER

RF OUT
ANT IN

Receiver or monitor/receiver

FIGURE 3-12 Ways of monitoring a recording.

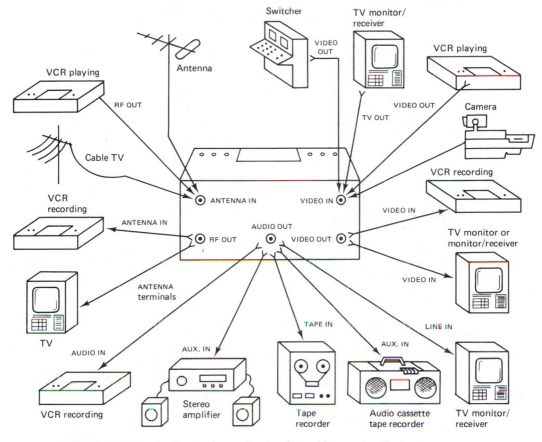

FIGURE 3–13 Reviewing the ins and outs of RF, video, and audio between a VCR and other equipment.

3. *Plug a monitoring device into the VCR* (as in Figure 3–12). Remember to switch the TV monitor's TERMINATOR to the 75-ohm position.

    The best way to monitor the sound is by using headphones connected to the VCR's HEADPHONE output.

Figure 3–13 reviews some of the things you can connect to your VCR.

Wiring Several TVs and a VCR Together

Connecting one antenna to one VCR to one TV is fairly straightforward. If you have cable TV, the wiring gets more complicated if you have to mess with that CONVERTER BOX. And you can add a whole new tangle to the ball of wires if you wish to connect several VCRs to your TV system. We'll save that migrane for Chap-

Method #1

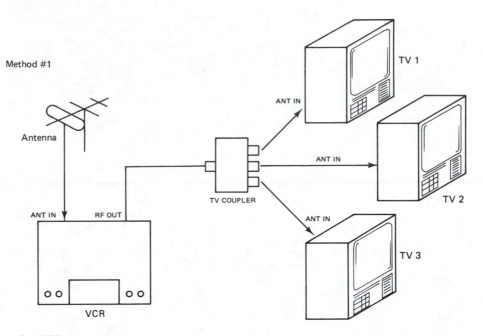

Capabilities:

1. With VCR's output switched to TV, all TV's can view any channel. The VCR can simultaneously record any channel. The recording cannot be viewed simultaneously.

2. With the VCR output switched to VCR, all TV's see only what the VCR is recording or playing. They must also be tuned to the VCR's channel (usually 3 or 4).

Note: If the antenna signal is weak, there may not be enough signal to feed three TV's especially if their wires are long. In such cases, instead of using a PASSIVE TV COUPLER (uses no power), buy an ACTIVE COUPLER (which amplifies the signal while splitting it). Or, insert an RF AMPLIFIER or ANTENNA AMPLIFIER or ANTENNA BOOSTER *between* the VCR and the COUPLER.

Method #2

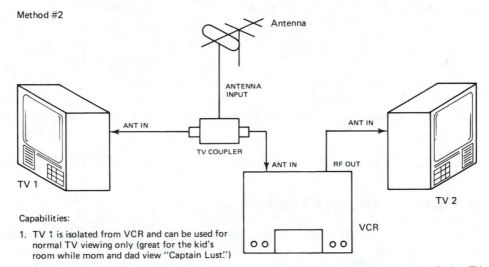

Capabilities:

1. TV 1 is isolated from VCR and can be used for normal TV viewing only (great for the kid's room while mom and dad view "Captain Lust.")

2. TV 2 displays regular TV channel if VCR's output is switched to TV. If output is switched to VCR, then TV views only what the VCR is recording or playing. TV must be tuned to VCR's channel to display the VCR's signal. *(continued)*

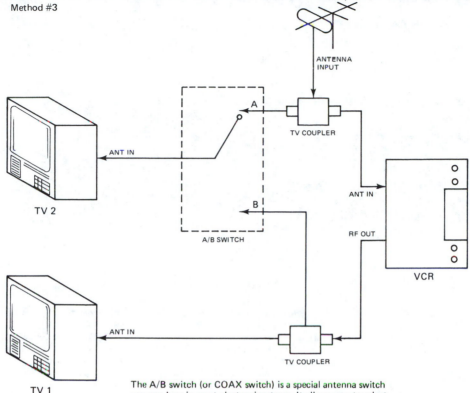

ANTENNA
INPUT

A

TV COUPLER

ANT IN

ANT IN

A/B SWITCH

TV 2

RF OUT

B

VCR

ANT IN

TV COUPLER

TV 1

The A/B switch (or COAX switch) is a special antenna switch you can buy in most electronics stores. It allows you to select one of two sources.

Capabilities:

1. With A/B switch on A, TV 2 is isolated from VCR and views regular broadcasts.

2. With A/B switch on B, TV 2 watches what the VCR is putting out, which could be (a) regular TV channels if the VCR output is switched to TV, or (b) whatever the VCR is recording or playing if the output is switched to VCR.

3. TV 1 can view regular broadcasts or taped program depending on position of VTR's output switch.

    In short, anything can be viewed on either TV with this setup, depending on where the switches are set.

FIGURE 3-14   Connecting your VCR to several TVs.

ter 9 and just concentrate here on a few common setups for one CABLE COMPATIBLE VCR and several CABLE COMPATIBLE TVs (Figure 3–14).

Always try to keep your wires as short as possible to avoid TV signal interference and to maintain a strong signal. Remember that each time you divide a TV signal, it becomes weaker. If you notice a grainy picture, you may wish to use an AMPLIFIED COUPLER (described in Chapter 1) to boost your signal before dividing it.

ENSURING A GOOD RECORDING

Start with a good strong signal. If it is weak, your recording will be equally bad.

Use brand name tape that's fairly new and hasn't been sitting around in hot or damp places. For your best recordings, use a high grade (HG) or other premium quality tape. Also, use your VCR's fastest speed (SP).

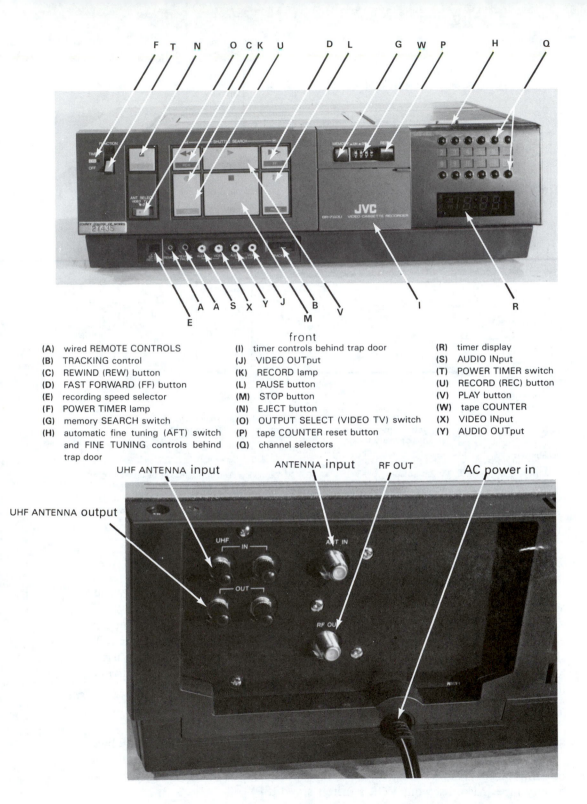

(A) wired REMOTE CONTROLS
(B) TRACKING control
(C) REWIND (REW) button
(D) FAST FORWARD (FF) button
(E) recording speed selector
(F) POWER TIMER lamp
(G) memory SEARCH switch
(H) automatic fine tuning (AFT) switch and FINE TUNING controls behind trap door

(I) timer controls behind trap door
(J) VIDEO OUTput
(K) RECORD lamp
(L) PAUSE button
(M) STOP button
(N) EJECT button
(O) OUTPUT SELECT (VIDEO TV) switch
(P) tape COUNTER reset button
(Q) channel selectors

(R) timer display
(S) AUDIO INput
(T) POWER TIMER switch
(U) RECORD (REC) button
(V) PLAY button
(W) tape COUNTER
(X) VIDEO INput
(Y) AUDIO OUTput

FIGURE 3–15 Location of inputs, outputs, and controls on one VCR.

You are not likely to heed this warning until the inevitable happens to you, but here's the warning anyway:

Before making your recording, make a short test recording and play it back to confirm proper functioning of the equipment. It is much easier to invest this moment of prevention than it is to redo an hour of production.

You may think that you are checking your recording if you watch the TV monitor while the recording is being made. Indeed, you are proving to yourself that the signal is going into the VCR. What you are not proving is whether the signal is being *recorded on the tape*. The only way that you can confirm that is by *playing back the recording*. Some things that ruin recordings and show up only on playback are dirt or scratches on the tape, wrinkles or creases in the tape, or defective video recording heads.

For important shows, it may be important to monitor audio during the recording process. There are two ways to do this:

1. Plug headphones into the VCR HEADPHONE output. This way you can hear what the VCR is hearing.
2. Use a monitor/receiver and listen to the audio on it while the recording is in progress. If the sound bothers others, you may be able to plug an earphone into the monitor/receiver (which cuts out the speaker).

OTHER VCR CONTROLS AND FEATURES

Simple inexpensive home and industrial videocassette players may have very few features. Top-of-the-line machines, however, have more bells and whistles than you'll ever have time to ring or blow. As you can see from Figure 3–15, a VCR can teem with inputs, outputs, and switches.

Remote Control

A REMOTE CONTROL (Figure 3–16) is a keypad which allows you to operate a VCR's controls at some distance. Most operate by sending infrared light signals through the air to a sensor on the VCR. To work, the WIRELESS REMOTE must be aimed like a flashlight in the general direction of the VCR, and the REMOTE's batteries must be alive (they last about a year).

Convenience Outlet

On the back of most VCRs you'll find an electrical outlet. This AC power socket is handy for plugging in small accessories such as separate timers, converters or decoders, or a small lamp. If the outlet says UNSWITCHED, it supplies power whether the VCR is turned on or not (handy for timers which must keep going after the VCR

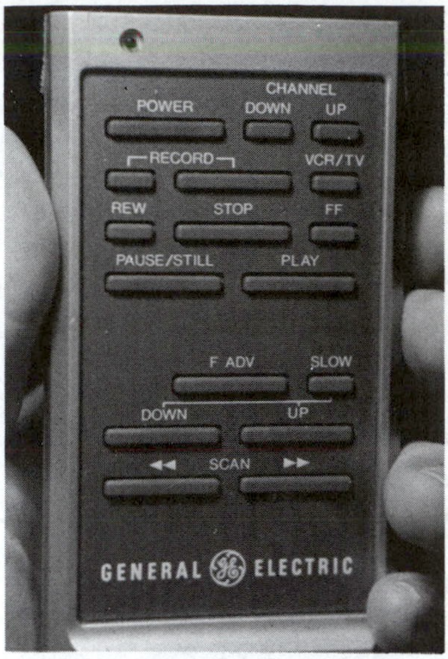

FIGURE 3-16 Remote Control.

is turned off). If the outlet is labeled SWITCHED, then it turns on and off with the VCR (handy for activating decoders during the time a show is being recorded).

These outlets are usually labeled something like "300w MAX" which means that they can feed up to 300 watts of power to an appliance (like three 100-watt light bulbs). Plug your 1,000-watt steam iron into it and you risk zapping your circuits or blowing a fuse inside of your machine. Depending on your TV's wattage, it is probably safe to plug your TV into this outlet.

Dew Indicator

For the VCR to operate properly, the tape has to slide smoothly through its internal mechanism. When the machine is cold and the air is humid, the surfaces become "sticky" and the tape risks getting hung up and damaged. The DEW INDICATOR senses this dampness (illuminating a light) and makes you wait until it is safe. If the DEW INDICATOR brings your TV production to a standstill, just leave the machine ON and wait for the light to go out. Sitting and staring at the machine will not shorten this process. When the light goes out, your VCR will function normally again.

Counter/Reset/Memory

We've already seen how the INDEX COUNTER can help us find things on a tape. Some counters have a MEMORY button which makes locating things even easier. The MEMORY button will stop the machine from rewinding whenever the INDEX COUNTER reaches 000. Here's how to use it: Say you are playing or recording a movie and you'd like to come back to an exciting scene. Set the COUNTER RESET to 000. Next, switch MEMORY on. You can do these things even with the tape running without harm to your recording. Let the tape continue playing (or recording). Later, when you want to find that spot again, simply press REWIND. When the counter reaches 000 the machine will automatically STOP. You are there. Incidentally, you must switch MEMORY OFF to rewind any farther than 000. Someday you will leave your MEMORY ON and wonder why you can't rewind your tape to the beginning.

One disadvantage of the MEMORY system is that when you press RESET mid-tape, you are no longer keeping chronological track of elapsed time. This may or may not be a problem depending upon whether you are trying to keep a log of what's where on the tape.

Some recent models of VCRs have a TAPE INDEXING feature whereby you can press a button to invisibly record a signal on the videotape marking a spot for you to come back to later. On fancier models, these spots may be numbered and you can later punch in the number 12 to skip ahead to the twelfth "mark" on the tape. Some machines automatically place a marker on the tape each time the tape stops. Thus you can quickly find the beginning of each program (assuming the machine recorded, stopped, recorded another show, stopped, and so on). These INDEXES can be erased and changed.

Speed Select

3/4U and industrial VCRs are designed for one standard speed only. VHS recorders are equipped with one, two, or three speeds: SP (two hours, standard play), LP (four hours, long play), and EP (six hours, extra play). Beta recorders similarly have up to three speeds: X1 (one hour), X2 (two hours), X3 (three hours). Of course, tapes of different lengths will change how long the VCR can record at a given speed.

You select the tape speed when recording. VCRs automatically sense and adjust themselves to the correct speed when playing back.

Many industrial, editing, and camcorder VCRs, in order to provide the best picture possible, work at only one speed—the fastest speed. If recording with a three-speed machine, you should select the fastest speed (the shortest recording time) for the higher quality recording and to assure your tape will be playable and editable on industrial machines.

Tracking

Tracking adjusts the VCR's ability to play a tape exactly the way it was recorded; the spinning video heads must follow exactly the same path taken by the record heads when the tape was made. Generally, you shouldn't have to adjust the TRACK-ING control on a VCR. Leave it in the FIX (center) position. When playing a tape, if your picture shows a band of hash across it as in Figure 3-17, or jiggles a lot, then it is time to adjust TRACKING. Turn it until the picture clears up.

The TRACKING control compensates for minor differences between similar FORMAT recorders and tapes. You are most likely to use it when playing a tape recorded on someone else's machine or even when playing your own tapes after your machine gets worn and out of adjustment. *This control does nothing when you are recording—only when you are playing tapes.*

8mm VCRs don't have a TRACKING control. They adjust themselves automatically.

FIGURE 3–17   TRACKING misadjustment.

Slow Tracking

Sometimes you get a smooth picture when PLAYING a tape but get a band of hash across the screen when the VCR is in PAUSE, STILL, or SLO MO. Adjust SLOW TRACKING to clear up the picture in these modes.

Audio Dub

When you record a program, you automatically record both picture and sound. With AUDIO DUB you can go back and rerecord *new* sound, erasing the old sound as you go, leaving the picture untouched.

    To activate AUDIO DUB,

1. Plug a microphone into MIC IN or some other audio signal source into AUDIO IN as described earlier. If using a portable VCR and camera, you can even use the microphone built into the camera.
2. You may wish to check your sound level before you start recording by listening to it through your system. You could
   a. Plug an earphone into the EARPHONE jack, if your VCR has one.
   b. Run RF to your TV and monitor your sound there.
   c. Connect your hi-fi to the AUDIO OUT jack on the VCR. On some decks you automatically will be able to hear the audio source with the VCR on STOP. On others you must press AUDIO DUB to send the sound through the monitoring outputs. On a few, the machine may actually have to be recording before you can hear your source.

       Some VCRs record with an AUTOMATIC VOLUME CONTROL. You don't have to adjust the recording volume, the machine does it for you. More advanced models may have MANUAL VOLUME CONTROLS which you can raise or lower by turning knobs or sliders on the VCR while watching a volume meter. Most MANUAL machines can also be switched to AUTO (or AGC, ALC, or AVC).
3. Find out where you wish to start dubbing new sound.
4. Press AUDIO DUB and PLAY together.

5. You will hear the new sound being recorded. The old sound is being erased as you go, and you won't hear it.

6. When done, press STOP.

Some VCRs have stereo sound and allow you to DUB one channel alone, or both channels simultaneously. On some machines you can listen to one channel (the one you are not dubbing) while you rerecord new sound on the other channel.

Older or inexpensive VCRs record low fidelity sound along LINEAR audio tracks at the edge of the tape, much like an audiocassette recorder records sound. Hi-fi VCRs, on the other hand, record the sound as part of the picture. While they are doing this, they *also* record the sound on their LINEAR audio tracks. Put another way, non-hi-fi machines record the sound one way while hi-fi machines record the sound two ways. If you make an AUDIO DUB on a non-hi-fi recording, you will erase the LINEAR audio track, replacing it with another LINEAR audio track. If, however, you make an AUDIO DUB on a hi-fi recording, you will not touch the hi-fi sound that was already recorded along with the picture. That sound will be part of the picture forever; you cannot get rid of it unless you erase the picture (recording a new picture and sound over it). When you make an AUDIO DUB on a hi-fi recording, you are really replacing the LINEAR audio tracks with new sound. When you are finished, you could play back the tape in the hi-fi mode, listening to the original sound with exquisite fidelity. Or you could switch off the hi-fi button and listen to the LINEAR (lo-fi) audio tracks. Since those were the tracks that you changed when you dubbed in new sound, those are the tracks that you wish to listen to. Make a note of this on your recordings so that you don't try to play your modified tape and wonder what happened to all the new sound you dubbed in.

Remember that an AUDIO DUB done on a hi-fi tape yields only low fidelity.

Still Frame

When playing a tape, STILL FRAME "freezes" the picture on the screen. Some VCRs do a better job than others at holding a clean, still picture on the screen. Sometimes that picture will stop with a horizontal band of hash across it (which looks exactly like the TRACKING problem shown back in Figure 3–17). The hash is called NOISE or a NOISE BAR. Just as in audio where "noise" is unwanted sound, in video "noise" can be unwanted stuff in the picture like hash, grain, snow, or specks.

Home VCRs with *two video heads* generally leave NOISE BARS in their STILL FRAMES. Home VCRs with three, four, or five video heads can make a NOISELESS STILL FRAME. Some VCRs automatically make the picture NOISELESS. Others require fidgeting with the SLOW TRACKING control.

Frame Advance

Once in the STILL FRAME mode, a second control allows you to advance to the next video picture and stay there. Or on some models, by holding the button down, you can continuously advance the tape slowly, picture by picture, like viewing a movie one frame at a time. On professional tape machines, this feature is often called JOG.

Variable Speed Slow Motion

Sometimes combined with STILL FRAME or FRAME ADVANCE features, VARIABLE SPEED SLOW MOTION allows the tape to proceed slowly forward at various speeds.

Search or Scan

SEARCH, SCAN, or HIGH SPEED PICTURE SEARCH shuttles the tape forward or reverse at 5, 10, or maybe 20 times the normal speed with its picture still showing. It's handy for finding things quickly on a tape.

Varactor Tuning

Some VCRs have about 14 tuning buttons on them. Each of these buttons needs to be manually preset to a certain TV station so that all you need to do is push a button to pick up that station. More advanced VCRs, however, have VARACTOR TUNING which is easier to use. If the buttons are labeled 0 through 9 on a calculator-type keypad, then you probably have VARACTOR, DIRECT ACCESS, or EXPRESS tuning. It allows you to go from channel 2 to channel 18, directly skipping the channels in between. On such a tuner, you can watch channel 2 by pressing the 0 and then the 2, and can watch channel 18 by pressing the 1 and then the 8.

Automatic Backspace

Portable VCRs and camcorders often have this feature. When you are recording and press PAUSE (perhaps to stop recording and line up a new shot), the VCR will automatically back itself up a little ways. When you UNPAUSE to start recording again, you will see the tail end of your last scene played to you for a few seconds and *then* the VCR will jump into RECORD. This makes a very clean edit, without a glitch on the TV screen, which is a problem you often get from VCRs not having this feature. The problem is that you have to plan for these extra few moments at the beginning of each scene. The VCR won't start recording the moment you expect it to, it will do this little backspacing dance first, so you'll have to wait a few moments before starting the action in your scene.

Stereo

Nearly all home VCRs and camcorders nowadays record and play back in stereo. This means that there are two audio tracks, one for the left channel (left ear) and one for the right channel (right ear).

There are several ways to get signals onto those two channels. One way is to send the signal to the left and right AUDIO INPUTS on the VCR. Another way is to use a stereo microphone connected to the camera or VCR while making your recording.

A stereo VCR cannot necessarily receive *off-the-air* stereo broadcasts. To do so, it needs a stereo TV tuner to decode the stereo broadcasts and make two-channel sound. This feature is called MTS (multichannel television sound) and is found on newer stereo TVs and VCRs. An MTS switch on your VCR will make it sensitive to these broadcast stereo signals so that they can be recorded. You can tell when it's working because a little pilot light will turn on, indicating that the VCR is receiving stereo signals. Many TV broadcasts are now in stereo.

If a TV *program* is monaural (single channel rather than stereo), then that is all your VCR will reproduce. Also, unless your TV set is able to play stereo, you will hear monaural sound from it even if the VCR and the tape are stereo. VCRs are designed so that stereo tapes will play on monaural machines and monaural tapes will play on stereo machines. In both cases the sound will be monaural.

The word *stereo* does not imply *high fidelity;* it only means that there are two audio channels—one for the left ear and one for the right ear. Those two channels can be stereo but still deliver mediocre sound quality as is usually the case with home VCRs (except the hi-fi versions which do an excellent job of making stereo sound).

8mm VCRs automatically record monaural hi-fi sound. You can also record (by using separate audio inputs and throwing a switch) stereo hi-fi sound. And if you wish to forgo the picture altogether and use a special VCR with this feature, you can record up to six hi-fi stereo sound channels on a tape (instead of the picture).

Dolby

DOLBY is a method of improving sound quality mostly by reducing background hiss on a tape recording. When making your recording, switch Dolby *on* to put the improved sound on the tape. When playing the tape back, also switch Dolby *on* to extract the best sound from the tape. A Dolby tape can be played on a non-Dolby machine and vice versa, but the sound will be slightly worse than normal quality.

If you are making a recording for someone who does not have Dolby, then switch your Dolby *off.* If you are playing a tape which was not recorded in Dolby, also switch Dolby *off* for best results.

Audio-1, Audio-2, Mix

3/4U VCRs and home stereo VCRs have two independent channels of audio called AUDIO-1 and AUDIO-2. You can record on the AUDIO-1 channel by plugging your source into the AUDIO-1 INPUT of the VCR. You can record on AUDIO-2 by plugging into the AUDIO-2 INPUT of the VCR. When playing back the tape, you flip the AUDIO/MONITOR switch to CH-1 to listen to the AUDIO-1 channel or to CH-2 to listen to the AUDIO-2 channel or to MIX to listen to both channels at the same time. Most people leave their VCRs on MIX, but there are times when, because audio dubbing has occurred on one channel, that you wish to listen only to that channel and not to the other.

Dub

DUB is not the same as AUDIO DUB. This is the feature found in editing and high quality VCRs. With the help of a special DUB CABLE connected between two VCRs, it allows extra sharp copies of videocassettes to be made. You'll see more about this in Chapter 9.

Video Dub

Just as it is possible to replace old sound with new sound using AUDIO DUB, it is possible to replace *only the picture* with a new picture. The better VCRs have this feature, which is explained more fully in Chapter 10.

Automatic Rewind

AUTOMATIC REWIND or REPEAT is a feature which allows a tape machine to play the same show over and over all day long. When the machine reaches the end of the tape or a certain point programmed into the tape, the machine will stop and rewind to 000 on its INDEX COUNTER and will switch to play. If you make a home recording someday and find your tape at its beginning the next day, it could mean one of two things:

1. That the recording never occurred.
2. The recording did occur but you ran out of tape before the end of the show and the machine rewound to the beginning.

Skew or Tape Tension

SKEW or TAPE TENSION is an adjustment on professional VCRs which tightens or loosens the tape as it plays. SKEW does not affect recording. Home VCRs have this control factory preset making it inaccessible to the user.

When tape shrinks or stretches or is pulled too tight by the VCR playing it, the picture bends at the top or flutters back and forth. This is called FLAGWAVING and is shown in Figure 3–18. In extreme cases, the picture collapses altogether into a mass of diagonal lines. Adjusting SKEW may straighten out the problem. If it doesn't or if your VCR lacks this control, try adjusting HORIZONTAL HOLD on your TV.

Insert Edit

The INSERT EDIT feature is found on editing videocassette recorders and will be described more fully in Chapter 10. Briefly, an INSERT EDIT is done in the *middle* of the program. It cuts a piece out of a show and puts a new piece in. Home VCRs with this feature will make a fairly neat jump from one scene to the other at the

FIGURE 3-18 FLAGWAVING—adjust SKEW.

edit point, leaving a very tiny glitch on the picture. Some 8mm VCRs and professional video editors will do the same without leaving any glitch at all.

Superbeta, VHS HQ, Super VHS, and ED Beta

Manufacturers have been struggling with ways to improve the picture quality on their VCRs without sacrificing compatibility with older models. Superbeta VCRs make a picture 25% sharper than regular beta *if* the tape is recorded *and* played back using Superbeta machines. At the flip of a switch, Superbeta VCRs can record and play regular beta tapes too, but without the improved quality. Normal beta VCRs can play Superbeta recordings, but the pictures look a little worse than normal. When using a Superbeta VCR to make tapes for your friends, flip your switch to the Superbeta mode if your friends have Superbeta players; otherwise, use the regular beta mode.

VHS HQ (high quality) is an enhanced VHS format where the picture isn't *really* sharper, but just *looks* sharper because there is less graininess and the edges of objects appear more abrupt (less fuzzy). To see the improvement, your tape has to be recorded *and* played back on VHS HQ machines. An HQ recording will play back on a normal VHS machine and vice versa, but the improvement will no longer be visible. VHS HQ and normal VHS tapes are otherwise totally compatible.

Super VHS (S-VHS) requires a special tape (also usable on normal VHS machines), but when an S-VHS recording is played back on an S-VHS machine, the picture is 75% sharper than regular VHS. S-VHS recordings are unplayable on normal VHS machines, but S-VHS machines can play normal VHS recordings. By flipping a switch, S-VHS VCRs can also make normal VHS recordings.

S-VHS machines, in addition to their normal VIDEO OUT, have an extra socket called an S connector. When used with a special monitor also having an S connector, the picture from the S-VHS machine will appear further improved. (Note: S-VHS pictures are super sharp even if you don't use the special monitor and connector.)

The special connector and monitor will allow the VCR to send its color signals separate from its luminance signals, and as a result the colors have sharper, smoother edges. This plug is sometimes also called a Y/C connector (where the Y stands for luminance and the C stands for color).

ED (extended definition) beta also records super sharp pictures on a special tape. The blank or recorded tapes are unusable on regular beta VCRs. ED beta VCRs have a switch to make them record or play normal beta tapes, too.

Digital Effects

Recent home VCRs are able to perform special effects such as picture-in-a-picture (PIP) which allows you to view one picture on your TV screen with a smaller picture inserted over it. This allows you to watch two shows at once.

Another DIGITAL EFFECT is a FREEZE FRAME which holds the picture still even though the tape isn't standing still. Incidentally, have you ever noticed that while playing your VCR and switching to PAUSE, the picture becomes slightly fuzzy? This is because you are seeing a STILL FIELD (although most call this a STILL FRAME). You may recall from Chapter 1 that a TV picture is made of odd and even lines interlaced together. When your VCR is on PAUSE, it is playing only the odd lines of your TV picture or only the even lines, but not both. Thus there are pieces of your picture which are missing and the result looks fuzzy. A digital FREEZE FRAME is done a different way. A circuit inside the VCR "grabs" all of the electronic data which makes up the picture and displays it for you as a single still picture. The process has nothing to do with the VCR playing back a picture from the tape over and over as is done with older VCRs.

There are other DIGITAL EFFECTS which, though dazzling, aren't very useful, such as POSTERIZATION and MOSAIC. POSTERIZATION will give a cartoon-like effect to the picture. MOSAIC will turn your picture into a checkerboard of tiny boxes.

Two significant improvements available in digital VCRs have to do with making the picture look better. In some models, the digital circuit will "look" for ghosts and other interference in your TV picture and will remove it. Such circuits can make a good picture excellent. These same circuits, however, tend to make a fair picture worse.

Another picture improvement available through digital processing has to do with DOUBLE SCANNING. The VCR will store an image for a sixtieth of a second and use it to "fill in between the lines" when the next picture is shown. Thus, a TV set which normally shows 262 1/2 horizontal scanning lines at a time will now show twice as many lines and will appear sharper.

GETTING MORE OUT OF A VCR

In the coming chapters you'll see dozens of tricks for making your video recordings better looking and easier to produce. Here are a few now.

Magnified version of
what a normal TV
shows in 1/60 second

Magnified view of what
digital double scanning
does to the picture

Digital double scanning, (a) Magnified version of what a normal TV shows in 1/60 second. (b) Magnified view of what DIGITAL DOUBLE SCANNING does to the picture.

Erasing Part of a Tape

Say you recorded a 60-minute special at home, viewed it, and didn't want it any more. Now, say you used that same tape to record a documentary for your school. The documentary runs only 30 minutes, leaving the last half of the special still on the tape. Since it is rather unpolished video etiquette to play a program to a class that ends with a sudden jump to unrelated trivial video leftovers, you would like to erase the last 30 minutes of the special.

The process is simple. Just record a new program over the special—a program of *nothing*. There are several ways to do this:

1. Switch the VCR to a vacant channel (snow) and set the timer to record for a half hour.
2. Better yet, switch the INPUT SELECTOR to CAMERA or VIDEO and make a half-hour recording. Since nothing is connected to those video and audio inputs, nothing will be recorded.
3. If you want the recording to be smooth black and silent, connect a TV camera to the VCR, but leave the lens cap on and don't plug in a microphone. Switch your INPUT SELECT to CAMERA and you will record a picture of black.

Drying out a VCR when the Dew Lamp Goes On

When you move your VCR from a cool place to a warmer, humid place, water condenses inside it making the mechanism sticky. This could damage your tape if the DEW sensor inside your VCR didn't shut your machine down, forcing you to wait until it dried out.

So what do you do? Just dig your blow drier out of the bathroom closet, switch it to its *lowest heat,* open the cassette compartment, and remove the cassette. Then, holding the drier about six inches from the hole, blow the mechanism dry. One minute may do the trick.

Note: Do not use *high* heat with the nozzle *stuck into* the cassette hole.

Squeezing out the Highest Quality Picture and Sound

Record your master tapes with the best machine you've got. One-inch is preferable to 3/4U. 3/4U, ED beta, and Super VHS are preferable to beta, VHS, or 8mm.

Start with a good picture and sound while recording. Use a strong enough antenna, properly aimed, good antenna wire, and tight connections. FINE TUNE your stations carefully. To really be sure your VCR is receiving a good signal, monitor the beginning of the recording through your TV.

Use the fastest speed (shortest recording time) for highest picture and sound quality on home VCRs.

If playing back through the antenna input of a TV, FINE TUNE the TV carefully.

For better sound, run the VCR's AUDIO OUT to the AUX inputs of your good $400 hi-fi sound system rather than your TV's $6 sound system.

For a 10% sharper picture, use a monitor or monitor/receiver and use the VCR's VIDEO OUT directly. Definitely use straight video when playing your VCR through a TV PROJECTOR. The RF fuzziness shows up even more when the picture is blown up.

Don't record anything on the first 10 seconds of your tape or your last 10 seconds of your tape. This LEADER assures that your precious recording occurs far from the threading-induced scratches on the tape. The LEADER plays an important role in editing, described in Chapter 10.

If you plan to make an *important* recording, first make a sample recording and play it back to make sure that everything is working. If you are recording long stretches of material with short breaks (perhaps commercials), use these respites to rewind and play back a little of your recording just to see how it is coming along. *Simply viewing your TV screen as the recording is being made doesn't completely guarantee that the recording is going onto the tape.*

VCRs (and this includes portables and camcorders) don't like to be tipped, rocked, rotated, or spun around while running. The spinning VIDEO HEADS inside the machine act like a gyroscope and fight the motion. This shifts the tape speed momentarily causing the picture to waver in what's called a GYROSCOPIC ERROR and causes FLAGWAVING.

If a show is going to run longer than one cassette, don't bother rewinding the first cassette at its end. EJECT it, pop in the new cassette, and start recording immediately. This will save you three minutes and forty seconds of missed program as you rewound the tape. You can rewind it later; it won't hurt the tape to wait.

Every time you record a tape, *label it.* I can't count the number of tapes that I've seen accidently erased because someone didn't label them, and they subsequently got misplaced or recorded over.

If you plan to swap home videocassettes with others, *again,* use the fastest speed for recording. The faster speeds make more stable tapes. Because tapes recorded on one home VCR will play less solidly on another VCR, it helps to start with the most stable signal you can get.

Y Adapters

A Y ADAPTER, Figure 3–19, is a wire which mixes two audio signals together. It's handy for mixing the stereo outputs from a VCR and sending them to a monaural amplifier. It can also mix the outputs from a stereo source and send the result to a monaural input or one channel of another VCR. The Y ADAPTER is also handy for taking a monaural signal and sending it simultaneously to two channels of a stereo VCR so that the signal may be recorded on both channels at once.

Some alert readers may have noticed that it would be possible to plug a Y ADAPTER into their VCR's VIDEO OUT and feed the signal to two places. Or conversely, use the adapter to feed two sources into one VIDEO IN. Feeding the signal to two places with a Y ADAPTER will work, but it will weaken your signal badly, creating a faint or snowy picture. Feeding two sources (like two VCRs) simultaneously into your VCR's VIDEO IN by the Y ADAPTER won't work at all; you'll just get mush.

The only proper way to share a VIDEO signal between several devices is to

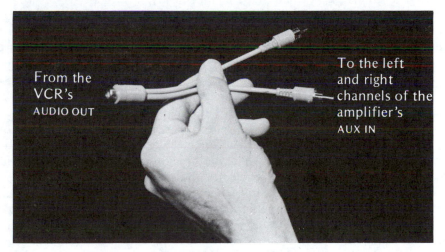

From the VCR's AUDIO OUT

To the left and right channels of the amplifier's AUX IN

FIGURE 3–19   Y ADAPTER

1. LOOP it from one to another.
2. Send the signal to a DISTRIBUTION AMPLIFIER (discussed in Chapter 12).
3. Send the signal to a VCR which has several outputs.

The same goes for the T ADAPTER shown back in Figure 1–27. Why do they make it if you shouldn't use it? That's a good question. I've never heard a good answer. Perhaps a T ADAPTER is for hooking things up wrong when you can't hook 'em up right.

If using a stereo home VCR for a monaural recording, record the sound on *both* channels and play it back from *both* channels. Recording on two tracks spreads the magnetism over twice the area of tape, making the total recorded signal stronger. When played back, this stronger signal will have less background hiss and will have better fidelity.

Clean Environment

VCRs don't like liquids, chalk dust, cat hairs, cigarette smoke, high humidity, beach sand or salt spray, bumps, vibrations, high heat, or sustained direct sunlight. A VCR is a delicate princess who should live in a cool, clean, dry, dust-free room, be fed clean videotape, and receive an annual checkup from the video doctor.

Recording a Series of Segments—Stop versus Pause

You'll see more on this subject in Chapter 10, but here's just a brief view of how to record several segments onto the same tape neatly.

If there is just a short wait between the scenes you are recording, simply press PAUSE, wait for the next scene to be set up, and then unpause when you wish to continue recording. Note that many VCRs back up a little bit when you press PAUSE and don't start recording immediately when you unpause. Build this extra delay into your plans. This inconvenient delay brings with it one advantage—clean edits—no hash, no snow, no rolling, no twisting, no rainbows, simply clean cuts from scene to scene. Some VCRs do this job better than others.

If you press STOP on a beta VCR when it is recording, the tape stops moving just like a VHS VCR does in PAUSE. A VHS machine, when you press STOP, however, will totally unthread itself. When you press RECORD again, the tape will rethread and start recording. The problem is that when a VHS machine unthreads itself, then rethreads itself, it doesn't come back to exactly the same spot on the tape. If it comes back to a place earlier than you left off, you end up recording over the end of your last segment, losing it. If it comes back later than where you left off, it ends up with a patch of snow (unrecorded tape) between your last segment and this one. In short, STOP edits are very messy and should be avoided on VHS VCRs.

Portable VCRs go almost anywhere.

If you must stop the VCR (say you recorded one segment yesterday and wi'
record another one today), then rewind the tape a little ways, press PLAY, let the
tape play up to one second before the end of the old scene, and then press PAUSE.
Next, press RECORD-PLAY. Next, unpause and the VCR will commence recording
from there (or it may back up a little ways, PLAY a little ways, and then commence
recording). Either way, the VCR will make a cleaner edit—not perfect—but cleaner.

Some portable VCRs, mostly VHS models, have a POWER SAVER or RECORD
LOCK feature which is very helpful when recording a series of segments with a long
wait between them. Here, when you switch to PAUSE, the machine turns off the
spinning video head so that it is not wearing against the tape. In fact the machine
doesn't even waste electricity in this mode. It is *almost* turned off but *ready to go.*
When you have set up your next scene, you simply reactivate the VCR and unpause
to continue your recording.

PORTABLE VCRS AND CAMERAS

Portable VCRs work much like console models do. They are usually smaller, have
more automatic circuits, have a multi-pin input for a camera, and will run on batteries. The features, functions, and feeding of portable recorders are nearly the same
as their tabletop brothers.

Why would you use a portable VCR and camera if you could find yourself a camcorder? Here are several reasons for using separate machines:

1. You wish to make a higher quality recording which requires you to use 3/4U video tape. Since there aren't any 3/4U camcorders, you have to use separate portable cameras and VCRs.

2. A camcorder limits you to the quality of the camera built into the VCR. If you want a better camera (with sharper picture, low light capability, wider angle zoom lens, more automatic features), you will need a separate camera. Excellent cameras can be rented for special occasion productions where quality is paramount.

3. You can sometimes pick up portable VCR and camera ensembles real cheap because they are no longer in vogue.

4. Sometimes, because of heat, vibration, or other environmental factors, the camera must be separate from the VCR.

5. A lightweight portable VCR (without camera) is handy for bringing a cassette TV production with you on the road. The portable VCR and tape fits easily in your briefcase and can be connected easily to a large, heavy TV set at your destination when you get there.

Planning a portable recording and assembling the paraphernalia for an *electronic field production* (EFP) will be covered in Chapter 11. Here we will just deal with how to use the equipment.

Operating a Portable VCR

Once someone else has set it up, operating a portable VCR is easy:

1. Find something to shoot, preferably not something in the dark.

2. Remove the camera's lens cap. Thereafter, don't aim the camera at anything too bright, like the sun.

3. About a minute before you are ready to begin taping, switch the VCR's power to ON. Since either the camera can pause the VCR (with its trigger) or the VCR's pause button can pause it, let's fix things so that the camera does the pausing; it's more convenient that way. To do this, you will first want the VCR's pause OFF and the camera's pause OFF. A methodical way to coordinate this is to press PLAY and look to see if the tape is moving. If it is, you are all set; the camera's trigger will pause for you. If it *isn't,* pull the camera trigger. If this unpauses you, you're all set. If it doesn't, unpause the VCR's button. If that doesn't get things started, pull the camera trigger again. Eventually you get the machine unpaused and playing.

4. Now pull the trigger to pause everything (after all that). Next, press RECORD.

The camera's viewfinder will light up either when you switch the VCR's power ON or when you press PLAY or RECORD. Either way, the camera will take 30 seconds to "warm up" and give you a picture. If the camera is an MOS (metal oxide semiconductor) or CCD (charge coupled device) type, it will give you an instant picture.

5. While in the pause mode, focus the lens, adjust the iris (f-stop), color temperature, and white balance controls. More on this in Chapter 4.

6. When ready to record, pull the camera trigger and the VCR will switch from pause to forward and will begin recording.

7. To stop recording temporarily, pull the trigger again and the VCR will switch to PAUSE.

8. To start recording once more, pull the trigger again.

9. To *finally* stop recording, switch the VCR to STOP (if you wish you may pause the recording first by pulling the camera trigger). In the pause mode, VCRs will consume electricity, wearing down your battery even though you are not making a recording. In the stop mode, some VCRs and cameras keep consuming electricity; others don't. To save your batteries, you may wish to switch the power OFF if the machine will be idle for a while. As mentioned before, some VCRs have a power saver switch which "powers down" the VCR while in the pause mode.

10. To play back a sample of what you recorded, just press REWIND and back up a ways. When the tape is rewound, press STOP.

11. To play, press PLAY and look into the tiny viewfinder on the camera. The image will appear there *if* your camera happens to have an electronic viewfinder (a tiny black-and-white TV set) in it. To hear sound, find the earphone. It usually lives in a little pocket in the carrying case. Stick the plug into the earphone socket on the VCR or the camera; the other end sticks into your ear.

Setting up a Portable VCR for Use

Recording from a camera   The camera connects to the VCR via a multi-pin plug. Just line it up, push it in, and screw the tightening collar to hold the plug in.

Next, check the VCR's INPUT SELECT switch. When operating with a camera, this switch must be in the CAMERA position.

On most portable TV cameras, sound is picked up by a sensitive mike built into the front of the camera and recorded automatically.

When using color cameras and VCR equipment, setting up takes a few moments. Color TV cameras often have to be "warmed up" and adjusted to give good color. Chapter 4 will tell more on how to adjust the camera for proper color.

Not all portable cameras will work with all portable VCRs. First, the plugs may be different. Beta equipment uses a 14-pin plug. VHS and most others use a 10-pin plug. Even if the plugs match, there is no guarantee that the right signal is traveling on the right wire. Recently made portable cameras and recorders generally put their audio and video and power signals on the same wires making it likely that your camera *will work* but might not be able to use all its fancy features. There are special CAMERA-TO-VCR adapters available to solve some of these problems. The more professional portable cameras and VCRs have their own battery power and use normal video and audio outputs and inputs.

Recording audio   Instead of using the mike built into the camera, you can substitute your own, (say a LAVALIER or a SHOTGUN mike described further in Chapter 7). These mikes plug into the MIC input of the VCR. Home VCRs usually take a MINI PLUG for their mikes. Professional VCRs take a three-pronged XLR mike plug. You may need an adapter to match your mike's plug to the machine's socket.

Using the mike built into the camera is very handy, but tends to cause sound with echoes because if the camera is eight feet from the performer, so is the microphone. Microphones pick up sound best when they are close to the performer. The only way to move the mike close to a performer without moving the camera too close is to use a separate microphone.

If the sound source is prerecorded and requires a HI LEVEL INPUT, look for an AUX or AUDIO IN socket on the VCR for this.

In most cases, the audio level is automatically adjusted. Fancier models have manual adjustments too.

AUDIO DUBS are possible by pushing the DUB button on the deck while switching the VCR to PLAY. The mike in the camera may be used in this process or you may plug in a second mike.

Recording off-air broadcasts   The big difference between console and portable VCRs is that consoles *include* the TV tuner, while the portables, for weight reasons, don't. The tuners are separate and connect to the VCR through a multi-pin umbilical cable or through several cables to the VIDEO IN, AUDIO IN, and REMOTE inputs. To pull in distant stations, tuners have ANTENNA inputs which connect to your rooftop antenna or cable TV.

Sometimes these tuners have PROGRAMMABLE TIMERS with all the features the console models have. Also included in most units is a power supply that runs your VCR without discharging your battery. In fact, most units *will charge* your VCR's battery. Of course they must be plugged into a wall outlet, connected to a VCR, and turned *on* to do this.

To really be sure that you've accurately tuned the tuner for a recording, you may wish to review the results on a TV set beforehand. The following explains how.

Attaching a TV set   Most portable VCRs have a socket labeled RF OUT. On older and industrial models, connect this to the TV's ANTENNA terminals. Switch the VCR's OUTPUT SELECTOR (if it has one) to VCR to send the VCR signal (rather than the antenna's) to the TV. Switch the TV to channel 3 (if that's what the VCR's RF GENERATOR puts out, that's all. It's a lot like your console VCR setup. Figure 3-20 diagrams the connection.

Older method:

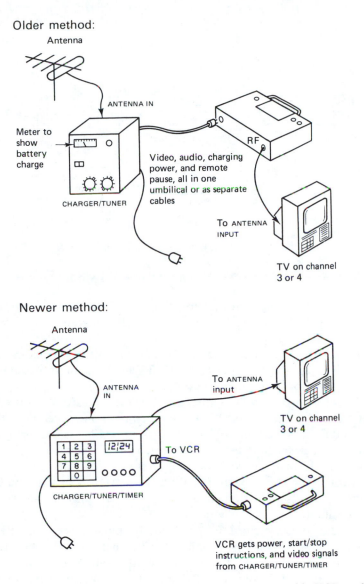

Newer method:

FIGURE 3-20   Tuner/power supply connections to portable VCR and a TV.

Newer models do it a slightly different way. The antenna runs to the tuner. The tuner runs a multi-pin cable to the VCR. The VCR sends its RF back to the tuner over the multi-pin cable. You plug your TV to the ANT OUTPUTs on the tuner. The OUTPUT SELECTOR is also on the tuner. Not much is really changed except the location of the TV connection and the OUTPUT SELECTOR. The tuner may also house the TIMER and an infrared REMOTE control sensor.

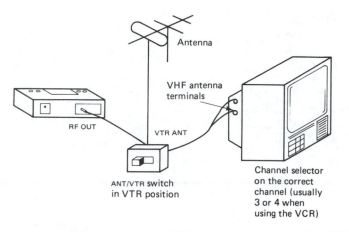

FIGURE 3-21   Receiving RF on a TV receiver from a portable VCR.

What's handy about both of the setups in Figure 3–20 is that only one or two cables have to be disconnected before you can run off with your portable VCR. The TV and antenna wires stay put.

With portables, as with console VCRs, it's possible to run both audio and video to an audio amplifier and speaker and a TV monitor, or you could run both signals to a TV monitor/receiver for viewing.

Sometimes the portable VCR isn't used with a tuner. Instead, it's used to make tapes out in the field (or the woods) and then it comes home to connect to the TV for viewing. Industrial VCRs and older and cheaper VCRs were designed to work this way and use an external ANTENNA/VTR switch when feeding a TV. Figure 3–21 shows the hookup. In fact, this kind of hookup is used for video games and many other devices which connect to your TV. With the ANTENNA switch, you can select whether your TV will "see" the antenna signal (ANT position) or "see" the VCR's signal (VCR position).

Why bother with the switch? Why not simply connect the VCR's RF cable to the TV's antenna terminals and then connect the TV antenna to the same terminals? Such a connection *would work,* although not awfully well. You could get a grainy, ghosty, signal on your TV. Here's why: RF doesn't care where it goes when it comes through the RF cable from the VCR. If the TV is still connected to its antenna, some of the RF signal will go into the TV, as it should, and the rest will detour out the antenna wires to the rooftop antenna. In fact, the RF going up the antenna will actually broadcast out the antenna a little and may interfere with other people's TVs. The Federal Communication Commission frowns on renegade TV broadcasters scattering signals willy-nilly over the airways.

Cable TV and master antenna systems face the same problem. If your TV set is still connected to your building antenna system when you pump RF into your set, everyone on your system will get interference from your signal.

Time for a true story. A young man and his wife bought a portable VCR and camera. After taking it back to their apartment, they decided to set up the camera to record themselves making love. When finished, they eagerly played the tape back on their home receiver. How exciting! The next morning, the couple noticed funny stares from other tenants in the lobby. Someone in the elevator asked, "Haven't I seen you somewhere before?" In their exuberance, the couple had neglected to disconnect the master antenna cable from their TV before attaching their VCR to it. It is not known exactly how many tenants had watched this X-rated gem on their TV sets that evening or had recognized their neighbors as the main characters.

The same danger exists (but not to the same degree of embarrassment) with video games that you connect to your TV antenna terminals. The games send out an RF signal that must go into the TV set *only* and not detour up the antenna wires for all to see.

In short, when sending RF to a TV set, make sure

1. The set is disconnected from its rooftop antenna.
2. The set is disconnected from any master antenna or cable system. Or,
3. If you have an ANT/VCR junction box with a switch, be sure the switch is in the VCR position.

Powering the VCR

For short, on-location shootings, a rechargeable battery which fits inside the VCR will power the VCR for up to one hour. See Figure 3–22. These batteries usually slide into a hole in the VCR somewhere and when clicked tightly into position, will make their own electrical contact. Other VCR batteries have a plug at the end which has to be inserted in the BATT or DC input after the battery has been inserted.

If you press RECORD and FORWARD but do not pull the camera trigger you still are using power even though the tape may be paused and not moving. Add this "standby" time to the time you spend actually shooting and you can estimate that your battery will probably power you through only a half-hour of actual recording.

As the battery gets older, it will serve shorter and shorter duty cycles. Usually the VCR has a battery level meter or there is an indicator light in your camera's viewfinder showing you how much battery life is left.

There are two popular kinds of VCR batteries. One is called GEL-CELL which works much like a car battery. The other is NICAD which stands for NIckel CADmium battery. NICADS are smaller, lighter, hold more power, recharge faster, and last longer than GEL-CELLS. They also cost about twice as much.

The VCR's battery must power the VCR *plus* the camera. How long the battery lasts will depend greatly upon how much juice the camera uses. CCD cameras and cameras without electronic viewfinders use the least power.

To operate a VCR on location for up to three hours, there are optional external chargeable battery packs that connect to the VCR. They plug into the VCR socket labeled DC or 12V IN or EXT BATT.

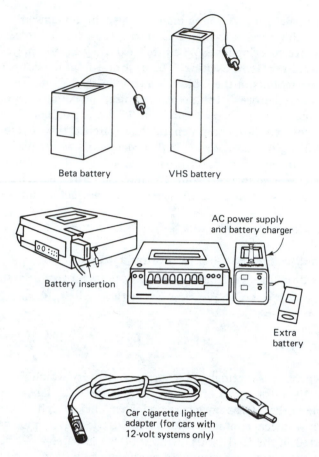

Beta battery   VHS battery

AC power supply
and battery charger

Battery insertion

Extra
battery

Car cigarette lighter
adapter (for cars with
12-volt systems only)

FIGURE 3–22   Powering the VCR.

To operate near vehicles using their battery power, there is a "cigarette lighter" plug and cable which can suck power from your car while you're shooting. Your car has to have a *12-volt* battery (most do). If your car battery is old, it may be wise to start your car and let it run every so often.

For extended shooting, bring along your AC adapter which can power the VCR from a wall outlet when your battery is used up. The adapter can also recharge the VCR's internal battery. Some AC adapters are shaped like VCR batteries and slip into the VCR without a trace except the AC cord.

None of the preceding power supplies is yet designed to power anything *other than* the VCR and its camera. TV monitor/receivers and other equipment must be powered separately either by batteries or by AC.

If you wish to play back some of your recording "in the field" (a good idea just to make sure everything is being recorded), nearly all cameras which have electronic viewfinders will allow you to view your tape through the viewfinder. Plug in an earphone for sound and you can see and hear your recordings without dragging along a separate TV. Take note that this playback also takes electricity and drains batteries.

Nonprofessional Camcorders

A CAMCORDER, as you know, is a camera and VCR in one box. The convenience of not having two separate items with a dangling cord between them is obvious. Also, great efforts have gone into making CAMCORDERS weigh six pounds or less. The two popular types of consumer CAMCORDERS use VHS or 8mm tape.

VHS and VHS-C   A VHS CAMCORDER can record two hours at the SP speed on a T-120 cassette (if the battery holds out). A few models can record at slower speeds yielding up to six hours of recording.

Since VHS cassettes are rather large, these full-sized camcorders are large and heavy also. Their big advantage is that the cassette can be slipped into any VHS machine—no muss, no fuss. For higher quality recordings you may wish to use a Super VHS camcorder.

If size and weight are important, you might select the VHS-C type of camcorder. The tiny cassettes are about the size of a deck of cards. The miniature cassette can be inserted into an adapter which fits normal VHS players. Thus the tape recorded on VHS-C machines is playable on standard VHS machines. A miniature TC-20 cassette can record 20 minutes at the SP speed or 1 hour at the EP speed. These are also available in the Super VHS format.

(Courtesy of Magnavox)

(Courtesy of Minolta)

Consumer CAMCORDERS (Courtesy of Panasonic)

8mm Smallest of all is the 8mm (1/4″) FORMAT. Cassettes hold 8mm wide metal evaporated tape which can record for two or four hours. Tiniest in the 8mm class is Sony's Handicam, weighing 2.2 pounds and fitting in the palm of your hand. With this model, you must play your tapes back on a separate 8mm VCR (included in the ensemble). Larger models weighing about five pounds include electronic viewfinders, inputs, and outputs, and *can* play the tapes back. All models record high fidelity sound.

Professional Camcorders

The nonprofessional camcorders cost about $1,000 and have picture quality about the same as beta and VHS VCRs. The professional CAMCORDERS, on the other hand, cost $15,000 and up and have a picture quality similar to a one-inch VCR.

There are two main types of professional CAMCORDERS. One uses beta-like cassettes, another uses VHS-like cassettes. Although the cassettes are very similar to beta and VHS, the recordings are totally *incompatible* with normal beta and VHS recorders. In both cases, COMPONENT COLORS are recorded on the videocassette rather than COMPOSITE VIDEO. The VCR lays down two tracks side by side. One track is the black-and-white picture and the second track contains instructions on how to paint the colors onto the black-and-white picture. In each of the CAMCORD-ERS, the camera and the VCR may be separated (unlike the nonprofessional CAM-

Betacam (Courtesy of Sony Broadcast Products Company)
Professional CAMCORDER.

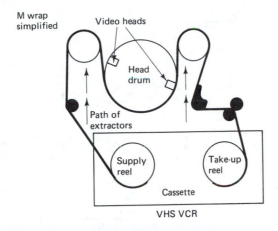

FIGURE 3-23 Videocassette threading pattern.

CORDERS where the camera and VCR are forever united in one box). Professional CAMCORDERS weigh about 20 pounds, 10 pounds for the camera part and 10 pounds for the recorder part.

Most popular is the Sony Betacam which can record 20 minutes on an HG-20 beta cassette. Second most popular is the M2 format which uses special VHS cassettes running at six times the normal speed lasting for 20 minutes.

If doing professional work which is to be edited later, the high quality Betacam and M2 CAMCORDERS are highly preferred. Their colors are sharp and the high quality picture can stand up to the rigors of copying and editing.

HOW VCRS WORK

Open up a VCR someday and look inside. You'll see a marvel of circuits, wheels, pulleys, brakes, sensors, and other gadgets. VCRs are so complex that it is amazing they work at all (sometimes they don't). If the opportunity comes your way, watch a VCR run with its lid off. It's a high tech thrill to see tiny robot fingers extract the tape from the videocassette and thread it around the guides and the spinning VIDEO RECORD HEADS. Figure 3–23 diagrams the process for VHS recorders.

The VIDEO RECORD HEAD is the heart of the system. To understand it, let's go back to a simpler system and see how audio tape is recorded.

To make an audio recording, sound vibrations go in a microphone and are changed to small electrical vibrations. These are sent to an AUDIO RECORD HEAD which is a block of metal with an electromagnet in it which changes the electrical

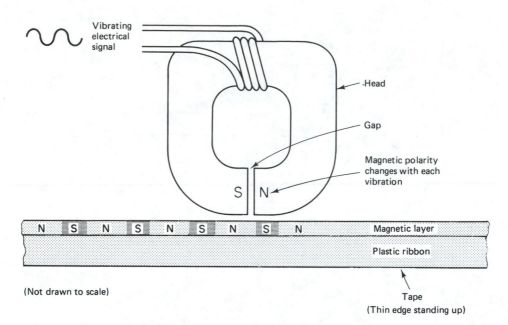

FIGURE 3-24   Record head magnetizing the tape.

vibrations to magnetic vibrations. In the recorder, a rotating spindle called a CAP-STAN pulls the tape through the machine. The tape is a plastic ribbon impregnated with metal particles which can be magnetized as the tape slides over the HEAD. Figure 3-24 diagrams the process.

When audio tape is played back, just the opposite happens. The magnetic vibrations on the tape slightly magnetize the head as they pass by it. This *generates* a tiny electrical signal in the head. The tiny electrical vibrations from the head are amplified in the tape recorder and can vibrate a speaker, making sound again.

The same technique is used by the VCR as it records the low fidelity LINEAR audio track on the tape. Because the tape moves so slowly, a lot of vibrations have to be packed into a small space and this reduces the fidelity of the recording. Hi-fi VCRs use a different method to record the sound.

Video signals are made of extremely high frequency (millions of vibrations per second). To fit all these vibrations on a tape, the tape must be moving very quickly relative to the record head. The VCR wizards in Japan who figured out how to do this decided to place the VIDEO HEADS on a spinning cylinder so that the heads could be moving very fast while the tape traveled slowly.

As the tape moves slowly through the machine, it passes over the HEAD DRUM which rotates 30 times per second. Attached to the drum, opposite each other, are the VIDEO HEADS as shown in Figure 3-25.

The VIDEO HEAD DRUM is tilted so that each head takes a diagonal swipe across the tape as the drum rotates. Since the tape is moving, one head makes one swipe and the next head makes another swipe right next to it. Each swipe records one picture. Figure 3–26 diagrams the path that the VIDEO HEAD takes across the tape.

While the recording is being made, an ERASE HEAD upstream of the VIDEO HEAD is erasing old material from the tape. At the same time, a stationary AUDIO HEAD is recording audio at the edge of the tape. At the opposite edge of the tape, a CONTROL HEAD is placing 60 pulses per second on the tape. These pulses correspond with the VERTICAL SYNC pulses on your TV picture. When the tape is played back, these pulses act like the sprocket holes in a movie film; they keep the picture centered so that it doesn't roll up or down. They also help guide the VIDEO HEADS so that as they play back a tape, each head follows exactly the same path the record heads took. The recorded control track is sort of a "drum beat" which is used by the VCR's motors so that they know how fast to play the tape and how fast to spin the VIDEO HEAD drum. The TRACKING control on the VCR adjusts where the video heads take each swipe. Adjusted perfectly, the heads precisely follow the recorded paths on the tape. When TRACKING is misadjusted, the VIDEO HEADS may play a little of the unrecorded space *between* the paths or even stray into the adjacent path.

Industrial VCRs have fatter VIDEO HEADS which make broader swipes across the tape than home VCRs do. As a result, these professional VCRs and tape duplicators make better pictures. The wider tape pathways are easier for other VCRs to follow, and when these broad pathways are played back on *another* VCR with "fat" heads, the signal is stronger, making a smoother, higher quality picture.

Now you can understand how a VCR makes a STILL FRAME. The tape stands still; the heads keep spinning, tracing the same picture path over and over again. Move the tape forward a tad and the next picture will show. Move the tape halfway between the pictures and the heads will play the mush between the tracks. Voilà, a

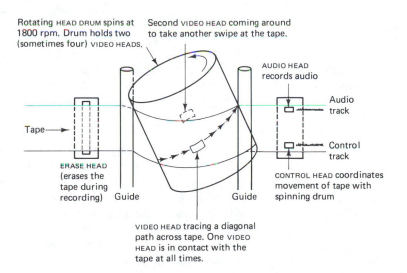

FIGURE 3-25 Spinning VIDEO HEAD recording a tape.

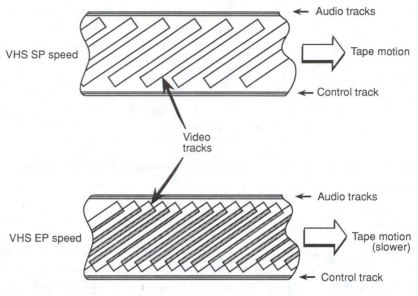

← Audio tracks

VHS SP speed

Tape motion

← Control track

Video
tracks

← Audio tracks

VHS EP speed

Tape motion
(slower)

← Control track

FIGURE 3-26   Path of VIDEO HEAD across the tape.

tracking problem like Figure 3–17. Leave the VCR in STILL FRAME too long in the same spot and the heads start to eat through the tape. The same phenomenon happens with the soles of shoes.

ALL ABOUT TAPE

Videotape is a thin plastic film impregnated with a fine magnetizable powder. You cannot see the magnetism; recorded tape looks no different than blank tape. The magnetic vibrations on the tape are transformed electronically into a picture and sounds by the magnetism-sensing playback HEADS of your VCR in conjunction with various electronic circuits.

Video recording tape must be built to exacting standards. The plastic ribbon must neither stretch nor shrink significantly yet be strong enough to withstand the wear and tear of threading and winding. The tape must be smooth enough not to abrade the delicate spinning VIDEO HEADS inside the machine. The magnetic powder must be very pure, uniform, and resistant to flaking or shedding from its base. Even the videocassette shells themselves must be built to exacting tolerances, with 36 parts to meter the flow of tape from one hub to the other without sticking or jamming.

Like audio tape, videotape can be erased (demagnetized) and used over. With healthy machines and a clean environment, this rerecording process may be repeated hundreds of times.

There is no such thing as ''color'' videotape. The *signals* that are recorded on the tape make the color, not the tape itself. There is no such thing as ''hi-fi'' video-tape. Again, it's the recorded *signals* that make the hi-fi sound.

Selecting Videotape

Some brands of videotape are better than others. Try a few and see what works best with your VCR. Stick with name brands that you recognize, such as

- BASF
- JVC
- Maxell
- Panasonic
- Scotch
- TDK
- Fuji
- Kodak
- Memorex
- RCA
- Sony

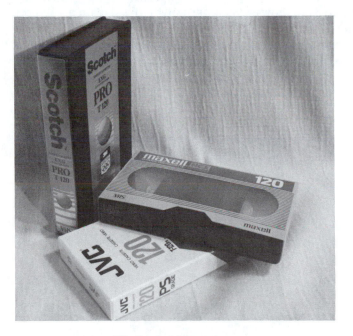

Kinds of video tape.

Name brand cassettes are built to high standards and are less likely to jam inside your VCR.

Some videocassettes are called HIGH GRADE (HG) or SUPER HIGH GRADE (SHG). Although this *usually* means a higher quality tape, the advertisers and manufacturers sometimes fool around with the words and end up packaging regular tape with the "super high grade" label on it. A genuine high grade tape will give you long service, even if edited and paused frequently, and will yield smooth colors with very little graininess.

Super VHS and ED beta VCRs, in order to provide the improved picture, require their own special videotapes. The cassettes look the same as regular VHS and beta videocassettes, but contain tape which is more magnetizable. An S-VHS ST-120 videocassette costs about $15 and will also work in a regular VCR, but won't improve the picture. An ED beta videocassette costs about $12 and will not work in a regular beta VCR.

The best videotapes will give smooth colors, especially in the solid reds and solid blues. The poorer tapes give a grainy picture and grain is especially noticeable in the colors.

Better tapes have fewer DROPOUTS. No, DROPOUTS aren't the jocks who hang around your daughter instead of doing their high school homework. DROPOUTS are specks of snow or streaks on a TV screen caused by a VIDEO HEAD passing over a "bare spot" on the tape where the magnetic powder has flaked off, leaving no signal (and no picture) behind. DROPOUTS also occur when flecks of dirt or tape debris cover the magnetic powder in places, impairing contact with the spinning VIDEO HEADS. Figure 3–27 shows what a DROPOUT looks like on a TV screen. Some DROPOUTS appear as a blink on the screen for a thousandth of a second and are gone before you see them. Others may last longer and are quite distracting. Better tape has fewer DROPOUTS, but all tape has some, especially at the beginning where the tape gets more abused from threading. It doesn't take much to cause a DROPOUT as you can see from Figure 3–28.

FIGURE 3-27   DROPOUT as it appears on a TV screen.

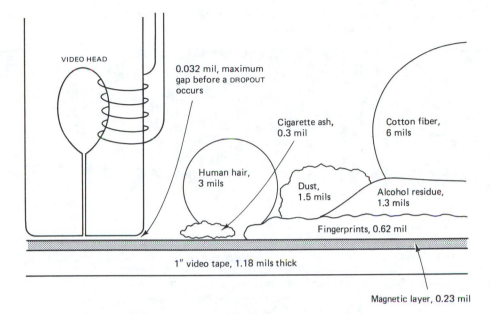

VIDEO HEAD

0.032 mil, maximum gap before a DROPOUT occurs

Cigarette ash, 0.3 mil

Cotton fiber, 6 mils

Human hair, 3 mils

Dust, 1.5 mils

Alcohol residue, 1.3 mils

Fingerprints, 0.62 mil

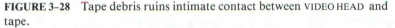

1" video tape, 1.18 mils thick

Magnetic layer, 0.23 mil

FIGURE 3-28 Tape debris ruins intimate contact between VIDEO HEAD and tape.

Length   Videocassettes come with various lengths of tape spooled into them. A common L-500 beta videocassette will last one, two, or three hours depending on the VCR's speed. In beta L-500, the 500 stands for the length of the tape in feet. A thinner L-750 tape will last 50% longer running up to four and a half hours at the beta-3 speed.

VHS videocassettes have model numbers which tell you their lengths in minutes at the SP speed. A T-120 videocassette will last 120 minutes (2 hours) at the SP speed. The same tape will run four hours at the LP speed and six hours at the EP speed. VHS videocassettes come in other lengths such as T-30 (30 minutes), T-60, T-140, and T-160 (which runs eight hours at the EP speed).

Super-thin tape may give you more playing time, but it has its disadvantages, too. Some tape is so thin that it stretches and snags easier than regular tape. If you want the best picture and sound, use the standard thickness tape (T-120, L-500, or lower numbered) and the fastest VCR speed. If you plan to do much winding, rewinding, pausing, scanning, starting, stopping, editing, or frequent ejecting or inserting, use the standard thickness tape. If, however, you plan to record a long passage from beginning to end and play it back nonstop from beginning to end, feel comfortable in using the thinner tapes.

If you play a cassette all the way through, you are likely to get a pleasant surprise. The manufacturers generally put more tape in the cassette than they advertised. A VHS T-120 cassette generally has as much as 15 extra minutes in it at the SP mode.

Turn tape over and pop out red button to protect cassette from being recorded over.
Reinsert button to restore recording ability to prevent erasure.

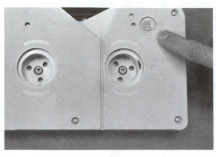

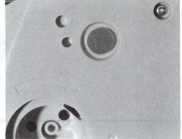

| tab | to prevent erasure | to record again |

VHS

To protect a recording from accidental erasure, break off the SAFETY TAB on the bottom of the
videocassette (BETA) or the near edge of the videocassette (VHS) using a screwdriver.
With the tab removed, the RECORD button won't go down and the tape is "safe" from erasure.
If you change your mind and wish to record, cover the hole with a piece of cellophane tape.

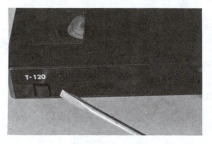

| tab | to prevent erasure | to record again |

BETA

| tab | to prevent erasure | to record again |

  FIGURE 3-29 Preventing accidental erasure.

Avoiding Accidental Erasure

Picture yourself recording a "Munsters" rerun and looking down at the cassette box to discover that you are recording over priceless camcorded sequences of Robert Redford changing his tire at the end of *your driveway*. Or, you can loan your only copy of "Casablanca" to your neighbor and get it back with his kids' recording of Saturday morning "Plastic Man" cartoons on it. Murphy's 108th Law of Recording states that junk recordings *never* get accidentally erased; prized ones *always* do. Nothing short of copying all of your tapes and keeping them in a vault will completely protect them. But two easy precautions will save you a lot of disappointments.

1. *Label everything as soon as it is recorded.* Don't guess what is on your tapes. You are likely to record over your wrong guesses.
2. *Remove the* SAFETY TAB *from the videocassette so that the tape cannot be recorded upon.* Figure 3–29 shows how.

On beta and VHS cassettes, break off the plastic safety tab from the edge of the cassette (don't bother keeping the tab; covering the hole with a piece of scotch tape will restore the cassette's recordability).

This procedure does not affect playback or any other feature of the VCR or tape. It just defeats the VCR's RECORDING function.

Care of Videotape

Longevity   Magnetic tape is not an archival medium. Although the magnetism recorded on it will last easily 50 years, the plastic ribbon itself stretches and contracts with heat and cold and "relaxes" with age causing the picture to bend at the top (FLAGWAVING).

Even under ideal environmental conditions, your tape may begin to suffer the "bends" after a year or so. Playing the tape once or twice a year will help, perhaps stretching this figure to ten years.

A tape can be played between a 100 and 200 times before the picture becomes noticeably degraded. PAUSING wears out the tape quickly.

If you record something that you expect to be valuable 50 years from now, consider whether anyone will be able to find a VCR to play it 50 years from now. VCR formats change with time. In the 70s, the popular video format was EIAJ reel-to-reel and IVC 1″. Almost none of these machines are around today, and if you do find one, it probably needs repair before it can be used.

Storage   The lifetime of your recording is directly related to how carefully it is *stored* and how gently it's *used*. Here are the rules of storage:

1. *Store cassettes upright, in a vertical position.* This prevents the edges of the tape "ribbon" from getting "roughed up" against the inside of the cassette as it lays on its side.

2. *Keep the cassettes in their boxes.* This keeps out dust and dirt which cause DROPOUTS.

3. *Store tapes at average temperature and humidity*—about 70°F (20°C) and 50% or less humidity. Temperatures below −40°F (−40°C) and above 140°F (60°C) will permanently damage the tape. A car trunk, passenger area or glove compartment on a hot day may easily exceed the 140°F maximum. Leaving a tape on the dashboard will definitely exceed the maximum temperature (the cassette may even shrivel up). Leaving the tape in the sun anywhere may also overheat it. Mildew will grow on damp tapes.

4. *Keep tapes away from magnetic fields,* such as hi-fi speakers, amplifiers, transformers, magnets, or big electric motors. The magnetism from these devices can partially erase your tape. Don't set your tape on top of the TV for long periods of time. Every time you switch on your TV set, it demagnetizes the tape a little. Incidentally, removing the tape's SAFETY TAB will not protect the tape from being erased by stray magnetism.

5. *Wind or rewind tapes before storage.* Don't store them partially rewound because you want the DROPOUT-causing threading process to occur at the beginning or end of your tape, not in the middle of your show.

   Some experts advise winding your tapes all the way to the end for long-term storage. This provides very uniform tension on the tape. Also, when you rewind the tape before playing it back, you "air it out," dehumidifying it so it will slip easily through the machine when it plays.

6. *Don't leave recorded tapes threaded in the VCR* for days or weeks; this creases them where they are bent around the tape guides.

7. *Remove the SAFETY TAB* on any tape you wish to "erase-proof."

Handling

1. *Treat cassettes gently.* Dropping them rubs the delicate tape edges against the cassette housings, abrading the tape.

   If you damage a cassette, don't try to play it. It may jam in your VCR. New videocassettes are cheap. VCR repairs are expensive.

2. *With VHS machines, use PAUSE rather than short STOPS.* It stretches the tape a little every time the VHS machine unthreads and rethreads on STOP. On PAUSE, the tape stays threaded. On beta machines, the tape stays threaded on STOP so it's okay to STOP betas.

3. *Don't PAUSE a tape more than a couple minutes.* After a while, the spinning VIDEO HEAD will wear out the tape or crease it, causing DROPOUTS in that part of the program.

Organizing a Tape Collection

Home video addicts have a tendency to record too much and store too much. Almost every program seems too valuable to be erased. So, another box of videocassettes gets purchased and another batch of "priceless" recordings goes on the shelf. The programs most likely to be recorded and never watched include graduations, school events and concerts, school plays, and birthday parties. Since you will never know what will be chaff and what will be cherished, you may end up recording many programs and having some of them sit on the shelves for ten years unwatched. So regardless of your filing system, it pays to examine your shelves once a year and "weed out" the unnecessary recordings. People who fail to "weed" their tape inventory tend to get buried in their recordings and have a hard time locating the important ones.

It is better to have a short pencil than a long memory. You will need some method of logging your recordings on paper. The most common method is logging and shelving by ACCESSION NUMBER.

Number your cassettes on the box and on the cassette shell itself (in case they get separated) from 1 to whatever. Thereafter, each new tape gets the next higher number. Get a loose-leaf or other type of notebook and number each page. List each tape's contents with COUNTER numbers on the corresponding page. You may wish to include length of show, date, time of recording (or broadcast), channel, tape speed, the cast, original recording or duplicate, recording quality, black-and-white or color, or other details on the page. For off-the-air recordings, you could easily slice out the *TV Guide* listing for the show and paste it on the page.

Later, you can sort the entries by title or subject and print up tape catalogues with alphabetized titles and tape numbers.

For large collections, computerized databases are very handy for sorting and listing the program titles alphabetically. The computer may also sort the list by subject or by kind of tape (that is, VHS, S-VHS, VHS-C, 8mm).

Storage boxes and labels   The boxes videocassettes come in are fine except that when you shelve all the various brands side by side, the mix of colors and trademarks starts to make your shelves look messy. Also the space available for titling is a bit cramped. Furthermore, some cardboard tape boxes fall apart rather easily.

Half-inch videocassette boxes are usually plastic; some snap shut and are sturdy enough to be mailed. They cost about $2 (Figure 3–30).

Many stationery stores sell blank 3/4″ × 3″ labels which can be typed and then stuck onto your present cassette boxes and cassettes. Placing same-sized labels on the boxes will keep your tape library looking uniform. Also, when you make a new recording over an old one, you can neatly affix a new label rather than erasing, scraping, or blow torching off the old label.

Remember, when numbering cassettes, to put your number on both the box *and* the cassette. Place the cassette's number so it will be visible through the re-

FIGURE 3–30 Videocassette storage boxes.

corder's window while the tape is in use. This way, you'll not lose track of what tape you're playing *now.*

And here's a special hint for fitting more tapes on those cramped shelves of yours: Most people store cassettes upright (long side faces out, like books on a library shelf). This way the cassette labels on the spines of the boxes are easy to read. The cassettes, however, take up a lot of shelf height and you get fewer shelves per cabinet or per wall. If, instead, you set the cassettes on their long edge, (spine facing the ceiling) they are not so tall and more shelves can be used for the same height. There may no longer be room enough to show the cassette's title but you can put the cassette ACCESSION NUMBERS on 3/4″ square labels and affix these to the short edge of the tape which now faces out. Figure 3–31 shows an example of such an arrangement.

Never mail videotapes in those paper-filled cushioned envelopes. The envelopes invariably tear inside releasing head-clogging dust and flakes. Use special mailing boxes or plastic "bubble" wrap packaging.

COMMON VCR AILMENTS AND CURES

You followed the directions (you thought). Everything is connected and rarin' to go. Only it doesn't. Before you run whimpering to the repair shop, there's a lot you can try to diagnose and solve your VCR's problem yourself.

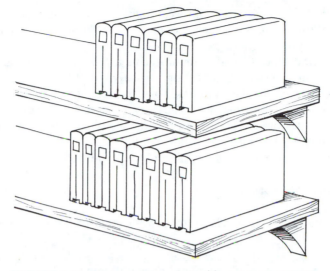

FIGURE 3–31   Store cassettes short-side-out to save space.

Common VCR ailments and cures.

After a while you will learn the eccentricities of your machines and will intuitively head right for the trouble when your VCR goes kaput. Until that time, you're going to have to use logic and patience.

You will find that 80% of your problems are because you failed to throw a switch, turn a dial, or connect something correctly. Another 10% of your problems will be minor defects, maybe in one of your connecting cables, perhaps a broken wire. Another 5% of the time, it's a dirty or broken switch somewhere—still an easy thing to replace or fix. Then 5% of your time the machine fails because *it* has a problem and needs technical attention.

Let's look at some common VCR problems and how to solve them.

Machine Control Problems

In these examples, the machine's buttons don't seem to do what they're supposed to.

1. *VCR fails to operate;* POWER *light does not come on.*
   a. Check to see if the VCR is plugged in.
   b. Is the socket it's plugged into operated by a wall switch somewhere? If in doubt, check the outlet using a lamp.
   c. TIMER may be switched to AUTO or ON and waiting for a scheduled time. Check which position manually activates the VCR, or try flipping it to another position and watching for signs of life.
   d. Turn TIMER/SLEEP switch OFF.
   e. Look for a REMOTE switch. Perhaps the machine only wants to listen to its remote control.
   f. Are you running on batteries? Are the batteries dead? Is there an AC/DC switch someplace telling the machine to operate off the batteries (which aren't installed) while you want it to operate off the AC power?
   g. A nearby lightning strike may have burned up your machine's power supply circuits (a good reason for unplugging your VCR during thunderstorms). If the machine seems completely dead, bring it to a repairperson, along with about $75.

2. POWER *light comes on but tape doesn't move when you switch to* PLAY.
   a. Check PAUSE; it should be OFF.
   b. Check the REMOTE socket; if anything is connected there, *it* may be PAUSED. (An earphone accidentally plugged into the REMOTE PAUSE socket will PAUSE the machine, too.)
   c. Is the DEW light on? If so, you'll have to wait until the machine dries out before it will work. Try the hair dryer trick mentioned in the ''Getting More Out of Your VCR'' section of this chapter.
      Is the machine cold (thus condensing humidity)? Move the machine to where it's warm and dry.

d. Is the cassette properly loaded? Are you trying to use a beta cassette in a VHS machine? That will never do.

e. On some VCRs, is the STANDBY light on? If so, give it a few moments to go off.

f. Maybe the tape is loose in the cassette; it should be taut. Often VCRs sense loose tape and switch themselves to STOP. Press REWIND, STOP, WIND, STOP, then PLAY. The rewinding and winding may tighten the tape.

g. Could it be that the tape is at its end and needs to be rewound? Some cassette machines have an AUTO OFF feature which stops the tape at the end of play. Some also have an AUTO OFF indicator that lights up to apprise you of this condition.

h. Are you using a portable VCR? Perhaps your battery died, or got too weak. Try another power supply. If using your portable in very cold weather, the oil in it could become gooey, slowing down the VCR's wheels. The VCR may sense this and shut itself down to avoid damage. The VCR may also sense whether its transistors are too cold to function, and will shut itself down.

i. Do you have a camera connected to the VCR? Perhaps its PAUSE trigger is pulled.

3. *Buttons won't depress.*
   a. Switch the power ON.
   b. Make sure you have a cassette in the VCR.
   c. Check everything in example 2.

4. RECORD *button won't depress or activate.*
   a. Check the cassette SAFETY TAB. If it's been removed, the tape cannot be recorded. See the section on avoiding accidental erasure earlier in this chapter.
   b. Check everything in examples 2 and 3.

5. AUDIO DUB *button won't depress or activate.* Same problem as example 4; most likely SAFETY TAB.

6. FAST FORWARD *does not function.*
   a. Maybe you're already at the tape's end. Rewind.
   b. Check everything in examples 2 and 3.

7. *VCR stops in* REWIND *before it reaches the beginning of the tape.* Turn the MEMORY or SEARCH switch *off.*

8. *Cassette won't insert into VCR.*
   a. Is it the right FORMAT (VHS, beta, or 3/4U) cassette?
   b. Are you holding it right? The trapdoor part points away from you; the reel hubs face down.
   c. Is there already a cassette in the VCR?

9. *Cassette* EJECT *doesn't work.* Switch power ON, press STOP, wait a moment, then try again.

10. *The tape moves slowly or moves backwards when you press* RECORD *or* PLAY. The belts in your VCR are tired, slippery, or broken. Call your repairperson.

11. *The tape rewinds or winds very slowly. (It should take less than three and a half minutes to completely wind or rewind a tape).* Tired belts; same as example 10. Air pollution and smoke tend to age belts quickly, causing them to glaze (get slippery), crack, or stretch.

12. *While playing or recording, the VCR mysteriously stops itself. It may even rewind itself, or rewind and begin playing/recording again.*
    a. Does the VCR have a REPEAT switch? If it's turned ON,
       • When the tape reaches its end, it will rewind and repeat.
       • When the INDEX COUNTER reaches 000 on some machines, they will rewind and start over.
    b. The tape may be scratched or perforated. VCRs have automatic shutoffs which sense this and stop. If the problem always occurs at the same spot on the tape, you might try removing the cassette and examining the tape for damage (explained further in Chapter 13).

Signal Control Problems

In these examples, you can't get a picture or sound where you want it to go. Often the culprit is a misflipped switch. If you do much connecting and disconnecting of cables, it may be a cable plugged in the wrong socket.

If the cables are moved often, the connectors sometimes get loose or the wires fray inside the plug. After trying the obvious (switches, correct connections), try wiggling the cable at the plug end, or rotating the plug in its socket (except for multipin plugs) and watch your TV for flashing and listen for crackling sounds on the TV speaker. A frayed wire or dirty or bent plug may make contact intermittently when wiggled, cutting your signal off and on. When you doubt a cable, try another if you have one. A successful substitution will prove the first cable defective. They are usually easy to fix (if you're the handy type) or fairly cheap to replace (except for the multi-pin cables—they're worth fixing because they're expensive).

Sometimes switches get dirty inside. When you switch, the TV shows a lot of breakup and hash, and the audio may crackle. Flipping the switch back and forth a dozen times may clean it somewhat, but a deteriorating switch will become more and more intermittent and unreliable. If you're handy, there are sprays you can squirt in there to clean a dirty switch. Otherwise, a technician may have to clean it for you.

Now let's see what else can go wrong.

1. *Can't get regular TV programs on the TV set.*
    a. Switch the VCR's OUTPUT SELECT, ANTENNA, or VTR/TV switch to TV.
    b. Is the VCR connected to the antenna? Is the TV's ANTENNA input connected to the VCR? They should be.

   c. If you're using the VCR's tuner to feed the TV, make sure *it* is FINE TUNED and your TV is FINE TUNED to the VCR's channel (3 or 4), and your VCR's INPUT SELECT is on TV and its OUTPUT SELECT is on VCR.

   d. If you are receiving cable TV, maybe the cable TV company has pooped out. Sometimes a lightning strike will knock them off the air.

2. *Can't get VCR to play through the TV.*

   a. VCR's OUTPUT SELECT must be in the VCR position.

   b. Check the connections between the VCR and the TV.

   c. Is your TV tuned to the same channel as your RF CONVERTER?

   d. If you're sending video and audio straight to a TV monitor/receiver, make sure the monitor/receiver is switched to LINE or VTR, not to AIR or TV.

   e. Check to see if the TV even works by switching the VCR's OUTPUT SELECT to TV or ANTENNA and tuning the TV to various broadcast channels. If nothing comes in, perhaps the VCR-to-TV connection is bad or the TV is bad. If stations are received, then the TV and its connections are okay. Switch the OUTPUT SELECT back to the VCR mode and check channels 3 or 4.

   f. Wiggle the cables while playing a tape and watch the TV for flashing to check for loose connections.

3. *Unable to record TV programs.*

   a. Flip the VCR's INPUT SELECTOR to TV.

   b. Make sure the cassette's SAFETY TAB is still there.

   c. Unplug the camera and microphone from the deck. They sometimes automatically override the TV inputs.

   d. Check to see if the VCR's tuner works by tuning the VCR to a station known to be good and monitoring the results on your TV set. If your TV had been able to pick up the station directly (with the VCR's OUTPUT SELECTOR on TV), but is now unable to tune in that same station with your VCR tuned to the station and its OUTPUT SELECTOR on VCR and the TV tuned to channel 3, then the tuner's blown. The culprit was probably a nearby lightning strike (on the cable wires or near your antenna wires). It's off to the repair shop to the tune of about $150. In the future, disconnect your VCR's antenna (or cable) input during thunderstorms.

4. *No sound while recording a TV broadcast.*

   a. You left the microphone plugged into the VCR, overriding the TV.

   b. Check any separate AUDIO IN connection for the same thing.

   c. If your portable VCR uses a separate tuner with separate AUDIO and VIDEO connections, the AUDIO wire may be loose.

   d. Maybe you have sound but you can't hear it. Can you get sound while playing other tapes or from off-the-air broadcasts? If not, maybe your TV has an earphone plugged into it, cutting off its speaker.

   e. Turn up the volume control on the TV. If the sound crackles on and off as you do, work the knob back and forth a couple of times or tap it. You may

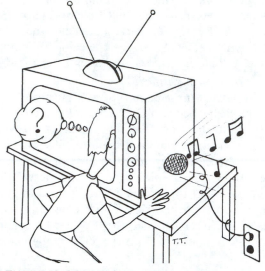

THERE IS SOUND BUT NO PICTURE

have a volume control that is dirty inside or has a "dead" spot. If you get the crackling volume control working for the time being, leave it. Later, have a technician look at it. It's generally easy to fix.

f. If you're using a monitor/receiver and sending separate audio and video to it, check your audio wire.

5. *No picture while recording a TV broadcast; sound is okay.*

a. The camera or a separate video input is still connected to the VCR.

b. On portable VCRs, check that the tuner's video cable is connected to the VCR's VIDEO IN.

6. *Camera or microphone signals won't record.*

a. Switch the VCR's input switch to CAMERA or VIDEO (away from TV or TUNER).

b. Are the microphone and camera plugged in? Is the camera turned on? Is the mike turned on? Some have ON/OFF switches.

Using your Monitors to Help Track Down Signal Problems

Home video usually involves a chain of equipment. If you happen to be missing audio or video at the end of this chain, you need to work your way back through the chain to find out where it was lost.

If audio happens to be missing, start at your audio source. Can you plug an earphone into it to see if it's even *making* sound? If not, your problem is with the source and you can spend your time troubleshooting there. If it is making sound, then your problem may be in the cables leading to the next device or in the next device. Can you plug your earphone into the next device and check for sound there? Try doing this all the way along your chain of equipment. Eventually you may find where the sound disappears and home in on the guilty party.

Another way to check your sound is with the AUDIO LEVEL meter found on some VCRs and other equipment. If the meter wiggles, that indicates you have sound.

Video works the same way. If you can connect a trusted TV monitor into your source and get a picture, then you know your source is working and your problem is somewhere downstream. Often the viewfinder on your camera is a good way to check whether the camera is putting out a good signal. If you see nothing on the viewfinder, then you should suspect the camera is at fault. If the viewfinder shows a good picture, the problem may be in the cable to the VCR or wherever the signal is going.

Of course it is difficult to monitor a video signal if you're using a TV monitor that is broken. Perhaps one way to check the monitor is to feed a known *good* signal into the monitor directly and see if the monitor works. If it does, now you can trust it and continue with the rest of your tests.

Special Audio Problems

Chapter 7 will sound off on this subject, but the following are some common gremlins to chase away:

1. *An uncalled for screech or howl comes out of the TV.*

    Turn down the volume on your TV receiver or sound monitor. You've got what is called FEEDBACK. What happens is this: Sound goes in the microphone, goes into the VCR, gets sent to the TV receiver, and comes out the speaker loudly enough to go back into the microphone again. Around and around the sound goes until you break the cycle by turning the volume down or moving the mike farther from the TV. Figure 3–32 diagrams this process.

2. *Sound that is hard to hear and full of echoes.*
    a. Move the mike closer to the subject.
    b. Move to a room with more carpet, curtains, and furniture. You have too many echoes from hard, bare walls.
    c. Turn the volume down on your TV; some of the sound is getting back to your mike.

3. *Microphone sound is weak, tinny, or has hum or hiss.*
    a. The mike is not right for your VCR. Read Chapter 7 and try another mike.
    b. The mike may be defective or of poor quality.
    c. The connection may be bad, or you may be using the wrong kind of mike wire.

4. *Using AUDIO IN, the sound distorts or sounds raspy; your audio signal is too strong; the sound may also have lots of hum and hiss.*

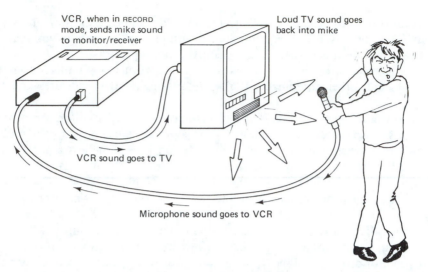

VCR, when in RECORD mode, sends mike sound to monitor/receiver

Loud TV sound goes back into mike

VCR sound goes to TV

Microphone sound goes to VCR

FIGURE 3-32 Audio FEEDBACK.

    a. Reduce the volume from the source.

    b. Attenuate the signal using methods described earlier in this chapter or in Chapter 7.

5. *While playing a tape, you get no sound, the wrong sound, two soundtracks at once, or what seems like half the sound.*

Videotapes can have two or even four soundtracks. You can listen to channel 1, 2, or a mixture of both. The trick is to play back the correct soundtrack. If you hear no sound, perhaps you're listening to the silent track. Try the other. If you're hearing Spanish and you want English, perhaps the tape is bilingual and you're listening to the wrong channel. Try the other. If you hear both languages together and you want only one, perhaps your AUDIO SELECT switch is on MIX. Switch it to CH-1 or CH-2. If you hear just sound effects when you should hear narration *and* effects, switch the selector to MIX.

If using RF or the VCR's headphone output, the AUDIO SELECT switch will probably take care of everything. If, however, you're running an audio cable from the CHANNEL 1 AUDIO OUT to a separate amplifier and loudspeaker, then CHANNEL 1 may be all the amp will hear. You may have to unplug the cable from the CHANNEL 1 output and stick it into the CHANNEL 2 socket to hear CHANNEL 2. The AUDIO SELECT switch won't make any difference here.

Hi-fi VCRs can take their sound either from the hi-fi tracks or from the low fidelity LINEAR tracks. You may select which tracks your VCR will play by throwing a switch probably marked HI-FI/LINEAR. Remember that if you've done AUDIO DUBS on your videotape, all of the changed sound is going to be on the low fidelity LINEAR tracks. Your hi-fi tracks remain unchanged.

Picture Quality Problems

1. *Picture is distorted, usually with a band of snow or* NOISE *through it. Figure 3-17 shows a mild case. Worst cases may look much like Figure 3-33. The picture may jiggle a lot.*

   Adjust the TRACKING control. This is perhaps the most frequent adjustment you will need to make on a VCR. Usually the picture is best when the TRACKING control is set in the middle at FIX, but tapes made on another recorder are most likely to require that the TRACKING knob be turned to some position other than FIX. Turn the TRACKING control until the breakup moves off the screen at either the top or bottom and the picture remains stable.

   Old, stretched, hot, cold, or damp tapes won't track well at all.

2. *On* PAUSE *or* STILL, *the VCR's picture has a band of noise through it as in Figure 3-17 or 3-33.*

   Similar to example 1, adjust the VCR's SLOW TRACKING control. You can see the results of your adjustments faster if you switch the VCR to the SLO MO mode while adjusting the SLOW TRACKING knob.

3. *No color or poor color when playing a tape.*
   a. Adjust the TV's FINE TUNING.
   b. Perhaps the VCR's FINE TUNING wasn't properly adjusted when the recording was made. If so, the program will never play in color.
   c. Are you sure this is a color program?
   d. Turn up the COLOR control on the TV set.
   e. Check to see the TV's ANTENNA input switch is set to 75 Ω if you're using coax cable, or 300 Ω if you're using twin lead.
   f. If you're using straight video into a TV monitor, make sure the set is properly terminated (as explained in Chapter 1).

FIGURE 3-33 Grainy picture caused by mistracking.

4. *Using AFT (automatic fine tuning) worsens reception.* You've tuned your VCR manually with the AFT *off* and everything looks great. You switch the AFT *on* and things get worse, or perhaps you lose color.

   a. Your AFT circuits need adjustment by a technician.

   b. In the meantime, leave it *off* and you'll get by.

5. *While playing a tape, the picture blanks out or temporarily distorts or shrinks.*

   a. Is there a power hungry motor, heater, microwave oven, or other appliance on your circuit sapping power? If this power interference occurred during the recording, the glitch is there to stay. If it happens only during playback, the tape is okay; go back and view again.

   b. If there's an air conditioner or big motor nearby, it can interfere with your video signal.

6. *Tape plays at the wrong speed.* The picture may roll, bend, tear, or collapse into diagonal lines.

   a. Is your SLOW MOTION feature engaged?

   b. Perhaps the machine is damp inside and the DEW SENSOR failed to stop the machine. Let it warm up a bit and try again.

   c. Your VCR's insides may be dirty. Run a CLEANING CASSETTE through (process described in Chapter 13) and see if it helps.

   d. Is your portable VCR's battery dying? Double check the AC power adapter connection. Does the power meter say it's getting enough juice?

   e. Are you using a cheap or nonbrand name cassette? It could be rubbing inside.

   f. Try another cassette tape. If the problem persists, perhaps the VCR's drive belts are old, tired, slippery, or need replacement.

   g. You would get speed problems if your AC power fluctuated in frequency. Do you have weird power? (I have a grandmother with weird powers).

   h. Was the tape recorded at a speed your VCR can't play? If the sound plays fast or slow, that's your tipoff that the machine and tape are different speeds.

7. *The picture bends or flutters at the top during playback.* FLAGWAVING (or TAPE TENSION ERROR or SKEW ERROR) is shown in Figure 3–18. it is usually caused by the tape being too tight, too loose, or too shrunken as it plays through the machine.

   a. Adjust the HORIZONTAL HOLD on your TV set.

   b. Adjust the SKEW or TAPE TENSION control on your VCR if it has one (most home models don't).

   c. If the problem happens on all tapes, have your VCR adjusted inside. If your TV is very old or has tubes, the picture will always look worse than it has to. If you have another TV, try that one.

   d. If the tape and/or VCR are cold, let them stabilize to room temperature.

   e. If the tape was recorded long ago, it probably has shrunk. Without adjusting the VCR inside, it will probably never play right. One thing you can try is winding the tape all the way to the end. Then, rewind it all the way to the beginning. Now try to play it. The winding may stretch or relax the tape a little, making a marginal tape playable.

f. Super-thin tapes stretch easily, especially in hot weather, causing FLAG-WAVING.

g. The problem may be similar to example 2 or 6 earlier. Try those maneuvers.

8. *The picture looks very grainy or even snowy on playback only. It looked fine when it was recorded (eliminating the possibility that you recorded a snowy picture to start with) and the sound is okay. Perhaps it looks like Figure 3–33.*

If the picture is very snowy, it could be due to a worn or dirty VIDEO HEAD. You can't easily see the dirt on a VIDEO HEAD, but a tiny speck of it can clog this very sensitive device. Usually a clogged HEAD will not completely obliterate the picture—some faint image may show through the snow. If this is what you see, you can be fairly sure your problem *is* a clogged HEAD.

What do you do for a clogged HEAD? You clean the HEAD with a special "cleaning cassette." Following the manufacturer's instructions, insert the cleaning cassette into the machine just as you would a normal cassette. Play the special cassette for about 30 seconds, then remove it without rewinding it. The HEADS should now be clean. Chapter 13 gives further details on this procedure.

9. *The TV used to work all right before you hooked up the VCR, and the VCR works okay elsewhere, but together they display interference or herringbone patterns on the TV screen or in the recording, as in Figure 3–34 or 3–35.*

The TV or the recorder is sending out a weak signal which is interfering with the other's tuner. Move the two farther apart—maybe three feet. If mov-

FIGURE 3-34 TV interference.

FIGURE 3-35 VCR's channel 3 is competing with a local station's channel 3 causing faint diagonal lines. Try switching RF converter to channel 4.

ing them apart isn't possible, try placing a grounded metal plate between the two. Sometimes tinfoil wrapped around part of the TV works (but don't cover its vent holes).

Also, avoid long antenna cables coiled up behind the equipment. Use good quality, well-shielded cables, and avoid excessive lengths.

10. *You used to get sharp cable TV pictures before you added the VCR and a few other video devices like switchers. Now you get a ghost on some channels (as in Figure 3–34).*

Nearby TV stations are broadcasting strong signals *directly into your equipment* while the cable company is sending you the same programs on the same channels slightly delayed (because their signals traverse so much wire). The unwanted direct signal "leaks into" your wires and into poorly shielded equipment to cause ghosts. Seal those invading signals out by using COAX or SHIELDED TWIN LEAD everywhere, and well-shielded, high quality switchers and other accessories.

11. *At every edit point, when the new scene begins, there is a rainbow of colors smeared across the picture which lasts for about five seconds and then disappears.*

When you are recording over something else that is on the tape using a nonediting VCR, it takes a few moments for the VCR to begin erasing the tape upon which you are recording the new picture. This picture-over-a-picture causes the color rainbow. It can't be helped; there's nothing wrong with your VCR. To get rid of the problem entirely, you need to buy a VCR with FLYING ERASE HEADS (described more fully in Chapter 10).

12. *You play a tape and find the picture to be contrasty, bending, or streaking in the bright places as in Figure 3–36.*
    a. You are probably playing an S-VHS recording on a normal VHS VCR.
    b. If using professional gear, you may be sending too strong a video signal to your VCR. If your VCR has a manual VIDEO LEVEL control, it may be turned up too high.

FIGURE 3-36   S-VHS tape played on a VHS machine.

FIGURE 3-37   Thin bands of snow across screen, usually a sign of damaged tape.

13. *While playing a tape, there are excessive* DROPOUTS *or thin bands of snow across screen, as in Figure 3–37.*
    a. If the band slides down the screen and eventually disappears off the screen as the tape plays, this is a tape defect. It could be a wrinkle, a tape splice, a dent in the tape, or a spot where the magnetic surface has flaked off. There is no cure; the tape will always play like this. If the problem is severe, and you can actually *hear* the bad part as it runs through the machine, you should consider not playing the tape again. The damaged tape could "snag" on the delicate video heads and damage them.
    b. If the band stays at the same height on the screen as the tape plays, the tape probably has a scratch on it.
       • The tape cassette could be scratching the tape. Perhaps it can be opened and fixed so it doesn't scratch *more* of this tape (the damage already done is irreversible).
       • The VCR could be scratching the tape. If so, it could scratch *all* your tapes. Try another tape of little importance. If the problem shows there too, it's the VCR's fault. Get it fixed pronto before it damages more tape.
    c. If tapes play okay on other machines but show the snowy streaks only on this one, there may be a dirty contact in the video head drum assembly. Have a technician clean it.
14. *Off-the-air TV signal looks okay when fed to a TV only, but when the VCR is wired into the system, the picture gets snowy, grainy, or color is lost.*
    a. The connections or the antenna wire between the VCR and its TV monitor might be bad. Check out the ends or try another wire.

b. If the TV signal is weak, giving it *two* machines to feed (the VCR and TV) may be enough to deplete it altogether. Try BOOSTING the signal first using an ANTENNA AMPLIFIER (which you can get from Radio Shack and other places). If you are dividing the signal between several TVs already, you may wish to use an AMPLIFIED COUPLER like the one shown in Figure 1–18.

15. *You play a prerecorded videocassette and the picture jitters and rolls.*
   a. Adjust TRACKING.
   b. Adjust your TV's VERTICAL HOLD.
   c. If this is a commercially made tape, it may be COPYGUARDED—its sync signals are messed up to keep people from duplicating it. These signals are messing up your VCR or TV. Send the tape back and ask for a non-COPYGUARDED edition.
   d. If a friend gave you this copy, which he or she made from a COPYGUARDED tape, naturally it shouldn't play. That was the tape producer's whole idea.
   e. Cheap, counterfeit, pirated, or nth generation (copies of somebody else's copies which were previously copied from somebody else's copy) tapes are likely to be of low tape quality, low cassette-shell quality, or low recording quality, and they just won't play well.
   f. Clean the HEADS with a CLEANING CASSETTE (process described in Chapter 13). Your CONTROL HEAD, which synchronizes the motors and tape movement, may be dirty. Also the CAPSTAN (the part that pulls the tape steadily through the machine) may be dirty. If you're handy, open the machine and clean these parts manually to do a better job.

16. *When playing a VCR using RF into a TV receiver, you see a ghost (a faint second image) or light or dark bars floating through the picture, as in Figures 3–34 or 3–35.*
   a. The RF GENERATOR in your VCR is using the same frequency (channel) as a nearby TV station, giving you CO-CHANNEL INTERFERENCE. Switch the RF GENERATOR and TV to another channel.
   b. You have a tangle of antenna wires, picking up interference. Organize them neatly and place them farther apart.
   c. Your antenna cables aren't well grounded or well shielded and are picking up interference.
   d. Your TV and VCR are too close together. One is interfering with the other. Review example 9.
   e. If you're using boosters, splitters, switchers, or other gadgets on your antenna wires, they may be poorly shielded and interference may be "leaking" into or out of them.

17. *Portable VCR mysteriously turns itself on when in its carrying case.* You probably bumped the carry case hard enough to push one of the "feather touch" function controls. Some buttons are mighty sensitive.

4

All about TV cameras and lenses

Why talk about separate cameras when camcorders are now the vogue? Here are some reasons:

1. Camcorders are also cameras, so the more you know about cameras, the more you know about camcorders.
2. Home camcorders are often compromises; you might not find the best camera built into a camcorder. Where high quality production is necessary, a separate camera and VCR should be used so that you can use the best camera for the job—maybe one with a super zoom lens.
3. For special occasions, an expensive high quality camera can be rented and attached to your VCR for more professional results.
4. Very good quality used TV cameras can be purchased.
5. You can set up a mini studio with a switcher and several separate TV cameras.
6. There are times when you want your TV camera separated from your VCR. Perhaps the camera has to be hidden, needs to be way up high, or needs to be in a place where vibrations, smoke, or dust would cause a VCR to malfunction.

What you'll read here about TV cameras will apply to camcorders just as well.

KINDS OF CAMERAS

The first television cameras were as big as a St. Bernard's dog house and took two strong men to aim and operate them. The St. Bernard hasn't changed over the years, but today's cameras can fit into a birdhouse—along with the VCR.

Although improved technology is lowering the cost of all TV cameras, it is generally true that the better quality TV cameras are more expensive. Color cameras range in price from $500 to $80,000. Naturally, the $80,000 camera gives a much sharper, purer, and more stable picture than its home video cousin. The quality of the picture depends on many factors in the camera's makeup. Where a home video camera uses a single 1/2-inch-wide CCD chip to create a full color picture, an industrial camera uses three pickup chips or tubes—one for each primary color—and those tubes are 2/3-inch wide or more to produce a sharper picture. Even the makeup of the tubes is different, making them more sensitive in low light, or resistant to bright lights. Additional camera circuits check on how the camera is seeing things and adjust the camera so that colors are pure and overlap each other in perfect registration.

PICKUP TUBES IN CAMERAS

A TV camera "sees" with its PICKUP TUBE (or PICKUP CHIP if it is using an MOS or CCD image sensor).

Some pickups are designed for monochrome and others for color. Some color pickups have fine colored stripes on their faces which allow them to sense all three primary colors at once, and are used in the less expensive SINGLE-TUBE or SINGLE-CHIP color cameras. Other color camera tubes are manufactured for use in THREE-

BURN-IN from aiming at the "THE END" sign too long. The image remains, even though the camera is now aiming at a new subject.

BURN-IN from aiming across a shiny object

FIGURE 4-1   BURN-INS

Picture "sticks" on screen as subject moves.

A flare lags behind her bright hand as it moves across the dark background.

FIGURE 4-2 STICKING and LAG in tubed cameras

TUBE or THREE-CHIP color cameras where each is destined to view but one primary color.

The internal design of the camera permits it to excel in certain ways. The "perfect" camera would

1. Have excellent resolution (picture sharpness).
2. Be sensitive in low light. This would allow the camera to produce a good picture without the need for many extra lights, handy for indoor situations where normal room lighting or perhaps one light is all that is available.
3. Resist BURN-INS. BURN-INS occur when a tube type TV camera is aimed at a bright light or the sun or a contrasty scene for too long. The bright parts of the scene "burn themselves into" the picture and remain there no matter where the camera is aimed. Mild BURN-INS go away in time, but serious ones, caused by very bright lights, may damage the tube forever. Figure 4–1 shows examples of BURN-INS. Cameras which are to be used by novices or outdoors need to be BURN-IN resistant.
4. Resist LAG, STICKING, or COMET-TAILING. When something moves in your picture, no trace of it should be left behind. LAG is a smear that follows a bright object moving over a dark background. STICKING describes an image which "sticks" on the screen after the camera has been moved to a new scene. COMET-TAILING is a streak that follows a bright light moving across the screen. Figure 4–2 shows examples of STICKING and LAG.
5. Reproduce color faithfully.
6. Be affordable.

The most common tube used in older inexpensive video cameras was the VIDI-CON (Figure 4–3). More expensive industrial video cameras use the SATICON tube

Things that are too bright for a tubed camera to look at are:

1. The sun, for even a second.
2. A movie or a TV light, for even a second.
3. A bright bare bulb.
4. Any chromed object reflecting the light from any of the first three above.
5. Mirrors or glass objects reflecting bright lights.
6. Atom bomb blasts.

Very bright lights will scar the light-sensitive surfce of older VIDICON TUBE cameras causing a permanent blemish there. These are called BURN-INS. Medium bright lights can cause temporary BURN-INS.

Avoid BURN-INS in tubed cameras

which gives a better picture. Newvicons give a better picture than SATICONS in low light situations, but in normal light, SATICONS win out. Today's home cameras use the MOS (metal oxide semiconductor) which is not a tube at all but is a transistorized light sensor the size of a postage stamp. A more expensive cousin used in higher quality cameras is the CCD (charged coupled device) which is also a light sensor on a circuit chip. Both are extremely rugged and tiny compared to camera tubes. Such cameras can be very small and lightweight and use very little power.

VIEWFINDERS

The VIEWFINDER is the thing you look through to see where your camera is aimed. Not all TV cameras have VIEWFINDERS. Many security and industrial cameras do not. Most portables do. Some color portables even have detachable VIEWFINDERS, handy for tight spaces.

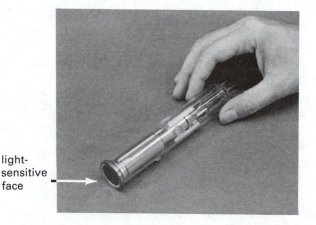

light-sensitive face

FIGURE 4–3 VIDICON tube from a TV camera

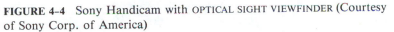

FIGURE 4-4 Sony Handicam with OPTICAL SIGHT VIEWFINDER (Courtesy of Sony Corp. of America)

Cameras may have three kinds of VIEWFINDERS: OPTICAL-SIGHT VIEWFINDER, THROUGH-THE-LENS VIEWFINDER, and ELECTRONIC VIEWFINDER.

Optical-Sight Viewfinder

The OPTICAL-SIGHT VIEWFINDER is an inexpensive little range finder that, like a weak telescope, shows you approximately where your camera is aimed. OPTICAL-SIGHT VIEWFINDERS are found on the least expensive or tiniest cameras like the Sony 8mm Handicam (Figure 4–4).

Although cameras with OPTICAL-SIGHT VIEWFINDERS are cheaper, smaller, lighter, and use less power, they have disadvantages: You don't automatically know if you are focused, and you can't tell where you are zoomed to. You can't tell if your picture is too contrasty, and you can't even check your recordings by playing them back through the camera. The OPTICAL VIEWFINDER is best where lightness and smallness are paramount.

Through-the-Lens Viewfinder

The THROUGH-THE-LENS (TTL) VIEWFINDER, much like your 35mm SLR (single lens reflex) slide camera displays the image which actually comes *through the lens* (ergo its catchy name). You see what the pickup tube sees. You know immediately if your picture is fuzzy or off center. You can tell exactly what is in a picture as you zoom.

TTL VIEWFINDERS are usually found on the less expensive home video cameras. They often have a few lights or meters built into them to indicate whether you have enough light, whether your battery is weak, and whether your VCR is paused or recording. Some TTL VIEWFINDERS have lights to tell you whether your WHITE BALANCE is properly adjusted (a process explained later).

As with the OPTICAL-SIGHT VIEWFINDER, the TTL VIEWFINDER uses no power, handy for when you need to conserve battery power while shooting with a portable VCR or camcorder.

The disadvantage of the TTL VIEWFINDER is that it doesn't show if your picture is too contrasty. Nor can you check your recordings by playing them back through your VIEWFINDER.

Electronic Viewfinder

ELECTRONIC VIEWFINDERS—small TV monitors attached to your cameras or camcorders—display the picture exactly the way it is being sent to the tape machine. Focus, framing, contrast, and zoom all manifest themselves in the picture you see.

Color is the one thing you don't see on your ELECTRONIC VIEWFINDER. With rare exceptions, ELECTRONIC VIEWFINDERS are black and white, even on color TV cameras. That's not a mistake. Black-and-white VIEWFINDERS give a sharper picture than color (of prime importance when focusing). They are smaller, lighter, much cheaper, and adequately perform their basic mission to display what you are shooting.

Many ELECTRONIC VIEWFINDERS have indicators for light level, pause, battery, and other functions of the camera and VCR.

One great advantage of the ELECTRONIC VIEWFINDER on a portable camera is that it can display the image *played back* from your VCR. So after recording a sequence, you can rewind the tape and play it through your VIEWFINDER to see how you were doing.

Most home video manufacturers build the VIEWFINDER into the camera which streamlines the package and makes it look much like a super 8 movie camera. Industrial cameras and the more expensive home video cameras have separate VIEWFINDERS which are detachable. Some advantages of the detachable VIEWFINDERS are as follows:

1. Once the VIEWFINDER is removed, the camera and VIEWFINDER are more easily packed and transported.

2. Detachable ELECTRONIC VIEWFINDERS are handy when in a pinch you need to conserve battery power while shooting—simply disconnect to save a watt.

3. Many ELECTRONIC VIEWFINDERS hitch up to either side of a portable camera (for left-eyed or right-eyed people) and some can be adjusted in many directions, freeing the camera operator to hold the camera above or below him or her. Some finders can be removed from the camera and attached to an extension cable for remote viewing—handy if your camera is up in a tree or in the middle of a cattle drive.

Usually, the heavier, higher quality, portable cameras come with ELECTRONIC VIEWFINDERS. These cameras, too heavy to be steadily held by the trigger handles, sit on the shoulder. The VIEWFINDER is attached near the front of the camera improving the balance and steadiness.

Portable TV cameras use miniature TV monitors with one-inch screens. You view the screen by placing your face against a rubber cushion, and looking through a magnifying lens built into the VIEWFINDER. This will make the picture big and easy to see. Often these viewfinders have a hinged lens/eyecup mechanism which can be flipped up out of your way allowing you to view the TV monitor directly with both eyes or with a friend. You'd both better have good eyes though, as the picture is not much bigger than a postage stamp.

Some TV cameras are designed for both studio and portable use. In the studio the camera is placed on a tripod, connected to a multi-wire umbilical cable which remotely controls its electronics, and has a four-inch-wide VIEWFINDER. To use the camera in portable situations, the large VIEWFINDER is detached and a miniature one is connected. The multi-wire umbilical is replaced with a battery pack and a cable leading to the VCR. The tripod is replaced with a cushioned shoulder mount. Figure 4–5 shows such a camera.

Camcorder with adjustable ELECTRONIC VIEWFINDER (Courtesy of Aiwa)

portable configuration   studio configuration

FIGURE 4–5   Industrial color camera designed for portable or studio use

MICROPHONES—BUILT-IN

All portable home video cameras and some of the lower cost industrial cameras have microphones built into them. These are usually ELECTRET CONDENSOR microphones which are very sensitive and give good sound quality, especially for conversation.

They do have one fault. Since your camera is likely to be six feet or more away from your subject, that means that your built-in mike is also six feet away. This results in echo-filled speech and a distracting amount of background noise such as doors slamming, dogs barking, traffic, wind, and even the sounds of the camera operator.

When really good sound is necessary, it is possible to override the built-in mike and use a separate microphone such as a lavalier which you hang around your talent's neck or attach to his or her lapel. The plug goes into the MIC input of the VCR. Because the subject speaks directly into the mike (a foot away) the sound is clearer. If the talent moves around too much for an attached mike, you could use a SHOT-GUN MIKE.

A SHOTGUN MIKE, so named because of its long shotgun-like barrel, "listens" in one direction only. Someone standing nearby could aim the SHOTGUN MIKE at the talent as he or she moved around.

Some cameras have SHOTGUN MIKES built into them. This is handy because the microphone automatically aims wherever the camera aims.

Another solution to the problem of the built-in microphone picking up the sounds of the camera operator is to use a BOOM microphone. This is usually a tele-scoping rod which allows the microphone to be stretched out ahead of the camera,

Camera with built-in SHOTGUN MIKE (Courtesy of Canon)

S-VHS-C CAMCORDER with built-in BOOM MIKE (Courtesy of Quasar)

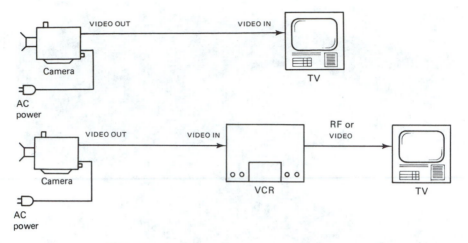

FIGURE 4-6 Connecting up a surveillance camera

farther from the sounds of the camera operator pulling the trigger, focusing (especially with motorized ELECTRIC FOCUSING cameras), zooming, and breathing.

The more professional cameras allow different microphones with different characteristics to be plugged into their VCRs as needed.

CONNECTING A CAMERA TO A VCR

The simplest TV camera is the black-and-white surveillance camera used to keep an eye on the baby or the front door stoop. These cameras cost about $100, use AC power, and make video signals just like their larger brothers. If you find one of these, you can hook it up as in Figure 4-6.

Portable color TV cameras range in price from about $500 to about $20,000. The home and many industrial models connect to the VCR with a multi-wire umbilical cable. This cable carries power to the camera, video from the camera to the VCR, audio from the camera to the VCR, video from the VCR to the viewfinder when the VCR is playing a tape back, as well as a plethora of other signals such as remote pause (operated from the camera's trigger). Some cameras not only PAUSE their VCRs, but can control all their VCR functions (PLAY, REWIND, FAST FORWARD, SCAN) from the camera. Some VCRs will send signals to the camera's viewfinder to warn you that your batteries are getting tired or that your tape has run out. All these signals travel over the multi-wire umbilical between the camera and the portable VCR. Naturally, for all these functions to work, the camera and VCR have to be designed to work with each other. If you switch cameras, the camera plug may fit into the VCR and you may even be able to record picture and sound, but remote control of the VCR and other features are likely to be lost.

Portable TV cameras do not *have* to be used portably. With the help of a CAMERA ADAPTER, they can be placed on a tripod and used in the studio just like any other camera. The CAMERA ADAPTER is a box which gets AC power from a wall outlet and makes all the signals the camera needs to operate. The CAMERA ADAPTER box has a standard VIDEO and AUDIO output and generally has a cable which sends a REMOTE PAUSE signal to a console VCR. Figure 4–7 shows how a portable camera can be connected to a VCR.

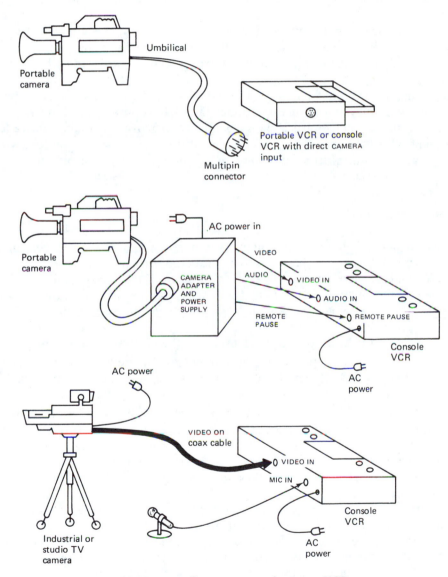

FIGURE 4-7 Camera connections to a VCR

ADJUSTMENTS ON THE CAMERA

In the old days, you would buy a camera, a lens, and a VCR separately. You could put a cheapie $20 lens on the camera or a fancy $3,000 super 10:1 zoom lens on the camera, depending upon your needs. The camera could be a cheap $100 black-and-white vidicon type, or it could be an outrageously expensive $40,000 three-tube plumbicon. After that you could choose the kind of VCR that best suited your needs—a heavy duty multifunction editing deck, or an inexpensive lightweight portable.

With camcorders, the mixing and matching of components goes out the window. You get the lens, camera, and VCR that the manufacturer chose for you. You get a nice tidy package with automatic controls for almost everything because all the parts are designed to work together. But you do lose the flexibility of using the best of lenses, the best of cameras, or the best of VCRs for your particular purpose.

For those of you who manage to get their hands on an older camera, or a more professional camera which allows manual control of the lens and camera features, and also for those of you who buy camcorders with manual overrides for some of these features, let's study some of the more popular controls and adjustments on a color camera.

Focus, Zoom, and Iris

The lens typically found on even a simple TV camera would be a ZOOM LENS Figure 4–8). There are three moving parts that can be adjusted on a ZOOM lens. When using a simple camera you reach around to the front of the camera and make your adjustments by rotating parts of the lens. Always check what you are doing by watching the VIEWFINDER or a TV monitor. The three adjustments are

1. FOCUS. Turning this part of the lens makes the picture sharp or blurry.
2. ZOOM. Turning this part of the lens makes the picture look closer or farther away. With electric zoom lenses you press a button rather than turn the lens to zoom.
3. IRIS. Turning this part of the lens in one direction allows lots of light to pass through the lens and increases the contrast in your picture. Turning it in the other direction, restricts the amount of light allowed through the lens and decreases the contrast making the picture look grayer. In general, you adjust the IRIS so that the picture looks good.

You will be using focus and zoom all the time. Usually you set the IRIS at the beginning of the show and don't touch it thereafter.

There is only one way to correctly focus a zoom lens. The method takes about five seconds and should be done before the scene actually starts. During the scene, you may not have time to use this proper method and will have to focus as best you can.

FIGURE 4–8   ZOOM lens

Proper method of focusing:

1. Zoom in all the way on your central subject making it look as close as you can.
2. Focus the lens.
3. Zoom back out to the kind of shot you want.

If you use this method, you can zoom in and out and your subject will stay in focus. If you don't use this method, your picture will go out of focus whenever you zoom in and you will have to keep refocusing repeatedly. In any case, if the distance between your subject and your camera changes—the subject moves or you move the camera or you pick another subject at a different distance from the camera—you will have to refocus if you want the picture to stay sharp throughout the entire zoom range of the lens.

We'll come back to the fine points of focusing, zooming, and adjusting the lens IRIS a little later in this chapter, but this should get us started.

Color Temperature

COLOR TEMPERATURE describes the warmth (redness) or chill (blueness) of a scene. For example, have you ever noticed how cold and sterile offices lit with fluorescent lights look? Or have you looked into a darkened room illuminated only by the light from a black-and-white TV set and noticed how stark and bluish everything seemed?

On the other hand, have you noticed the warmth in a home lit by incandescent lamps or the warmth of a supper lit by candlelight, or the richness of the whole outdoors during an August sunset? These differences are caused by the COLOR TEMPERATURE of the light.

Under different lighting conditions, the color of things changes drastically even though you may not be aware of it with your naked eye. The eye of the camera, however, sees these differences and makes them even more pronounced. A face that looked red and rosy when lit by a sunset will look deathly pale when photographed on a foggy day. Somehow the color camera must be adjusted to compensate for these differences in lighting so that colors will look familiar and proper. This is called COLOR BALANCE.

Some color cameras have a built-in set of colored glass lenses that counteract the ''coldness'' of the light and bring it into proper balance. The COLOR TEMPERATURE control on most cameras is a three-position or four-position thumb-wheel (Figure 4–9). Next to the wheel is usually a chart listing which position to set the wheel for various lighting conditions. Sometimes these conditions are described by little pictures and sometimes they are described in more technical terms. The precise measurement of COLOR TEMPERATURE will be discussed more in Chapter 6 but for now just follow this chart of where to turn the wheel for various lighting situations.

Not all cameras will use the same filters or numbers for their COLOR TEMPERATURE controls. Some may simply have a two-position switch marked INDOORS/OUTDOORS. Less expensive home cameras may lack this adjustment altogether; their colors will always be a little off.

White Balance

Every time you use your camera or change lighting conditions (like moving from indoors to outdoors or even from scene to scene sometimes) you have to ''teach'' your camera what color *white* is.

FIGURE 4–9   COLOR TEMPERATURE wheel on a JVC camera

Position	COLOR TEMPERATURE (degrees K)	Lighting Situation
1	3,200	For shooting scenes under studio lamps or outside during a sunrise or sunset—all "warm" light conditions.
2	4,500	For fluorescent lamp lighting.
3	6,000	For bright or hazy sunshine.
4	8,000	For shooting outdoors in cloudy or rainy weather or with a clear blue sky without direct sunshine.

You remember how a colored picture is the composite of three pictures—one green, one red, and one blue? A certain mix of these three primary colors is needed to make pure white. If the mix is off, you get tinted white. Sometimes things that are supposed to be white (a white piece of paper on a desk) turn out not to be white at all (the desk is in an orange room, casting orange light on the paper). Still you'd like the paper to look white on camera, so by adjusting WHITE BALANCE, you adjust that mix of primary colors to *make* it white. WHITE BALANCE, WHITE LEVEL SET, or WHITE SET is often adjusted as follows:

1. Adjust your COLOR TEMPERATURE filter *first*.
2. In the area you plan to shoot (and in its light), place a white card in front of the color camera close enough to fill the camera's VIEWFINDER screen. If you don't have a white card, then aim the camera close to a white teeshirt or some other white surface. Some cameras come equipped with a milky white camera lens cap which you can place over the lens and use that as your white surface.
3. Press the AUTO WHITE BALANCE button on the camera and hold it for about four seconds while the circuits inside the camera make the adjustment.

Which Adjustment Comes When

Which do you adjust first, the WHITE BALANCE, the IRIS, or the COLOR TEMPERATURE?

When preparing a color TV camera for use, make the adjustments in the following order:

1. Iris.   2. Color temperature.   3. White balance.

You will see how to do this shortly.

Automatic Controls

Many of today's cameras and camcorders have automatic controls for FOCUS, IRIS, and WHITE BALANCE. With these cameras you don't have to do any thinking—just aim and shoot. The camera will automatically focus, automatically adjust the iris to let in the amount of light necessary for a contrasty enough picture, and will continuously adjust the WHITE BALANCE to give a generally good picture.

The trouble with automatic controls is that they are sometimes fooled, giving you a terrible looking picture. Other times, they take away your artistic control where you may wish to have a picture do something unusual. This is when it is nice to have manual overrides so that you may adjust the FOCUS, IRIS, and WHITE BALANCE to suit your needs. Let's study these automatic controls in a little more detail.

Auto focus   There are three ways to make an auto focus camera and each has its own weakness. Most cameras use an *infrared* beam of light which bounces off the subject, and returns to tell the camera how far away the subject is and where to focus the lens. This kind of automatic focusing goes awry when you are shooting through leaves, bushes, or fencing which may reflect back some light from nearby, focusing your lens for near instead of far. The infrared focuser also gets confused when you're shooting a large flat surface, like a shiny floor, which reflects the infrared beam away from you rather than back to you. Also the infrared beam gets absorbed by dark surfaces like dark carpets, drapes, or velvet. In these situations, you will want to use manual focusing.

Ultrasonic focusing is another range finding technique. A high-pitched sound (beyond human hearing) is emitted from the camera and bounces back from the subject telling the camera how far away the subject is. This camera runs amuck when the sound is bounced *away* or is absorbed by sound-absorbing material like drapes or snow. Shooting through a window is impossible because the sound bounces off the window and focuses the lens on the glass rather than the subject.

Another scheme focuses the camera electronically. It "looks" for sharp edges in the picture and tries to make them sharper. This works fine when there are sharp edges in the picture, but some pictures such as clouds, carpeting, foggy scenes, and special effect scenes have no sharp edges and drive the camera crazy.

All of the foregoing focusing methods sometimes have difficulty distinguishing which is the subject and which is the background in the picture. The camera can't tell whether to focus on the flower 4 feet away from you, the person 10 feet away from you, or the trees 100 feet away from you. Some cameras will even "hunt" back and forth from one subject to the next, really mucking up your shot. In all of these cases, you have to take charge and switch to MANUAL FOCUS, making the camera do what *you* want it to do.

Auto Iris

AUTO IRIS has a similar problem distinguishing what part of the picture is important to you. If a person is standing in front of a bright background, the AUTO IRIS is likely to adjust the lens to give you a lovely picture of the background and a silhouette of the person standing in the foreground, as shown in Figure 4–10. In these cases, you need to manually override the AUTO IRIS and open the lens f-stop further to make the person look good even though the background may be too white (Figure 4–11).

FIGURE 4-10 Light background "fools" AUTO IRIS

FIGURE 4-11 Background sacrificed for foreground

Some cameras even have a button called BACKLIGHT which, when pressed, makes this adjustment for you.

Continuous White Balance

Here the camera continuously adjusts its WHITE BALANCE automatically as your camera moves from scene to scene. It does a pretty good job, but when it gets fooled, your subjects' faces will turn from one color to another because of a change in background color. The best way to WHITE BALANCE a camera is the hard way:

1. Light your scene.
2. Adjust your IRIS.
3. Adjust COLOR TEMPERATURE.
4. Manually adjust WHITE BALANCE using a white card or milky lens cap. This should give you "perfect" white balance.

Now let's go to some other controls you may find on your camera or camcorder.

Viewfinder Controls

VIEWFINDERS are just tiny TV monitors. They sample a little of the camera's video signal before sending it out to its destination. Like other monitors, they have controls for BRIGHTNESS, CONTRAST, HORIZONTAL, and VERTICAL. These controls do not affect the picture that is being recorded. They only make the picture comfortable for the camera operator's eyes. Many home cameras have their viewfinder controls hidden while others may have screwdriver-type adjustments for BRIGHTNESS and CONTRAST.

Some VIEWFINDERS have lens adjustments for nearsighted individuals or those with glasses. These adjustments only change the focusing of the VIEWFINDER lens (making the picture sharp or fuzzy in the viewfinder) and do not affect the recording whatsoever.

+6 dB, +12dB Boost

Cameras are designed to work with a certain amount of light. When the light gets too dim, the image from the camera gets dim and murky. The colors will look especially dingy. The BOOST control found on the professional and the better home cameras will make the camera more sensitive in dim light. This is handy when you get into situations where you have no choice but to use the existing light or one small portable light to shoot with.

You never get something for nothing. When you boost the sensitivity of the camera, you also boost the NOISE or graininess in the picture. The BOOST control should always be left *off* unless it is absolutely needed.

Usually, the switch is labeled with a number (like +6 dB) to tell you how much BOOST you are getting. The bigger the number, the bigger the BOOST.

Auto Fade

AUTO FADE is a control found on some home video cameras which allows you to fade the picture out by pressing a button. This is often a neat way to end a scene, fading to black. AUTO FADE can also be used the other way to open a scene fading up from black to the full picture.

Variable Shutter

Normal TV cameras have a shutter speed of 1/60 second. When things zip by they appear a bit blurry. Newer MOS and CCD cameras have VARIABLE SPEED SHUTTERS which will capture an image in maybe 1/500 or 1/1000 second. The sharper pictures make it easier to analyze a golf swing or a bird's flight. Because the camera "takes" the pictures quicker, it requires more light (just like a film camera). Use the faster SHUTTER speed only when necessary (when you plan to STILL FRAME the image for study) and when you have plenty of light.

Character Generator/Timer

One way to put titles on the TV screen is to painstakingly letter them onto a piece of paper and aim the camera at it. A quicker way to put words on the TV screen is to use a CHARACTER GENERATOR built into some of the more expensive home video cameras. By pressing buttons on the camera, you can electronically select letters to appear on the TV screen. On many models, these letters will even appear over your picture (as was shown back in Figure 2–1). Some cameras even have a built-in clock

6dB, 12dB, BOOST

which will record the date and time along with your picture. This would be handy for instance if you were documenting when a factory was polluting the air. Your videotape would show the smoke coming out the stacks while the time and date would be shown on the screen.

The date/time generator could also be useful if you were shooting a legal deposition in a courtroom. The date and time on the screen would assure that no editing had occurred, thus legitimizing the tape.

Using these CHARACTER GENERATORS is fairly easy. You would switch on the CHARACTER GENERATOR circuit, then select the position for the first letter and then select the letter. Repeat the process for all the letters of your title. Then you store the title in "memory" and call the entire title out at the push of a button when you want it to appear on your tape. Some generators are easier to use than others. They have a separate button for each letter. Others have only two buttons—FORWARD and BACKWARD. If the first letter you wanted was a "D," you would press the FORWARD button four times. You would then advance the CURSOR (positioner) to the next position and press the FORWARD button 11 more times to advance to "O." You'd then move the cursor ahead one more step and press the REVERSE button nine times to get back to "G." Voilà! It may sound hard, but remember that magic markers and paper aren't easy either.

Such CHARACTER-GENERATED text looks a bit chunky (as you could see back in Figure 2–1). The unadorned block letters may be satisfactory for amateur and some school uses, but wouldn't look right in a professional production.

Electric Zoom

It is sometimes difficult to reach around in front of a portable TV camera and grasp the lens to zoom it. To simplify matters, some manufacturers have built ELECTRIC ZOOM controls into their cameras, usually in the form of a ROCKER SWITCH (Figure 4–12). Press one end of the ROCKER SWITCH and a miniature motor will zoom the lens in for a close-up. Press the other end of the switch and the lens zooms out. On the better cameras, a gentle press of the ROCKER SWITCH zooms the lens slowly while a firm press of the button zooms you quickly. Others have only one speed.

STUDIO CAMERAS

As your hobby gets more professional, you may toy with the thought of building a small studio with several cameras and a switcher, perhaps with special effects like dissolve, wipe, corner insert, and chromakey. How to do all this is beyond the scope of this book. But there are a few things you should know before spending any money on equipment.

Cameras which have to work together in a studio need to be synchronized electronically. All the cameras have to scan their pictures in step to an EXTERNAL SYNC GENERATOR before their pictures can be switched, mixed, or manipulated as special effects. Such specialized cameras have a socket on them called EXTERNAL SYNC or GENLOCK IN. When a signal from a SYNC GENERATOR is sent to the GENLOCK IN of a camera, the camera's circuits "listen" and synchronize themselves to that signal. These synchronized video signals can now be sent to a switcher and be manipulated.

You can find more on this subject in *Video User's Handbook* or in *Today's Video,* both published by Prentice Hall.

CAMERA CARE

1. Never aim the camera into a bright light and beware of shiny objects which could reflect a bright light. Chrome, glass, water, and shiny tubas can reflect enough light on a sunny day to BURN-IN a VIDICON tube. Welding torches and studio lamps also create too much light for even the more resistant SATICON tube. CCD and MOS cameras are almost indestructible, but it's not wise to press your luck.

2. Lock your camera pedestal controls when your camera is idle. Someone brushing against an unattended camera could point it into a bright light. Worse yet, a camera with a heavy lens might suddenly tilt down, slamming its lens against the tripod, breaking the lens, or tipping over the whole works.

3. Cap your lens when the camera is idle. This protects not only the lens glass but the pickup tube. It's amazing where bright lights come from when nobody is looking.

4. When you move a camera from place to place, keep its lens capped or watch the viewfinder constantly to avoid accidentally aiming into bright lights.

5. Never leave tube cameras pointed at a very contrasty subject for a long period of time. The bright parts of the image will BURN-IN the tube and will remain in the picture later when you use the camera to shoot something else.

FIGURE 4-12 ROCKER SWITCH to control ELECTRIC ZOOM

6. Don't knock the camera around. It is fragile and easily misaligned.

7. Avoid extremes in temperature. The heat in the trunk of a parked car on a sunny day could damage the circuits. In frigid weather, the zoom lens may get "sticky" and may fail to rotate smoothly. Incidentally, damp fingers on a subfreezing lens barrel might instantly freeze to the lens barrel.

8. Avoid dampness.

9. If traveling by air, don't check your camera with your baggage. Remember the luggage ad with the ape tossing around the suitcases?

COMMON TV CAMERA AILMENTS AND CURES

The first step, as always, is to home in on the problem. If your camera has a viewfinder and can send its signal to a TV monitor, you are equipped to track down the elusive camera gremlins. Although there are 100 things that can go wrong with a camera, there are probably only 10 things that go wrong 90% of the time. Figuring out *where* the problem occurs tells you a lot about *what* the problem might be. Try to narrow the problem down to whether it's caused by the camera, the viewfinder, the cables, the VCR, or your monitor. Now let's attack some specific problems.

Picture Problems

1. *No picture on* ELECTRIC VIEWFINDER *or TV set.*
   a. Is the camera turned on?
   b. Is the VCR turned on?
   c. If using an AC POWER ADAPTER with your camera, is *it* turned on?

    d. Is the lens uncapped? This is not as silly an oversight as you may think.

    e. Is the lens IRIS open enough? Turn it to low f numbers.

    f. Is the camera designed to work with this VCR?

    g. Is the camera's FADE button depressed? It may be faded out.

    h. Is the camera switched to the CHARACTER GENERATOR mode showing you a screen of text that hasn't been made yet (black screen)?

    i. Is there a dark lens FILTER attached to the lens from a prior shoot?

2. *Good picture in the* VIEWFINDER; *no picture on the monitor.*

    a. Wiggle each end of the camera cable near the plug. If the picture flashes on and off the screen, you have a broken wire—very common on simple camera setups.

    b. Are the VCR's INPUT and OUTPUT selectors set to their proper positions?

    c. Is the camera designed to work with this VCR?

    d. Your monitor may be malfunctioning. Check its switches or send it a signal from somewhere else.

    e. The monitor cable may be malfunctioning. Substitute another cable.

3. *Picture is faded on both the monitor and the* VIEWFINDER.

    a. Perhaps there is insufficient light on the subject.

    b. Is the lens IRIS closed too much. Turn to the lower f numbers.

    c. Is the camera's FADE button pressed?

    d. Is the lens covered with water or salt spray, or did you leave a dark FILTER attached to the lens?

4. *Picture is good in the* VIEWFINDER, *but faded on the TV monitor.*

    a. The TV's BRIGHTNESS or CONTRAST may be too low.

    b. The video signal may have been improperly split, LOOPED, or TERMINATED, losing some of its "punch."

5. *Camera's picture is fuzzy on both the* VIEWFINDER *and the TV monitor.*

    a. Focus the lens.

    b. Are you using a MACRO lens or a close-up lens attachment while viewing a distant subject (more on this later in the chapter)?

    c. Are you aimed at something too close for your particular lens? Aim at something farther away and see what happens.

6. *Ghost of the same image stays on TV and* VIEWFINDER *screens no matter where you point the camera* (Figure 4-1). You have a BURN-IN from having the camera "see" the same contrasty picture for too long, or it has been aimed into a bright light. Mild BURN-INS can be removed by

    a. Turning the camera off and waiting a day or so before you use it again.

    b. Turning on the camera and aiming it at a smooth white (not shiny) object like an out-of-focus close-up of a well-illuminated sheet or dull white paper. The white image *must fill* the screen. The BURN-IN may go away in about an hour or so.

    c. Check your lens to see if there is anything on it. If you cover the lens, and a mark or streak remains, it's a BURN-IN. If the streak disappears, your lens or VIDICON tube is probably dirty. Chapter 13 tells how to clean them.

d. Have a technician remove the pickup tube and replace it with a new one.

7. *Picture won't stay in focus throughout the zoom range*
   a. Have you focused correctly (zoom in, focus, then zoom out)?
   b. Do you have a close-up lens attachment or is your lens in the MACRO mode? Return the lens to normal.
   c. Are you trying to focus on something too close for your particular lens? Read the focus etchings on the lens; the lowest distance marked is the closest distance to which the lens will normally focus.
   d. Has the camera been bumped or knocked around? If so, the pickup tube may have jarred out of alignment. A technician can readjust this alignment.

8. THREE-TUBE *color camera makes pictures with colored ridges around the edges. The ridges are especially noticeable around white objects in front of black backgrounds.* Your camera is out of CONVERGENCE. To make a proper picture, it must precisely lay the green, red, and blue pictures atop one another. If CONVERGENCE is misadjusted, then the three pictures don't match up. Repair requires a technician.

Color TV sets also become misconverged. If you get colored ridges on pictures coming from rental tapes or broadcast TV shows, have your set CONVERGED by a technician.

Other Problems

1. *When you pull the camera trigger, the VCR fails to start.*
   a. Have you pressed RECORD/PLAY as you should?
   b. If using a separate camera and VCR, check to see that the VCR *itself* isn't PAUSED. Its PAUSE button must be off for the camera's PAUSE to work.
   c. Is something (an earphone, perhaps) plugged into the REMOTE input on the VCR? Unplug anything from the REMOTE jack.
   d. Does this VCR go with this camera?
   e. Is there a CAMERA or REMOTE switch on the VCR flipped to the wrong position? Sometimes the VCR has to be told to listen to its CAMERA input.

2. *Weak or no audio is being recorded from the camera; picture is okay.* To monitor your audio, connect a TV to the VCR while the camera and VCR are in RECORD. If you don't hear sound from the TV speaker, double check the sound by trying an earphone in the EARPHONE or HEADPHONE OUT socket of the VCR. Once you're sure that the sound is deficient,
   a. Check the MIC IN or AUDIO IN. Nothing should be connected there if you are recording from the camera's built-in microphone.
   b. Does this camera go with this VCR? Some ensembles don't work together.
   c. Is your VCR's INPUT SELECT in the VCR or TV mode? Switch it to VCR.
   d. Are you using an external microphone? If so,
      • Make sure its ON/OFF switch (some have them) is tuned ON.
      • Some mikes have batteries inside. Is its battery dead?

CAMERA MOUNTING EQUIPMENT

Really smooth camera movement requires a tripod. It also alleviates arm fatigue during long shooting sessions at weddings or sports events. During "trick" shots, it holds the camera still long enough for edits to be unobtrusive (more on this in Chapter 10).

Figure 4–13 shows a tripod with a HEAD and DOLLY. If you decide to build a mini-studio in your basement, this will be a necessity. The HEAD part at the top (not to be confused with the heads on a VCR which are something else altogether) connects to your camera and allows you to aim it using a long handle. The tripod part usually has an adjustable PEDESTAL raised and lowered by a crank to allow for high and low shots. The tripod legs often telescope to make the unit compact for travel and storage. On the bottom is the DOLLY—a set of wheels which allows the tripod to glide smoothly over the floor. There are less expensive and less flexible units available. Unless you are the type who would mount a diamond in a plastic setting, you may not want to trust your $1,200 camcorder to a $29 "precarious pod."

If you leave the camera, tighten the HEAD controls. The weight of the camera makes it want to tilt. If it squirms loose while unattended, it could tilt down abruptly and smash its lens against the tripod. When you *do* decide to move the camera, be

FIGURE 4-13 Portable tripod with HEAD and DOLLY (Courtesy of Comprehensive Video Supply Corp.)

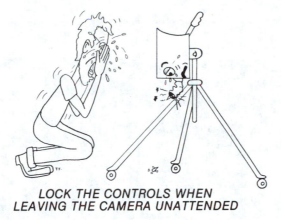

*LOCK THE CONTROLS WHEN
LEAVING THE CAMERA UNATTENDED*

sure to loosen the controls first. Otherwise the flimsy parts of the HEAD and PEDESTAL will strip and wear out quickly.

Attaching the camera to the HEAD is sometimes tricky. There is a threaded hole in the base of the camera or the base of the trigger handle. In the HEAD is a captive bolt which shouldn't fall out. Somehow that bolt has to screw into the hole in the camera's base. It's not easy to get the bolt started straight. Starting it crooked will strip the threads, so be patient. Once the bolt has a good grab on the camera, you may twist the tightener ring to tighten everything down as shown in Figure 4–14.

Step 1: Line up bolt with threaded hole in camera.

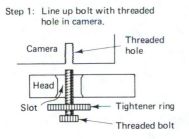

Step 2: Screw bolt into camera all the way, then unscrew it one turn so it's not held tightly to head.

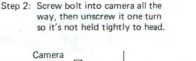

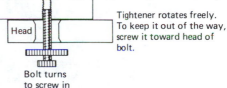

Step 3: Slide camera and bolt forward or backward on head for best balance.

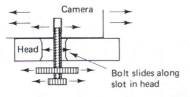

Step 4: Once the camera is balanced, tighten the tightener ring against the head to firmly hold the camera in place.

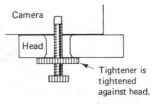

FIGURE 4-14 Steps for fastening camera to head

FIGURE 4-15 QUICK RELEASE camera mount allowing the camera to be easily removed from the tripod HEAD.

FIGURE 4-16 MONOPOD (Courtesy of Comprehensive Video Supply Corp.)

Some of the better tripods have a QUICK RELEASE camera mount, a little plate which screws firmly onto the base of your camera and can be quickly clamped onto your camera head (Figure 4–15). It is especially handy when you need to pick up your camera and run, and then later wish to set it down on the tripod without messing with the tightener rings, and so on.

Lighter, more portable, and cheaper than the tripod is the MONOPOD, a one-legged tripod (Figure 4–16). Although it can't stand up by itself, it takes a lot of weight off your arms and steadies your shots as you hold it upright. It moves with you quickly with a minimum of setup (for when you are shooting wild scenes of that tornado ripping the town apart a block ahead of you.)

And next, there is the CENTIPOD, a furry little worm with a hundred legs.

Most tripods are built for still cameras. Although they can be aimed around, they do not aim smoothly, making your panning and tilting shots sort of jerky. There are better quality TRIPOD HEADS available which dampen out the jerkiness. The best among these is the FLUID HEAD (Figure 4–17) which contains a viscous oil to smooth out your moves. FLUID HEADS are expensive and you may find a SEMI-FLUID design to be a satisfactory compromise.

Improvised Mounts

When shooting on location, you usually don't have room to carry much mounting equipment. Most camera mounting gear is quite bulky. Here are a few tricks of the trade.

BASIC TRIPOD CONTROLS AND MOVEMENTS

TILT: To aim the camera up and down on a vertical axis, like nodding your head "yes." *Tilt up* means to shoot higher, toward the ceiling. *Tilt down* means to aim lower, toward the floor.

PAN: To aim the camera back and forth on a horizontal axis, like shaking your head "no." *Pan left* means to turn the camera to your left. *Pan right*, of course, means to turn it to the right.

To DOLLY: To travel forward or backward across the floor with the camera. *Dolly in* means to move the camera forward, tripod and all, closer to the subject. *Dolly out* means to pull back.

To TRUCK or CRAB: To travel from side to side across the floor with the camera, tripod and all. *Truck right* means to travel to your right, and *truck left* tells you to go in the other direction.

To PEDESTAL: To adjust the elevation of the camera above floor level. *Pedestal up* means to make the elevation greater. *Pedestal down* means to decrease the height of the camera.

DOLLY, TRUCK, PEDESTAL: When used as nouns, these words refer to parts of the camera tripod mechanism. The dolly or truck is the base with wheels which supports the actual tripod. The pedestal is the vertical shaft that raises or lowers the camera.

Basic tripod controls and movements

FIGURE 4-17 FLUID HEAD for portability and smooth moves.

Wobbly camera shots will make your scenes look amateurish. Steady your camera by leaning it against the hood of a car, a fence, or a notch in a tree. If that's too hard, then hold the camera and brace yourself against something solid. Perhaps you can set your elbows on a desk or lean your shoulder against a doorway.

A pillow or bean bag is indispensible when doing a lot of on-location shooting. It does a wonderful job of cradling a camera for steady shots. You can lie prone on the ground and use it to steady your low angle shots. It's great for sinking your elbows into when you've propped yourself over the hood of a car. If you're shooting children, you'll find yourself taking many medium-low angle shots, probably while kneeling. A pillow or bean bag saves untold bruised kneecaps.

There are a lot of ways to move without a DOLLY. Wheelchairs glide smoothly, even over irregular surfaces. One person pushes while the other sits and holds the camera.

If you're shooting near shopping centers, the ubiquitous shopping cart gives a smooth ride over indoor floors (if you can find one with casters which aren't square).

How would you shoot a bowling ball as it rolled down the alley? Try lying on an upside down carpet remnant while two helpers push you with brooms.

A pillow or bean bag will help you steady your shots.

You can shoot from the window of a moving car, from the tailgate of a pickup truck, from an electric company cherrypicker (a bucket on a long mast capable of lifting a person high into the air), or from a fire truck ladder. Speedboats, roller coasters, and hot air balloons are all possible sources of creative camera angles. If the bumpiness of the ride makes your picture jiggle too much, try to zoom the lens out as far as you can. This will hide most of the wobbles.

Tai Chi Stance

If tripods are too cumbersome for you or you are moving a lot, there are several methods for steadying a hand-held camera. Figure 4–18 shows the Tai Chi stance (from oriental martial arts) which minimizes natural body sway while putting you in excellent position for smooth moves in most directions. Stand with your legs 18″ apart, slightly pigeon-toed, with knees slightly bent. Keep your neck and the camera in close to your body. From the Tai Chi position, you can PAN by turning at the waist, you can TILT using your whole torso, you can PEDESTAL DOWN by further bending your knees, and you can DOLLY in or out by proceeding to walk, bent over in the Groucho Marx style, sliding your feet along, letting your knees absorb all the ups and downs while your torso glides smoothly through the air. Perhaps it sounds

FIGURE 4-18 Tai Chi position for holding camera

FIGURE 4–19 VIEWFINDER adjusted for a low-angle shot

more like torture than good camera posture and indeed it gets uncomfortable over time, but with a little practice, this silly looking stance will deliver nice-looking pictures.

And while we are on the subject of walking with the camera, here's a good habit to get into, one practiced by professional microscope and telescope users—stick one eye to the eyepiece, but *keep both eyes open*. It may be awkward at first, but a half-hour of practice will teach your "unused" eye not to see. Thereafter, you don't have to tire your face squinting one eye closed *and* you reap an unexpected benefit when you try to walk. Your "unused" eye starts keeping track of curbsides, low limbs, and trip cables as you march hither, thither, and yon.

A camera that rests on your shoulder will give a more stable picture than one with the common pistol grip. With the shoulder cameras, the camera gains stability by being pressed against you at several points: the eyecup (or forehead), the side of the face, the shoulder, the trigger grip, and the lens. The pistol grip camera, on the other hand, is held at the end of your bobbing arm. If using a pistol grip camera, stabilize your arms by pressing your elbows against your chest. Press the eyecup against your brow and hold onto the lens. Again, uncomfortable, but stable.

As mentioned before, it will be more restful and more stable if you can brace yourself or your camera against something while shooting. Sit down, lean against a wall, brace the camera against a pole, hold it against a car hood or a rock for rock-solid shots.

For really low shots, the movable ELECTRONIC VIEWFINDER will make it easy to look straight down into the finder while cradling the camera beneath you, perhaps at knee height (Figure 4–19). If you can connect to a TV set to view your shots, you may not need the VIEWFINDER at all, freeing you to hold the camera anywhere. Low shots are also easily done by hugging the camera to your waist and aiming it while viewing the TV screen.

Electronic Image Stabilization

Philips and Panasonic have introduced camcorders with ELECTRONIC IMAGE STABI-LIZATION, special jitter correcting circuitry which reduces the bouncing effect occurring when you shoot sans tripod. Sensors in the camera detect camera wiggles and compensate (to a degree) by electrically reaiming the lens. This is no substitute for a tripod, but helps smooth out your hand-held camera shots.

MORE ABOUT TV CAMERA LENSES

Anybody who wears glasses knows how important lenses are. The lens is the camera's window to the world and could be a $20 chunk of plastic or a $2,000 high grade zoom lens. The principles for using and caring for both kinds of lenses will be the same.

Iris or f-Stop

The F-STOPS measure the ability of a lens to allow light through it. The IRIS ring, a rotatable collar somewhere on the lens, has numbers etched on it—typically these are 1.4, 2.0, 2.8, 4, 5.6, 8, 11, 16, and 22. It may seem backward, but the higher the number the *less* light is allowed through the lens. In general, you'd keep the lens "wide open" (set at the lowest f number) if you are shooting inside with minimal light. Outdoors in bright sunshine, you'd "stop down" to a small lens opening (a high f number) to allow limited light.

In summary, the iris is adjusted to the f number that allows in *enough light* for your camera to "see" to make a good picture, but *not too much light* which will result in too contrasty a picture or poor DEPTH-OF-FIELD. So what's DEPTH-OF-FIELD?

(Courtesy of Panasonic)

Depth-of-Field

DEPTH-OF-FIELD is the range of distance over which a picture will remain in focus. Good DEPTH-OF-FIELD occurs when something near you and something far from you can both be sharply in focus at the same time. Poor DEPTH-OF-FIELD is the opposite. Things go badly out of focus when their distance from you is changed. Figure 4–20 diagrams this relationship.

Generally, one wants to maintain good DEPTH-OF-FIELD so that all aspects of the picture are sharp. There are times, however, when for artistic reasons, one would prefer to have the foreground of the picture (the part of the picture which is up close) sharp while the background is blurry. Such a condition focuses the viewer's attention on the central attraction in the foreground or middleground while making the fuzzy background unobtrusive. And, it's especially handy for hiding the inevitable scratches and smudges on your TV scenery. In such cases, poor DEPTH-OF-FIELD is an advantage.

The mechanism for adjusting the DEPTH-OF-FIELD is our old friend, the IRIS. As you see from Figure 4–21, low f numbers give poor DEPTH-OF-FIELD while high f numbers give excellent DEPTH-OF-FIELD.

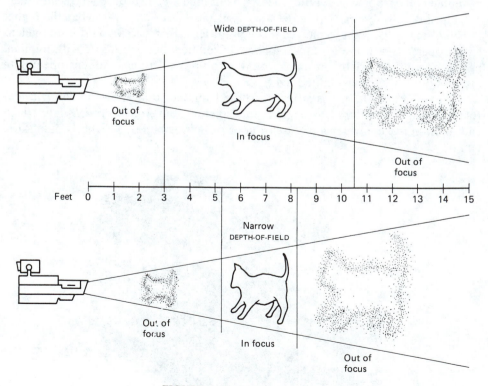

FIGURE 4–20 DEPTH-OF-FIELD

F4: A good compromise

F16: Excellent DEPTH-OF-FIELD but picture is too faded

F2.8: Contrast to spare but poor DEPTH-OF-FIELD

F8: Sometimes okay

FIGURE 4-21 How a TV camera responds to different IRIS settings; the camera is focused at 5 feet

Notice how you never get something for nothing. As you improve your DEPTH-OF-FIELD by increasing your f number, you simultaneously reduce the amount of light permitted through the lens. So while f22 may give you excellent DEPTH-OF-FIELD, it will let in very little light for a gray, dull picture. F2.8 would let in plenty of light for a brilliant, contrasty picture, but your DEPTH-OF-FIELD would be very limited. What can one do to get the best of both worlds?

1. Try to get as much light on the subject as possible. This will make up for some of the light that the high f numbers cut out.
2. Decide where to compromise. Usually, people go for the bright enough picture and sacrifice DEPTH-OF-FIELD.
3. One can make the camera work harder to compensate for the insufficient light associated with the high f number by hitting the +6 dB or +12 dB BOOST switch, if your camera has one. Beware that this will make your picture grainier.

A good compromise in the outdoor setting is to provide plenty of light, and set the lens at f4 for moderate DEPTH-OF-FIELD and moderate contrast. Indoor shooting may generally require f2.0. Bright daytime shooting outdoors may permit f8 to be used.

FIGURE 4–22 WIDE ANGLE lens (low FOCAL LENGTH number) gives a LONG SHOT

FIGURE 4–23 25mm FOCAL LENGTH gives a MEDIUM SHOT

FIGURE 4–24 TELEPHOTO lens gives a CLOSE-UP picture

Zoom Lenses

FOCAL LENGTH describes a zoom lens's magnification. A 12mm FOCAL LENGTH would give a wide angle shot as in Figure 4–22. A 25mm FOCAL LENGTH lens gives a MEDIUM SHOT as in Figure 4–23. A 50mm (or greater) FOCAL LENGTH yields a TELEPHOTO shot like the one in Figure 4–24.

Zoom lenses can be changed from wide angle to telephoto shots. Cheap ones may go from 20mm to 60mm giving a lousy 3:1 ZOOM RATIO. Most camcorder lenses are better than that by offering a 6:1 ratio allowing you to make something look six times closer. A really good lens with a broad 10:1 ratio would be very flexible, allowing you to get a very wide angle shot as well as a tight close-up out of the same lens.

Changing the FOCAL LENGTH of a lens does more than simply change the magnification of the picture. Other subtle changes occur. The greater the focal length, the greater the magnification of the picture, the narrower the field of view, the flatter the scene looks, and the narrower the DEPTH-OF-FIELD becomes.

You are probably familiar with the telephoto shots at baseball games where the players in the outfield look as though they are standing on top of the pitcher who looks inches away from the batter. if you want to compress distance so that far away things look closer to nearby things, then use a TELEPHOTO LENS. If you'd like to stress the difference between nearby and faraway things, use a WIDE ANGLE SHOT (Figure 4–25). If a vehicle or person is coming toward you and you wish to make their motion appear slower or wish to hold them in the scene longer, then have them start from far away and use a TELEPHOTO LENS. However, if you wish to exaggerate their speed or progress, use a WIDE ANGLE lens. Once near you, the subject will appear to whip by.

WIDE ANGLE shots have excellent DEPTH-OF-FIELD and TELEPHOTO shots have poor DEPTH-OF-FIELD (Figure 4–26). This sometimes makes it hard to shoot moving objects with a TELEPHOTO lens; they are constantly wiggling out of focus on you. A WIDE ANGLE lens, on the other hand, hides the focusing errors. WIDE ANGLE shots are useful when you have to run with the camera or shoot without taking time to focus.

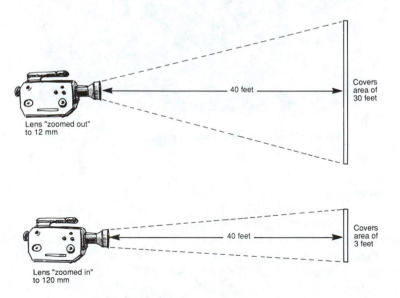

Angle of view from a zoom lens

Telephoto   Wide Angle

FIGURE 4–25   TELEPHOTO lens compresses distance while WIDE ANGLE lens
emphasizes it

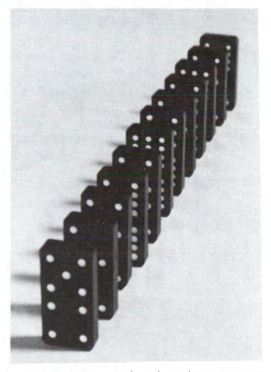

Telephoto shot gives narrow DEPTH-OF-FIELD   Wide Angle shot gives broad DEPTH-OF-FIELD

FIGURE 4–26   How FOCAL LENGTH affects DEPTH-OF-FIELD

Focusing Tricks

The rules of focusing are

1. Zoom in all the way on the subject.
2. Focus the lens.
3. Zoom out to the shot you want.

Obviously, this list of steps is only useful when you have plenty of time and a still subject. Nevertheless, this is the only way to get a sharp picture of things which *have* to be perfectly focused such as graphics, or close-ups of small items.

What do you do when you have a subject who moves around a lot? How do you stay in focus? Here are some possibilities:

1. If you are a good focuser, just stay alert and adjust for every movement. Most of us are not good focusers, however.
2. Flood the subject with light so that you can use high f numbers for broad DEPTH-OF-FIELD.
3. Stay zoomed out. Focusing inaccuracies are most noticeable in close-ups. When you are zoomed out, nearly everything appears sharp.
4. Try to get the subject to move *laterally* to you, not toward or away from you. Since the subject stays roughly the same distance from the camera, you will not have to refocus, just aim.
5. Try to use big subjects so that you can zoom out or can stay farther away from them. Why are big, zoomed-out subjects easier to focus? To fill a TV screen, little objects must be magnified. You do this by zooming in or by moving the camera closer to them. A zoomed-in lens blows up all the little focusing inaccuracies, especially if an object is itself deep or is moving toward or away from the camera. A camera close to an object also exaggerates the focusing problems. Zooming in on a postage stamp held in somebody's hand three feet away will display formidable focusing problems as the hand moves. But zooming out on a giant poster of a postage stamp held 30 feet away poses no focusing problems even if the poster moves a foot.
6. Last and least, try to confine your subjects by seating them, encumbering them with microphone cables, or marking a spot on the floor where they must stand.

Selective focusing   A tricky way to move the viewer's attention from one object to another is by SELECTIVE FOCUS. First you focus on an object in, say, the foreground, leaving the background blurry. Next you refocus for the background, blurring the foreground. Your viewer's eyes will stay riveted to whichever part of the picture is in focus at the time. Figure 4–27 shows how your attention can be moved from the time on the clock to the person asleep in bed. Another SELECTIVE

Your attention is drawn to the alarm clock.

Your attention is drawn to the sleeper.

FIGURE 4–27 Selective focus

FOCUS technique is used with long rows of objects (soldiers, flowers, toys on an assembly line). Focus first on the closest items and slowly refocus to the farthest ones. One by one, each will pull into focus and then retreat into a blur as your eye follows down the line to the end. This is a technique called PULL FOCUS, focusing from one object to another while the camera is "on."

To intensify the SELECTIVE FOCUS effect, it is good to have a narrow DEPTH-OF-FIELD. Zoom way in, try to use a low f-stop, and try to keep the nearby objects as near as possible and the far ones as far as possible.

Close-up Shooting

Normally if you try to shoot something closer than four or five feet from your camera, the picture will be blurry. If you must get closer to your work, the following options are available:

1. Buy a camera or camcorder with a MACRO lens.
2. Affix a CLOSE-UP LENS ATTACHMENT to your present camera or camcorder.

Macro lenses   In their "normal" (nonMACRO) mode, most of these lenses work like any other lens focusing down to four feet or so. They'll also zoom normally. To change them to MACRO, you generally throw a "safety catch" (which prevents the lens from going into this mode accidentally) and then refocus on a very near object. Sometimes the zoom control becomes the MACRO focus control. Many MACRO lenses can be refocused easily from a super close-up back out to normal distances, opening the possibility of "arty" or creative transitional effects.

Unfortunately, MACROS cost more and while in the MACRO mode, they cannot zoom.

Close-up lens attachments   The regular zoom lens on your camera or camcorder can generally be made to focus on closer subjects by the mere addition of a CLOSE-UP LENS ATTACHMENT as shown in Figure 4–28. You would attach these by unscrewing the lens shade and screwing on the CLOSE-UP LENS ATTACHMENT in its place. The curved surface of the attachment should face *away* from the camera. *Do not* screw the close lens attachment down tight; they easily seize up and become hard to remove. The lens shade may now be screwed onto the close-up attachment. Leave this slightly loose, too.

With the close-up lens attachment on your zoom lens, you can zoom the full range without going out of focus, assuming that you are the right distance from your subject and that you followed proper focusing procedure to start with. This is the greatest advantage of CLOSE-UP LENS ATTACHMENTS over MACRO lenses.

To select a proper CLOSE-UP LENS ATTACHMENT, you need to know two things:

1. The magnification you want.
2. The attachment's compatibility with your present lens.

CLOSE-UP LENS ATTACHMENTS don't magnify an image *per se;* they merely permit you to bring your camera closer to your subject without going out of focus. They essentially make your camera nearsighted.

The power of a CLOSE-UP LENS ATTACHMENT is measured in DIOPTERS. The bigger the DIOPTER number, the stronger the lens and the closer your camera can "see" with it on. The weaker ones are +1 and +2. The +3 power is a good compromise. +4 and higher powers are often too strong.

Getting the CLOSE-UP LENS ATTACHMENT to fit your present lens is sometimes difficult. The attachment needs to be the same diameter and have the same screw threads as your present lens. If you are lucky, your local camera shop may be able to measure your lens and order an attachment for you. Another solution might be to buy a STEPPING RING, an inexpensive device with screw threads to fit your camera

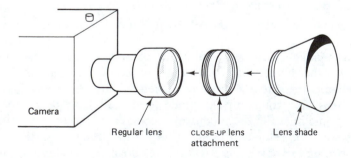

Camera

Regular lens   CLOSE-UP lens   Lens shade
                  attachment

FIGURE 4–28   CLOSE-UP LENS ATTACHMENT

CLOSE-UP SHOOTING

lens at one end and another size screw threads to fit your CLOSE-UP LENS ATTACH-MENT at the other end. Figure 4–29 shows one. Thus you put the STEPPING RING onto your camera lens and may now affix other lens attachments and filters to it.

Telephoto and Wide Angle Converters

One problem with autofocus cameras and camcorders is that you are stuck with the lens that the manufacturers gave you. You can't take telephoto close-ups of football players on the field or wild tigers in the jungle without getting dangerously close. On the other hand, you can't take the beautiful wide angled panoramas that bring

FIGURE 4–29 STEPPING RING adapts one size lens to a slightly different sized lens attachment

"2X TelXtender®" TELEPHOTO CONVERTER

Normal view

View with "2X TelXtender®"

"Curvatar™" WIDE-ANGLE CONVERTER

Normal view

With "Curvatar™"

FIGURE 4-30 TELEPHOTO and WIDE ANGLE CONVERTERS (Courtesy of Spiratone, Inc.)

a lump to your throat when you visit the Rocky Mountains or the Grand Canyon.

One solution is to visit your camera store or pour through optics catalogs to find TELEPHOTO CONVERTERS or WIDE ANGLE CONVERTERS which may attach to your lens. Whatever the focal length of your zoom lens, these attachments will make it greater or smaller, thus yielding a wider view or a more magnified view of your subjects. Figure 4–30 shows a WIDE ANGLE and TELEPHOTO CONVERTER and the image you get when using them.

Lens Filters

A FILTER blocks something unwanted and let through something wanted. Lens filters attach to the outside of your lens and block out unwanted colors, brightness, or glare.

Some FILTERS can create fancy effects like those in Figure 4–31 while others can reduce the contrast of your picture as shown in Figure 4–32. These filters give a soft portrait effect to your pictures and can even give you a nice fog effect, saving you a jet flight to London.

You can fake some of these effects yourself with a piece of glass and a few items around the house. You can make the center-sharp lens attachment by rubbing a little vaseline in a circle on a clear piece of glass without touching the center of

"Center Sharp" lens attachment   "Multimage 5C" prism attachment   "Crostar ISQ" lens attachment

Resulting CENTER FOCUS image   Resulting multiple image   Resulting STAR PATTERN image

FIGURE 4–31   Camera lens effects (Courtesy of Spiratone, Inc.)

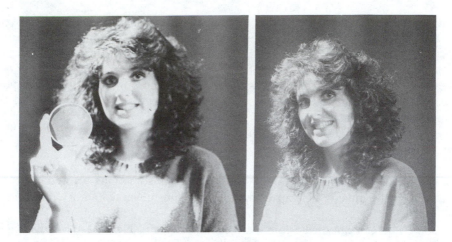

FIGURE 4-32 Contrast reduction filter

the glass. When held up in front of the lens, the vaseline will "soften" the outside edges of your picture.

You can build your own star pattern filter by placing a wire screen in front of your camera lens or by using a tiny smudge of baby oil streaked in one or two directions across the surface of a clear glass in front of your lens. And you can build your own low contrast filter by placing gauze or lady's nylon hose over the lens, adding layers to increase the effect as in Figure 4-33.

Table 4-1 lists some of the more popular filters you can buy.

LENS AILMENTS AND CURES

1. *Camera is out of focus all the time.*
   a. Is the lens still wearing a CLOSE-UP LENS ATTACHMENT? Look very carefully. Sometimes these attachments look so much like the lens that you can't tell that they are there. If you are aiming at something closer or farther than the attachment is designed for (some work in a very narrow range, like 10″ to 20″), everything will be blurry. Remove the attachment, use a different power attachment, or move your subject into the attachment's focus range.
   b. Is your lens switched to the MACRO mode?
   c. Are you using a detachable lens which is not screwed tightly into its camera mount?
   d. Are you trying to focus on something closer than the lens can "see"?
   e. Perhaps the camera has been severely bumped, misaligning it.
2. *Corners of the picture seem dark.*
   a. Has your removable lens been swapped with another? Perhaps the other lens is too small.

FIGURE 4–33 Homemade low contrast filter using gauze

TABLE 4–1 FILTERS

COLOR CAMERA FILTERS:

Skylight (1A), or Haze (UV)—Nearly clear lens absorbs ultraviolet light. Removes excessive blues from open shade. Excellent for protecting camera lens from blowing sand, water, fingerprints, and so on, and may be left on all the time.

Polarizing—Reduces outdoor reflections in glass, chrome, water. Deepens blue sky and whitens clouds. Reduces bright light. Take off when not needed.

#85—Orange FILTER makes camera think it's seeing indoor incandescent light even though it's outdoors. Use on cameras without indoor/outdoor COLOR TEMPERATURE adjustments.

Graduated—Half the lens is tinted, then gradually changes to clear glass for the other half. A blue tint at the top half of the lens, for instance, would create a blue sky while the lower foreground looked normal.

BLACK-AND-WHITE CAMERA FILTERS:

Yellow (K2)—yellow. Lightens yellow, darkens blue, increases contrast slightly. Reduces haze, especially on distance shots.

Orange (G)—Goes one step further than preceding FILTER, darkening skies, sunsets, sea-scapes.

Red (25A)—Goes the whole route, darkening sky to black, increasing contrast. Good for psuedo-night scenes.

Green (X1)—Darkens reds, lightens greens, emphasizes flesh tones.

Neutral Density (ND-X1, X2, X3. . .)—Simply reduces the light in a bright scene. The higher the "X" number, the darker the FILTER.

FILTERS must be bought in sizes which fit the diameter and threads of your present lens. If this is a difficulty, or you already have FILTERS from your photo equipment, buy a STEPPING RING which adapts your lens to your FILTER.

b. Are you using several CLOSE-UP LENS ATTACHMENTS at once? They tend to make the corners dark.
c. Is your LENS SHADE too small? It may be getting in the picture.

3. *White spots or octagonal figures float through the picture as you move the camera* (Figure 4–34). Light is shining into your lens.
a. Reposition your camera so that light doesn't shine into your lens.
b. Use a bigger LENS SHADE to protect your lens from the direct light.
c. Hold a square of cardboard near the lens so that it casts a shadow on the lens.
d. Move the light farther away from the subject.
e. Use a very expensive lens with professional lens coating. These lenses are less susceptible to FLARE from lights.
f. Use a NEUTRAL DENSITY FILTER and open the IRIS to a low f-stop.

4. *Specks of dust appear in your picture.*
a. If they move only when you rotate the outer lens surface (while focusing), then that is the dirty part of your lens. Brush or blow it clean.
b. If the dust only moves when you unscrew the entire lens, then it is most likely on the camera end of the lens. Remove the lens and brush or blow it clean.
c. If the blemish disappears when you cover the lens, it is probably dust on your image sensor. Unscrew the lens and brush or blow the pickup tube clean. Incidentally, the tiniest flakes of dust seem very large to a tiny pickup. You have to look very closely or use a magnifying glass to see them.
d. If the blemish doesn't go away when you cover the lens, then it may be a BURN-IN. Your pickup tube may have to be replaced.
e. CCD and MOS image sensors sometimes have inherent blemishes usually in the form of tiny white dots. These blemishes cannot be fixed outside of replacing the sensors with higher quality models (at higher expense).
f. If the dust or dirt cannot be blown or brushed off, try wiping the lens or image pickup with a lint-free cloth dampened with window cleaner. Remember not to leave any soapy film behind. Chapter 13 tells more about lens care.

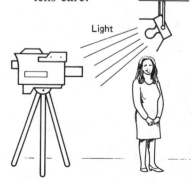

FIGURE 4-34 Lights shining into the lens

5

Camera techniques and picture composition

So far, we've studied only how to operate the equipment. Now that we can work our machinery, let's focus on how to use it to make professional-looking pictures.

Anyone can pick up a camera and make a boring, fuzzy videotape that plays like the typical home movie. Videophiles by the score stockpile dust laden videocassettes of programs so dull and dry that nobody wants to watch them. It's easy to get so involved in the mechanics of producing a TV program that you forget to make it interesting, forget to make it visual, forget to make it memorable.

Many people may share in the production of a TV program, but the buck stops with the camera operator. What *you* get is what everyone will see. (Unfortunately, the spendable bucks never seem to stop anywhere near the camera operator.)

As you become more expert at camera work, you will be developing skills in lighting, audio, directing, and stage management. These crafts are all related, and proficiency at one adds to your competency at the others.

Our stairway to expertise will have three steps:

1. Mechanics of skillful camera handling.
2. Aesthetics of picture composition.
3. Camera "tricks" which add visual interest or create a mood.

It is the nature of art that sometimes you will balance on several steps at once, using a camera "trick" to compose an appealing shot or using raw mechanical skill to create a desired illusion.

TV is all illusion anyway; making your audience see something that really isn't there is part of the magic of television. *A bigger part of the magic, however, is making something look like it really is*. It doesn't just happen.

Much of TV is illusion

You'll be shown a lot of "rules" on the aesthetics of picture composition and camera movement. These "rules" are meant to be broken at times—but *after they've been learned*. You'll be master of your tools if you can "do it right" whenever you need to, then, "do it your way" whenever you *want* to.

Once you become aware of these "rules," "tricks," and techniques, a funny thing will happen to you; you will never be able to watch TV again without becoming conscious of the camera angles and shot composition. You'll see the "rules" being followed and sometimes broken. You'll have become a gourmet of visual craftsmanship. You'll be "video literate."

CAMERA MOVES

First let's review the lingo. Figure 5-1 shows the fundamental moves the camera can make. They apply whether you are using a tripod or holding the camera by hand.

All camera movements should be smooth and gentle. Unless there is a special reason for not doing so, *your pictures should always be in focus and centered*. You generally should follow the motion as it occurs and zoom appropriately to keep the important action in the picture.

In more complicated shots where your camera would be taking only part of the final picture, you may have to consciously break these "rules." For instance,

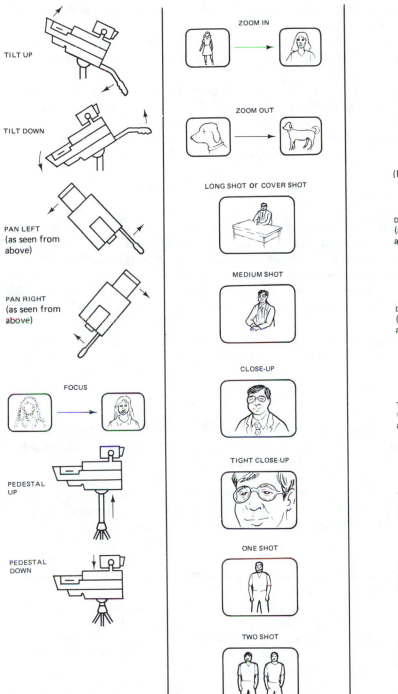

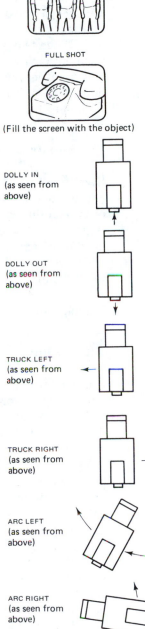

FIGURE 5-1 Basic camera moves

you may have to keep the performer in the right-hand half of your screen so that a moment later, someone may walk into the left-hand part of the screen.

Keep the tops of people's heads near the top of your viewfinder. Don't leave an airy space above them when they sit down, or decapitate your performers when they stand up.

When two people are on your screen (a TWO SHOT), zoom out enough to keep them both in the picture most of the time. However, if two people are in the picture and one is leaving, let that person walk out of the picture. Don't try to zoom way out and keep them both visible. It is very natural for a person to leave someone and walk out of the picture. To the viewer, it's as if the person simply left the room.

The Steady Camera

Every move you make during taping will be seen and perhaps unconsciously become part of your message. A picture that bobs around, even a little, betrays amateurism or implies that you are looking through somebody else's eyes. The camera, for instance, would follow someone down a flight of stairs, becoming the pursuer. Jumpy, hand-held camera work can also imply peril, reality (as in newsreels), and frenzy. Unless you intend to portray these moods, you'll want to keep the camera rock solid while taping.

For this reason, many cameras spend most of their time sitting on tripods. Here are some tips on using them.

Tilt and Pan

If using a tripod, think ahead to loosen the controls so that your camera will move effortlessly. If you expect frequent, fast moves such as with sports, loosen the pan and tilt locks all the way. If you're doing slow, gentle moves, leave a little drag on the controls to dampen some of the jiggles.

If, however, you find yourself shooting a motionless scene for a long time, your arms will get awfully tired holding the camera steady. It will be much easier to lock the controls and let the camera hold itself. You must forever remain alert for an upcoming pan or tilt so that you can get your controls unlocked in time to carry out the move.

If working hand-held, use the Tai Chi position (Figure 4–18) and move your whole torso when you tilt or pan.

If you expect to move the camera somewhere while recording, figure out where you want to go first. This avoids zigzagging and "searching" kinds of shots. If you can, PAUSE the VCR first and try out the move to practice it and also decide on the picture composition. Then UNPAUSE and carry out your practiced move.

I recall, as a amateur, filming panoramic scenes of the Grand Canyon. I started at the ridge, moved down the wall of the canyon to the base, panned right for a ways, tilted back up to the rim, panned right some more across the rim, and then panned left for a long sweep. I was so awed by the scenery that I constantly felt as if I were missing something. I therefore crisscrossed and zigzagged my poor viewers' eyeballs out. The proper technique would have been to *select* the part of the canyon I was going to show first. Next, plan a strategy for moving from one part of the panorama to the other. Next, carry out your plan in one smooth, leisurely sweep. Be patient. Don't ruin the shot you are taking now in order to "get it all in." Strangely, your audience will never miss the shots you don't take, but they will abhor the hasty pans and the plummeting tilts you take as you try to photograph every weed and boulder.

It sometimes helps to pick an interesting beginning and end to a sweeping panoramic shot. Perhaps starting with a view of one canyon ridge, framed by some nearby tree limbs would do. In fact you could start with the limbs in focus and the background blurry and PULL FOCUS, bringing the canyon into focus. The out-of-focus tree nearby will actually add depth and dimensionality to your picture (another case where something out-of-focus *adds* attractiveness to the picture). Next, carry out a slow pan across the ridge, ending with a shot of tourists by your side, leaning over the guardrail, taking pictures of the canyon. Such a scene provides an ending to the shot, a comfortable place to jump to another shot.

Dolly, Truck, and Arc

If using a tripod on a dolly over a smooth floor, the process of traveling is easy. Do think ahead to unlock your wheels and to sweep cables and obstructions out of the way so you don't drive bumpity-bump over them.

If time permits, aim the wheel casters in the right direction so a gentle push is all that is needed to get the camera moving. A single wayward caster will do wonders at swaying you off course during a DOLLY or TRUCK maneuver.

If traveling hand-held, it is best to first zoom out to a wide angle. A telephoto shot greatly magnifies camera wiggles while wide angle shots hide them. Use the Tai Chi posture to start from, then glide like Groucho.

Everyone likes to take a journey. Travel will give your pictures motion and reveals new things to see as we move. The DOLLY and TRUCK are excellent vehicles for such excursions. Camera motion can seem very natural and does not wear thin too quickly. The camera could, for instance, DOLLY in, then ARC around a desk as the person behind the desk speaks. This move not only presents us with a new view, but also moves us from the formal across-the-desk position to a more casual face-to-face (desk to the side) position.

An ARCING shot is handy for showing two people talking together. By slowly circling the two, you can start with one's face (and the back of the other's head) and ARC around to the other's face, gently swinging the audience's attention from one performer to the other.

Moving the camera behind props, through bushes, or through windows or doors gives a strong three-dimensional feel to the picture.

A shot taken over a steep cliff may not convince the viewer of the canyon's depth. TRUCKING a camera up to the cliff's edge while looking down (and seeing the edge of the cliff disappear underfoot) can take the audience's breath away (take triple precautions so that you don't go over the edge with your camera and end up taking *really* spectacular shots).

Wheelchairs, shopping carts, or any number of wheeled or sliding vehicles can serve nicely as a temporary dolly. Be creative. Skis, toboggans, ice skates, mechanic's creepers, rubber rafts, parachutes, and construction cranes make fascinating (though dangerous) camera mounts.

If your VCR is separate from your camera, have someone else carry it so that you are more free to move your camera. That friend can also serve as a "guide dog" for you while you're walking (eyes glued to the viewfinder) as well as keeping your camera cord from dragging or tangling.

Avoid swinging the VCR around too much as you shoot. It won't hurt the machine (unless you bumped it hard), but it's likely to affect the quality of your picture. Inside the VCR, the spinning video heads and so on act a little like a gyro-

Television is a close-up medium. Get in close.

Zoomed out, the viewer observes the action.

Zoomed in, the viewer participates in it.

FIGURE 5–2 CLOSE-UPS capture the excitement of a scene

scope and resist changes in direction. Forced reorientation of the machine changes recording speed, causing a slight horizontal shift of the TV picture. When possible, set the VCR down, use a long cable, and move only the camera.

As long as it's not bumped, the *camera* doesn't care what position it's shooting in or whether it's moving.

Focus and Zoom

Know your lens controls. Know by "feel" which part of the lens does what. Know instinctively which way to turn the lens (or which button to push) to zoom in. A typical amateurish shot is the "false zoom"—a slight in-then-out move made because the camera operator didn't immediately know which button to push to zoom out. *Know* which button zooms out; don't experiment while recording. The same goes for focus; if something comes toward you, *know* which button to push or whether to turn the lens clockwise or counterclockwise to FOLLOW FOCUS.

What's FOLLOW FOCUS? That's a technique used by professional camera operators as they shoot moving objects. With a little practice you can do it, too. Zoom in on someone and have them walk toward you from 30 feet away. Try to keep their image sharp as they move. It isn't easy. With practice, you can develop the skill of following a moving target, keeping it centered, keeping it focused, and even keeping it the right size on the screen (by zooming) as it moves around.

But if you can't get the hang of it, stay zoomed out on fast moving objects. That way your focusing errors won't be as noticeable and you'll have less trouble keeping your moving target on the screen.

Assuming you've mastered keeping your zoomed-in shots sharp and centered, *use them; television is a close-up medium.*

LONG SHOTS, although easy to shoot, turn into monotonous mush on the TV screen. CLOSE-UPS capture the expressions, the detail, the excitement of a scene. Check out Figure 5–2 and notice how the CLOSE-UP is more interesting than the LONG SHOT.

And now a word about that zoom lens of yours. Everyone who gets his or her hands on one loves playing with it. In and out, in and out, your audience's eyeballs feel like yo-yos. Zoom to your heart's content while practicing. *Then go out and force yourself to shoot without zooming.* If you want a close-up of something, then PAUSE, zoom in to a close-up, then UNPAUSE your recording. Do you want to create a sense of travel, motion, or exploration? Then move the whole camera. That will create a *real* sense of travel, not the overworn zoom. Although a zoom and a DOLLY both can make things look closer or farther away, only the DOLLY changes perspective as it happens. Neither still pictures or words can do justice to this concept. You need to see the motion on the screen to really believe it. Try this experiment: Stand on a wooded pathway and zoom in down the pathway. Next, zoom back out and walk down the pathway carrying your camera. Look at the two scenes. The first scene is *okay,* but the second one is *fun.*

One handy use for the zoom lens is to fill the TV screen with action when you can't move the camera. Picture a youngster up to bat. Pitcher and batter are both on the screen. The wind up, the throw—it's a hit. You follow the ball into the outfield, *zooming in* as you go. When the outfielder fumbles it, you'll be zoomed in close to *see* the fumble rather than seeing a dot surrounded by a whole outfield. Here the zoom lens helps you fill the screen with action. To get that nice shot, however, you need to zoom *and* aim *and* refocus simultaneously—no easy task for the unpracticed.

Manipulating all the camera controls at once takes some practice.

Think Ahead

The following advice may seem too obvious to deserve attention, but it does deserve attention. It separates the masters from the mediocre:

As a camera operator, *try to anticipate every move*. Be ready to tilt up if somebody is about to stand up. Be ready to zoom out if someone is about to move from one place to another. Being zoomed out makes it easier to follow unpredictable or quick movements. If someone is about to move to the left, start moving a little before your subject does. This will make a "space" for the subject to move into. Such a camera move also creates an unconscious anticipation in your viewers. They will expect the performer to move when the camera moves.

Reviewing some previous commandments for emphasis: Have your controls unlocked if you expect to pan, tilt, or PEDESTAL. If you'll have to DOLLY or TRUCK, get the things out of your path and orient your casters. If shooting panoramas, plan a shot to start with, a route to take, and a shot to finish with.

CAMERA ANGLES AND PICTURE COMPOSITION

Basic Camera Angles and the Moods They Portray

You have already seen the results of dollying, zooming, and selective focusing. Figure 5–3 shows examples of some more basic camera angles and describes their impact.

When the camera is low, the performer looks domineering, strong, forceful, and authoritative. Political advertisers use this camera angle to strengthen the image of politicians.

When the camera is higher than eye level, the performer looks submissive, docile, unassertive, obedient, weak, or frightened. These camera angles do not have to be obvious. Slight camera height adjustments will leave a subconscious message with the viewer.

To avoid tainting the image with any special meaning, keep the camera at eye level. This is appropriate for newscasts, interviews, panel discussions, and instructional presentations. Sometimes you will find it necessary to elevate the performers on risers so that when they sit down they won't be lower than the camera can go. If this isn't possible, then keep the camera far from the performers so that the angle of view is not steep.

Dominance is also implied by screen position and size. If you have two shots, one of the host and one of the guest, use a slightly larger close-up of the host to portray the host as the more influential of the two. If during an argument between two actors, one is getting the upper hand, frame your TWO SHOTS with that actor closer to the camera. It is said that the upper right quadrant of the TV screen is more "powerful" than the lower left. To symbolically shift power from one TV

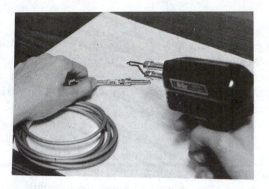

If trying to teach something, favor the doer's point of view.

Zoomed way out. Subject looks insignificant and dominated by surroundings.

FIGURE 5-3 Camera angles

character to another, frame the dominant one in the upper right-hand part of the screen where his or her presence is stronger.

People walking or running need space to move into; don't center them on your screen. People speaking need space to speak into. If you know someone is going to begin walking, zoom out far enough and start panning to give them a space to walk into before they even begin. This mentally prepares the viewer for the action and makes the shot look very natural. If a person is about to turn to the side and start speaking, you would similarly pan to the side just a moment before he or she starts.

Tilted shots imply danger or threat. You could use a tilted shot of someone being chased.

Camera low. Subject looks domineering.

Camera high. Subject looks weak or subservient.

Camera at eye level. Viewer feels neutral, person-to-person relationship with performer.

People walking need space to walk into.

People speaking need space to speak into.

Tilted shots give an aura of danger, frenzy, threat. Combined with moving, hand-held camera, shows a panicked subject's viewpoint; the viewer is running, the viewer is searching, etc.

(Fig. 5-3 Continued)

Long wide shots make the performer look insignificant and weak.

There are two ways to show someone how to do something. One is from the viewpoint of an onlooker; the other is from the viewpoint of the "doer." Educational studies have shown that over-the-shoulder shots from the performer's viewpoint are more instructive.

Assorted camera angles add variety to presentations and make them more enjoyable to watch, as long as they *do not distract the viewer from the show*. Strive to balance creativity with singleness of purpose.

Camera Placement and Backgrounds

Two questions should come first to mind as you set up a camera shot:

1. Where is the light?
2. What's in the background?

Lighting   When you are driving into the sunset, it is hard to see the road. The sun glares into your eyes and makes you squint and it creates reflections on your windshield. For cameras, the same is true only worse. Bright lights near or behind your subject force your camera's automatic circuits to "squint" creating a very dark picture as in Figure 5–4. Light also reflects off the lens ELEMENTS, creating white dots and geometric shapes as you saw in Figure 4–34.

In general, try to keep all the light behind the camera—none behind the subject (with the exception of carefully controlled backlighting which will be discussed in Chapter 6). In situations where you *must* shoot toward (not at) the light, the following steps might minimize the problem:

1. Use a bigger lens shade. The lens shade (shown in Figure 4–8) is the funnel-like scoop on the outside of the lens that shields the lens from ambient light. Or you could make a shade with some paper and adhesive tape.
2. Zoom in some to avoid as much of the extraneous light as possible. A tight CLOSE-UP of the face in Figure 5–4 for instance, would eliminate much of the glare from the window (but it may be easier to close the windowshade than it is to maintain a good CLOSE-UP of a moving face).
3. Using extra lights, throw more light on the foreground (the face in Figure 5–4) to offset the background light.
4. The bright lights are fooling the automatic iris controls into "squinting." So, turn the controls to MANUAL and adjust the camera to make the subject look good even though the window behind the subject may appear overexposed or look washed out. Some cameras have a BACKLIGHT button which does just this; it overexposes a light background so that the darker main subject looks best.

Window shade closed   Window shade open

FIGURE 5-4   Excessive lighting from behind the subject

Note that if the light from behind is too bright, a damaging burn-in can occur *if* you're using a tube-type camera. The preceding steps are applicable if the light is bright enough to affect the picture but too moderate to damage your camera's pickup tube. Things that are too bright for a pickup tube *ever* to look at are

1. The sun.
2. A movie or TV light.
3. Any bright, bare bulb.
4. Any chromed object reflecting light from any of the first three.
5. Mirrors or glass objects that are reflecting bright lights.

Later in this chapter you will learn a couple of safe routes around these restrictions.

Things that camera pickup tubes can stand to look at (but not for long periods of time) are

1. An open window that looks outdoors (but not into the sun).
2. Fluorescent lamps.
3. Table lamps with translucent shades.
4. A flashlight or other weak light.
5. A dimmed house light if dimmed or diffused enough.
6. Shiny automobiles on a hazy day.

KEEP THE SUN BEHIND THE CAMERA.
AVOID BURN-INS

7. White clothing.
8. A TV screen image.

Backgrounds   The good camera operator should also take into account what is behind the subject. With just the wrong camera placement, the bush in the background could appear to grow out of the subject's ear or a desk lamp could become the subject's antenna as in Figure 5–5. Avoid busy or distracting backgrounds unless they serve a purpose in your program. Clocks are especially distracting because the viewer automatically notes what time it is and chuckles at the discrepancy.

Watch for window reflections which betray the fact that a camera and lights are present. Also, make sure that cameras and microphones don't cast shadows—especially moving ones—on the set or performers.

When shooting outdoors, be especially aware of the line of the horizon. You may get so involved in shooting your subject that you forget to notice that your horizon isn't level. A level horizon is stable and unobtrusive. Unless you're looking for special effects, the horizon should always be level.

A slightly nonlevel horizon gives a heightened energy to the picture. The same applies for vertical objects like tall buildings. If they are tilted, they lend urgency or excitement to the picture. Figure 5-6 gives some examples.

There are times when you want to hide the horizon. Imagine taking pictures in a rocking boat. Your tripod is firmly planted on the deck. You thought your pictures would be stable, but when you view them later, you see the ocean tilting back and forth. A few minutes of this is enough to make you seasick. To solve this problem, simply zoom your camera in on the subject, avoiding the rocking background.

Sometimes the background is the subject of your picture. Backgrounds could be scenes of raging oceans, peaceful valleys, or majestic mountains, or they could be giant machines, thundering waterfalls, towering pyramids, or sprawling shopping

Lamp in background looks as if it were
growing out of the subject's head.

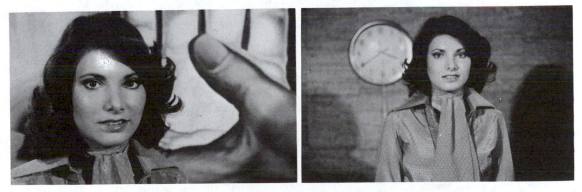

More distracting backgrounds (Courtesy Imero Fiorentino Associates).

FIGURE 5-5 Distracting backgrounds

Level, stable, unobtrusive horizon.

Angled horizon attracts attention, heightens energy.

FIGURE 5-6 Beware of your horizon line

centers. In each case, the actual size of the background subject is too large to appreciate, especially on a tiny TV screen. To give your screen depth, include something in the foreground of your shot like a tree, a wagon wheel, a person—something of recognizable size. Better yet, try to include something in the foreground and middleground of the shot to show even more dimensionality. It doesn't really matter a lot if the foreground object is a little blurry (as may be the case if you have focused on the distant background). The blurriness will further emphasize the farness of the background and *because* of the blurriness, won't distract attention from the background. Figure 5-7 shows some examples.

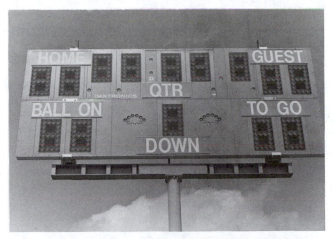

Vertical tall structure appears stable, solid.

Angled tall structure implies danger, action.

(Fig. 5–6 Continued)

Don't's and Do's of Camera Angles

Now we get deeper into the aesthetics of picture composition. Before we merely concerned ourselves with keeping subjects sharp, close, centered, and level without wiggling. If you can do that, you score 75%, but still Frances Ford Coppola you're not. To score 100%, your TV screen must portray precisely the message you want it to. The image must embrace the subconscious nuances you desire yet eliminate unwanted distractions. Figure 5–8 shows some more "rules" of picture composition. Can you see why the "don't's" should be avoided?

background alone

foreground object

middleground and foreground object

FIGURE 5-7 Using a foreground object to emphasize the size or distance of the background

eyes, nose, mouth, chin

bust

hands

knees
hem line

ankles

Cut off a person at any of these natural divisions

Cut off feet

Include feet

Cut off neck

Leave in part of the body leading to the next part. The mind will complete the rest of the body.

FIGURE 5-8 Don'ts and do's of the camera angles

Cut a person off where she contacts her surroundings. Here the talent looks like she's leaning on the side of the TV screen

Provide enough surroundings for shot to explain itself: the talent is in a chair

Provide insufficient headroom.

Leave just a little space so talent doesn't "bump her head"

(Fig. 5–8 Continued)

Change angle without changing shot size. Twists performer without apparent purpose.

Change shot size as you change angle to add variety and interest.

DON'T	**DO**

Use many LONG SHOTS.

Television is a CLOSE-UP medium.

JUMP CUT between long shots and closeups without changing angle. With a cut, the viewer expects a substantial change in visual information but doesn't get it.

Change angle about 30° when cutting. Adds variety and smooths transition. Builds a fuller perception of subject.

Place most important picture element in the dead center of the screen.

Use the so-called RULE OF THIRDS placing important picture elements one-third down or one-third up the screen.

(Fig. 5-8 Continued)

 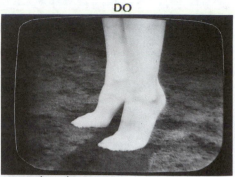

centered   ⅓ up from bottom

Place eyes in the middle of the screen.   Place eyes one-third down the screen.

Place the face in the middle of the screen. Too much headroom. Note also how shot cuts body at the bust, also a no-no.   Place face one-third down the screen.

(Fig. 5-8 Continued)

The mouth and eyes are important. Here they follow the RULE OF THIRDS, where the eyes are one-third down the screen and the mouth one-third up. Here the missing chin and forehead will be mentally filled in by a psychological process called CLOSURE.

208

DO

If possible, cut from shot to shot when necessary

DON'T

Allow talent to wiggle object around while looking at TV monitor, trying to center it for the camera. Also, here the talent can't see object well enough to point to detail.

Hold object to side of face, steadily. Let camera operator do the centering. Detail is easy to see and point to.

Or, set it on something stationary and hold it there.

(Fig. 5-8 Continued)

You shouldn't cut a person off at a natural body divison such as the ankles, the bust, or the chin. It makes the body look as though there is something missing. If, however, you leave in part of the body leading to the next part, the mind will complete the rest of the body using a psychological quirk called CLOSURE. Similarly, if your talent is sitting on or leaning against something, a part of that something should be showing. Again, the mind, by seeing part of the object will complete the rest of it.

The RULE OF THIRDS suggests that your center of attention should not be in the dead center of the TV screen. The picture looks best when your eye is attracted to areas just off the center of the screen such as one third down from the top, one third up from the bottom, or one third in from either side.

Performers should be taught how to hold items they are displaying to the camera. The talent shouldn't be looking into a monitor and trying to center a picture for the camera operator. Centering and focusing is the camera person's job. Instead, the talent should place an object near his or her face and hold it as still as possible. Here the performer can easily see the detail he or she wishes to point to. Another technique is to place the object on a table (which holds it very still for close-up shooting) and to point out details without moving the object.

More Do's of Camera Angles

Seat people close together   One of the oddities of television is how it distorts space. A five-foot-wide SET becomes the entire universe for your TV show. Your audience never sees the mess of lights, cables, and clutter just a foot "off screen." To them, what they see is all that exists. Visit a TV newsroom which you've grown accustomed to viewing only on TV and you'll be shocked at how little there is to it.

One aspect of this distortion of space involves people in conversation. Normal Americans converse at about three or four feet from each other and sit even farther from each other. Not on TV. Three or four feet seems like across the room on TV (see Figure 5–9). Squeeze your people in tight to look "normal." Note that it may take some practice before your performers feel comfortable conversing from less than two feet apart.

Seat host to one side of guests   This way you avoid giving the host "tennis neck" as he or she ping-pongs attention first the guest on the left and then to the guest on the right. Cameras and viewers alike go bouncing back and forth to follow the discussion.

Placing the host between the guests has another disadvantage. If you later edit together the TWO SHOTS, which include the host and one guest, (as in Figure 5–10), then the host and the other guest, the host snaps from the left side of the frame to the right side. First the host is looking to the right; then suddenly to the left. Figure 5–11 is more comfortable.

Talent may look fine in the studio but . . .

. . . are too far apart for a good MEDIUM

FIGURE 5-9 Seat the talent close together

First the host is on the left . . .

. . . then the host is suddenly on the right.

FIGURE 5-10 Panel discussion with host between guests

FIGURE 5-11 Panel discussion with host to one side of guests

Nose to nose implies adversary relationship.

Line-up gives no relationship between guests.

Angled is comfortable.

FIGURE 5–12 Angle the guests

Angle the guests   This applies to any shot with two or more persons in it. People facing each other nose-to-nose suggests an adversarial relationship. It is a great way to portray an argument. But in a panel discussion, the shots imply disagreement or debate. Conversely, people lined up facing the camera look like a team of contestants. They appear ready to perform individually for the camera but not ready to react with each other. The most comfortable seating arrangement has people angled toward each other as shown in Figure 5–12.

Reverse angle shots   No one wants to look at the back of somebody's head. But people usually face each other when speaking and unless you like profiles, you're always going to be shooting somebody from behind.

There are lots of ways to get a dialogue with two people facing the camera, like people on a park bench, sitting in a car, watching TV or a fireplace, or with one in front of a mirror. In fact, you'd be surprised at how many natural-looking scenes there are in the soaps showing someone facing *away* from the person they are talking with. Nevertheless, at some point, you're going have to face the problem of how to shoot faces facing faces.

One way is the over-the-shoulder shot as shown in Figure 5–13. Shooting over one person's shoulder, we get a close-up of the second person's face as he or she speaks. When the first person speaks, we swap everything around making a medium shot of the first person over the shoulder of the second.

If you are using a single camera and editing as you go, you'll find yourself getting a lot of exercise traveling back and forth to get a face shot for each actor's lines. If shooting RAW FOOTAGE for later editing, you could save steps by shooting the entire sequence twice—once facing one actor (or actress) and once facing the other. In fact, each sequence could be recorded on a separate cassette. When editing later, all you do is change tapes to change camera angle and get a face shot of the person speaking.

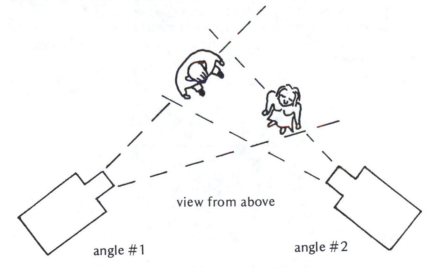

FIGURE 5–13 Over-the-shoulder shot

Over-the-shoulder shots are not always easy to do. Performers seem to have a away of stepping to the side and blocking your shot. To counteract this, you must always be ready to ARC your camera to the left or right to unblock the shot.

Reverse angle shots may be great for two people talking, but not for cuts between hands or props and the person holding them. If a performer is angled to the right in a MEDIUM SHOT, his or her *hands* should be angled to the right when you cut to a CLOSE-UP. To have the hands or prop suddenly change direction would be jarring to the audience. The same is true for the general flow of motion in a scene. If the action is moving to the right in one shot, it should be moving to the right in the next, at least for the start of the shot. If panning left in one shot, the following shot should continue the motion. These are examples of why the camera operator should know *how* the shots are going to be used, so that they may be recorded with the later edits in mind.

Avoid slightly off-camera looks Have your performers play directly *to* the camera *or* react to each other or the props disregarding the camera completely. Direct eye contact is very engaging, making the viewer feel as if the performer is talking to *him* or *her* alone. Profile and off-angle shots make the viewer feel like an observer to the action. Both kinds of shots have their advantages. But avoid splitting the difference. The slightly off-camera shot in Figure 5–14 makes the performer look insincere and shifty-eyed or makes the performer look as though she's reading something.

As combination camera operator and acting coach, it may be your responsibility to remind the performers that they are supposed to look *into* your camera; they shouldn't be talking to the floor, the wall, or the studio monitor. You can remind them by reaching out from behind your camera and pointing your finger at your lens. I have found that with amateur talent, 10 such reminders in a single show are not too many. Eventually, the performer learns good eye contact.

If you have a TV monitor which seems to catch your talent's eye during the performance, then turn it off. They don't need to see what they are doing, and their off-stage glances look bad on TV.

FIGURE 5-14 Avoid slightly off-camera looks

FIGURE 5–15   Foreground figure to give scale to landscape shot

Use a familiar object to create a sense of scale   Extreme CLOSE-UPS and majestic landscape shots suffer one problem in common. The viewer cannot appreciate the smallness or largeness of the subject without a "visual yardstick" to gauge it by. Figure 1–25 used a hand to define the size of a plug. Figure 5–15 uses a familiar object in the foreground to add dimension and meaning to the landscape in the background. Often a bush, a tree, a person, or an old wagon wheel serves nicely to create scale, balance, and visual variety in a scenic view.

Shooting children   Photographing little people requires getting low. If you shoot them from the same height as you do adults, you inadvertently introduce the domination-weakness impression (refer to the example in Figure 5–3). To keep your shots neutral and unbiased, get down and shoot children at their own eye level.

The same goes when adults interview children. The adult should bend down to the same height as the child so that the camera sees both their heads at about the same level. Otherwise, you get a shot of

a. The child's body and the adult's knees.
b. The adult's torso and the child's head.
c. An uninteresting LONG SHOT of both of them.

When the adult gets down to the level of the child, there is better eye contact and a warmer relationship is implied. See Figure 5–16.

camera high

eye level

FIGURE 5-16 Shooting children

CREATIVE CAMERA ANGLES

Popular Alternatives to the Simple Shot

There are lots of ways to show the same thing. The real skill comes in knowing when fancy shots will add spice to the scene and when they will distract the viewer and ruin the scene. Your decision will be a delicate balance between two forces. One is the pressure to "show off" many of the tricks and skills you can perform. I have seen students contrive ways to ring and blow every bell and whistle they can find on their equipment. The opposite force is the "let's-get-it-done-quick-and-dirty"

adult interviewing from above

adult at child's level

(Fig. 5–16 Continued)

approach. You get so involved in cranking out the required shots on your list that you forget to make your program visually interesting. Knowing when to be fancy and when to be straightforward makes you a master of this trade.

Focus shift   Something (or someone) is in the foreground. Something else (or someone else) is in the background. Usually one of these two has to be out of focus for the other to be sharp. Okay, use this to your advantage. As two people talk, focus back and forth on whichever person is speaking. It's better than panning back and forth, and better than a LONG SHOT trying to get both performers into the picture at once. Perhaps the foreground person's expression is paramount (for example, tears welling in the eyes) while the background person is secondary, even distracting. So focus on the foreground making the background blurry. Then when the background person's action becomes important, (staggering to the cupboard and pouring another drink) *that* is pulled into focus, diverting attention from the face. Yet both characters can be seen at once as you shoot past the tearful face four feet from the camera and in the other half of the screen get a LONG SHOT of the drinker twenty feet away. Attention can be focused on one or the other performer, yet the viewer can *keep track of* both. Figure 4–27 showed an example of FOCUS SHIFT.

FOCUS SHIFT is also a popular way to display a long line of something—soldiers, flowers, gravestones, fenceposts, and so on. Position yourself next to one member of the lineup and shoot toward the farthest member. Focus on the closest (or farthest) at first and then, as you change focus, different members will, in turn, become sharp, then blurry as other members become sharp.

Low f numbers and longer focal length lenses make this focus-defocus effect more pronounced.

If you have a macro lens, you're equipped to carry out a super FOCUS SHIFT from three inches out to 20 feet. Picture how this could work with a beginning title. You letter your title onto a foot-square piece of clear glass, plastic, or acetate transparency (like those used in schools for overhead projectors). You macro focus on that title inches away from your lens (make sure you make the title the right size for this). In the background, so out-of-focus that you can't see it, is your first scene. You refocus from the title to the distant scene as the action begins. The title will go so far out of focus that it almost disappears, making it a nice cheap dissolve effect using only one camera.

The same technique may be used for 35mm slides taped to the front of the macro lens or for FOCUS SHIFTS from miniature soldiers or plane models out to your live actors.

Mirror Shots

This is another way to slip twice as much into your picture without resorting to dull LONG SHOTS. Imagine this—a CLOSE-UP of a woman putting on lipstick. The camera slowly zooms (or dollies) out revealing that her face is a reflection in a mirror. You see the side of her head in the foreground. As the camera pulls back further, you see someone else reflected in the mirror. It's a man getting dressed across the room. As he speaks, she turns now facing toward the camera. He steps closer tying his tie as he walks. Now your camera has two people talking *to* each other, *facing* each other, yet you see *both faces at once*. Nice trick. How else can you get two full face shots at once?

Mirrors are useful any time you want to show both sides of something like an engine, a statue, or some complex device. They're useful for dramatic effects (an actor looks up and in the mirror sees someone climbing through the window). Occasionally, they serve as just another way of formulating a shot.

A mirror hung at an angle over the kitchen stove allows you to get straight-down-into-the-pan shots without the risk of having your camera fall into your tomato sauce. Conversely, a mirror slipped under the car allows you to document defective ball joints on autos awaiting recall.

Mirrors are a handy way to get a bird's-eye view of medical operations without the risk of your camera operator fainting onto someone's intestines.

Mirrors are not the only things that reflect images. Imagine a CLOSE-UP of a man's face slowly turning toward the camera. He is wearing those mirror-like sunglasses. You know what he's looking at when the twin likenesses of a sunbather appear in the lenses.

Windows and water reflect, too. Windows have an added advantage of being able to mix two scenes together for you: the figure behind the glass and the one reflected by it. In fact, one tricky way to dissolve from one picture to another without an expensive video FADER and two cameras is as follows: First, illuminate the figure behind the glass while keeping the reflected subject in the dark. Then, dim the behind-the-glass scene while simultaneously brightening the reflected scene. The old scene will melt away, being replaced by the new. Makes a nice trick shot for a sci-fi drama, too.

Mirrors don't even have to be flat to work. Nice effects can be had by shooting a CLOSE-UP of someone's face reflected in a shiny Christmas tree decoration, teapot, or chrome bumper. Remember all those serving dishes you got as wedding presents but never had occasion to use in the thirty-one years that you've been married? Hallelujah, the time has come! Use them now for twisting the world into funhouse contortions. It is a good way to start a scene before zooming out and panning to the real world.

Again, be careful not to reflect any bright lights into your camera when you use mirrors. They may cause burn-ins.

Reflection in a shiny object

Parallel movement Joggers, bicyclists, waterskiers, snowmobilers, and horseback riders all pose the same problem for the camera. They are fun to watch but they're gone an instant later. To really catch the action, move with them. Videotape that jogger from your car (preferably with someone else driving). Shoot that waterskier from the back of the tow boat or by moving along next to the action in a separate boat; the waterskier stays with you while the background slips by.

Adding movement to still objects Photos and model ships don't move. That doesn't mean that the camera can't make them come alive. Imagine a close-up of a *photo* of a parade. By panning across the picture to the sound of a marching band, the people will *seem* to be marching.

Imagine a slow *zoom in* on a painting, starting first with the whole town but ending with a "stroll" down the main street.

Picture the museum's dinosaur display filling the screen. Cut to a close-up of one of the models. Take the shot from slightly below the creature so it looks domineering and dangerous. ARC the camera around the model making it seem to turn its head. Add some tension by tilting the camera sideways a little as you go.

Zoom in on a still photo of a horse race with the sound of crowds cheering in the background. Shake the camera as you zero in on the lead horse. You can almost see the mud flying from the hooves.

To the beat of rock music, quickly zoom in and out, in and out, on a singer's face from the record jacket. Dance him or her around at the microphone by angling the camera left and right to the music. This will heighten energy in the scene and if the shots are quick enough, the viewer will never notice that the performer isn't moving.

Pan across photos of antique cars. Move the camera so that the cars appear to be traveling forward. You won't fool anybody into thinking that the cars are

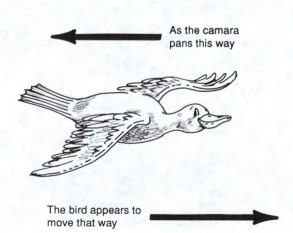

As the camara pans this way

The bird appears to move that way

The bird appears to move

really moving, but viewers are often inattentive. Leaving them with the *impression* that the cars are moving is all that is necessary.

The same trick works with photographs of birds. Pan across a photo of a bird in flight; it will appear to be gliding through the sky.

Wall shadow   In the movie *Goodbye Girl,* the young lady is forced to accept a male roommate in her apartment. She's had it with his guitar playing and barges into his bedroom to complain. Seems he strums in the nude. How would you show such a scene without going R-rated?

In the movie they aimed the camera at the flustered lady standing by the door with the shadow of a man projected on the wall. It all seemed very natural and the scene was creative and novel.

You can use this technique to show sinister shadows, lantern cast shadows, or just for a stylistic view of something before you actually see it (like a shot of the bicycle shadow on the pavement followed by a tilt up to the bicycle).

Shadows make nice surprise revelations. Consider a lady's shadow cast upon a doorway. Then into view comes the shadow's owner: a fellow dressed ridiculously in women's clothing in order to sneak past a detective.

Arty Tricks

Here you are limited only by your creativity. Try experimenting with these ideas and soon you will be developing ones of your own.

Flashy opening   Every notice how when you first power up a tube type camera, all kinds of exotic colors and ghost-like images fill the screen for a moment and then melt away to reveal your picture? Use this. Start your VCR recording and turn on the camera. The dazzling images will unfold into your opening scene as the camera "warms up."

Lag and comet-tailing   The dancer swings her arms and a streak follows them like a flowing sleeve. She slips across the floor leaving a faint trail behind her which evaporates in a second. This is comet-tailing caused by

1. Bright objects.
2. Dark backgrounds.
3. Very low light level.
4. Cheap vidicon cameras.

What you're doing is intensifying the tube camera's natural LAG caused by insufficient light on contrasty scenes. Older vidicon cameras easily display a lot of LAG in their pictures, as you saw in Figure 4–2.

Lens flare   Figure 4–34 showed what happens when you aim too close to a light. The geometric patterns and spots that you get are called LENS FLARE and are usually reduced by the lens shade. But what if you *want* LENS FLARE for artistic affects? Well, remove the lens shade. Play around with your zoom and iris further to enhance the effect, but watch out that you don't shoot directly into a light and burn-in your pickup tube.

If you'd like to get one of those dreamy sails-across-the-sunset shots or sun-eclipsed-by-the-glider views, it's still possible—if you are careful: Place a dark, neutral density filter over your lens and stop down you lens to f16. Take a quick zip past the sun with your camera and see if it is leaving a streak. If there's no evidence of temporary burn-in, and your picture is altogether too dark to use, open your lens one stop at a time and repeat the experiment until you notice that the sun is starting to leave a mild *temporary* streak. That's as far as you can go safely with a tube type camera. Such a shot should yield nice halos, rings, rainbows, and geometric patterns yet probably a dim silhouetted shot of that sailboat or glider. This technique works well with sun reflections on water, sunsets, tall buildings with the sun just behind them, the sun peeking through the trees as you look up from a stroll on a wooded path, and almost-into-the-sun shots.

If you *must* shoot directly into the sun:

1. Use a film camera for the shots. The film camera won't be harmed and the film can later be transferred to videotape (see Chapter 8). This way you take no chances.
2. Use a CCD or MOS camera which is less likely to be harmed by bright light.

Gun barrels, drain pipes, kaleidoscopes   Remember the title scenes of James Bond 007 where you are looking *through* a gun barrel at James? You could even see the spiral rifling of the barrel's interior. You can do this or something similar by placing tinfoil or cardboard over your lens and making a pin hole in its center. Then aim your camera through the gun barrel or whatever and *flood* your subject with light. Because the pin hole "stopped down" your lens to perhaps f64, you'll have nearly infinite depth-of-field but will need lots of light.

Chrome-plated sink drain pipes are interesting to shoot through. Kaleidoscopes, too. You can pull the end off your kid's scope (or wait until three days after Christmas when he or she has done this) and get kaleidoscopic views through your home camera.

Silhouette   Hang a large, seamless, white sheet from a wall extending it in a smooth curve to the floor. Perhaps place another on the floor overlapping with the first. Darken the room and flood the sheets with light. Have your performer stand in front of the sheets, *but not in the light*. The strong backlighting will create a silhouette effect as shown in Figure 5–17.

FIGURE 5–17 Silhouette effect by brightly illuminating background

Painting with a camera   Most of the warm, red sunrises and sunsets you've seen on TV weren't as warm as they looked. The camera shot the scene through an orange lens filter or with its COLOR BALANCE controls misadjusted to "paint" the scene redder than it really was. You can "cool" a scene by "painting" it blue with the opposite adjustment. Science fiction scenes can be done with this effect making all the colors unusual and foreign. Faces become green, water becomes magenta. You can imitate the sepia tone of old time movies by adjusting your camera's color controls for perfect WHITE BALANCE while *aiming it at something light blue.* This will trick the camera into making whites look sepia.

Lost horizon   We touched on this subject before while discussing how a slightly angled horizon can add energy or frenzy to a shot. Now, let's carry angled shots to the extreme.

The viewer who can't see the horizon can be easily fooled, much like the way you can be fooled in a funhouse in a tilted room where *everything* is tilted—except you—and you soon become tilted, too.

Shoot straight down at someone climbing on his belly (panting and groaning) over a gently sloped cliff of rocks. The viewer will think the cliff goes straight down. Include the appropriate glances "downward", with an occasional "slip" of the foot, and the-face-pressed-against-the-rock look to add credibility.

Walls that look like floors and vice versa are splendid sets for such camera tricks. And imagine someone hanging onto a window ledge ready to jump 30 floors—or is it really 30 inches? The camera will never tell.

Picture a rope in the gym backed by a nondescript cinderblock wall. Have an athlete climb up a ways, get turned head down, then slide slowly down toward the floor. Only shoot this all with the camera upside down. Imagine your viewers seeing someone slither to the "top" of a rope and teeter at its free end like an Indian rope trick.

Nail up a sheet of wall paneling—at a 30° angle. Prop a table or desk and chair at the same angle. Stick in a performer holding himself or herself at a 30° tilt and place your camera 30° from level. Now have your actor pour a glass of milk. Guess where the milk will go?

To make a car or runner seem to speed powerfully up a hill, tilt the camera so that the road is at an uphill angle. Shoot with a neutral background avoiding telltale trees, signs, and houses. This shot is very common in car and truck commercials. The runaway wagon, on the other hand, will look as though it is careening down a much steeper slope than it is with the help of a camera tilt in the downhill direction.

A tilted camera can make an airplane "dive" to earth. A back and forth tilt can make a boat endure great sea swells.

Reflections and refractions   Try shooting through a wavy glass for a dreamy or underwater effect. Edmund Scientific, an optics company, sells such glass and all kinds of crazy lenses. So do many photo shops.

Try shooting through a glass of water or a fish tank or just above a hot radiator or parallel to hot pavement for some nice effects.

How about shooting at a steep angle into a puddle of water, a pan of water, or a lake to catch ripply reflections before you tilt up to the actual subject.

For a dreamy effect, project a scene onto a screen or even a white sheet in a darkened room. Place a pan of water in front of the screen image and shoot the

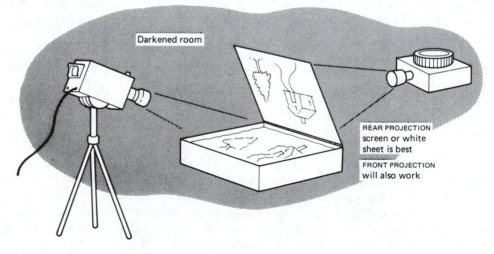

FIGURE 5-18 Dreamy effect from reflection off water

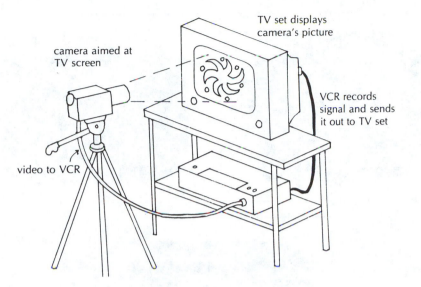

FIGURE 5-19   Camera setup for VIDEO FEEDBACK

reflected image (with ripples in the water). To make the reflected scene right side up, invert the slide in the projector. Figure 5–18 shows the setup.

Video feedback   What do you suppose would happen if you aimed your TV camera at your TV monitor which was displaying your TV camera's picture? What your camera saw, your set would show, and your camera would see, and your set would then show, and 'round and 'round the signals would go in a FEEDBACK LOOP. This is called VIDEO FEEDBACK.

The visual effects are so limitless that one could sit all night tilting the camera a little, zooming a little, twiddling the TV's color and brightness controls as well as the camera's white balance controls, and then sticking one's hand in front of the TV screen to see what happens. You're unlikely to see exactly the same effect twice and just as unlikely to be able to reproduce a given effect at will.

Tilted cameras produce pinwheel and kaleidoscope patterns which spin, freeze, reverse direction, and break up into separate pinwheels. Iris changes create shrinking and growing blobs of light. Color these blobs with your TV and camera's color controls.

And when you've taped a couple hours of this fantasy, go back and dub in an appropriate sound track. Hard rock or heavy classical scores set to the same visual piece can create completely different moods.

The effect of watching such a recording is much like gazing into the fireplace while listening to the stereo. Your eyes are rivoted but your mind is free to wander. The name given to these kinds of abstract TV productions is VISUAL WALLPAPER. Figure 5–19 shows the setup and Figure 5–20 shows some examples.

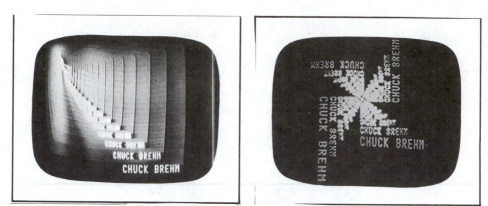

FIGURE 5-20 VIDEO FEEDBACK

CREATING MOODS AND IMPRESSIONS WITH THE CAMERA

How you show something tells as much of your story as *what* you show. You've learned that by changing camera height, you can make a performer look strong or weak. You've seen how tilted shots create suspense, and how soft focus and foggy lenses create a dreamy effect. Close-ups, as you've seen, involve the viewer directly with the action. Here are some more mood creating shots.

Progress versus Frustration

A jackrabbit is racing to the right. The camera pans along with it but slowly falls behind so that the bunny moves forward in the frame. That's progress. A mountain lion pursues to the right. Here the camera pans slightly faster than the lion can run leaving more space in front of it. That's frustration. Score: jackrabbit one, lion zero.

A runner in a telephoto shot approaches and approaches and approaches in a vain attempt to reach the camera. Frustration. Shot at a wide angle, the mild-mannered accountant strolls by the camera and appears to loom forward as she nears the camera lens. The look is one of decisive action. Progress.

Suspense

Our hero creeps backwards and the audience cringes waiting for him to back into something awful. He looks up slowly; something terrible is bound to drop on him. He pokes his head ito an air duct; what's going to grab his face? He draws open the curtains, what monster will leap from behind them? As he sleeps, a large shadow slips across the bedroom wall—what is it? He washes his hands, he looks up, and through the sink window, inches from his face there is a. . . . He sits at the dressing table and looks up into the mirror, what unholy creature will he see behind him? He casually shaves while we dolly in from behind him, stopping just over his shoulder; what unwelcome surprise awaits him in seconds?

In each case, your attention is drawn to what you *don't* see, out of the camera's view, behind the curtain, in the mirror, or behind the camera as it moves closer. For a crash course in suspense shots, see the movie *Alien*. It uses every trick in the handbook.

Anger, Secrets

Pose your performers almost nose to nose and have them shout. Voilà, anger. As they move about, keep their heads very close together.

This closeness *without* the shouting implies intimacy or secretiveness.

Speed

Keep the camera low to the ground (so you can see the ground rushing towards you) and use a wide angle lens to portray speed. A camera on a skateboard moving at one mile per hour looks as though it's moving at 60. A camera shooting from the roof of a tall truck at 60 miles an hour looks as though it's only traveling at 20.

I once shot a traffic safety tape by mounting a TV camera on the fender of a car and driving it around a congested campus. The scenes made it look as though I performed speeding maneuvers and daredevil near misses at every turn. Potholes loomed up like canyons. Casual pedestrians looked like kamikaze jaywalkers. Yet all these shots were taken at a calm 15 miles per hour or less.

Night

Naturally, if you shoot in the dark, you don't get a picture. The object is to make the scene *look like night* but with plenty of light for the camera.

If shooting outdoors in the daylight, pick a cloudless day with blue sky and harsh shadows. Place a red filter in front of the lens to make the blue sky very dark. Either shoot with a black-and-white camera or misadjust the camera's color controls to undo the redness you've just added to the scene. Incidentally, night scenes normally have very little color in them anyway. They do not look abnormal in black and white. Use a neutral density filter or stop down your lens to darken the scene more. One way to darken the sky without messing up your colors is to use a polarizing filter. If the effect isn't noticeable enough, try using the polarizing filter *and* the red filter together. (Review Table 4–1 on lens filters.)

One really tricky filter that the pros use is a GRADUATED FILTER. It's dark (or colored) at the top and clear at the bottom, much like some popular styles of sunglasses or like the tinted windshields on cars. The colored part of the lens may cover the sky, making it very blue, or very dark, or orange like a sunset, while the bottom of the picture looks normal.

Keep performers in shadows or "puddles" of light as they move from place to place. Shoot with the sun halfway or three-quarters behind the performer, creating frequent silhouettes. The sun will also appear to "moonlight" the scene. Be very careful not to shoot directly into the sun unless you have a sufficient neutral density filter in place and your lens is at a high f number or you are using a CCD or MOS pickup. The process is very difficult to do well.

If shooting a "night scene" at night outdoors, use one or two harsh lights creating distinct shadows. Try to BACKLIGHT the performers (described further in Chapter 6) to form a white ridge outlining them. Again, watch out for burn-ins.

If shooting a night scene outdoors, create harsh shadows and puddles of light by using one or two bare light bulbs hidden from the camera by props. BACKLIGHT the performers to create silhouettes. If you give your actors lanterns or candles, you have an excuse to beam some light on their faces to catch expressions and so on. The face light doesn't *really* have to come from their lanterns, you could carefully beam some light on their faces from off-camera making it look as though the light came from the lantern.

SURREPTITIOUS RECORDING

If something is important enough to risk your life or (more important) your equipment for, that's your business. The camera operator is usually the one attacked when people want to hide what they are doing. Also, you may be the one sued when their privacy has been invaded.

It is generally considered legally permissible to record anyone in public areas (not counting toilets). Streets, sidewalks, parking areas, and public buildings are pretty much unrestricted. One rule of thumb to use when deciding whether you are illegally invading someone's privacy is to consider the following: Do the unwitting participants have a good reason for believing their activities are totally private and visible to no one else? A football fan making a big gambling payoff in the bleachers

SURREPTITIOUS RECORDING

is fair game. The same transaction shot with a telephoto lens through the person's living room window is off limits.

The courts give investigative reporters and film crews more leeway than people shooting documentaries or entertainment programs. Using a hidden camera to catch a shop mechanic puncturing someone's tire is treated differently from comedy shots of hospital patients frantically trying to open jammed bathroom doors.

If you're doing a Candid Camera type of production, you will be required to secure permission from the participants before you can distribute or publically perform your production. Warnings over, now let's get on with how to do it.

One way to catch people off guard is to focus quickly for medium distance, zoom out all the way, and hold the camera by your side, perhaps under your shoulder, perhaps at arm's length, held by the camera handle. The VCR is still running but no one knows it. The camera is still taking pictures (but not of the sun or other bright objects, we hope). Since the camera is not up to your eye, people think that it is turned off. Try to divert attention away from the equipment by turning yourself away from the camera. You might set the unit down (running) on a table. You could pretend to switch it off and then button up the carrying case. Just make sure your "dirty tricks" are worth the possible consequences if you are found out.

There are special "peephole" lenses which are very small and permit cameras to hide behind a hole in a wall or behind clutter with just the tiny lens snout sticking out. I can remember once investigating storeroom thefts and wondering how to hide the camera and its regular lens. I hit upon the idea of stuffing the camera into a cardboard box of plastic drinking cups and sticking one cup over the lens. The image through the base of the clear plastic cup was excellent and no one noticed the half open box of cups peering out from the shelf. Lesson: Be creative.

It's best to use black-and-white cameras with wide angle standard lenses for detective work like this. A black-and-white camera works well with low light and gives sharp pictures. The wide lenses pick up all the action and if your "spy" gets stolen, you're not out a $1,200 camcorder.

And after all this, you play back your tape the next day and see the thief in action—wearing a mask.

SHOOTING SPORTS EVENTS

For field sports, get as high up as you can (without using drugs). Mount your camera atop a school bus or on some kind of tower. Face away from the sun. If the team is practicing moves for later review, the camera's view is of paramount importance. Have the practice moved to where the camera can see best, such as on a lawn near a building. Here you can shoot from the window or a roof.

Feel free to zoom in or out on the action while the players are moving. Don't bother zooming in to a close-up of a player standing still.

For football, place the ball carrier to the rear of the frame with the blockers in the front. As the ball carrier passes the line of scrimmage, gradually center him so you get the action both ahead of and behind him. If the runner makes it through the secondary defense men, gradually let him out-run your pan thus positioning him in the front edge of the screen so you can reveal as much of the rear action as possible.

On passing plays, cover the passer until the ball is thrown. Then pan to the intended receiver while zooming out some. As the ball is caught, continue zooming out enough to get the other players in his zone. On punts, cover the kicker. When the ball is kicked, stay with the kicker a moment to watch for roughing. Then, pan to the receiver (you'll probably have time for this, as the ball generally stays in the air awhile).

The general technique in sports videography is to catch the *main* event while recording the secondary action as well. No one cares what's happening *behind* the kicker during an extra point attempt, so you frame him off center with space in front. Meanwhile, you're including the charging defense at the other edge of the viewfinder.

If you are shooting games for entertainment and for coaching purposes, don't forget to include a quick shot of the scoreboard after a touchdown or the down indicator or referee signals just to clarify what's going on and provide a visual respite.

If your VCR makes good PAUSE edits, try to cut out the chaff, like the huddle breaks. Start the tape rolling when the call of the play begins.

When you get near the end of a cassette, eject it during a break in the action and start a new cassette. You don't want to run out of tape in the middle of the game's best play (and Murphy's 109th Law says that the play you missed is the best play of the game).

Perhaps this is a large enough dose of camera angles and techniques for one sitting. We'll be coming back for another taste of camera and shooting strategies later in Chapter 10 when we cover editing techniques and how to get one shot to flow smoothly into another.

6

Lighting

The human eye is an amazing thing. It can make wide angle, crystal sharp images in color under the worst conditions. The eye is sensitive enough to see by candlelight, and tough enough to perform in sunlight 20,000 times brighter than a candle's light.

The television camera is frail in comparison. It needs plenty of light, but too much light can damage tube-type cameras. It can display only a two-dimensional image which looks flat and dull compared with the 3-D panorama our eyes give us with each glance. Where the eye can discern a thousand different levels of brightness, the best cameras under the best conditions can distinguish only 30 or fewer shades of gray.

Lighting serves two purposes:

1. It illuminates the scene so that the camera can at least "see" it.
2. It enhances the scene to make up for television's visual shortcomings.

THE KIND OF LIGHT THE CAMERA NEEDS

When the networks pay $20,000 or more for a TV camera, they get a machine that is hardly bothered by bright lights and dark shadows. *They'll work better* with the proper lighting, but they don't mess up too badly when the lighting is wrong. Industrial and home cameras, on the other hand, need all the help they can get. For them, good lighting is essential.

Cameras which work in minimal light generally cost considerably more than cameras which need more light. So which is better? To spend $2,000 extra for a super sensitive camera or to spend $100 extra for two lights?

This chapter will list a lot of "rules" of lighting. Some of them matter a lot and some not very much. It all depends on how tolerant your camera and your audience are. No matter what camera you are using, the picture will always look better if you follow the "rules."

Enough Light

For most cameras, normal home lighting is barely sufficient to yield a picture. Although faces and objects will be recognizable, the image will be rough, grainy, or very gray and flat looking.

Office and classroom lighting is generally sufficient for shooting. Depending on the circumstances, you may even be able to "stop down" your lens from its lowest f number to its next lowest f number, realizing a little better depth-of-field in the process. Office lighting, though it provides sufficient light to create a picture, doesn't create the shadows and contrast to yield a vivid picture; it will still look somewhat flat and lifeless. The colors may also look drab.

On a cloudy day outdoors, the light is adequate for shooting. You may be able to use f4 to f5.6 for good depth-of-field.

A slightly hazy day is perfect for shooting outdoors. Shiny objects won't be dangerously bright (endangering your camera tube) and there will be plenty of contrast at f8, yet shadows won't be too pronounced.

Full sunny days are pretty good for shooting. Avoid highly reflective objects. Use f11 or so. The picture will be bright and vivid but may appear too contrasty. Shadows especially may look too dark and anything lurking in them may be obliterated.

The sun or its reflection off highly polished surfaces, a welder's torch in action, or direct views of an atomic blomb blast constitute excessive light for all tube-type cameras and must be avoided at all costs (unless special light filtering lens attachments are used). Bright lights will make temporary vertical streaks in the picture when CCD cameras are used.

Home video cameras will work well with office and classroom lighting and will work pretty well in home lighting. In home situations, the color and contrast will always be improved if you can find a way to throw more light on the subject. Notice the differences in the pictures in Figure 6–1 as light is added to the scene.

Lighting Ratio

Place something very bright next to something very, very bright, next to something very dark, next to something very, very dark and you will be able to distinguish one from another readily. A TV camera, on the other hand, will see only two white objects and two black objects. Although your eye can handle something a thousand times brighter than something else in the same scene, and although photographic film can distinguish between an object one hundred times brighter than another in the same scene, a TV camera can accept a LIGHT RATIO of only 30. With home video equipment this number may be as low as 15.

Scene lit with regular incandescent home lighting

Scene lit by overhead office fluorescent lamps

Scene with just one extra 250-watt lamp added near camera

Scene with three, well placed, extra lamps

FIGURE 6-1   Ambient lighting vs extra lighting

The brightest thing in the picture should not be more than 30 times brighter than the darkest object in the same scene. Here's what this means in practice. You wish to tape a person standing in front of an open window during the day. What your camera will see was shown back in Figure 5–4. Since the light from the window is very bright, everything else looks dark and silhouetted by comparison. The gradations of gray in the clothing and face are all lost. If you close the shade (see the figure again), now the whitest thing in the picture is the wall and some of the clothing. They are only about 10 times brighter than the hair and other dark parts of the picture. As a result, everything between the blacks of the hair and the whites of the wall gets a chance to be seen as some gradation of gray rather than end up black as they did before. In short, things which are exceedingly bright must be avoided. The brightest part of the scene should be less than 30 times brighter than the darkest part of the scene. Shafts of light coming in the windows, shiny buttons, chrome hardware, and shadowy areas outdoors under the trees should be avoided or subdued.

Lighting Placement

You want most of the light to come from behind you (the camera). Avoid light coming from behind the subject (bright windows and so on) as that will silhouette your performer as shown back in Figure 5–4. On the other hand, try not to have all your light coming from *too near* the camera or you'll lose your shadows, making everything look flat and dull as in Figure 6–2.

Sometimes because you are moving around from room to room, you have no choice but to carry your light with you. Try to mount the light above and to the side of the camera about a foot away if possible. Figure 6–3 shows a lighting contraption which is inexpensive and easy to make that clips to your camera for traveling shots.

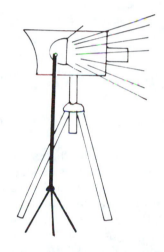

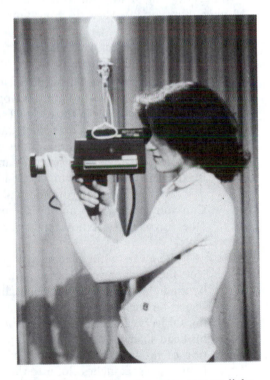

FIGURE 6–2 One light placed near the camera yields a flat picture with almost no shadows on the subject

FIGURE 6–3 Cheapie roving camera light

Lighting Color

Unless you are after special effects, you'll be using white light. But white light isn't always white. Fluorescent lights are blue-greenish. The incandescent lights in your home are reddish. You don't see this difference with your naked eye, but your camera does. The COLOR TEMPERATURE and WHITE BALANCE controls on your color camera can make up for much of this variation. But your controls can't salvage a scene that's lit on one side with fluorescent or sunlight and on the other side with incandescent or studio lights. The majority of the light in your scene has to be of the same COLOR TEMPERATURE or else you'll confuse your poor camera into giving you half red and half blue faces.

BASIC LIGHTING TECHNIQUES

Existing Indoor Light Only

You're shooting on location and didn't bring lights (maybe you're traveling light, if I may abuse a pun). How do you illuminate your subject?

1. Place your subject where the existing illumination is best, such as outdoors (in the daytime, of course) or under office lighting.
2. If the camera with its lens wide open (lowest f setting) still shows a poor picture because of insufficient light, seek out other light sources, such as desk lamps. Turn on every lamp in the room. Take the shades off any lamps not appearing in your scene just to boost the lighting more. Move lamps closer to the scene if possible. Replace the light bulbs in lamps with the largest wattage rated for the lamp (if using extension cords and lots of lamps, do not exceed the wattage maximums for the building's wiring and extension cords).

    Every light that you add will add punch and contrast to your picture. Can you scrounge up any lights nearby? How about an outdoor floodlight? Does anyone have a movie light packed away since their super 8 movie making days?

    Be aware while placing such lamps that the closer they are to your subject, the brighter your subject will be illuminated; however, the area covered by the light will be smaller. This can be a problem if your subject is a moving one as he might slip out of the small bright area you have created. Also, moving subjects cause a brightness problem with close lights. If the subject moves his head six inches closer to a lamp four feet away, the change in the illumination of his face will be unnoticeable. But if someone two feet away from a lamp moves six inches closer to the lamp, the illumination on his face increases sharply, causing a pronounced flare or shine on his forehead and cheeks.

3. Avoid bright windows or lights in the background of the shot. If you wish to use light from a window, get between it and the subject so that the subject, not you, is looking into the window light.

Most of the preceding ideas pose COLOR TEMPERATURE problems, but at least you'll have enough light to take your pictures.

Outdoor Lighting

The big challenge with outdoor shooting is shadow control. Picture a bright sunny day. The baby chases the family cat across the green lawn and under a tree. Suddenly a baby's rosy pink cheeks turn muddy gray. Your orange cat turns muddy gray. The green lawn turns muddy gray. Every once in a while you can see a white flash as the child's outfit is caught in a stray beam of sunlight piercing the leaves. The trick here is to fill in the shadows.

1. Shoot on hazy days when shadows are soft.
2. Shoot with the sun mostly to your back so shadows are partially hidden.
3. Stop down your lens as far as possible to reduce excessive contrast.
4. Glue some wrinkled tinfoil to a sheet of posterboard and "fill in" the shadows with reflected light or plain white posterboard (or a sheet) will do if near enough to your subject.
5. Shoot with a bright light near the camera, even in broad daylight. Place the light in such a way as to "fill in" the shadows caused by the sun. To avoid COLOR TEMPERATURE problems, use a "daylight" photoflood, or use a colored filter over the bulb to convert the light to 5,600°K.

Bright sunlight has a way of driving a camera's AUTO IRIS crazy. The automatic control "locks onto" the brightest part of the scene while everything else looks dark relative to it. Whenever possible, size up the lighting situation and switch to MANUAL IRIS. Let your eye and viewfinder be the judge of what is most important in the scene and make *that* look good, even if something else gets a little over- or underexposed.

PHOTOFLOOD bulbs make daylight COLOR TEMPERATURE

Outdoor light reflector of aluminum foil over posterboard helps fill in shadows.

This technique is commonly applied when shooting *toward* the sun: In this case, the sun acts as a strong BACK LIGHT, rimming the performer, while you use a separate lamp or a reflector to illuminate the talent's face. The background or rim may be too white, darkening the talent's face. Here you would manually open the IRIS a little (or press a BACKLIGHT button on the camera which does the same thing) to overexpose the background while properly exposing the face. You can only "cheat" like this by one or two f-stops before you overburden the camera's electronics with excessive light. Sometimes it helps to zoom in on the face a bit to decrease the amount of bright background visible.

If you're shooting early in the morning or late in the afternoon, WHITE BALANCE your camera often. As the sun nears the horizon, its COLOR TEMPERATURE drops rapidly toward the red. This change can sneak up and bite you if you're too preoccupied with your shoot to notice the changing sun.

One Light Only

You're shooting on location and you brought only one light (perhaps that's all that would fit under your airline seat). Where do you place it?

Don't place it next to the camera because that will give a flat picture without shadows as in Figure 6–2. In most cases, shadows are desirable as they create a sense of depth and texture to the image. Place the lamp at an angle 20° to 45° to the right and 30° to 45° above the subject, as shown in Figure 6–4.

What kind of lighting instrument should be used? Figure 6-5 shows several popular portable lamps used for video and filmmaking. Some can be held by hand and others clamp to telescoping stands.

If you're practicing pennypinching teleproductions, all is not lost. Improvise. Buy one (or more) clip-on lights and extension cords at your hardware store. For a daylight color balance, equip them with PHOTOFLOOD light bulbs from a photo store. The lamp can be clipped almost anywhere including the top of your camera to make a roving camera/light ensemble like the one in Figure 6-3. Although that clip-on setup is handy, the shadows it creates aren't too gorgeous.

Dig around in the back of your closet or go to a church rummage sale and you may come up with a movie light (Figure 6-6). They are portable, very bright, and yield a reasonable COLOR TEMPERATURE. Set your camera for 3,200°K or IN-CANDESCENT.

Shooting with only one light has its liabilities. It is possible that the light may be so bright, compared to other light in the scene, that it "washes out" light-colored

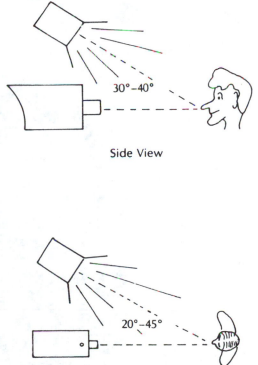

Side View

Top View (Lamp could be to left or to right.)

FIGURE 6-4 Optimal placement of single lamp to create depth through shadows

Hand-held light   Camera-mounted light

Brace holds camera-mounted light farther from
camera for better shadows.

FIGURE 6–5 Portable TV lights (Courtesy Quality/Universal)

FIGURE 6–6 A movie light makes a handy portable video light

FIGURE 6–7 Excessive LIGHTING RATIO.

parts of the scene and creates harsh shadows. This is called EXCESSIVE LIGHTING RATIO and typically occurs when a very bright light is placed too near the subject. Figure 6–7 shows an example.

The cure for EXCESSIVE LIGHTING RATIO is to find some way to dim or diffuse the light and to create or reflect some light into the shadow areas. Moving the light farther from your subject may be easiest. Another solution may be to place a metal screen, called a SCRIM, in front of the light to diffuse it. Figure 6–8 shows a SCRIM which clips onto the front of a light fixture.

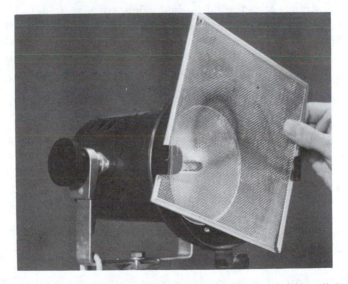

FIGURE 6–8 SCRIM clips onto light fixture to reduce and diffuse light intensity

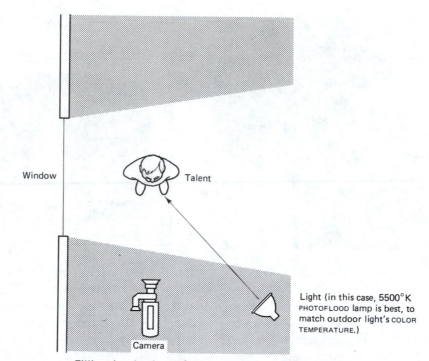

Filling in shadows from a room's natural light.

Another alternative is to aim the light at a white ceiling or white wall and illuminate your subject with the fairly shadowless BOUNCE light.

If the room's natural lighting seems to illuminate the left side of the face the most, you should place your professional light on the right side of the face. This way the existing room lighting has a job to do; it fills in the shadows created by your professional light.

Two Lights Only

The professional solution to dark shadows is to use two lights. One light makes the shadows, the other one decreases their intensity, bringing the LIGHTING RATIO back to where the camera can handle it.

Where should you place the two lights? The first light should go 20° to 45° to the side and 30° to 45° up, as described in Figure 6–4. You place the second light similarly up and to the *other* side of the camera as in Figure 6–9.

The brighter of the two lights acts as the KEY light providing most of the illumination on the subject while the weaker lamp becomes the FILL light filling in the shadows somewhat and softening the picture.

If both lights are of equal brightness, one can be made into a FILL light by

1. Moving it farther away from the subject.
2. Placing a SCRIM in front of it to diffuse the light.
3. Aiming the light at something reflective nearby (a white posterboard, wall, or some aluminum foil). The diffused reflected light will then fill in the shadows.

Individual taste and circumstances play a large role in setting up lights. There is no law that says a light must be 20° up and 30° over. No law says one lamp must be brighter than the other so that one is the KEY and the other is the FILL; they could be equal. The ideas set forth here are generalities, not rules.

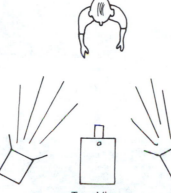

Top View

FIGURE 6-9   Using two lights

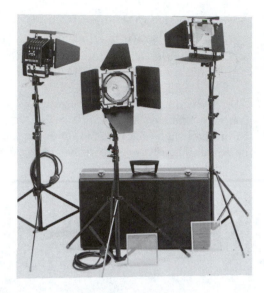

FIGURE 6-10 Homemade FILL light

FIGURE 6-11 Portable lighting kit (Courtesy of Quality/Universal)

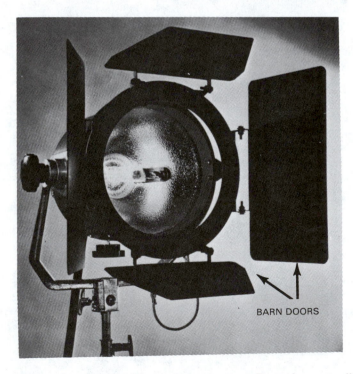

BARN DOORS

FIGURE 6-12 Instrument with BARN DOORS, generally used as a KEY light

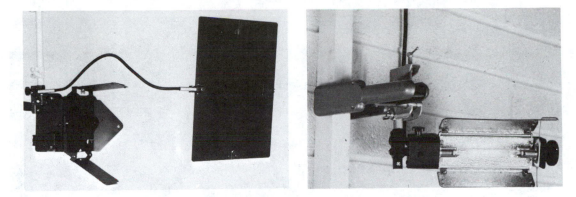

Some portable lights with clamps (From B. Fuller, *Single Camera Video Production: Techniques, Equipment, and Resources for Producing Quality Video Programs,* Prentice Hall, Englewood Cliffs, N.J., 1983)

If working without professional lights, you could make a FILL light out of a clamp-on utility lamp with a large reflector as in Figure 6–10. You can further soften the light by covering the opening with layers of metal window screen. A PHOTO-FLOOD bulb will give a higher COLOR TEMPERATURE light than the standard home light bulb and will also provide plenty of brightness.

If you want all shadows to be harsh, deep, and noticeable, and if you want textures to appear rough and super three-dimensional, omit the FILL light. In most cases, however, you don't want *black* shadows, just the dark gentle hint of shadows.

The better lighting kits (Figure 6–11) usually come with attachable BARN DOORS (Figure 6–12), flaps which you can adjust to direct the light away from certain parts of your scene. The BARN DOORS are helpful when your light is reflecting off metal or some bright part of the picture making that part too bright. The BARN DOORS also help you create special effects by closing the flaps and allowing a small beam of light to illuminate someone's eyes or a specific object.

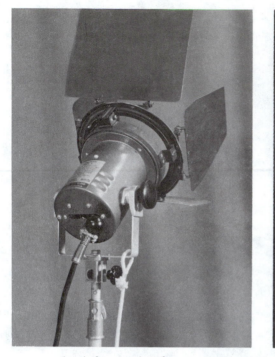

knob for varying focus   loop for varying focus

FIGURE 6–13   Focus controls

Professional lights usually have a focus knob (Figure 6–13) which allows you to vary the beam from a brightly focused SPOT to a widely dispersed FLOOD as shown in Figure 6–14. The FLOOD position covers more area but the light is weaker. The SPOT position gives plenty of light, but over a small area. If your lamp is too bright and you do not wish to move it farther away, you might try adjusting it to FLOOD where the light is weaker.

The softer and more diffuse the light, the sexier and more informal your picture will look. To get the effect shown in Figure 6–15, you will have to bounce your light off a large white surface.

When shooting outdoors, the sun usually acts as your KEY light and you have to dream up something for your FILL. You could bring along an electric light and position it to fill in the shadows. Or you could hold up a square of white poster-board and position it to reflect some of the sun's light onto the shaded side of your subject.

Three Lights

If you can afford to employ three lights, the third one should be your BACK light. The BACK light is responsible for most of the dimensionality of the TV picture.

Light focused for SPOT   Light focused for FLOOD

FIGURE 6–14 SPOT versus FLOOD

FIGURE 6–15 Soft indirect lighting (Courtesy of LEE Colortron, Inc.)

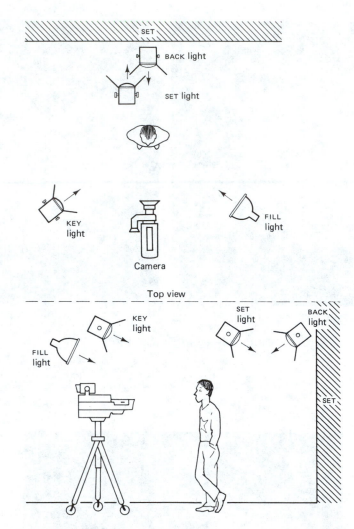

FIGURE 6-16 Typical lighting layout

Without it, the image is flat and dull. With it, the image stands out from its background and has punch.

The BACK light's job is to rim foreground subjects, separating them from the background. The light should strike from above and behind at an angle of 45° to 75° up from the horizontal. The higher and farther back the lamp, the better because the light being aimed *toward* the cameras has a tendency to shine into the lenses. This causes undesired optical effects like the lens flare in Figure 4–34 and risks burn-ins on tube-type cameras if careless camera operators tilt too far up. Often the BARN DOORS help by shading the cameras from the lights while directing the light only on the performers. Figure 6–16 shows a typical lighting layout with KEY, FILL, and BACK lights. Figure 6–17 shows the effect of these lights in a darkened room.

KEY light alone

FILL light alone

KEY and FILL together

BACK light alone

KEY, FILL, and BACK together

SET light alone

KEY, FILL, BACK, and SET together

FIGURE 6–17 Various lighting effects in a darkened room

FIGURE 6–18   BACK light aimed straight down on subject

KEY and FILL only   KEY, FILL, and MODELING

FIGURE 6–19   MODELING light

The BACK light shouldn't look straight down on the subject (as in Figure 6–18) for it will illuminate the performer's nose (like Rudolf the Red Nosed Reindeer) every time the head tilts back. Be sure to keep the BACK light *behind* the performer.

If you can't get the BACK light where it belongs (perhaps the ceiling is in the way), then try using the BACK light from the side. Technically, it is now called a MODELING light. Although not as effective, it can still add punch and dimensionality to your picture as shown in Figure 6–19. Unlike the BACK light, the MODELING light

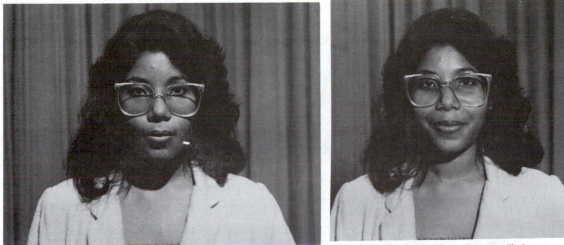

Sometimes a high KEY light can cause problems, like prominent eye shadows or shadows from eyeglass rims.

Try lowering the KEY light.

FIGURE 6–20 Shadows caused by glasses

doesn't have to be behind the performer; it works pretty well from the side. For best results, don't use it at full brightness; let its contribution be subtle.

If your performers wear glasses, sometimes your KEY light reflects in their lenses or casts shadows from their eyeglasses frames as shown in Figure 6–20. You might avoid the reflection by either raising your camera or having your performer raise the stems on the glasses higher above the ear so the lenses reflect downward more. This minor change won't be visible to the camera. To get rid of eyeglass rim shadows, try lowering your KEY light, raising the shadow up to where it is less visible. Another solution is to SCRIM your light, softening it and making the shadows softer.

Try not to allow too much of your light to spill onto your background set. Your eye is naturally attracted to the brightest part of the picture which should be your performer, not your background. *Very* light backgrounds, like white walls, make you picture even worse, especially if your performers are wearing white as in Figure 6–21. Here the performer tends to blend in with the background like a chameleon taking on the color of his rocky home.

LIGHTING COLOR

Your biggest problem with color lighting will involve COLOR TEMPERATURE. It is hard to set up situations which don't mix fluorescent lights with homestyle incandescent lights or with daylight. When all three converge on your picture at the same time, the fluorescent creates a blue-greenish hue, the incandescent light creates a reddish hue, and the daylight creates a bluish hue. These differences may not be

FIGURE 6–21 Light background

noticed except when you are showing faces. We are used to seeing Caucasian faces being a certain shade of flesh tone and when the skin looks greenish or reddish, the lighting error becomes obvious.

If you can't illuminate the whole area with just one kind of light, all is not lost. Sometimes one light is so bright it drowns out the colors of the other lights so that you can adjust your camera for the main light source and never notice the problem caused by the remaining lights. The professionals don't take any chances and bring along GELS—sheets of specially colored plastic, which will color their lights to the desired COLOR TEMPERATURE. They might GEL a window to make the light from the window look redder to match the indoor lights. Or, they may GEL their indoor lamps to look bluer to match the outdoor light.

The colored GEL can slip into your portable light as shown in Figure 6–22. Extra colored GELS can be purchased at theatrical supply shops.

You can also use GELS to make colors for special effects. Blue lights can give the impression of nighttime, darkness, or cold. Red lighting may convey warmth, happiness, or fire. Lighting an object with different colored lights from different angles offers dimensionality and visual appeal. Since the eye doesn't see color exactly the same way the camera does, you should observe your color monitor when making your lighting setups so that you can see the actual effect the way it will be recorded.

Background color, like a blue beam of light sweeping across a wall or curtain, can be used to add dimensionality to a scene. Choose background colors which are complementary to your foreground.

Rules of Color

Although TV color is a matter of artistic taste, the following rules apply most of the time:

1. Avoid pure whites. They will be too bright for most color cameras. Avoid pale yellow and light off-whites as they will probably all end up white on the camera anyway. Medium tone colors reproduce best. Dark colors such as maroon, black, and purple may all appear as black on TV.
2. Try to avoid mixing different COLOR TEMPERATURE lighting on your scene.
3. The background for a colored object should be either gray or a complementary color. For instance, red looks best before a blue-green background; yellow in front of blue; green in front of magenta; orange in front of green; and flesh tones look best with a cyan background.
4. Bright, multicolored subjects look best before a smooth, neutral background. Especially, avoid "busy" backgrounds as they distract the eye from the main subject.

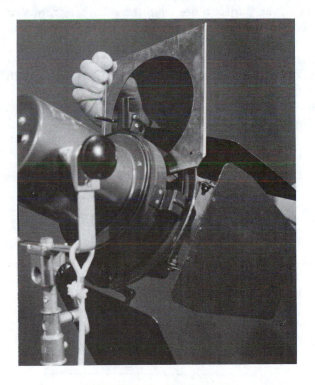

FIGURE 6-22   Colored GEL

5. Attention is attracted to items with saturated (pure or solid) color. Pastels attract less attention and are good for backgrounds.

6. Colors appear brighter and more saturated when illuminated by hard light as opposed to those illuminated by soft, diffuse light.

MOOD LIGHTING AND SPECIAL EFFECTS

Now for some lighting trickery.

For the evil look, aim the lamp up from under the chin as shown in Figure 6–23. A weaker low angle light will give a more subtle effect. Lighting from below builds an unconscious suspense to the shot perhaps making the performer look untrustworthy or devious.

For the soft, sexy bedroom look, use reflected light only, either by aiming the instruments at white boards or shooting your light through a white sheet (don't put your lamp too close to the sheet or you will singe the sheet).

Hard, direct light does just the opposite; it accentuates texture and flaws in smooth surfaces. To get hard lighting, like that in Figure 6–24, avoid lamps with big reflectors. Use a typical KEY light as your FILL light or maybe no FILL at all. Have the lights hit the subject more from the side than from straight on to accent the shadows. The texture of a surface becomes more pronounced as the light skims along it from the edge.

A small lamp placed near the camera's lens and shone into the talent's face will add a sparkle to his or her eyes. Be conservative; too much light will add tears to his or her eyes and complaints to your ears.

Comedies demand upbeat, happy lighting. This is generally done by providing plenty of brightness and FILL lighting. Shadows are minimized and backgrounds are fairly bright.

FIGURE 6–23   Evil look with lamp from below

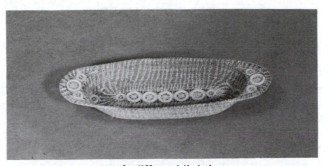

soft diffused lighting

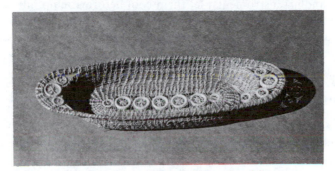

hard, direct lighting from the side

FIGURE 6–24 Hard, direct lighting emphasizes texture

Mysteries and dramas are the opposite. Backgrounds are darker, shadows deeper, and overall illumination is lower. The scene may have dark areas and "puddles" of light through which the performers travel. Don't be afraid to allow your performers to pass in and out of the light, to move through shadows, or to be totally backlit, obscuring their features. A drama isn't a newscast; the viewer doesn't expect a perfectly lit view of the talent. The shadows and vagueries improve the scene.

Lighting can sometimes provide a quick-and-dirty way to create the illusion of something being there when it really isn't. Are people supposed to be driving in a car? Park the car somewhere with a blank background (like in an open area), and have somebody wave a light across the car (from front to back) once in a while to imply movement.

Are folks chatting next to a fire? Wave some red or yellow lights around so flames dance across their faces.

With imagination you can project plants, rain effects, explosions, rocket take-offs, police car flashers, lighthouse beacons, colored spacecraft control panel reflections, green radar scope reflections, all kinds of things, on your performers and their backgrounds.

CARE OF LAMPS

Fixtures Get Hot

And boy do they! They make as much heat as a toaster and can toast you if you don't stay clear. Keep the instrument away from anything combustible or meltable. Make sure that the power cord for the fixture isn't draped over the instrument (it could melt). Watch where the lamp is aimed. You can feel the heat of a 1,000-watt lamp from 10 feet away, so imagine how hot it will be a foot in front of it. For instance, aiming the lamp at a wall or curtain less than one foot away or so could start a fire in a matter of minutes.

When handling instruments, let them cool before attempting to change bulbs or SCRIMS (unless you go around wearing asbestos gloves). Do not attempt to store instruments until they have cooled adequately. Don't be too surprised if the paint burns off the BARN DOORS sometimes; it doesn't look pretty but it's common wear and tear.

Moving Lamps

Do not jar, shake, bump, or attempt to move a lamp while it is lit. The filament in the light bulb is white hot and *extremely* fragile. When the lamp is not glowing, the filament is solid again and is fairly rugged. When you turn off a lamp, always let it cool for a few seconds before moving it. Yes, a few seconds is all that is necessary.

Changing Bulbs

You can assume that a lamp is burned out when it stops working. To confirm that it has expired, first *turn off the power to the instrument*. Take a close look at the bulb. If it has a big bulge, if it is blackened, if it is cloudy inside, or if the filament is clearly broken, the bulb is shot. If none of the preceding is true, perhaps the bulb is good and the instrument, switch, extension cord, or wall outlet isn't getting power.

Unplug the instrument before changing the bulb. If, by accident, the lamp were still ON (some switches don't have the "ON" clearly marked), it would flash to life in your hand as you inserted it in its socket.

Bulbs last between 10 and 500 hours depending upon the manufacturer and type. PHOTOFLOODS last about 10 hours.

Never touch a good bulb with your fingers or it won't be much good anymore. Traces of oil from your fingers can chemically change the glass when the bulb heats up. The glass devitrifies and fails right where the fingerprints were. Handle bulbs with a clean cloth or with the packing that came with the bulb.

Replace bulbs with exactly the same type of bulb or its equivalent. Some lamps can take bulbs of different power and brightness. *Do not exceed the power rating of the instrument.* Removing a 600-watt bulb from a fixture designed for a 600-watt bulb and putting in a 2,000-watt bulb will give you more light—until the fixture and its wires burn up.

Fixtures get hot

To help you find a replacement bulb, hang onto the one you just took out of the lamp. If you examine its base, it will probably have a three-letter code which designates an exact replacement for the bulb. See Figure 6–25. Bulb boxes usually have this three-letter code emblazened on them as well as other details like wattage. Some lighting instruments have a tag on them telling the bulb type appropriate for the fixture. If yours don't, it might be handy to make your own label and attach it to the lamp.

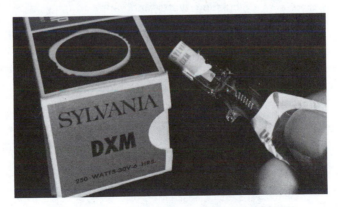

FIGURE 6–25 Three-letter code on base of bulb

A blown bulb can mess up a whole day's shooting. Stock up on bulbs so that you are always one ahead. Like a good Boy Scout, be prepared.

Power Requirements

AMPS times VOLTS equals WATTS. Homes and schools in the U.S. run on 120 VOLTS, so if a circuit is good for 15 AMPS (as is typical in older homes) then you may use up to 15 × 120 = 1,800 WATTS of power on that circuit. If a circuit is rated at 20 AMPS (schools and businesses usually are), then you can use 20 × 120 = 2400 WATTS. In short, the house current you get from the wall socket in your home is good for about 1,800 WATTS. Institutional electrical outlets can sustain about 2400 WATTS. So how many 1,000-WATT lamps can you use at home without blowing a fuse or burning the house down? Table 6–1 reviews how to calculate and estimate WATTS and AMPS.

Before turning on any light, check to see what else is on the same circuit and is also using power. Check also to make sure that you aren't running several lights off one extension cord. An extension cord rated for 15 AMPS (a label on it may say 15A, 120V meaning that it can take 15 AMPS of electric current) can carry only 1,800 WATTS of power. Even if you are working in a school whose outlets are rated for 20 AMPS (2400 WATTS) your extension cord would safely handle only 1,800 WATTS.

Once you are set up for a remote production and are satisfied that you aren't overburdening the wiring, you're ready to go. Switch the lights on *one at a time* rather than all at once because they use abnormally high amounts of power at the moment when they are just lighting up. Switching all the lights on at once could cause a "surge" of power and blow a fuse. If you switch the lights on one at a time, the smaller surges are spaced out and are less likely to overburden the wiring.

One last note, from experience: Don't operate right at the limit of your power capacity. Murphy's 44th Law of Lighting states that lighting systems will work during rehearsal but will fail during the show. The likelihood of failure increases with the importance of the show.

TABLE 6–1 Calculating watts and amps roughly in your head

The exact calculation goes like this:

$$watts = amps \times volts$$

Nearly everyone in the United States uses 120-volt power, so

$$watts = 120 \times amps \quad \text{or}$$
$$amps = watts \div 120$$

The quickie approximation:
   To change watts to amps, divide by 100.
   To change amps to watts, multiply by 100.
   Or 100 watts equals an amp (sort of).

7

Audio

Unless you are producing old time movie classics, you are going to need sound. Although this book is about video, audio is half the show and deserves a chapter of its own.

THE BASIC BASICS

In Figures 3-24 and 3-25 you saw where the VCR's AUDIO RECORD HEAD put the audio signal on the tape. How did the audio signal get into the VCR to start with? If you recorded a show off the air, then your VCR's tuner took care of everything, separating the antenna's RF signal into video and audio and sending the audio to the AUDIO RECORD HEAD automatically. If you used a portable TV camera to record a scene, most likely the built-in mike on the camera took care of everything, sending the right amount of audio signal to the right place automatically. It is when you start playing around with extra microphones, record players, stereos, and other goodies that you need to know about audio and how it works.

The microphone picks up sound vibrations and turns them into a tiny electrical signal that travels down a wire into your VCR. Automatic controls in the VCR adjust the volume of the sound being recorded. Some VCRs allow you to adjust the volume manually.

What kind of mike should you use? The mike on your camera is pretty good. Any mike with a plug that fits your VCR's MIC IN is also likely to work. Try it. You can't hurt anything by trying it. Even if the plug doesn't fit, you can buy an adapter plug that will mate your mike to your machine. If the mike is designed for hanging around the neck and the performer wants to hold it or put it on a stand, it will still work. The mike will still pick up sound. If the mike is designed for stand use and the performer wants it to hang around his or her neck, get some string and tie the mike around the person's neck. It will still work.

What if the mike doesn't work? If you get no sound from a mike after having done all the things described in Chapter 3—pressing record and checking to see that your mike cable is plugged in—try the old standbys of wiggling the wire near the plug, wiggling the plug, or trying another microphone. Also, check to see whether the mike itself has an ON/OFF switch on it that is turned to OFF.

In a pinch, you can even record sound without a microphone. Yep, if you take your common stereo headphones, plug them into your MIC IN, and talk into the tiny headphone speakers, the sound will be recorded. It may sound tinny, it may hum a bit, and may not even work at all. But for an emergency, when you have no mike, this will get you by sometimes.

These are the basic basics of audio. With them you will be successful at recording the sounds you want most of the time. The rest of this chapter is dedicated to helping you make the sound perfectly right. If your sound is poor, it will distract the viewers from the message. If the sound is mediocre, the presentation will appear amateurish. Professional-sounding audio is like paint on a car. The car drives okay

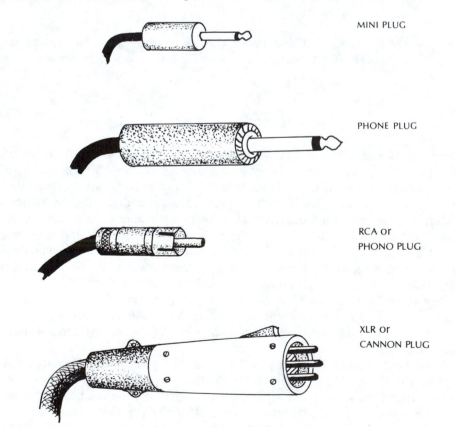

MINI PLUG

PHONE PLUG

RCA or
PHONO PLUG

XLR or
CANNON PLUG

FIGURE 7-1   Common audio plugs

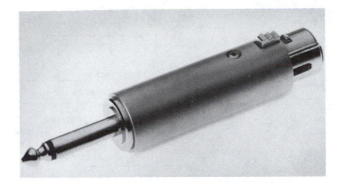

FIGURE 7-2   Audio IMPEDANCE MATCHING TRANSFORMER adapter

without it, but that extra shine is what turns people's heads. How impressive do you want your show to be?

PLUGS AND ADAPTERS

It seems as though every type of machine requires a different kind of plug. The three most common plugs (Figure 7–1) are

1. MINI—Tiniest of the audio plugs, the MINI plug is used on some microphones, most earphones, and most portable audio gear.
2. PHONE—The largest of audio plugs, the PHONE plug is common on microphones, headphones, and speakers.
3. RCA—Sometimes used on microphones, the RCA (or PHONO plug as it is sometimes called) generally connects two audio devices together such as a phonograph turntable and a stereo amplifier, an FM tuner and an amplifier, or the AUDIO OUT from one tape recorder to the AUDIO IN of another for copying tapes.

    Not only are they commonly used for audio on VCRs, but RCAs are used for video, too. Just because the same plugs are used doesn't mean that you should use video and audio cables interchangeably. You can run audio through the video cable alright, but the video loses strength and picks up interference if run through the audio cable. How can you tell a video cable with RCAs on each end from an audio cable with RCAs? Video cables are stiffer and thicker than audio cables. Also, the video cables are likely to have printing on them saying "75 OHM."

A fourth and less popular kind of plug is the CANNON or XLR plug. This plug is used on industrial and professional audio equipment. If using a device with such a plug, buy a MATCHING TRANSFORMER like the one shown in Figure 7–2. This will adapt your wiring from the professional system to the home system.

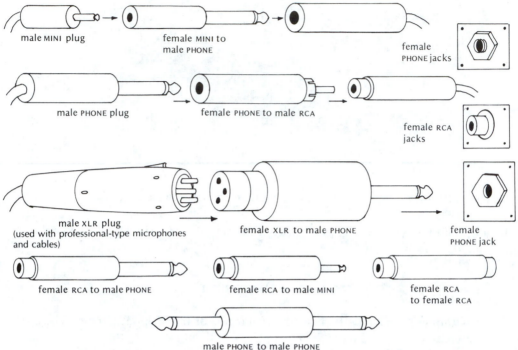

FIGURE 7-3 Audio adapters and their names

Since there are so many different kinds of plugs and sockets that have to mate, there must be adapters to make it possible to connect one thing to another.

Figure 7–3 diagrams some of the most common audio adapters and names them. It wouldn't hurt to learn these names and stock up on a couple of adapters if you plan to mate your equipment with anybody else's.

GETTING THE BEST AUDIO SIGNAL

Lavalier and Hand-Held Mikes

The mike built into your camera will give satisfactory sound. The worst thing about it is that it *must* go where the camera goes. If you move the camera away from the performer, the mike will also be far from the performer. A faraway mike picks up a lot of room echoes, background sounds of cars, breathing, motors, footsteps, and so on, and gives a rather tinny rendition of the person speaking.

Perfectionists get around this by using a separate microphone with a long cable. They plug one end into the MIC IN jack on their VCR or camera. They hand the other to their talent. I'll leave it to your imagination which end goes where.

Two popular mikes used for tape recording are the LAVALIER (hung around the neck by a string) and the LAPEL (clipped to the clothing) microphone. Figure

7–4 shows where to attach them to your performers. A third popular mike is the HAND-HELD, STAND, or DESK microphone shown in Figure 7–5. HAND-HELD mikes can be clipped to a mike stand or carried about newspaper reporter fashion. Good HAND-HELD mikes are usually CARDIOID, rejecting unwanted sounds and echoes (more on this shortly).

FIGURE 7-4   LAVALIER and LAPEL mike placement

FIGURE 7-5   HAND HELD or STAND or DESK microphones

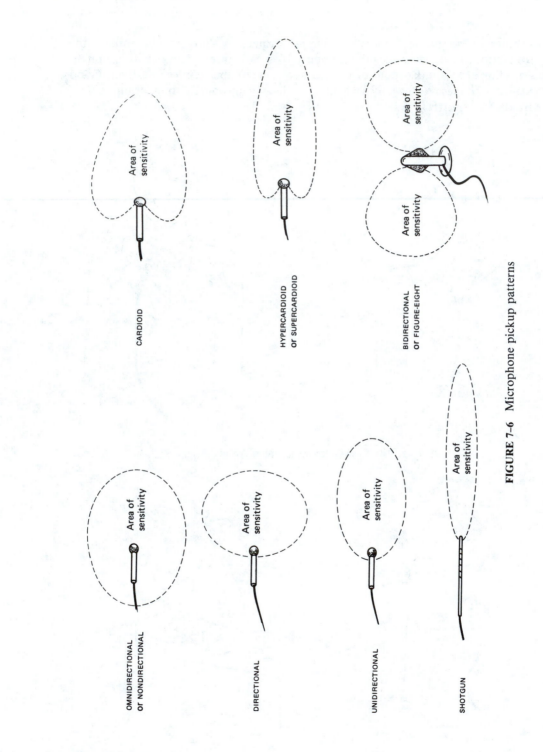

FIGURE 7-6 Microphone pickup patterns

CARDIOID

HYPERCARDIOID
or SUPERCARDIOID

BIDIRECTIONAL
or FIGURE-EIGHT

OMNIDIRECTIONAL
or NONDIRECTIONAL

DIRECTIONAL

UNIDIRECTIONAL

SHOTGUN

Area of
sensitivity

Good quality LAV mikes are designed specifically for use as LAVALIERS and give tinny sound when gripped in the hand. Some less specialized mikes (less expensive with less quality) may be used as LAVs but are really HAND-HELD mikes that come with a string for hanging them around your neck.

Kinds of Microphones

Microphones are designed to listen in various directions. Sometimes you want them to work like your ears and listen in all directions equally. Sometimes you want them to be like binoculars and listen in only one direction, rejecting noises from behind and to the side. Figure 7–6 diagrams how various microphones pick up sound from certain directions.

The OMNIDIRECTIONAL microphone is equally sensitive to sound from all directions. OMNIS are less expensive than their directional brothers and are the type usually built into home cameras. Figure 7–7 shows a $6 OMNIDIRECTIONAL microphone which you can pick up at Radio Shack or similar stores.

OMNIS are excellent for close work. If a person turns his or her face to the side or the microphone moves a little, the sound is relatively unchanged because the microphone can "listen" in all directions. This becomes a disadvantage when the microphone is used to pick up a distant sound because the microphone will hear the room echoes and off-stage sounds as well as the sound of your performer.

DIRECTIONAL is a general term indicating that a microphone has greater sensitivity in one direction than it does in another. DIRECTIONAL microphones are good for picking up small groups of people where you want all of them to be heard, but you don't want to hear room echoes and other background sounds. DIRECTIONAL microphones have also been used on podiums where they pick up the sound of a person speaking, but reject the sound of the audience or any loudspeakers in the audience area.

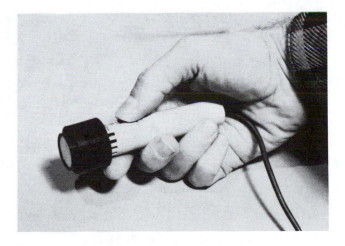

FIGURE 7-7 CRYSTAL or CERAMIC microphone

FIGURE 7–8 PRESSURE ZONE microphone (PZM)

One DIRECTIONAL microphone is the unusual-shaped PRESSURE ZONE MICRO-PHONE or PZM (Figure 7–8). It is generally placed on a desk or attached to a flat surface which reflects the sound waves into the microphone. It can also be hung with a flat plate attached to it for funneling the sound.

PZMs have a hemispheric pickup pattern (they listen to everything above them) which makes them ideal for picking up large group discussions and audience reactions. For instance, a PZM sitting in the middle of the table will pick up the voices of all the people sitting around the table. Unfortunately, the PZM will also pick up the sound of finger tapping and paper rustling or the thumps of people knocking their knees against the table legs.

UNIDIRECTIONAL and CARDIOID microphones are very sensitive in the direction they are pointed and are insensitive to the sides and rear. They make it possible to move the microphone a little farther from the talent (perhaps getting the mike out of the picture) yet still pick up the sound of the talent loud and clear. They also

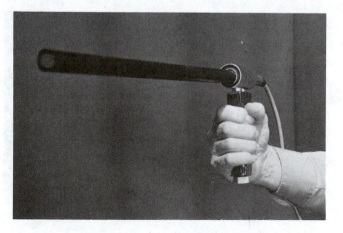

FIGURE 7–9 SHOTGUN microphone

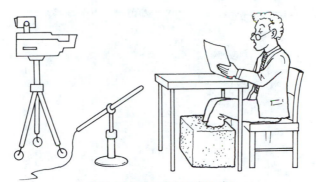

If the talent stays in one place, the SHOTGUN can be mounted on a stand outside of the camera's view. . .

Otherwise, someone has to aim the mike to follow the action.

SHOTGUN mike needs careful aiming

reject room echoes. They are so sensitive that when used close to a person speaking, if the microphone is turned slightly away from the person, the person moves from the center of the microphone's domain, or the person turns to the side and speaks, the sound of his or her voice will drop noticeably. UNIDIRECTIONAL mikes can be used up close only if your talent is tied down and has a stiff neck.

More expensive, but very directional, is the SHOTGUN microphone (Figure 7–9). You can see how it gets its name. It is a very UNIDIRECTIONAL microphone, rejecting all sounds except those coming from where it is pointed. These microphones are especially useful in noisy environments and in situations where you have to pick up sound from some distance away.

SHOTGUN microphones are so effective at rejecting off-center sounds that accurate aiming becomes a constant hassle. If a person moves or two people are speaking, the SHOTGUN microphone has to be aimed precisely at the speaker's face or else he or she may not be heard at all.

The SHOTGUN microphone can reject loud sounds to its side, but a weak sound in front of it still remains a weak sound. To pick up weak and distant sounds, you may need a PARABOLIC microphone.

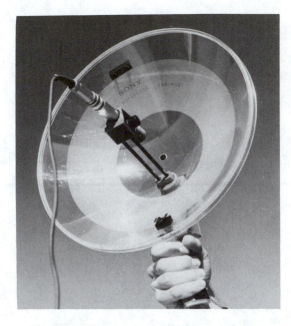

FIGURE 7-10 PARABOLIC microphone

A PARABOLIC microphone (Figure 7-10) has a conventional microphone mounted at the focal point of a large parabolic reflector. The larger the reflector, the more sensitive the device. In fact these microphones can often pick up the sound of people conversing a block away (what a great way to spy on your friends). You often see PARABOLICS used at football games to pick up the grunts, groans, and bone crushing blows of the players.

PARABOLICS usually have poor low frequency response making them sound a bit tinny. Many also tend to pick up the sounds of the person holding and aiming the microphone as well as distant echoes of cars going by and wind blowing in the trees.

To pick up stereophonic sound, you can use two microphones. Sometimes it is handier to use a single STEREO microphone which is actually two microphones built into the same body so that it looks like a single microphone. Half the microphone listens in one direction and sends the signal to the left channel through a stereo plug at the other end. The other half sends its signal out through another conductor on the same plug. Figure 7-11 shows a STEREO microphone.

If your talent moves around too much, they are likely to get tangled up in their cords. This is where an FM WIRELESS MIKE is handy. The microphone contains a small radio transmitter which sends its signal through the air to a small receiver (as in Figure 7-12) which is connected by a short wire to your VCR or camcorder.

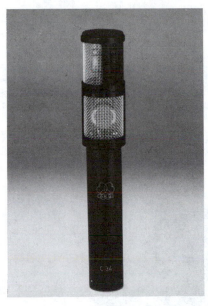

FIGURE 7-11 STEREO microphone (Courtesy of Quality/Universal)

Sometimes a WIRELESS mike can give you more freedom to move

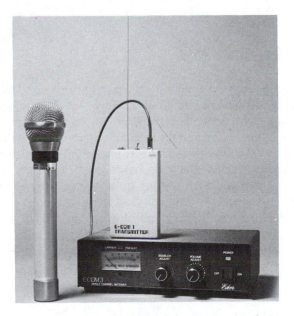

FIGURE 7-12 WIRELESS microphone, transmitter, and receiver (Courtesy of Edcor and B. Fuller, *Single-Camera Video Production: Techniques, Equipment, and Resources for Producing Quality Video Programs,* Prentice Hall, Englewood Cliffs, N.J., 1983)

Duct tape

Inside the Microphone

You usually don't care very much how the microphone operates inside, but here are some words to know in case you go out to buy one. A DYNAMIC MICROPHONE is a fairly rugged mike with good sound quality, but fairly high price. Professionals use them because they can withstand the tremendous volume one inch away from a rock singer's lips. CRYSTAL or CERAMIC microphones, like the one in Figure 7–7, are cheap and give poor fidelity. They are okay for voice and are very sensitive to weak sounds, making them good for picking up a lecture from the fifth row in a classroom. Very popular today is the ELECTRET CONDENSOR microphone which uses a small battery to activate a tiny circuit in the microphone. They have excellent fidelity and good sensitivity, but if you forget to turn off their power when finished using them, their batteries end up dead the next time you use them. ELECTRET CONDENSOR mikes don't like humidity or rough handling.

Cable Care

Mike cables have an affinity for tying themselves and their talent in knots. They snag on everything and wrap around folks faster than a starved boa constrictor. Here are some helpful hints on how to handle this horrible harness:

1. If the performer expects to move around a lot, it is good to attach the mike wire to his body or have him hold some wire in his hand so that it will trail along easily.

2. Loop the performer's lavalier mike cable through the performer's belt so that as he or she moves, the cable isn't tugging directly on the microphone.

3. Keep people from tripping over your cables by tying them (the cables—not the people) to your mike stand base, as in Figure 7–13.

4. If using extension cables for your mike, knot the ends at the plug (Figure 7–13 again) so they don't pull themselves loose.

5. In high traffic areas, it might even be wise to tape your cables to the floor (Figure 7–13 a third time). Trip-ups are dangerous and expensive. Duct tape, available in hardware stores, is strong, flexible, easily torn by hand, and sticks anywhere, making it perfect for trip-proofing cables.

Microphone Placement

Sometimes, for dramatic purposes, you prefer the microphone to remain hidden. To make a LAV mike disappear, its cable can be threaded up a pant's leg or under a shirt. You can hang it just beneath the shirt or, better yet, you can sneak the "head" of the mike out between the top two buttons on the shirt so that the sound is not muffled by the shirt. Mikes can be hidden at the cleavage in a brassiere,

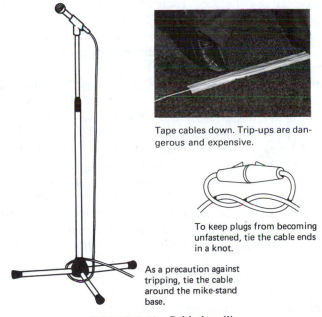

Tape cables down. Trip-ups are dangerous and expensive.

To keep plugs from becoming unfastened, tie the cable ends in a knot.

As a precaution against tripping, tie the cable around the mike-stand base.

FIGURE 7-13 Cable handling

Watch your cables, especially when mikes are attached to clothing

under a carnation, in lots of places. There are stories to tell about the places where microphones have been hidden.

If your desk mike must remain out of view of the camera, try hiding it in a prop, perhaps among the flowers in a centerpiece, or camouflaged as part of some tabletop artwork.

As mentioned before, for cleanest sound, keep the mike close to the performer—six to 18 inches is a good distance. Some performers insist on holding the mike close to their lips like rock stars. This is *too* close. As a result, two things happen: When the performer speaks loudly, the sound distorts. When the performer pronounces the letters, t, b, and especially p, it sounds like bombs bursting in air. Teach performers to trust the mike. Have them keep their distance. If reasoning doesn't work, cover the top of the mike with erect porcupine needles. And if the performer *still* "pops his or her p's" place the mike *at an angle to the side* rather than directly in front of the mouth (as shown in Figure 7–14). The offensive consonants will fly straight forward hurting no one, missing the microphone. CARDIOID microphones exhibit this p-popping problem more often than OMNIDIRECTIONALS do.

Some more sound tips:

1. When possible, use CARDIOID mikes to reject room noise when the mike cannot be kept close to the performer.

2. Keep the performer from handling the mike and mike cord during the recording or you will end up with creeking and thumping noises throughout your show.

3. If recording outdoors in the wind, the blowing wind will make a loud rumble unless you shield the mike with a WIND SCREEN (Figure 7–15). You can make your own out of a chunk of foam rubber or an old sock. Be ready for comments like, ''Your sound stinks!''

FIGURE 7–14 Microphones placement to avoid ''popping p's'' at close range

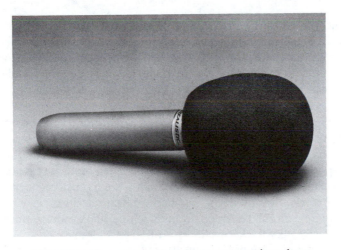

FIGURE 7–15 WIND or ''pop'' screen on microphone

Homemade WINDSCREEN

4. If your desk stand or floor stand mike is picking up noises from arms on the desk or feet vibrations from the floor, place the stand on something soft like a carpet square, some foam rubber, or a warm spongy pizza.

5. Use a quiet room to record in. Turn off fans, air conditioners, and other machines while taping. Close windows and doors. Pick a room with curtains, carpet, and soft furniture to reduce echoes.

Any time you can get the microphone closer to your performer, your sound will be clearer. Often you can place a microphone on a pole to get it closer to the action, as long as you can find someone to aim the pole around. In stage situations, you can use a BABY BOOM which is a small extension to a floor stand able to hold your microphone out in front of your performer without getting in the way.

Wireless FM mikes For the very active performer, the FM or WIRELESS microphone may be the answer. Instead of sending its signal down a wire to the VCR, the FM mike changes the signal into a radio wave and broadcasts this wave to an FM receiver up to 400 feet away. The FM receiver then sends a regular audio signal to the VCR as diagrammed in Figure 7–16. Such systems cost between $70 and $250 ($2,000+ for professional models). They are unbeatable in cases where the talent dances while singing, circulates among other people, interviews members of an audience, rides a bicycle, skydives, or climbs around machinery.

FM WIRELESS microphones do have their faults. Unless selected or tuned carefully, they may pick up commercial FM radio broadcasts, walkie talkies, or other

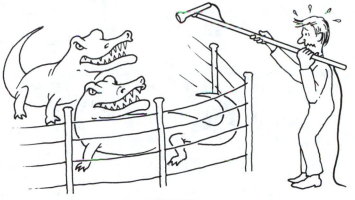

FISH POLE

COUNTERWEIGHTED BOOM

Baby BOOM

FISHPOLE and BOOMS

275

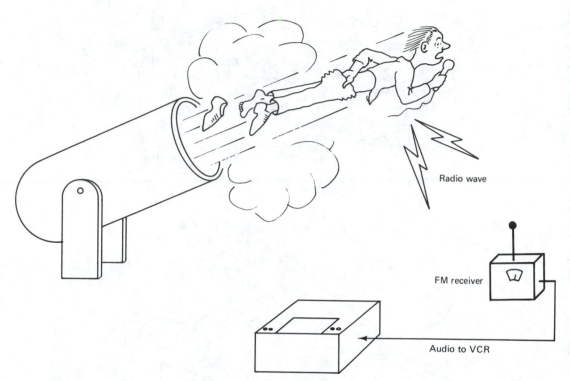

Radio wave

FM receiver

Audio to VCR

FIGURE 7-16 FM or WIRELESS mike

interference in your neighborhood. Before throwing away your receipt, make sure your new mike operates on an unoccupied frequency.

When used indoors or near metal, WIRELESS microphones sometimes bounce their signals off something before reaching the receiver. These bounced signals sometimes interfere with the direct signal, weakening it or canceling it out altogether. As the performer moves and turns, you will hear short bursts of hiss or silence in place of your good sound. The result sounds like what you sometimes hear on a stereo FM radio in a car traveling through a city, under an overpass, or in the mountains. The sound will be great most of the time, but every so often it fades out.

The more expensive WIRELESS microphones go to great lengths to reduce these annoying dropouts. For best results, try to keep a direct line of sight between the transmitter and the receiver.

Musical recording   If the performers are singing, fidelity is paramount. LA-VALIER mikes are generally designed for speech and are therefore inappropriate. The best fidelity usually comes from the larger HAND-HELD mike (which also can be used on a MIKE STAND or a BOOM). If possible, mike each singer separately for individualized volume control and keep each performer one or two feet from their mike. If you run out of mikes, group the singers.

Musical recording is a science in itself. If it is necessary to group the musicians, do it so that the lead has a separate mike from the rest, the rhythm gets a mike, the bass gets a mike, the chorus shares a mike, and related instruments share a microphone. This way you have independent control of the volumes from each *section* of the band. This will require a MIXER (described shortly).

If you can, use a VCR or camcorder with hi-fi sound for a better fidelity recording.

Stereo microphones   Simply plug one mike into the left MIC IN and another into the right MIC IN and shoot. Whatever is picked up by the left mike is recorded on the left channel and what goes in the right mike is recorded on the right channel (assuming you have a stereo VCR).

Separating the mikes so that they each hear something different will improve the stereo effect. Figure 7–17 diagrams the hookup.

A strange problem sometimes occurs when using two microphones spread apart. Because it takes time for sound to travel through the air, the vibrations can get OUT OF PHASE, making one mike's signal counteract the other mike's signal. When using two microphones, carefully listen to the result over your headphones to see if the sound is hollow, tinny, or strange. Repositioning the mikes will probably

Musical recording

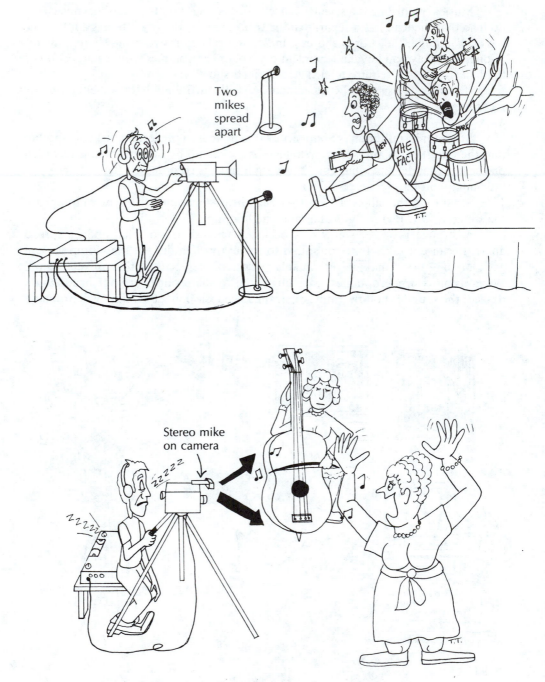

FIGURE 7-17 Recording stereo from microphones

FIGURE 7-18 Wrong way to use two mikes on one person

FIGURE 7-19 Right way to set up two mikes on a single person

fix the problem. If using two microphones to record somebody giving a speech, place the "heads" of the two mikes very close together, almost touching. Figures 7-18 and 7-19 show the wrong way and the right way to set up two mikes on a podium.

RECORDING SOUND FROM OTHER SOURCES

Sometimes you'd like to record music from a record, tape, radio, or some device other than a microphone. If narration or music has already been recorded with good fidelity, you wish to copy it with the best fidelity you can. This is best done by using PATCH CORDS and taking the electronic signal from the source and running it directly into your VCR's AUDIO INPUT. Although it would be possible to place your microphone in front of your radio or hi-fi speaker to pick up the sound, it would decrease your fidelity and also add room echoes (it would also pick up your private conversations and other noises around the house). Copying the signal straight through a wire avoids all that, keeping the signal clean and pure.

A PATCH CORD is simply a wire with appropriate plugs on both ends to connect an audio device up to your VCR to play the sound into it. You may already have used a PATCH CORD to connect something to the AUDIO IN or AUDIO OUT of your VCR back in Chapter 3.

Once you've connected the PATCH CORDS, play the record or tape, hit DUB or RECORD on the VCR and the electric genies do the rest. Figure 7-20 diagrams the hookup.

PATCH CORD

If the sound comes out weak, try turning the volume up at the source. If the volume is strong, distorted, or raspy, try turning it down at the source. If you have volume controls on both your source *and* your VCR, try not to have one of them way up high while the other is way down low. For best results, they both should be low, medium, or high together. Sometimes a source's volume control does not affect the signal coming from its audio outputs; it only affects your speakers or headphones. In such a case, the only adjustments you can make are on your VCR.

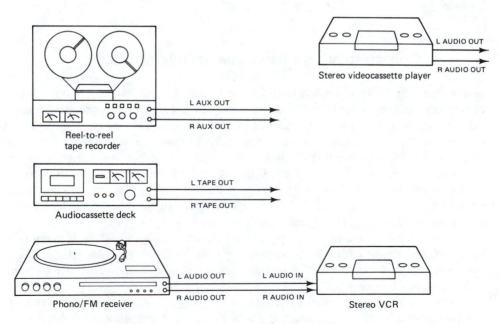

FIGURE 7-20 Recording stereo from records and tapes

MIXING SOUNDS

Sometimes you'd like to mix two sounds together such as music and narration. The professionals (and dedicated home video crazies) use a MIXER. This little console has inputs for microphones, tape players, phonographs, and so on, and with a turn of the knob can mix these signals in the right proportions and send the result to your VCR. Figure 7–21 shows this setup.

Using Mixers

The MIXER accepts weak signals from microphones or turntables into its LOW LEVEL or MIC inputs. It accepts stronger signals from tuners, tape players, and so on into its HI LEVEL or AUX inputs. For each input plug in the back of the MIXER, there is a corresponding knob on the front to adjust its volume. Sometimes there are switches on the back of the MIXER to change the input from LO LEVEL to HI LEVEL

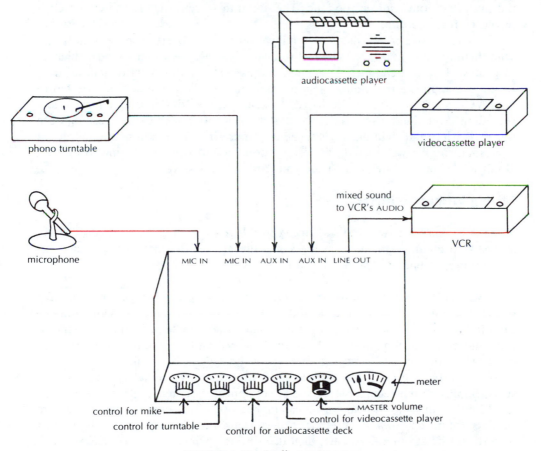

FIGURE 7-21 Audio MIXER setup

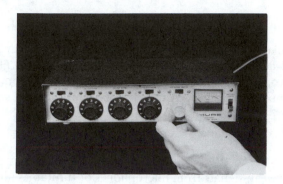

Portable audio MIXER

so you can plug different things into it. You can adjust all of the volumes up or down together with the MASTER volume control. If the MIXER has a meter, adjust the volume so that the meter wiggles but rarely dips into the red area. The red area indicates that your audio is too loud. The sound mixture is then fed to your VCR's AUDIO IN for recording.

There are stereo MIXERS which allow you to mix together some sounds and send them to your VCR's left channel while mixing together other sounds which go to your VCR's right channel. The common inexpensive MIXERS are monaural, mixing *all* the sounds and sending them out one output. This output could be fed to your VCR's left AUDIO IN or to its right AUDIO IN, resulting in a monaural sound recording. You could also send the MIXER'S output to a Y ADAPTER, feeding both the VCR's left and right channels together. The result would still be monaural.

Incidentally, well-mixed, interesting mono sound is very pleasing to the ear. Don't let the lack of stereo dissuade you from using a MIXER.

Mixing Without a Mixer

Sometimes you have two sound sources you'd love to mix together, but don't have a MIXER to combine them. Here are some alternatives that *may* work, but come with no money-back guarantee that they will work well.

Acoustical mixing   Picture yourself driving through Dodge City with the twang of country music on the car radio. A passenger is taping the sights out the car window to send back East to the folks. The camera mike picks up the sound of the radio and adds that western flavor to the view. And when a narration or comment seems appropriate, you just lower the radio volume and talk.

Similarly, you can DUB narration and musical background over existing visuals. Simply find a record player and select appropriate music. Set up your mike (or the mike built into the camera—it can make AUDIO DUBS even though the camera isn't recording any new picture) close to you and the phonograph. Perhaps start with the music at normal volume, then fade it down while you speak. Fade it back up when you've finished speaking. Although the sound fidelity won't be too great, the music and voice mix will add pizazz to your tape. Also, you are likely to enjoy the thrill of being a true DJ as you attempt to coordinate the switching on the VCR, starting the record, fading the volume, and making sense as you try to speak at the same time.

Mixing with inputs   This isn't really mixing, but may be a way to "fake it." If you have a stereo VCR with manual volume controls, you could hitch one source (say your mike) up to the VCR's left input and hitch another source (say an audio-cassette player) to the right input. Now make a recording or a stereo AUDIO DUB. Manipulate the two volume controls to raise and lower your mike volume or to raise and lower the audiocassette's volume. When played back, the result will be mixed just as you wanted, if played into your mono TV receiver using RF. And if you play the tape into a stereo TV or stereo hi-fi, the mike sounds will come out your left speaker and the audiocassette sounds will come out your right speaker.

Y adapter   Figure 3–19 showed how this little widget could take your VCR's one audio output and send it to your stereo's two inputs. A Y ADAPTER with the right plugs can work the same way in reverse, taking two sources and combining their signals to send to one VCR input.

For this to work well, both sources must have about the same strength signal, such as two microphones or two similar audio outputs from VCRs or audiocassette tape players. Since the Y ADAPTER has no volume controls of its own, you may have trouble stopping a strong source from overpowering a weaker source. Try adjusting the source volume controls.

To use the Y ADAPTER, simply connect it to your VCR's input and connect the other two sources to the other two ends of the Y ADAPTER. Play the two sound sources and listen to the result over your VCR's headphone. Adjust and mix the volume of the sources as you go.

Stereo amplifier   Most stereo hi-fis today have lots of inputs in the back for tape players, tuners, phonographs, and even microphones. By turning your ampli-fier's INPUT SELECT switch to one of these positions, your amp will "listen" to that pair of inputs. Often you can plug a microphone into one of the inputs (MIC input works best but others may work too—experiment) and talk through your hi-fi. Aim your speakers away from you or else the sound from the speakers will get back into your microphone and create the loud squeal of FEEDBACK.

Since stereos have two inputs (left and right channels) for every source, you could plug a *second* mike into the twin input and talk through *two* microphones. By adjusting the left and right channel volume controls, or by adjusting the BAL-ANCE control on your amp, you can vary the loudness of each mike.

Now to get the signal into your VCR: Find an output on your amplifier that you can connect to the AUDIO IN of your VCR. This output may be labeled TAPE OUT, AUX OUT, LINE OUT, or PREAMP OUT, or if there are no outputs, use the HEAD-

PHONE socket (you may need to buy an adapter or a special audio cable for this). Now you have a stereo output to send to your VCR. If your VCR is stereo, you could send the hi-fi's left output to the VCR's left input and send the right to the right. Another option would be to switch your stereo to MONO, sending exactly the same signal to both channels on your VCR.

If you really wanted to get fancy, you could send a microphone signal directly to the left channel of your VCR while sending the MONO output from your hi-fi to the right channel of your VCR. Remember that the hi-fi's output will be a mix of two sounds (its two channels), giving you a grand total of three sounds mixed together.

If your VCR isn't stereo, you should switch your amp to MONO which will mix the two signals together. Now by connecting just one of the outputs (it doesn't matter which one) to your VCR, you will get the mixed sound. Another way to achieve the same effect is to use another Y ADAPTER to take the left and right signals from your hi-fi, mix them, and run them down one wire to the VCR. Either way, you now control the volume of two sources using your amplifier's volume controls and send the result to your VCR for recording.

Audiocassette deck   Many stereo audiocassette decks have microphone and auxiliary inputs and independent volume controls. By plugging your mikes into the audio deck, pressing RECORD and PAUSE, twiddling the controls, and sending the deck's output to your VCR, you can mix audio sources the way you can with your stereo amplifier. A stereo audiocassette deck can send stereo signals to a stereo VCR, or by using a Y ADAPTER you can combine the deck's stereo outputs into a single channel.

SOUND MIXING TECHNIQUES

There is no substitute for creativity. There are some basics, however, that could help. In fact, your library may have several books written solely on the basics of audio; it gets that involved.

Segue

SEGUE (pronounced SEG-way) is a fade from one sound to another. For instance, the sounds of machinery can be smoothly replaced with music. The machinery's volume control is lowered at the same time that the music volume control is being raised. This is often done between two pieces of music, as one finishes, the other is being faded up.

A more sophisticated SEGUE uses an intermediate sound when changing from one audio passage to another. For instance, to go from one scene in a play to another, after the last line in the first scene come a few bars of appropriate music (called a BRIDGE). As the music fades out, the first line in the next scene is delivered.

Briefer things like jokes or single statements may deserve a sound effect, laughter, applause, or a single note or chord of music (such a musical passage is called a STING) between them.

Some SEGUES prepare the listener for things to come, like faint machinery noise before we open the engine room door or the sound of windshield wipers before the actors begin to speak in the car on a rainy night. A famous Hitchcock SEGUE is a woman's scream suddenly changing to the scream of a train's whistle as it chugs into the next scene. Another popular SEGUE is the dance troupe rehearsing to "one, two, three, four, one, two, . . ." as we dissolve the picture and sound to the actual on-stage performance of the number with all the glitter and music.

Music Under, Sound Mix, Voiceover

Your production begins with a snappy musical selection. The title fades in and then cuts to the opening scene. Someone is about to speak. The music fades down just before the first words are heard. This is a MUSIC UNDER. The music became subordinate to the speech and is played *under* it.

Sometimes you have to decide whether to fade the music out entirely when the action starts or to MUSIC UNDER holding in the background throughout the scene. If the music is needed for dramatic effect, either to create a mood or just to provide continuity through long gaps in action or conversation, then keep it in. If, however, the action or conversation is very important, then don't distract your audience with background music.

So how loud should the background music be? The answer, of course, depends on the particular situation. There's no hard rule. In general, keep in mind that background music is *background* music. Keep the volume low—lower than your natural inclinations would have you set it. How many amateur productions have you sat through straining to hear the dialog through that "noise" in the background?

Again, these are just generalities. Some musical selections are inherently more obtrusive than others. For instance, while listening to a narration, the viewer may hardly be aware of instrumental music in the background. Conversely, a song with words competes with the narration for the viewer's attention. Because singing with words is so distracting, it's best to avoid it in favor of instrumentals.

Not all background sound is music. Street sounds, machines, sirens, motors, gunfire—all can be background to your dialog. Some of these sounds may not be background at all, but are interjected between dialogue such as "thud," "crash," and the like.

Sometimes you start with a videotape or film and wish to add narration. The original sound on the tape will be kept but only as background for the narration. Adding narration is called a VOICEOVER. The voice you're adding is imposed over, and is louder than, the original sounds. Here is an example of how it is done.

Mr. Expert brings in a tape showing his foundry in action. The tape shows the busy machines while you hear them foundering away in the background. Mr. Expert also brings a script that he wishes to read through parts of the recording. To do this, you set up a VCR to copy his original tape from a VCP (videocassette player). The VCP's video goes directly to the VCR. The audio from the VCP goes to a mixer. Mr. Expert's microphone also feeds to the mixer. The mixer combines and regulates the two sources and feeds the combination to the VCR. As the VCP plays, the VCR records, copying the picture and whatever original sound the mixer lets through. Mr. Expert reads his script as he keeps one eye on the VCP's monitor screen. You adjust audio levels, sometimes favoring the background sounds (when the narrator is silent) and sometimes lowering them (when the narrator speaks). That's a VOICEOVER. If he doesn't like the way the final tape comes out, you can erase it and do it over, since his original tape was not altered in the process. You can do this over and over again until you get it exactly right.

Sometimes the script is narrated by someone far away or long ago. You'll get a videocassette with background sounds and an audiocassette with the narrator's story. Here the process is about the same except an audio tape player is providing the narration rather than a live person. Instead of the narrator slowing down, speeding up, or stopping his reading to coincide with the pictures he sees from the VCP, you must stop and start the audio tape player to coincide with the pictures. If you have the script or memorize the narration, you will be able to choose good places to stop the audio tape from playing without catching the narrator between words.

Cueing Up Sounds

Professional audio equipment is designed to allow the audio director to press a button and have a sound come out perfectly. Home audio equipment isn't designed for this, making the process more difficult. For instance, if you wish to play just part of a song on a record, you would have trouble stopping the record in the middle of the song, getting your VCR started, and then getting the record started again without having the sound on the record go r-r-r-w-r-w-wing as it gets up to speed. Your only choice with home record players is to either use a song from the beginning, where you can stop the record with the needle in the silent grooves between songs, or you can start the music playing, turn the volume off, and then turn it back up mid-song when you are ready to use it. You might not fade up at exactly the right part in the song, but at least fading the music up and down won't sound like a mistake.

Audiocassette players are slightly easier to CUE. You could, for instance, listen to your music or sound a few times, memorize it, and then play it up to the point where the desired segment begins. Hit PAUSE on your audiocassette tape machine. When ready to record that sound into your video recording, simply UNPAUSE your audiocassette recorder and the music should start. Hit PAUSE again on the audiocassette recorder to kill the music. This process is somewhat hard to do with audiocassette players because their PAUSE controls are not very accurate. It works better with speech than with music because there are often pauses between words where you can stop the tape without anybody hearing weird sounds.

CD players, especially the programmable kind, can be paused and unpaused quite accurately.

If taking sound from another VCR, you use the same technique as with an audiocassette tape recorder. You study the sound a few times so that you know when to hit PAUSE on the videocassette player. The trouble with many videocassette players is that they back up a little ways and don't come out of PAUSE in exactly the same place you put them into PAUSE. If this inaccuracy is a problem, you have to fall back on the old trick of turning your volume down first, UNPAUSING the videocassette player, and then fading the volume up at just the right time. At least with VCRs you have a picture to help guide you.

There is an excellent book, *Recording Great Audio,* available from Radio Shack that tells more on how to get professional sound from amateur gear. And I'll give you three guesses who the author is.

8

Television graphics

What is it that makes a professional TV production look "different" from the home TV epic? Smooth camera work? Yes. Snappy lighting? That, too. Background music and crisp sound? Definitely. But there is something that happens at the very beginning of a show that tells the viewers that they are about to see something professional looking—and that's a classy title. Later, as your show includes charts, text, cartoons, and photos, it takes on an air of authority and confidence. It becomes visually engaging. Consider the added flexibility available to you, the producer, as you now use all the other media available—super 8 movies, 35mm slides, snapshots, and drawings.

THE BASICS

The essence of TV graphics boils down to three rules:

1. Make it fit the shape of the TV screen.
2. Keep it simple.
3. Make it bold.

FITTING YOUR GRAPHIC TO THE TV SCREEN

A TV screen is a box that is a little wider than it is tall. If the screen were 16″ wide, it would be 12″ tall. If it were 4″ wide, it would be 3″ tall. However wide it is, it is three-quarters as tall. This is called a 3:4 (three-by-four) ASPECT RATIO and is diagrammed in Figure 8–1.

As a consequence, visuals for television should have a 3:4 ASPECT RATIO if they are to fill the screen evenly. Panoramas don't fill this ratio because they are too wide. Telephone poles don't fit because they are too tall. Strictly speaking, even a square box is too tall to fit perfectly on a TV screen.

When showing a panorama on a TV screen, one must either display a long, long shot of it, showing a lot of sky and foreground, or one must sacrifice some of the width of the panorama, getting just a fraction of it. To display the square box, one must decide whether to cut off its top and bottom in the TV picture, or whether to get all of it, leaving an empty space on its left and right.

Just because your TV screen is a box doesn't mean that you can only shoot box-shaped things. If your scene, or a photograph of your scene, is very tall as in Figure 8–2, there are three ways to show it.

1. Zoom out to get it all in, but with wasted space on the left and right.
2. Zoom in to fill the screen with the most important part of the picture, sacrificing the remainder of the picture.
3. Zoom in on one part of the picture, perhaps near the bottom, and slowly tilt up to take in the rest of the picture.

The first method is somewhat obtrusive and works best when the audience is prepared for it, such as viewing snapshots from an album. The second solution is fine if losing part of your picture doesn't hurt your message. The third method has the advantage of adding motion to your scene, but it is sometimes hard to find a meaningful starting and ending point for your tilt.

For wide scenes, use a similar technique:

1. Zoom out, leaving a margin at the top and bottom of the picture.
2. Zoom in on part of the picture, sacrificing the rest.
3. Zoom in on one part of the picture and pan to another part.

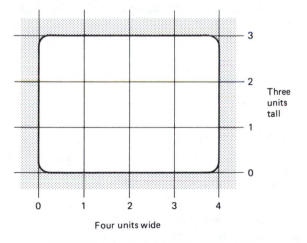

FIGURE 8-1   ASPECT RATIO of TV screen

Method 1

Zoom out, showing entire picture
but with wasted space at sides.
Mount the photo on a neutral
background so the side margins
do not distract from the
central picture.

Method 2

Zoom in on most
important part of
picture, sacrificing
the rest.

Method 3

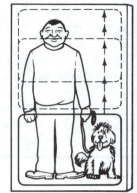

Zoom in on one
part of picture
and tilt to take
in rest of picture.

FIGURE 8-2 Making a vertical picture fit TV's ASPECT RATIO

MAKING WORDS FIT THE TV SCREEN

The composition of words, titles, and logos (a logo is your company or program's symbol or trademark) leaves us more flexibility than we have with pictures. One can arrange the words or whatever to fit the 3:4 dimensions of the screen. Figure 8-3 shows some good and bad graphic compositions.

When accurate workmanship is necessary, it is good to measure out, in faint lines, the 3:4 shape of the TV screen on your blank art paper before you or your graphic artist begins to draw. The lines will act as a guide and can later be erased. When such care is not warranted, one may simply "think boxes" when planning graphic composition.

SAFE TITLE AREA

Two things you *don't* want to do are

1. Show your audience the edge of your graphic or title sign.
2. Have a piece of the title disappear behind the edge of the viewer's TV screen.

Both problems can be avoided by

1. Leaving an adequate margin around the title or drawing.
2. Shooting the graphic so as to leave a little extra space around all sides of its image on your TV monitor.

Poor

Good

GIVE SOME PEOPLE AN INCH
AND THEY THINK THEY'RE A RULER

GIVE SOME PEOPLE
AN INCH AND
THEY THINK
THEY'RE A RULER

THE END

THE
END

Words shown
as ideas, like
apples on
a tree

WORDS SHOWN
AS IDEAS, LIKE
APPLES ON
A TREE

*A very long subtitle permitted
to ramble across the TV screen*

SUBTITLE ACROSS THE
BOTTOM OF SCREEN

FIGURE 8-3 ASPECT RATIO of words on screen

This extra space allows for the fact that the camera viewfinder generally shows the *whole* TV picture, while your TV set cuts off the edges. Some home (and school) TV sets are poorly adjusted anyway, causing even further loss of the TV picture on the edges. To allow for this, the SAFE TITLE AREA is used, principally confining all important matter to the middle portion of the TV screen. See Figure 8–4.

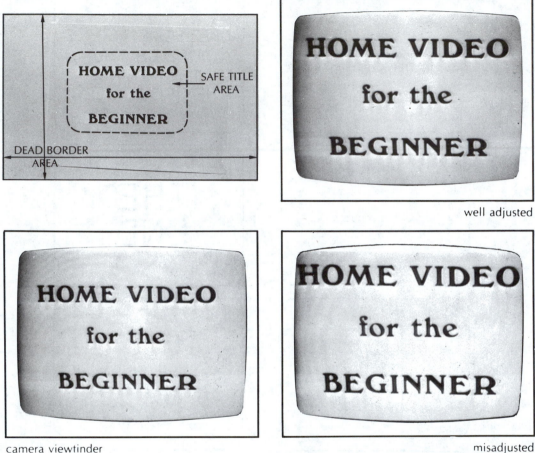

HOME TV SETS

well adjusted

camera viewtinder

misadjusted

misadjusted

FIGURE 8–4   Picture areas compared

Use the SAFE TITLE AREA

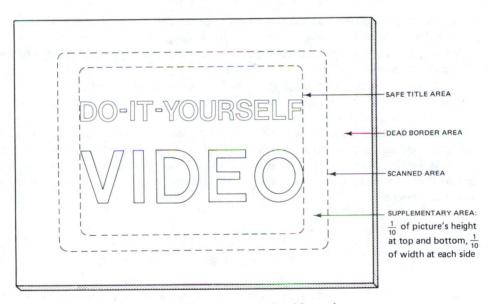

FIGURE 8-5 Areas of a title card

The SAFE TITLE AREA holds the essential information which should *always* show on the home viewer's screen. The DEAD BORDER AREA is the blank part of your title card which *never* shows on the TV screen. In fact, along its edge you may place little notes or picture sequence numbers to help you arrange and position the cards. Between the DEAD BORDER AREA and the SAFE TITLE AREA is the nether world of the SCANNED AREA. The SCANNED AREA shows on some TV sets but not on others. Since this part of the picture can't be counted on, it should not contain anything important. Figure 8-5 shows the SCANNED AREA, SAFE TITLE AREA, SUPPLEMENTARY AREA, and DEAD BORDER AREA of a title card.

Outside the ESSENTIAL or SAFE TITLE AREA, put unimportant stuff,
like background

The DEAD BORDER AREA is the camera operator's margin. It doesn't matter if
the border is an inch or three inches in width as long as it's large enough to make
it easy for the camera operator to shoot the picture without getting the edge of the
title card in the shot.

If you are doing a lot of graphics shooting, you may wish to mark on your
camera's viewfinder a little template like that shown in Figure 8–6 to remind you to
stay within the SAFE TITLE AREA.

When making titles and visuals, it is sometimes convenient to make them all
about the same size. Although the titles, regardless of their actual size, may all come
out looking the same once you have zoomed in or out on the title, it is easier if you
do not have to make this adjustment each time—especially if the visuals come in
rapid succession.

SLIDES

You may already have a mess of slides from 10 years of vacations or maybe you
still take slides because the slide camera is easier to carry around or you enjoy the
vivid detail as you blow the slides up on a large screen. Whatever the reason, there
are times when you wish to convert these slides to video. Several techniques will be
described later. What we should consider now is how to *take* your pictures so that
they show up well on TV.

A slide has a wider ASPECT RATIO than a TV screen which means that the
slide's picture is wider than your TV's picture. Generally speaking, a little bit of the
left and right side of your slide will be cut off when converted to video. Keep this
in mind when shooting your slides. Avoid shooting anything important at the left
or right edges of your slide camera's viewfinder. Also try to keep the SAFE TITLE

AREA in mind so that the important stuff resides in the middle section of your viewfinder.

Never take vertically oriented slides, the ones where you hold the camera sideways and the slide comes out tall and narrow. These slides *never* look good on TV.

If you're stuck using vertically oriented slides from the past, you will find yourself with three bad choices:

1. Zoom out and get the whole picture with the blank border on both sides.
2. Zoom in on the essential information disregarding the rest of the slide (almost half of it).
3. Zoom in on one part of the slide and tilt to another part.

BOLDNESS AND SIMPLICITY

Unlike cinema, slides, photographs, and the printed page, TV is a fuzzy medium. Fine detail turns into blurry grays and hazy shadows. With your eyes alone, look at a newspaper three feet away; you can probably read the entire page. Fill a TV screen with that same page and you can read only the main headlines and even they don't jump out and grab you. Figure 8–7 shows what I mean.

Visuals for TV need to be bold, simple, and uncluttered. Figure 8–8 compares some examples of poor and good visuals for TV.

Titling for TV needs to be brief, broad, and bold to have impact. Wordy subtitles that need to be small and unobtrusive should be limited to *no more than 25 to 30 characters per line* to remain legible. Remember, too, that something that looks

FIGURE 8-6 Mark your SAFE TITLE AREA on your camera viewfinder

FIGURE 8-7 Comparison of regular photograph with same shot played back on a VCR. Notice how TV loses a lot of detail.

pretty sharp in your camera viewfinder will lose a lot of oomph once it is recorded, edited, and copied, and the copy is played back on an inexpensive video player through RF into a casually adjusted TV set. It's a wonder that there is any picture left at all, much less a sharp one. Figure 8-9 shows what happens to character generated text which has run the gauntlet from camera to editor to playback of a tape copy.

One way to test for boldness is to step back from your proposed visual, squint your eyes, and look at it through your eyelashes. This is what it will look like when the viewer sees the image. Give every title, drawing, and photograph the old "squint test" and two things are bound to happen: your visuals will stand up to the rigors of the TV medium, and your friends will arrange optometrist appointments for you.

One thing to avoid in graphics, photos, and your talent's wardrobe is patterns of fine lines or herringbones. They sometimes vibrate with a shimmering rainbow of colors.

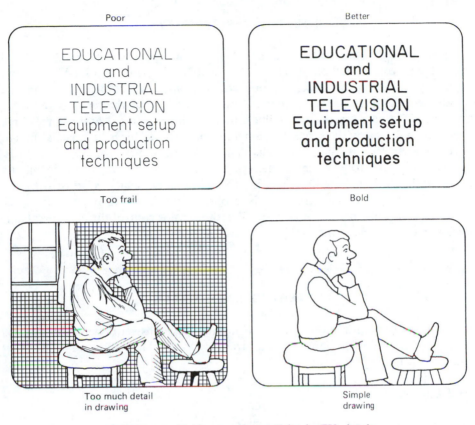

FIGURE 8-8 Boldness and simplicity in TV visuals

FIGURE 8-9 Limit your long text passages to 10 lines of 25 characters per line

COLOR COMPATIBILITY

If you place a light blue card next to a light green card next to a light red card and look at them, you can tell one from another easily (unless you're color-blind). Aim a color TV camera at the three, and observe the results on a color TV set and you will still be able to tell the three apart. If however, you view the result on a black-and-white TV (there are over 83 million of them in the United States), the three cards may look exactly the same, blending into one mass. This is because, although the colors are different, the cards' relative brightnesses are the same.

To avoid this problem, choose lettering which is substantially brighter than its background. When making drawings for TV, select colors which contrast with one another. One way to check your work is to observe the results through your black-and-white viewfinder or on your color TV with its color control turned down (so it shows a black-and-white picture).

LETTERING YOUR TITLES

What do you use to print your titles and subtitles? The answer depends on quality, budget, and purpose. Do you have a lot to say? Do you have a lot to spend? How good must it look?

Hand Lettering

If you are blessed with a good hand for lettering, you can create some pretty snappy titles quickly with a broad felt pen. Avoid longhand and fancy letters, again adhering to the principles of boldness and simplicity. Black letters on off-white backgrounds look best; but with experimentation, you may find other workable combinations.

Scrabble Board

Looking for some handy letters around the house? In the basement, behind the furnace, you'll probably find an old Scrabble game.

You can arrange the letters on the board for a true Scrabble look or you can lay the titles on a sheet of paper or across a towel or carpet for varied backgrounds. The letters are easily moved and rearranged. Unless there is a Scrabble theme to your show, this type of lettering may look a little hokey. Maybe you can think of some other games around the house that come with little letter squares. How about kid's building blocks?

These methods are appropriate only for short titles as you will probably run out of letters (and patience) after just a few lines.

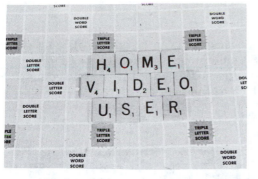
scrabble board letters

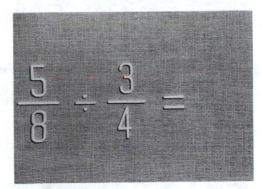
three-dimensional letters

rub-on letters

Lettering techniques

Three-Dimensional Letters

These letters may be made of plastic and may have pins or magnets in them for attaching them to a lettering board. The method is simple, bold, and quick. The letters are reusable (until you lose them) and have the added advantage that lighting may be used to cast fancy shadows from the letters or to highlight their edges. This method is appropriate for short titles only.

Spaghetti Board

The spaghetti board technique is used primarily by restaurants displaying their menus on grooved, felt boards with movable plastic letters. The method is fairly bold, neat, and rapid to set up. The letters are reusable. Care must be taken to adjust the TV camera in a way that will not show the grooves from the lettering board. This method is appropriate only for short titles.

Rub-on Letters

These are waxed coated letters that come in a sheet and can be rubbed off onto a sheet of paper or posterboard. The process is quite simple and the letters are neat, bold, and very professional looking. The wax sheets are inexpensive and no equipment is necessary except for a stick with which to rub the letters.

FIGURE 8–10   Typed titles

FIGURE 8-11   Stencilling

Typing

Thirfty, but lacking somewhat in boldness is our old friend the typewriter. MACRO lenses or close-up lens attachments permit the TV camera to take very tight close-ups of the typing. Just remember to zoom in to keep the lettering big and don't try to put too many words on the TV screen at once. Typing on various paper surfaces yields an assortment of background possibilities. As you might guess, typing is useful for both short and long textual passages. See Figure 8-10.

One disadvantage of the typed title method, however, is the likelihood that a minor flaw in the card's preparation will be exaggerated when the small picture area is magnified to large TV screen size.

Stenciling

Cheapest and perhaps most familiar is stenciling. A template with punched out letters guides the sign maker as he or she outlines the letters with pencil. The letters can then be filled in with ink or marker.

Stencils may also be spray painted, but this method may destroy the templates and the paint often seeps under the stencil, smudging the letters.

If you must use stencils, fill in the breaks in the letters afterward for a more professional look. Compare the examples in Figure 8-11.

Stenciling is a tedious process, good for short titles only.

Professional Typesetting

Modern print shops are equipped with ways of making bold, flawless type in seconds through the use of a typewriter connected to a computer that is in turn connected to an instant photographic type-making device. Lettering comes out evenly spaced with straight, even margins and can be made in a wide variety of size and

Letters with skinny parts. The skinnys may disappear.

Letters with a SERIF. Although in this case the SERIF may be fat enough not to disappear, it complicates the legibility of the letters.

Type with multiple lines. These lines vibrate on TV. Some may disappear.

"Tempo black" style here is too bold. Holes in letters close up.

Type nicely expresses the mood of the title, but may be too ornate (especially upper case lettering) for TV.

FIGURE 8-12 Type styles which are troublesome on TV

type FONTS. Costs run about $50 per page and a lot can be put on a page. With the use of MACRO and close-up lens attachments, columns of lettering can be blown up to fill the TV screen. Choosing a narrow column width of 25 characters allows lists, credits, sentences, paragraphs, and other long passages to be moved vertically through the screen for easy reading. Overall, professional typesetting may be the cheapest way to get professional-looking titles for the occasional production.

Be sure to select simple and bold type styles. The fancy ones shown in Figure 8-12 look pretty to the eye but drive the camera crazy.

Titling Camera

Some home cameras and camcorders have miniature CHARACTER GENERATORS built in. By pushing buttons on the camera, you can electronically type out short titles and record them on your VCR from the camera. You can generally type up to five lines with 12 characters per line, store the title in your camera's "memory," and then record the title. You may even insert the title over a picture. Figure 2-1 shows an example.

The lettering is a bit chunky and perhaps inappropriate for professional use, but is neat and convenient for home video epics.

Character Generator

Serious TV buffs may wish to buy a small CHARACTER GENERATOR costing about $400. These are electronic typing consoles with special video outputs for putting words on the TV screen. The more you spend for a CHARACTER GENERATOR, the smoother the lettering becomes and the more features you get such as DROP SHADOW and BORDER (Figure 8-13).

CHARACTER GENERATOR

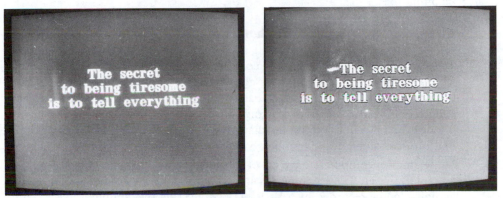

Text without border   . . . with border

. . . with shadow

FIGURE 8–13 Electronic text with BORDER and DROP SHADOW

Home Computer

If you have a home computer, I'm sure it has occurred to you that transferring the text from your computer screen to your VCR would be convenient and neat. Unfortuately the process is complicated.

1. Computers generally put 80 characters per line on the screen. VCRs can only record about 24 characters per line before the letters become too small and fuzzy.
2. Home computers generally do not have video outputs which can be sent to the VIDEO IN of your VCR.
3. The signal which creates the image on your computer screen is very different from a video signal. The frequencies are different, making the signals quite incompatible.

All is not lost. Here are a few solutions to these problems:

1. Try aiming your TV camera at the computer screen. Zoom in so that the letters are large and bold. Type your passages in narrow columns and space them in little boxes so that the camera can zoom in on just a few lines at a time. You will need to darken the room to avoid reflections off the TV screen. The results are neat and have an interesting character of their own, but are slightly fuzzy and unprofessional looking unless your TV show has a computer motif.
2. Some smaller computers have an RF OUT which goes to the antenna input of a regular TV set. These computers are likely to make the kind of signals which actually can be recorded by a VCR. Try connecting the computer as shown in Figure 8–14 and see if the recorded image plays back okay. Sometimes it will and sometimes it won't.
3. Buy a computer specifically designed for use with video. The $1,300 Commodore Amiga will make excellent video signals. You simply type or draw what you want on the screen and output your signal to your VCR as if your computer were a camera. An additional $300 device called the Model 1300 GEN-LOCK adapter will allow you to superimpose your graphics or words over existing video such as throwing words over the image from your camera before you record it or putting words over a videotape while you're making a copy of it.

    The Apple II-G also makes video signals which are recordable, but they are not 100% standard. For best results, you should record black on your tape first and then go back and INSERT EDIT the signals from your Apple II-G computer. The reasons for this may become more clear in Chapter 10.

    The Atari 800 makes TV signals which are recordable, and so does the Commodore 64. Buy an additional $24 stabilizer with your Commodore 64 to perfect the image for recording.

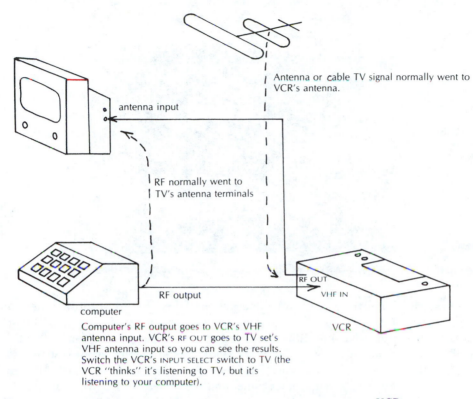

Antenna or cable TV signal normally went to VCR's antenna.

antenna input

RF normally went to TV's antenna terminals

RF output

RF OUT

VHF IN

computer

VCR

Computer's RF output goes to VCR's VHF antenna input. VCR's RF OUT goes to TV set's VHF antenna input so you can see the results. Switch the VCR's INPUT SELECT switch to TV (the VCR "thinks" it's listening to TV, but it's listening to your computer).

FIGURE 8-14 Connecting a home computer to your VCR

There are other more expensive solutions to interfacing computers with VCRs. AT&T makes a TARGA board which fits in an IBM PC. The board will digitize a video picture, changing your camera signal to a computer signal, then mix other computer signals with it (graphics or text), and then spit the signal back out as video for recording. Unfortunately, the board costs $3,000. Matrox is another company which makes a graphics board for IBM computers. Its EGA/video board costs $1,000 and makes video signals out of computer signals.

Most flexible of all is the Telecomp 2000, a $1,600 box which takes computer signals and mixes them, combines them, or superimposes them over video signals and makes a video output. This device (available from Quality Video Supplies Inc. in Hackensack, NJ) allows you to convert any computer's image to standard video signals for recording on a VCR, or you can superimpose the computer image over the signal from a camera or another VCR while rerecording the result.

One of the fun things about using home computers is that by using a GRAPHICS TABLET and electronic pen, you can "draw" pictures and modify them electronically

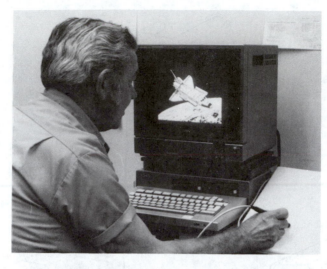

FIGURE 8–15 GRAPHICS TABLET and electronic pen

on the screen, color them, and sometimes animate them before recording them on tape. The least expensive system that allows you to do this is the Commodore Amiga. More expensive and more advanced systems are available for $2,000 and up. Professional models such as the Alias Research and Dubner paint systems cost nearly $100,000 (including software and mortgage). Figures 8–15 and 8–16 show examples of an inexpensive graphics tablet and the images which you can create.

GRAPHIC DESIGN

Title Placement and Background

As you saw in Figure 2–1, a white title pretty much disappears when placed over a white background. Placing a title over a darker part of a picture makes the title show up better. Similarly, a dark title should be moved to a light part of the picture to show up well.

Some backgrounds—especially the busy, bright, and contrasty ones—compete with titles no matter what color they are. Figure 8–17 shows an example.

You should avoid busy backgrounds. If you have no choice, then try darkening the background, perhaps with the camera's IRIS control. Another possibility might be to defocus the background. This will make the foreground stand out more. If carefully planned, you can have the title disappear as the background picture comes into focus. You'll see a technique for doing this shortly. At the end of your production, you could have the picture defocus as the title or credits appear.

A title should not look like a bumper sticker wrapped across someone's face as in Figure 8–18. Instead, try to find a place for the face and a place for the title so they don't fight with each other.

FIGURE 8-16 Images created from a GRAPHICS TABLET

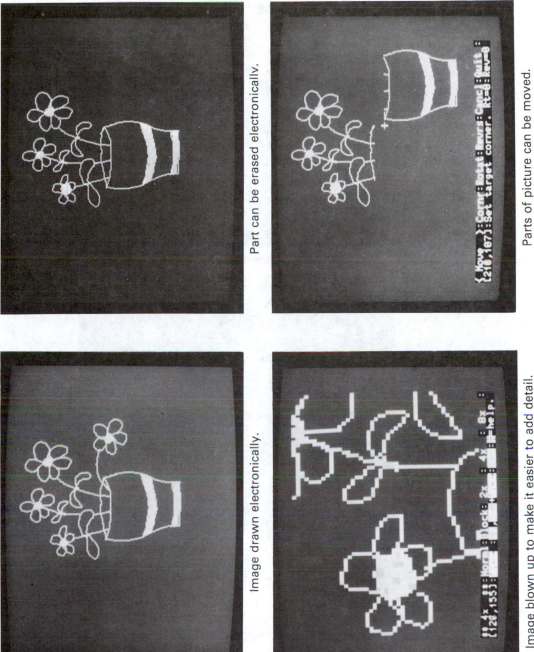

Image drawn electronically.

Part can be erased electronically.

Parts of picture can be moved.

Image blown up to make it easier to add detail.

Busy, bright, contrasty background obscures text.

Darken background so text stands out.

FIGURE 8-17 Text competing with background

All these warnings should not make you afraid of adding backgrounds to your titles. A drawing or photo can add meaning and pizzazz to a title. In fact the picture may be remembered long after the words have been forgotten, so this powerful visual tool should not be dismissed offhandedly.

If possible, always leave a large border around your title graphic so that you have the choice of zooming in (making the letters large and bold, filling the screen) or zooming out (making the title smaller and easy to fit in a quiet part of the screen). If your title card lacks a large border, when you zoom out you may overshoot the title card and get part of your kitchen in your shot. As mentioned earlier, it doesn't

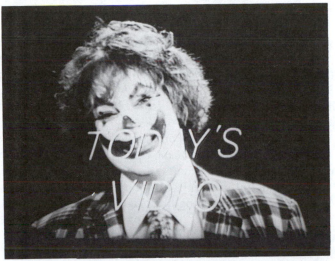

Title fights with face.

Move face and title.

FIGURE 8-18 Title across face

matter a whole lot whether the lettering on your title is large or small since you can always zoom in or zoom out to make it the size you want.

Making Graphics Come Alive

Those of us blessed with creativity will have no trouble making graphics come alive. Good artists and photographers can find ways to make almost anything look real or interesting.

There is no law which says that a still picture must remain stationary. A camera can pan, tilt, and zoom over a photograph or over a painting as if it were shooting something "live." Quick cutting and active movements can make the pictures themselves seem to be moving. Still photographs become movies; battle scenes become the actual battles (with the help of sound effects); birds glide through the sky; ships roll back and forth; earthquake scenes shake up and down; amusement park rides streak by while the lights of the midway grow blurry and dissolve into the next scene.

Cutouts can be placed over visuals and moved, simulating animation. Scenes can have holes cut in them with movement behind the holes, simulating running water, snow, vehicles passing by, or whatever.

Detailed photographs and paintings offer an excellent opportunity to zoom in on one part of the picture and slowly pan, taking a trip from one part of the scene to another. Your audience can slowly stroll down a street in Luxembourg or be barraged with close-ups of Civil War cannon fire and soldiers diving for cover. All of these shots may be taken from the same picture, just using close-ups of different parts, panning from one area to another, and zooming in on centers of interest.

When you wish to show something complicated or unfamiliar, it is often best to begin with a wide establishing shot of the item and its surroundings. Then you zoom in on the specific part of the picture detailing the concept you wish to highlight.

Visual Tricks

There's a bagful of tricks to this trade. Because TV is a two-dimensional medium there are many tricks that can be played with the nearness and farness of things. A person standing next to a mural of a house on a mountain may appear to be observing a real house on a distant mountain. A model robot near the camera lens may look like a life-sized attacker.

The author recalls having fun with a videotape of a college president giving a speech. The speech was played on a 21″ TV monitor so that the president's head was nearly life size. A TV camera was carefully focused on the TV screen image and its signal sent to a second VCR to record the results. In front of the TV screen a "live" hand (I'll never tell whose) appeared and reached up to pick the president's nose and to make unsavory gestures to the audience. The hand looked real. The resulting tape was a riot (though never shown publicly). Viewers couldn't tell the TV image from the real one. More tricks:

Lighting changes can make three-dimensional objects seem to move. Strong back light with very little key or fill light simulates night scenes. Raising the key and fill lights ushers in the day. Puppets, when not sharing the scene with real people, may begin to look like full-sized people themselves. Visuals or models may be burned on camera. Title lettering may be blown away. Delicate hands may enter the scene and may turn over a tarot card revealing titles or credits. Smoke in the foreground can lead to the final fade out. Blood (simulated of course) may drip onto a title. The camera zooms in on the drip filling the screen as the next visual is revealed in the redness of the drip.

Title backgrounds (Drawings by Jose Marjolin and Sheila Teeluck, courtesy of Joseph Sauder)

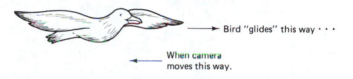

Panning across a still picture to create illusion of motion.

If your camera has a MACRO lens, print a tiny title on a slide or acetate sheet and mount it on or near your lens. By changing focus form near to far, you will make the sharp title fuzz away to nothing (like a dissolve effect) while the blurry background comes into focus and your action begins.

Creativity—it's the fun part of television. Use it. At the same time, however, keep the objectives of your production in mind and don't let the fancy stuff carry you away.

MOUNTING GRAPHICS

Photographs and flimsy paper will always curl up under hot television lights. The graphic then goes out of focus and causes uncontrollable reflections. It has to be held stiff and flat. Try tearing off a two-inch strip of masking tape and bending it into a loop so that both ends stick together looking like a small sticky wheel. Press the loop against the corners of the back of your picture and flatten them out some.

FIGURE 8–19   Covering the white borders of a photo with black PHOTO-GRAPHIC tape while also mounting the photo. (From Graphics for Television, Prentice Hall, Englewood Cliffs, N.J.)

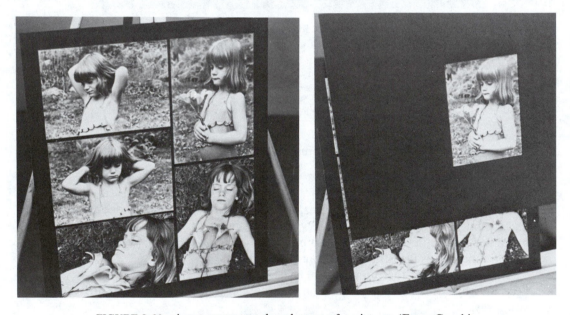

FIGURE 8–20   A cut MASK reveals only part of a picture. (From Graphics for Television, Prentice Hall, Englewood Cliffs, N.J.)

Thus the tape sticks to the picture yet there is a sticky side still facing out. Place the picture on a mounting board, press it down, and it should stay put. Beware that if you do not remove the tape within a year or so the masking tape will bleed its gooey stickum through the paper, leaving a yellow stain on the front of your picture.

From your photo store you can purchase black PHOTOGRAPHIC TAPE, handy for neatly mounting graphics on black backgrounds as demonstrated in Figure 8–19.

The tape not only holds down your graphic, but it nicely covers the white borders of photographs. The tape gives a sharp, straight edge to ragged pictures, and several rows of tape can be applied to crop a picture smaller. PHOTOGRAPHIC TAPE can reshape a 4″ × 5″ or 8″ × 10″ photograph into the TV's 3:4 ASPECT RATIO.

When pictures are part of a book or are already mounted in a combination or when you only want one part of a picture, you may need a MASK to cover the parts you don't want. A MASK is simply a black (or gray) cardboard cut to the desired shape (perhaps 3:4 ASPECT RATIO) with a razor knife. The edges of the hole can be blackened with a felt marker. You then lay the MASK over the desired part of the picture, as shown in Figure 8–20.

LIGHTING GRAPHICS

A professional-looking title is generally one which leaves no hint about how it was constructed. Curly edges on letters and grainy paper fibers in the background make titles look amateurish. Even flat smooth titles have minor scratches, ridges, and lumps in them which remain hidden until they are revealed by the all-seeing TV camera.

Some of these flaws can be deemphasized by the use of flat, shadowless lighting. As shown in Figure 8–21, lamps are set up to the left and right of the camera and aimed at the graphic. Each light "washes out" some of the shadows created by the other light making the image fairly shadowless. The "softer" (more diffused) the lights, the better.

Two 100-watt desk lamps with frosted bulbs and large reflector shades may work very well for black and white. Photofloods or professional lights may be necessary for perfect color.

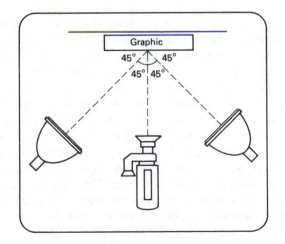

FIGURE 8-21 Lighting graphics (top view)

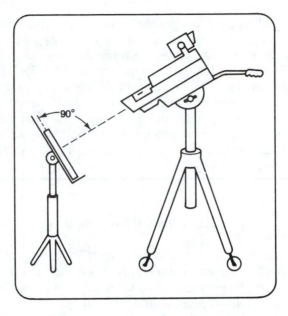

FIGURE 8–22   Graphic kept perpendicular to camera's line of sight

The angle of the lights is not too critical. If, however, they are too close to the camera, glossy or shiny paper or lettering surfaces may reflect light into the camera lens. Placed at too great an angle from the camera, the lights begin to create shadows and may also illuminate the visual unevenly. An angle of 45° from the camera/visual axis, as shown in the figure, is usually satisfactory.

FOCUSING ON GRAPHICS

All of the focusing procedures in the previous chapters also apply to focusing on graphics; however, small things like graphics are harder to focus on than larger things. Although one foot may make little difference from 20 feet away, one inch makes a big difference six inches away from the camera lens.

One way to minimize the focusing problem is to first assure that the graphic is exactly perpendicular to the camera's line of sight, as shown in Figure 8–22. This way, all parts of the graphic are equidistant (almost) from the camera lens and are therefore all in focus at the same time. You can take the guesswork out of this alignment process by laying a small mirror over the graphic. As you look in your TV camera viewfinder, you should see the reflection of your camera's lens. If the center of the lens appears in the center of your viewfinder, you are all set.

Another way to minimize the focusing problem is to flood the visual with light and to "stop down" the camera lens to a higher f number for maximum depth-of-field. In very tight close-ups, it may be impossible to focus all parts of the visual accurately because the edges of the visual are a shade farther away from the camera lens than the center of the visual. In such cases, stopping down the lens may be your only recourse for an all around sharp picture. Remember that heat from intense lights too close to the visual—especially a photograph—for too long, may curl your visual or its mount. At close range, this will throw your focusing off.

SHOWING A SERIES OF VISUALS

If your VCR can make clean edits, then you can easily show one visual, PAUSE the tape, change the visual, UNPAUSE the tape, and continue this process until you have displayed all your visuals.

If you must change visuals before the viewer's eyes, try mounting them all on the same size posterboards and find a way to flip from one board to another. You can stack your graphics one card in front of another and, one by one, flip the front card down, revealing the next. Be careful not to wiggle the cards while doing this.

Crawl and Roll

A CRAWL is a *sideways* movement of text across the TV screen (like a news bulletin), while a ROLL is the *vertical* movement of words through the screen (like titles, credits, or lists). Some video titlers and character generators move the text across the screen electronically. They will vary the speed of the roll or crawl and can stop it at any point.

Small studios without a CRAWL or a character generator can simulate the effect in a couple of cheapo ways. One is to type the desired text in a narrow column on a strip of paper. Then disengage the typewriter's ratchet so that the page can roll smoothly through the typewriter as you twist the roller. Using a close-up lens, aim your TV camera at the text where it exits the typewriter. Try to keep the paper flat in the area you are shooting. To "roll credits," simply hand turn the roller slowly as the camera looks on.

Another cheapie technique is shown in Figure 8–23. Here the camera is wheeled up to a wall on which is mounted the titles, list, or whatever on a long strip of paper. The strip should be evenly lit from top to bottom. Use a close-up lens if the print is small. Align the camera and list so that the camera may be aimed at the top of the list (or even above the top) and on cue, slowly and evenly crank the pedestal down, lowering the camera. The words will appear to rise through the screen and disappear at the top. Leaving a blank space at the bottom of the screen allows you to crank the last words off, leaving a blank screen.

Simply tilting the camera will not work. First, it is very hard to slowly and smoothly tilt a camera across something small like text. Second, since the top and bottom of the strip are farther from the lens than the middle of the strip, they will be out of focus. Third, for strips of any length, the image will begin to keystone, making the farther words smaller and the nearer words larger.

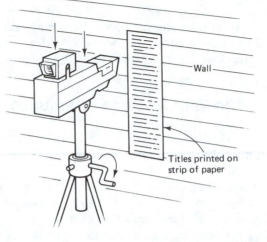

FIGURE 8-23   Simulated CRAWL using the camera's pedestal elevator

FILM-TO-TAPE TRANSFER

Advantages and Disadvantages

Both at home and at school the inconvenience of dragging out projection screens and projectors, or smashing your shins while crossing your darkened "theatre" makes you want to convert all your slides, filmstrips, and movies into video. Perhaps you would prefer the sound of background music and polished narration to the cement mixer roar of your projector fan. Or maybe a travel collection composed of 20 different media—some slides, some snapshots, some super 8 movies, a few audiocassette tapes, a reel-to-reel audio tape, some postcards, and Fibber Magee knows what else are just too difficult to show in a class or business meeting. Furthermore, you'd like to organize and consolidate this mess into a single, neat videocassette that runs itself.

Are you convinced that all your films should be transferred to video? Don't be. Before you start blowing dust off the film cans, take another peek at Figure 8-7. Look at the detail you will lose. Granted, by zooming in and panning across pictures at close range, you can preserve much of the important detail, but in cases where you wish to see the whole picture at once, with all its fine print, all its subtle highlights, all its true colors, and be able to distinguish every feather, every hair, every leaf and grain of sand individually, then keep your photos as photos. Until HDTV (high definition television) comes along; video just isn't a sharp enough medium to do the job.

Video is simply a trade-off—convenience for sharpness.

Do-It-Yourself Methods

If you've decided to transfer your slides, filmstrips, and photographs to videotape, here are some methods to do it.

Front screen projection   This method is cheap, flexible, and nearly as good as any other method. You simply aim your projector at a screen and aim your camera at the image to record it as shown in Figure 8–24.

Use a flat, white posterboard as your screen. Any smooth, matte-finished (not shiny), very white, flat surface will also do. Regular projection screens tend to reflect "hot spots"—overly bright areas on the screen—while allowing the edges and corners to look dim.

Position the projector so that the projected image is about 18″ tall. Larger images start to become too dim. Smaller images accentuate the minor imperfections in the screen's surface. Experiment. Be sure to focus the projector *very well*.

Mount your camera on a sturdy tripod. Position it as near the projector as possible so that you don't get KEYSTONING of your image. Turn out *all* lights (or close curtains) so that *no* light seeps in to "wash out" your projected image.

Focus the TV camera, adjust your camera's iris, color temperature, and white balance controls as usual. The "indoor" setting on the color temperature control may work best. Experiment. Watch your viewfinder or TV monitor.

Dark areas of the picture may tend to blend together as a solid mass. To cure this problem, add a small amount of light to the room while watching the result on your camera viewfinder. The room light will add just a little more brightness to the darkest areas, bringing them up to a level that the camera can register.

Adjust your camera's zoom lens so that the projected image fills the TV screen. Because film pictures have a wider ASPECT RATIO than video, this will mean the loss of a little of the left and right borders of your scene. Feel free, however, to

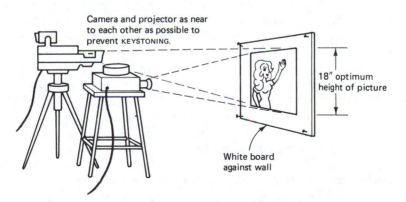

FIGURE 8-24   FRONT SCREEN PROJECTION method for transferring film to tape

TELECINE ADAPTERS Left, Magnavox TeleCine converter for video camera, Model 9057 (Courtesy of Magnavox) Right, Quasar TeleCine converter for TV camera, Model KT 502QF (Courtesy of Quasar)

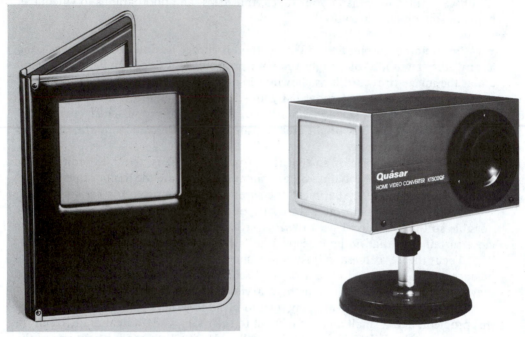

Accessory TELECINE ADAPTERS

zoom, pan, tilt, fade, or defocus your camera to focus attention on the main event, to add movement when needed, or to dress up the transitions between scenes.

With home video equipment and a single slide projector, you will get a blank or black screen between slides. If your VCR edits cleanly, you can omit that blank screen by pausing your VCR at the changeover point. You can also pause while changing movie reels.

If you plan to add an audio track to a silent slide show, don't try to do it while you are trying to record the video. You can rehearse your narration while recording if you want, just to get a sense of timing, but save the actual narration for a later audio dub. You have plenty to handle right now, whereas later, giving audio your full attention, you're likely to do a smoother, more creative job. Also, you won't have projection fans roaring in the background.

Rear screen projection   REAR PROJECTION has one advantage over FRONT PROJECTION. The image is brighter and that means you can leave a dim light on in the room (your shins will thank you for that). Also, there is no keystoning to deal with. Several video accessories companies sell TELECINE ADAPTERS which consist of a mirror and translucent (smokey) screen. If you don't have a professional rear projection screen, try some translucent tracing or vellum paper to project onto. Note that because you are projecting from behind the screen, your pictures will come out reversed, left to right. This is easily corrected on slide projectors where the slides can be put into the projector backwards. Movies, however, are harder or impossible to reverse. You will need to use a mirror as shown in Figure 8–25. The accessory home video projection screens contain the mirror which automatically makes this correction.

If you wish to dissolve from slide to slide, there is a cheap way to do it using only one camera. Rent (or borrow from a school) a DISSOLVE UNIT, a device that fades down the brightness of one slide projector while fading up the brightness of another. You would aim the projectors at a REAR or FRONT PROJECTION screen while your TV camera records the images as they dissolve from one slide to the next. Figure 8–26 diagrams the process using a REAR PROJECTION SCREEN.

You can also buy for about $75 a handy device that clips onto the lens of your camera and allows you to slip slides into it one at a time. The gadget is convenient; you simply aim your camera out the window and stuff slides into it to record them. It, however, doesn't allow you to zoom or pan across any of the pictures as you could with FRONT or REAR PROJECTION.

Movies There's one annoying problem faced by anyone trying to transfer a movie to videotape and that's SHUTTER BAR. Your video image flickers or has a

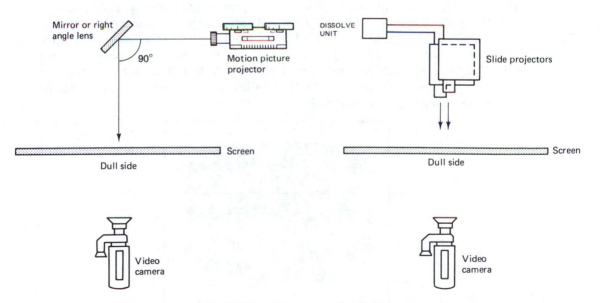

FIGURE 8–25 A mirror or right angle lens can correct image reversal problems on a REAR PROJECTION screen

FIGURE 8–26 Using a DISSOLVE unit and two slide projectors

dark horizontal band running through it, perhaps moving, sometimes stationary (Figure 8–27). Here's the cause.

Movie projectors beam their light through their shutters at 18 or 24 frames per second. Your camera makes its pictures at 60 per second. Your camera, therefore, is sometimes making a picture when none is on the projection screen (the projector is inbetween pictures). Although your eyes cannot see the problem, your *camera can.*

Professional TV setups like studios and commercial film-to-tape transfer shops use special projectors which synchronize their projected pictures with the camera.

Here are a few more tips for transferring slides and movies to video tape.

1. Adjust your camera's COLOR TEMPERATURE for "indoor."
2. Have your narrator stand far from the projector using a separate microphone to avoid picking up projector noise. Remember that you can always go back and AUDIO DUB in the narration later without the projector roaring in the background.

Commercial Services

Check to see if your local college has a TV studio. If so, it may have a *film chain* capable of making the proper transfer at a nominal (or no) charge. Professionally made film chains do quite a satisfactory job. If so equipped, they can duplicate 16mm, 8mm, or super 8mm movies with or without sound. Some are equipped with filmstrip projectors as well as *dual drum* slide projectors. Dual drum slide projectors, unlike regular projectors which leave a black screen for a half-second while they change slides, change slides almost immediately. They really consist of two projectors with an electrically operated mirror which shows the slide from the first projector and then switches instantly to the slide from the second while projector one is busy changing to its next slide.

FIGURE 8–27 SHUTTER BAR

Some camera shops and some video rental shops are equipped to make film-to-tape transfers. The better shops have professional duplicating machines with proper projectors, cameras, and so on to make a clean transfer for about $.08 per foot of movie film (videocassette extra). Avoid the shops that aim an 8mm projector at a wall, record the results with a TV camera, and tell you the result is "just as good" as the professional equipment. It just ain't so.

Commercial systems such as the Froelich Foto Video Transfer System and the Hope Industry System will make special effects such as fades, dissolves, and wipes. You may pay extra for music or the addition of titles. With these systems you can mix media such as slides, 8mm, 16mm, and also have multiple copies of your cassette made. They also do color correction which is especially helpful if you are using older slides or movies which have faded over the years.

Fotomat charges about $50 to transfer 30 minutes of regular or super 8 movie film or about $70 to transfer one hour of film (cassette included). All of these companies provide high quality, flickerless transfers.

If your film is extremely valuable, you could take it to a commercial TV production or postproduction house available in most large cities. Facilities such as Adwar, Devlin, and Windsor Total Video in New York use broadcast quality equipment such as FLYING SPOT SCANNERS instead of movie projectors to make super clean copies at about $400 per hour plus tape plus extras.

Remember that when sending your slides or movie films out to Fotomat or other consumer outlets, you lose nearly all "creative control" over the result. There would be no panning, zooming, fancy transitions, or mixture of media (a slide, a movie, than a snapshot) that you could do yourself. Also, vertically oriented slides would be recorded "as is" without regard for ASPECT RATIO.

After all this talk, graphics still boil down to three rules:

1. Make it fit the shape of a TV screen.
2. Keep it simple.
3. Make it bold.

9

Copying
a videotape

By this time you may already know how to copy a videotape and this subject may seem too simple to deserve a chapter of its own. But if you consider that nearly every videotaped program a viewer ever sees is actually a copy, you will realize that it is by our copies we are judged, not our originals. A poorly made copy will reflect on the entire production.

Copies are fairly quick to make (it takes one hour to copy a one-hour tape) and you can make just one copy if that is all you want. All it takes is two VCRs and some wire to connect them. If you had four VCRs, you could make three copies at once. To make video copies by the hundreds, you should send your MASTER tape to a DUPLICATION HOUSE (Figure 9–1) where hundreds of VCRs (SLAVES) copy it at the same time.

Incidentally, a DUPLICATION HOUSE will charge less per copy the more copies you make. Ten VHS copies of a 30-minute tape will cost about $110 total. One hundred would cost $800 and 1,000 copies would cost $3,150. Imagine how long it would take you to copy 1,000 tapes using two VCRs in your basement (and imagine how many VCRs you'd wear out).

THE BASICS

Here's how to copy a tape: Get two VCRs. Using separate audio and video cables, connect the audio and video OUTPUTS of the player (called the MASTER machine or VCP, for videocassette player) to the audio and video INPUTS of the recorder (called a SLAVE in video circles). Connect the TV set to the SLAVE's RF output so that you can monitor the results (Figure 9–2). Chuck your original cassette into the MASTER

Copying a video tape

Nation's largest is Video Corporation of America, located outside Chicago. It can make 2000 copies in one hour

FIGURE 9–1 Videocassette duplication facility (Courtesy of JVC Company of America)

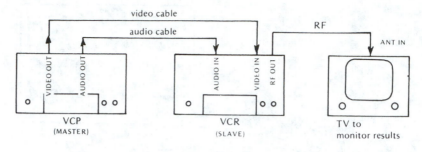

FIGURE 9-2 Simple hookup for copying a videocassette

player and a blank videocassette into the SLAVE. Adjust the INPUT SELECT switch on the SLAVE so that it "listens" to the MASTER. Select the desired tape speed. Hit PLAY on the MASTER and RECORD on the SLAVE and let the machines do the rest.

Copies never look as good as originals, so don't expect dazzling copies. The process, however, merely involves playing a tape on one machine while recording the signal on another.

One nice thing about video is that you can copy a tape from one format to another. Although different format *tapes* may not be compatible, their video signals are. By using a 3/4U VCR and a VHS VCR, you can make a VHS copy of the 3/4U tape.

MAKING THE BEST POSSIBLE SIGNAL FOR COPYING

Your Best Original

The tape you record can be no better than the tape you are copying from. If your original tape is fuzzy, grainy, or jittery, your copy of this tape will be fuzzier, grainier, and jitterier. So the first step is to start with good tape. Use your highest quality *name brand* tape, perhaps HG (HIGH GRADE) tape for recording your original. Use virgin (unrecorded) tape or tape that has only been used a few times. Avoid very long thin tape; stick to the standard length tapes like T-120 or L-500.

Next, record your original at your VCR's *fastest* speed. This ensures the highest quality picture and sound to start with. Record your original tape from a good strong antenna signal meticulously fine tuned, or with a well lit, carefully miked setup. Again, the better your original signal, the better your copy will be.

Your Player and Recorder

The machines you pick for playing the original and recording the copy should be in tip-top shape. If possible, play the original tape on the same VCR that made it. Tapes always play back better on "mother." If you can't play the tape on the machine that originally recorded it, then pay particular attention to TRACKING as you play your MASTER. This may have to be adjusted to yield a smooth, steady picture.

Your SLAVE recorder should be set at its fastest speed for making as stable a copy as possible.

To avoid accidentally erasing your master tape, remove the plastic erase-protect tab on the cassette as shown back in Figure 3–29. Another way to avoid getting mixed up is to place a piece of masking tape over the RECORD button on the MASTER VCP. That way, you won't accidentally try to record on the wrong machine.

For important productions, try not to master on VHS; the picture quality just won't stand up to several generations of recording. Instead, use Super VHS, 3/4U, 3/4U-SP, or one of the professional formats like Type-C, Betacam, or M2. The machines are much more expensive (and probably will have to be rented), but the final result will look much better. Table 9–1 shows the number of generations you can get from different format VCRs. Figure 9–3 shows how copies look worse than originals, especially in the home video formats.

Cables

Connect your VCP and VCR with the best cables you can buy. Use the shortest cables possible so that your signal passes through them at maximum strength.

VCRs with dub feature   There's another method of copying a videocassette that is even better than the ones listed, but it requires higher quality video tape machines with a DUB input (or output). Figure 9–4 shows the connection. Inciden-

TABLE 9–1   COMPARING GENERATIONAL LOSSES OF
DIFFERENT FORMATS

Format	Number of Acceptable Generations Possible[a]
VHS (SP)	1–2
VHS (LP, SLP)	1
Super Beta, VHS HQ	2
Beta 1	2
Beta 2	1–2
Beta 3	1
3/4U (using video)	2–3
ED beta	3
Super VHS	3
3/4U (using DUB)	3
C	5
Betacam	6
M2	6–8
Digital	20+

[a]Where 1 equals master only, 2 equals copy of master, 3 equals copy of copy, etc.

A) Original; As seen by camera

B) First generation; Same scene recorded and played back on VHS machine at 2-hour speed

C) First generation . . . and at 6-hour speed

D) Second generation; Copy of example B made at 2-hour mode

E) Third generation; Copy of example D made at 2-hour mode

FIGURE 9-3 Copies look worse than originals. Also, home VCRs make better pictures at the fastest speed

---

A RIDDLE

A teacher shot some videotapes at a school and gave them to her AV department to edit together electronically into one tape. The tape came out so well that the AV director immediately made a SAFE COPY of it in case the precious original ever got damaged. When the school board asked for copies, the AV director wisely used the SAFE COPY as a WORKING MASTER (the MASTER you usually make copies from) to avoid risking the original MASTER. One school-board member copied his copy of the tape and sent it to another school. The teachers liked it and had their librarian make a copy of it for classroom viewing. A student liked it and copied the teacher's copy to play to his folks on his home videocassette recorder. His folks liked it, copied it, and sent the copy off to Grandma, who also had a VCR. The question now is: What did Grandma see?

Answer: *crud.*

Why? Every time a tape is duplicated, it loses quality. The more generations you go down, the worse the picture and stability become. The moral of the story is this: *Try to stay as close to the original as possible.* Make copies from the original whenever possible. Make copies from a WORKING MASTER only when it is really necessary to protect the original and when using professional equipment which affords the luxury of going down one more generation.

A RIDDLE

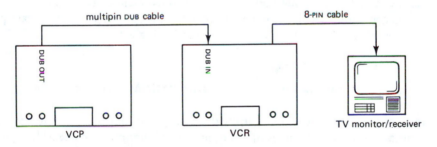

FIGURE 9–4   Setup for copying a video tape using VCRs with DUB feature.

tally, the word "dub" means "copy." Earlier, you saw the word "dub" used in conjunction with a VCR's AUDIO DUB feature whereby a new sound track could be recorded (perhaps "copied" from somewhere), erasing the old sound track. In this new context, however, the DUB feature refers to a special input/output on the VCR made especially for efficiently copying videotapes.

This system uses a multi-wire cable which carries the color over a separate wire from the black-and-white parts of the picture, bypassing a number of circuits which fuzz up the picture.

When using the DUB feature, be sure to throw a switch on the VCP to the DUB position to bypass the unneeded circuits. The result is a cleaner copy. Switch DUB off when using the VCP normally.

VCRs connected to cable TV or antennas Sometimes you may wish to use home VCRs to record shows off the air, copy tapes from one VCR to another, and also allow simultaneous TV viewing of either the VCR's signal or the broadcast signal. Figure 9–5 shows several ways to achieve this.

In each case, let's assume that an antenna signal is used or a cable TV signal is used which has either been UPCONVERTED to UHF or is being fed to VCRs and TVs which are CABLE COMPATIBLE. Otherwise we have to face the additional complication of wiring in a cable TV CONVERTER BOX.

In method A, the TV signal is split and goes to VCR 1 and VCR 2. Either VCR can record that antenna signal (with its INPUT SELECT on TV) or can record a signal from the other VCR (with its INPUT SELECT on VCR). Either VCR can record from or play back a tape to the other. TV 1 can pick up the antenna signal if VCR 1's OUTPUT SELECT is switched to TV. This will be true no matter whether VCR 1 is recording, playing back, or copying a tape. TV 1 can display what VCR 1 is doing by switching VCR 1's OUTPUT SELECT to VCR. Similarly, TV 2 can do the same things with VCR 2's signals.

If only one TV is available, then method B can be used. Here, an ANTENNA switch selects which VCR the TV will listen to. Either VCR can have its OUTPUT SELECT switched to the TV mode allowing the TV to view broadcast channels even when the VCRs are dubbing a tape.

Method C is the worst method of all. Here, only VCR 2 can do the recording. Also, the degenerated RF signal is being copied. The TV can view broadcast programs only while the VCRs aren't occupied duplicating a tape.

SIGNAL PROCESSING EQUIPMENT

You can't copy a sow's ear and end up with a silk purse, but there are devices that can accentuate desirable attributes of your picture and diminish the negative aspects. They are PROCESSING AMPLIFIERS that stabilize your video signal and IMAGE ENHANCERS that crispen the picture. These devices which are connected in the path of the signal as it goes from the MASTER to the SLAVE will be covered in Chapter 12.

SCAN CONVERSION

Sometimes your original tape is of such poor quality that it cannot be copied. The tape will play alright into your TV set, but if you try to copy it, the copy will not play back. Possible causes:

1. The tape is bad or was poorly recorded.
2. The tape is an nth generation copy that is very unstable.
3. The tape could be copy protected and has been rendered electronically uncopyable (more on this shortly).

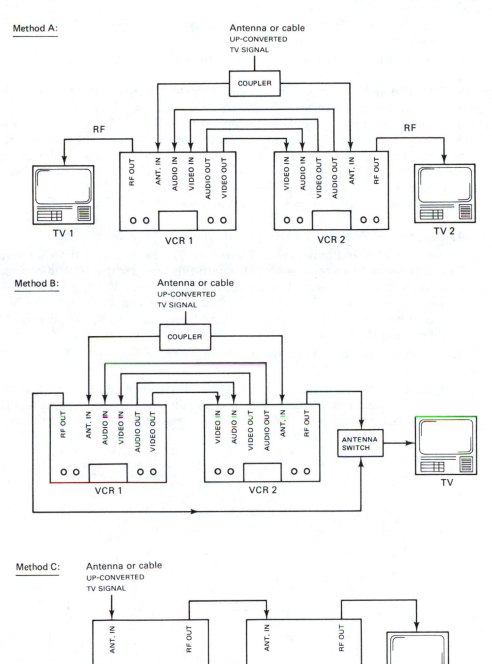

FIGURE 9-5 Home VCRs with antenna or cable

4. The tape was made in a foreign standard (like PAL or SECAM) and will play back only on foreign equipment.

5. You don't have the right cables to copy the tape directly.

The solution is to use a technique called OPTICAL CONVERSION or SCAN CONVERSION which is no more than displaying the tape on a TV set and with your camera and another VCR, recording the program from the TV screen as in Figure 9-6. This process will result in a video copy whose picture is stable but is about 20% fuzzier and has poorer color and poorer contrast than the original. Although the picture quality suffers, you may have no other choice if the five problems listed have rendered the original tape otherwise uncopyable.

Here's how to carry out a SCAN CONVERSION:

1. Find a good VCP and a TV to play your MASTER tape on.

2. Set up a VCR and camera as in Figure 9-6. The camera faces the TV screen and is zoomed to a FULL SHOT (TV screen fills the viewfinder). Audio is run directly from the MASTER VCR's AUDIO OUT to the SLAVE VCR's AUDIO IN (if you don't have an audio cable, you could play the sound out of the TV and record it from the camera's built-in microphone, but the sound quality will be echoey and tinny).

3. If possible, set up a VCR monitor from which to judge your final picture quality.

4. Play some of the program and adjust the TV picture controls. Note that the TV screen image that looks best to your eye does not necessarily look best to the TV camera. Adjust the TV screen's brightness and contrast to make a good

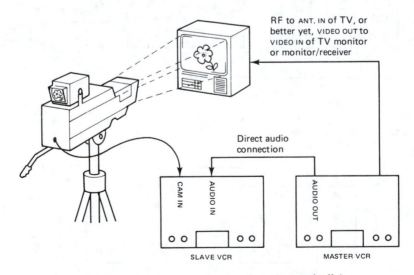

FIGURE 9-6 SCAN CONVERSION (copying optically)

picture *for the camera,* regardless of how it looks to your eye. Use the VCR monitor as a guide to the best picture settings. There's a lot of experimentation in this process.

If you notice faint diagonal or curved lines on the image from the camera (called moire), try tilting the camera a little.

5. When ready, turn out the lights to avoid reflections in the TV screen face, start the VCR recording, start the VCP playing, and cross your fingers.

TIPS ON MAKING VIDEO COPIES

Before you start, once you've decided which machine is to *play* and which machine is to *record,* take this one precaution which will save you apologies and a pint of stomach acid. *Place masking tape (or some other reminder) over the record button on the machine that will do the playing so you don't accidentally push the button and erase something on the* MASTER. You don't want to forget which machine is which and suddenly find yourself with a gap in the tape.

Actually, making a copy of a tape is straightforward:

1. Connect the VCRs and monitors as shown in Figures 9–2, 9–4, or 9–5.
2. Switch the SLAVE VCR's INPUT SELECT to "listen" to the other VCR. Choose the desired recording speed—preferably a fast speed.
3. Play a sample of tape from the MASTER and adjust the TRACKING if necessary. Once everything looks good, rewind the cassette to the program's start.
4. Press RECORD/PLAY on the SLAVE and let it run for about five seconds to get past the threading-caused dropouts at the beginning of the tape. Then, hit PAUSE.
5. Press PLAY on the MASTER.
6. Watch your TV monitor. At the first sign of clear program, UNPAUSE the SLAVE.
7. If you have any reason to believe the process may not work, stop copying after a minute and view the results. If okay, rewind both VCRs and make the copy for real.
8. When you are finished making a copy, view a little of the *end* of it. If your video heads clogged during the process, it's the end that is likely to be bad.

Now that you have successfully copied that videotape, what do you do next? Sit down and have a smoke right? Wrong! You label the copy and make sure you put the word *copy* on that label. Copies and originals look too much alike to be easily sorted out—but they are not *really* alike and should not be treated as equals. So, label and separate them. Besides, smoking is bad for your lungs.

COPYING AND COPYRIGHT

Commercially prerecorded videocassettes generally cost $2 and up to rent and $50 and up to buy. Wouldn't it be cheaper just to rent a tape and copy it for yourself? Or borrow a friend's tape and copy that? Yes, it would, but when the program is copyrighted (and most recent ones are), duplicating it without permission from the copyright holder is illegal. It is also immoral considering the copyright holder spent money producing the show to *sell* to you not to have you simply take.

Will you go to jail if you copy a commercially prerecorded copyrighted tape or videodisc? Probably not. The single copy that you make in your own home doesn't seem to interest the program owners. Besides, how would they find out? If, however, you trade, distribute, or, worse yet, sell your unsanctioned recordings, you are playing Russian roulette with the law.

Is it legal to record TV broadcasts off the air for use in the home? Yes. Even though these broadcasts are copyrighted. In 1984 the Supreme Court decided that home taping of broadcast and cable TV programs was legal. This doesn't mean, however, that you can duplicate copies of your tapes and distribute them.

The copyright laws not only cover entire programs, but parts of programs such as pictures and music. If you wish to use parts of other people's programs or photos from a magazine or book in your production, or you wish to use popular music in your titles or background music, it's okay as long as you are making the production only for yourself and family. If you intend to distribute this extravaganza commer-

ALTHOUGH IT IS UNLAWFUL TO COPY A COPYRIGHTED PROGRAM, THERE IS NO GRAND CAMPAIGN AFOOT TO CATCH HOME-COPIERS.

cially, your music and pictures all must be original or purchased. To do this, you could send a letter to the copyright holder of whatever material you are using and ask permission to use it in your production. Sometimes the permission is granted for free, sometimes it's rejected altogether, and sometimes there is a fee.

There are companies like De Wolfe Music Library Inc., Associated Production Music, or Valentino Inc. (all in New York) who sell records with the rights to use the music in video productions.

One company which (for a fee) will assist you in obtaining rights and permissions to photos, music, video, film, and literary works is

> BZ/Rights & Permissions, Inc.
> 145 West 86th Street
> New York, NY 10024

Copyrighting Your Own Work

If you or your school or business produces a program which you (or they) would like to distribute and profit from, you will need to copyright the work to protect it from duplication and sale by others. Here's how you go about copyrighting something:

1. At the beginning titles or ending credits of your tape include words like "Copyright 1989, Poverty Productions, Inc."
2. The cassette label and the cassette box label should also have the title of the program followed by "Copyright 1989, Poverty Productions, Inc." (or whatever the year and company).

   If you take no further steps, your program will be covered by a weak copyright law that states that you cannot sue an infringer to recover damages but you can make the infringers stop copying your production. To make your copyright ironclad, continue with the following steps.
3. Have the Copyright Office send you the forms and instructions on how to file a copyright application. Their address is

   > United States Copyright Office
   > Library of Congress
   > Washington, DC 20559
   > (202) 287-9100

4. File the application noting whether the production was yours *in its entirety* and the exact date the production was completed. (If you hired people to help you and told them what to do, you may still consider the program yours.)
5. Make a copy of the production and send it with your application and a $10 fee back to the Copyright Office for processing.

With these steps you secure the sole right to duplicate and distribute your production and have the right to sue anyone who duplicates your show without your permission.

ANTI-PIRACY MEASURES

When you copy a copyrighted tape without permission, the producers call it "piracy." To thwart the unlicensed duplication of their wares, many distributors do something to the video signal to make it uncopyable. These anti-piracy signals go under the names "Copyguard," "Videoguard," "Macrovision," and others.

They usually involve messing up the tape's video sync signal or its video level so that your VCR can *play* the tape, your TV can *show* it, but another VCR can't "lock on" to the signal to record it. Unfortunately for legitimate tape purchasers, the sync is sometimes too far out of whack for their VCRs to play or their TVs to show. They get diagonal lines, vertical rolling, jittering, a black line crawling

Many rental tape distributors put antipiracy signals on their tapes to discourage copying.

through the picture, or the contrast jumping up and down from bright to dark. Sometimes these problems are fixed by adjusting the vertical or horizontal hold on your TV set. If not, you can often bring the unplayable tape back to the dealer in exchange for an "unguarded" tape. If this isn't possible, reputable dealers will usually refund your money (one good reason for knowing from whom you are buying your tapes).

What do you do if (a) you can't even get guarded tapes to *play* on your VCR, or (b) you wish to duplicate a guarded tape (copyright holder's wishes not withstanding)? You buy yourself a VIDEO STABILIZER for $80 to $250. It's a little box that goes between your video player and your recorder (or TV) and usually fixes the problem. More on this and other video gadgets in Chapter 12.

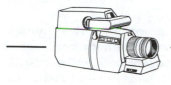

10

Editing
a videotape

In the professional video world, video editing is carried out on specially designed EDITING VIDEOCASSETTE RECORDERS capable of erasing *precisely* certain video "pictures" and replacing them *exactly* with new ones, all without a "glitch." Sometimes these more expensive VCRs are teamed up with computer controlled EDITING CONSOLES (Figure 10–1) which make sure exactly the *selected* pictures are deleted and the chosen substitutes reinserted.

The home video user, his PAUSE button atwitter, is equipped to perform quasi-edits by stopping and starting the tape during the recording process. The resulting program may look satisfactory in the home to friends and relatives, but it should be understood that "PAUSE button" edits are not true edits. They leave glitches—momentary interruptions of the smooth picture. They are sometimes tiny, but the glitches are still there. Professionals and broadcasters look down their noses at these "homestyle edits" and don't consider them to be *true* edits. Unless you intend to spend big bucks for "professional" editing equipment, PAUSE edits will have to be good enough. They are easy to do, look pretty good for home use, and add a whole world of flexibility to your video recordings. Let's see how.

EDITING WITHOUT AN EDITING VIDEOTAPE RECORDER

If you desire perfect glitch-free edits, you require special recorders that can edit electronically. If such machines are unavailable, you must make the personal choice between:

1. Making a tape with *no* glitches, which means recording the tape all the way through nonstop. This may limit what kinds of scenes you can put together (no jumping from location to location) and everything must be shot in sequence (no room for mistakes, additions, or deletions).
2. Producing a tape with glitches, but with content unbound by the aforementioned constraints. Shooting could be out of sequence, segments done days apart, and parts of a production could be done over and over in an attempt to achieve greater perfection.

If your tape is ever to be broadcast, shown to large audiences, or copied and used extensively, or if it will cost a lot to produce, then *no* glitches—not even small ones—are tolerable. Tape copying equipment chokes on glitches, broadcasters are forbidden to transmit glitches, and discriminating audiences will not take glitchy programs seriously.

Whether small budget productions for nondiscriminating nonbroadcast audiences should have glitches should depend perhaps on how bad the glitches are. Are

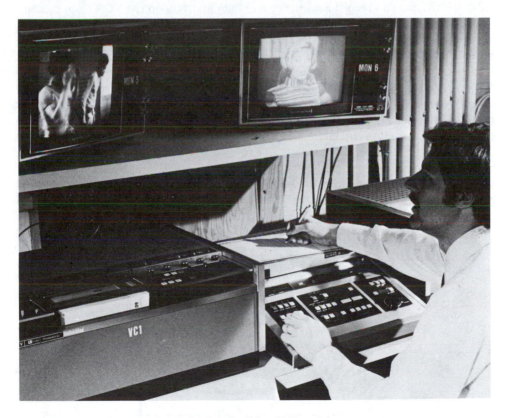

FIGURE 10-1 Professional editing VCRs and EDITING CONSOLE

they wide expanses of snowy picture or are they little blips gone in a second? The size and obtrusiveness of these glitches range from terrible to imperceptible depending on

1. The method of editing used.
2. The kind of VCR used and its condition.
3. Luck.

Let's start with "terrible" and work our way up to "perfect." Most people consider the word "*edit*" to imply a "good quality" edit. Since a true electronic editing VCR is not being used in these first primitive cases, what we get hardly deserves the name edit. Pretty or not, for the lack of a better word, let's call them edits anyway. Here are some methods of editing without specialized equipment.

Stop Edits

In STOP EDITING you record a sequence and then hit STOP on the VCR. You practice the next sequence and when ready to tape it, press RECORD/PLAY and proceed with the recording. When that scene is finished, STOP the machine again. Continue the process until you have assembled your whole show. This method works pretty well with beta VCRs, 8mm VCRs, and a few models of VHS VCRs, but not with most VHS or 3/4 U recorders. When the latter machines STOP, they unthread themselves, losing your place on the tape. When you hit RECORD/PLAY again, the machines rethread themselves—*but not to exactly same place where they left off*—and resume recording. You can end up with a pretty big glitch between edits. Beta VCRs don't unthread themselves when you hit STOP, so you don't lose your place and the glitch in your picture is small.

If you reshoot a scene in the *middle* of a tape using STOP EDITS, your EDIT-IN point (the beginning of your edit) will have a glitch. Your EDIT-OUT point, on com-

FIGURE 10-2   The end of a STOP EDIT

mon home VCRs, will have a terrible looking glitch with a band of snow running through it as in Figure 10–2.

Because of the tape rethreading problem, STOP EDITS are hard to accurately place. Add this to the fact that the glitches are hideous, and you have every reason to avoid this type of editing unless using an EDITING VCR designed for this purpose.

Pause Edits

In PAUSE EDITING you record a sequence, hit PAUSE, set up the next sequence, un-pause to continue recording, and so on until the end of the show. This is probably the method you've been using to delete the commercials from TV broadcasts (you hit PAUSE when the commercial began and unpaused to resume recording when the ad was over).

PAUSE edits are "cleaner" than STOP edits, and they display a barely percepti-ble blink on the TV screen. The edits are generally better when made at the VCR's fastest speed.

Why are PAUSE EDITS better looking? Because PAUSE EDITS, unlike STOP EDITS, don't unthread the tape. You stay put right where you left off—almost. There are exceptions. Some VHS VCRs automatically backspace (run the tape backward) a couple seconds when you hit PAUSE. They do this for mechanical reasons to ensure a smooth, almost glitchless edit. That's nice for smoothness, but a little rough on planning. On such machines, you have to learn to unpause your tape a couple sec-onds *before* the next scene begins. When you unpause, the machine will play you the last couple seconds of your previous scene in your camera viewfinder and then switch itself to RECORD/PLAY. Plan for this delay and your PAUSE EDITS will run smoothly.

One problem with PAUSE EDITS is that you can't leave your VCR in PAUSE very long because the spinning video head wears down the tape in the spot where you PAUSED. Many home VCRs will automatically switch from PAUSE to STOP after a couple minutes to protect the videotape and heads. This limits the amount of time you have to arrange your next scene, plan your next shot, or get your next camera angle.

Some home VCRs allow you to switch the VCR's POWER off (thus stopping the spinning video heads) while remaining in PAUSE. This allows you to take your time setting up between segments. It also saves battery power on portable VCRs. Different manufacturers call this feature "power saver" or "record lock."

Home VCRs and camcorders perform PAUSE EDITS when you pull the camera trigger while recording. A light in the viewfinder tells you when the tape is running and when it is PAUSED. Some models require that you keep the trigger pulled to continue recording. On other models, you pull the trigger and let go to start record-ing, and when you pull the trigger a second time, it PAUSES. Thus, you don't get a tired trigger finger.

Remember that you are using power and wearing down the tape while your VCR is PAUSED between scenes, so make your setups quickly.

Recording Something Over

Sometimes the only choice is to rewind a ways and replace an unsavory or unwanted scene with something else. So you rewind, play, and watch your viewfinder for a good breaking off point and hit PAUSE. Next hit RECORD/PLAY. Unpause when the next satisfactory scene comes up.

You may notice that such edits aren't as pretty as PAUSE EDITS. There may be a few seconds of herringbone lines wiggling through the picture, looking much like Figure 10-3. There may also be a rainbow or smear of colors lasting a few seconds.

This disruption is normal under the circumstances and is not the fault of you or your machine. If you must record over something, two things you can do to minimize the glitch are

1. Use the fastest tape speed for recording.
2. Make your edits on pauses in conversations or lapses in action. Then viewers don't feel as though they're missing something important.

Insert Editing

You've taken great pains to produce a full-length home video version of *Nicholas Nickleby*. Upon playback you discover an error in the middle of your show and wish to delete it. You wish to allow the material before and after the error to remain intact and you just want to replace one segment of the recording with new picture and sound.

FIGURE 10-3 Herringbone glitch as a VCR tries to record over old video

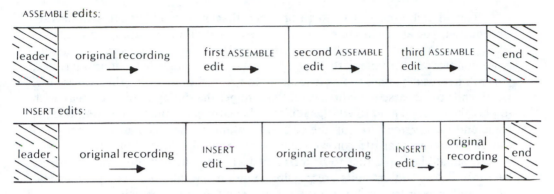

FIGURE 10-4   DIFFERENCE BETWEEN ASSEMBLE and INSERT edits

This is what is called an INSERT EDIT where you exchange an existing scene for a new one the same length. The order of the remaining scenes on the tape doesn't change; they are untouched. The whole production remains the same length, too. You are simply recording a new scene over an old one (erasing it). Figure 10–4 diagrams the concept. Here's the process:

How to insert edit   First you play the tape to find the error. Next you back up the tape a ways searching for a good point to EDIT IN or begin the edit. A point where activity pauses is best. Remember this spot and jot down the tape indicator number so that you can come back to the spot easily.

Now play ahead to find an appropriate place to EDIT OUT; that is, to terminate the new recording and go back to the original presentation. Again, a pause in action and conversation is usually a good place to come back to the old material from your new edit. Once you find the place, note the number from your tape index counter.

Essentially, you will want to record the new passage starting with the first index number and end it with the second number. This means that the performance must be timed out to last *exactly* the length of tape you wish to delete. If the replacement scene is too short, you end up with a long pregnant stare at someone's smiling face while you wait for the index number to come up. You must wait for the number because, if you terminate the edit too soon, you'll end up not deleting the tail end of the segment you want removed. If the replacement scene is too long, you end up erasing your way into the following material that you wanted to keep

This process is not easy. Besides being mechanically difficult, it requires precision timing from the performers and the VCR operator alike. To make things worse, the tape footage counter isn't all that accurate and will throw you off by a second or so anyway. A stopwatch might be helpful if you are handy running two devices at once. Instead of marking the footage for the EDIT-OUT point, mark the elapsed time from the EDIT-IN to the EDIT-OUT point. Then you can let the timepiece be your guide for when to EDIT OUT.

The difficult aspect of INSERT EDITING is that once you have pressed the REC-ORD button, you are flying blind. You can't see what you are erasing; you only see what you are recording. You have no visual cue for when to stop other than your index counter or your timepiece. If you make a mistake and edit too long a passage, you will irrevocably erase the next scene as you record over it. For this reason, it is worthwhile to rehearse the edit several times to get the timing exact. You may wish to play the tape, *pretend* to edit (as it plays), have the performers dress rehearse the scene and then *pretend* to stop the edit. By looking at the scene at this point, you can determine how far off you were and what should be done about it.

It should be noted that to be a *true* INSERT EDIT, the edit must be glitch free. Perfectly "clean" insert edits are possible only on specially designed professional VCRs and camcorders with FLYING ERASE HEADS (described shortly).

Now that the cautions are over, here's how you make the edits happen. To EDIT IN,

1. Play the tape to find the edit place.
2. Pause the tape.
3. Push RECORD.
4. When ready, UNPAUSE, and start acting.
5. Near the end of the replacement passage, get ready to EDIT OUT by placing your finger over the PAUSE button.
6. Watch your index counter or stopwatch, being aware that you may have to delay or hasten your action for a second to accommodate your performers. When the time comes, hit PAUSE, then STOP. You are done.

What does the edit look like? The EDIT IN has squiggly lines, double audio, and some picture breakup as in Figure 10–3. The EDIT OUT will look even worse. The picture will break into snow which may last two to eight seconds (depending upon tape speed). The snow will gradually slide off the screen during this period, followed by a clean picture once again. It looks a lot like what you saw in Figure 10–2.

Some VCR makers have recently improved the INSERT EDITS from their machines. VCRs with FLYING ERASE HEADS and the INSERT EDIT feature don't have a screenful of snow after the edit.

One last reminder about INSERT EDITS: They cannot be used merely to delete something. Something must be recorded in place of the part being removed. The program doesn't become shorter when you make an INSERT EDIT. It just has a new segment substituted for an existing segment.

Audio Dubbing

The AUDIO DUB feature on your VCR allows you to erase an old soundtrack while substituting a new one. Say you wanted to dump your existing soundtrack of Uncle Victor singing Christmas carols and substitute some real music for the entire duration of the tape. The process would go something like this:

1. Connect your new audio source to your VCR as described in Chapter 7. Make a test to assure that your sound quality is good.
2. Find the beginning of Uncle Victor's song. PAUSE your VCR right there.
3. Cue up the music (that is, get it ready to start at the beginning of that song).
4. Press the AUDIO DUB button. The VCR should remain PAUSED.
5. When ready, hit PLAY on the source to start the music playing while UNPAUSING the VCR to start *it* recording.
6. Perhaps fade out the music at the end of the video segment.

If you want to replace only a portion of the soundtrack, you use the same method but with more concern for the timing and placement of the DUB. The process is much like the INSERT EDIT in that you need to determine not only where to *start* the DUB, but you must also know where to *stop* the process lest you erase part of the audio in the following scene. To narrate a particular scene, for instance, the process would go like this:

1. Set up your microphone and do an audio check to assure that everything sounds good.
2. Find the beginning of the scene noting the tape index number.
3. Play the scene perhaps timing it as it plays. At the scene's end, note the tape index or the timing and familiarize yourself with the TV picture at the exact place where you wish to stop.
4. Prepare a narration that runs the alotted time. Practice the narration with the tape playing as a "dress rehearsal."
5. When ready, again find the place where the DUB should start.
6. To start DUBBING, hit PLAY while holding the AUDIO DUB button down. Start the narration. Another, more accurate way to start DUBBING would be to PLAY the tape and press PAUSE when you reach the spot where you wish to start DUBBING. Then press AUDIO DUB, and when ready to start narrating, UNPAUSE and the process will begin.
7. Prepare yourself to switch the VCR to STOP as you approach the appropriate index number.
8. Using the TV screen as a more accurate guide to the exact place to stop, (assuming that the scene offers visual cues you could use as a guide) and praying that the narration will end on time, stop the VCR at the end of the DUBBING sequence.

Don't forget: AUDIO DUBS like INSERT EDITS *replace* material; they don't add or subtract it. The total program always remains the same length. Also, you'll lose the old sound as you record the new sound. There are exceptions to this rule. Some stereo VCRs will replace *one* soundtrack as you DUB, but will leave the other alone allowing you to play back the old sound, the new sound, or a mix of both.

Note that on hi-fi, beta, and VHS VCRs, all AUDIO DUBS are done on the low fidelity linear audio tracks. The hi-fi audio tracks are part of the original picture and can never be changed without recording a new picture. Therefore, what you gain in flexibility and creativity you lose in quality because your new sound is low fi. Remember also that when playing back an AUDIO DUBBED tape, you should switch the VCR to ''listen'' to its linear audio tracks rather than ''listen'' to its unchanged hi-fi track.

Sound-on-sound   Some stereo VCRs will allow you to record new sound on one channel while leaving the other channel untouched. Hi-fi VCRs always do this because they don't erase their hi-fi sound when you make an AUDIO DUB.

This allows you to carry out a neat trick called SOUND-ON-SOUND or OVERDUB-BING. It allows you to take the sound already on your tape, mix it with new sound, and record the final result back on your tape.

Say you finished making your original recording using the lo fi channels 1 and 2 for your audio. They contain essentially the same information. You now wish to add narration and/or music to the original sound in just the proper proportions to make the finished product. To do this, you will need to, for instance, play back the channel 1 audio, mix it with the music and/or narration sources and record this combination on channel 2 through the VCR's AUDIO DUB. The process goes like this:

1. Connect the VCP's audio channel 1 output to an input of an audio mixer.
2. Also connect your music and narration sources to the mixer.
3. Make an audio level check from all three sources.
4. Connect the mixer's LINE OUT to the VCR's channel 2 AUX IN.
5. By putting channel 2 *only* in the AUDIO DUB mode, get an audio check on the VCR using a sample signal from the mixer.
6. When ready, switch the VCR to PLAY while pressing the AUDIO 2 DUB button.
7. The old song along with the music and narration will all go into the mixer where you can fade, balance, and adjust them as desired. This combination of sounds gets recorded onto track 2 of your videotape. If a mistake is made, go back and repeat the process; the track 1 audio is still intact, while the linear track 2 audio will automatically be erased as you record over it the next time. Figure 10–5 diagrams the connection.

Some VCRs won't allow you to record on one track while playing the other. Maybe they have one AUDIO DUB button but no way to distinguish which track gets recorded (they both will). The solution here is to use two VCRs. Essentially you copy the tape from one VCR to another using a connection like Figure 9–2. Only you run the audio from the VCR, into a mixer, along with your narration or music. The mixer then feeds the AUDIO IN on the VCR. As the VCP plays, the VCR records the picture and the new sound mix.

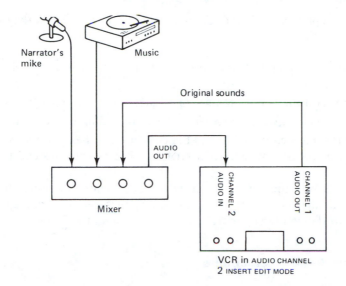

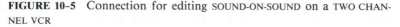

FIGURE 10-5 Connection for editing SOUND-ON-SOUND on a TWO CHAN-NEL VCR

Video-Only Inserts

Some of the better VCRs will allow you to INSERT a video segment while leaving the old audio untouched. This is called a VIDEO DUB or a VIDEO-ONLY INSERT.

Say you were recording your daughter's wedding ceremony. She's walking down the aisle to strains of "Here Comes the Bride" and while you are walking backward, eyes intent on your viewfinder, you stumble into one of the altar flower arrangements. (What are those dumb things doing in the way anyhow?) Like a pro, you keep on shooting but you'd like to substitute something else for that spinning shot of the church ceiling blurring to a close-up of rose stems scattered across the carpet. Maybe a brief shot of the organist playing "Here Comes the Bride" would do the trick. Here's how you'd go about replacing the bad scene:

1. After the ceremony is over, offer the organist $10 to sit down at the organ again and pretend to play "Here Comes the Bride" (remember you are only replacing video; the old sound of the song remains on the tape).
2. Rewind and play the tape up to the accident point and take note of the index number.
3. Play further and find out where the picture gets good again. Take note of the index number.

At this point, you wish to "dress rehearse" the edit, especially if the action you're substituting needs to finish within a certain time. As in the case of the AUDIO

DUB, you would pretend to do the edit and would watch to see how the timing comes out. Now to continue for real:

4. Rewind the tape and play it up to the EDIT IN point (the first index number you noted earlier). Hit PAUSE.
5. Press VIDEO DUB, VIDEO INSERT, or whatever buttons engage this feature.
6. Start the organist, then UNPAUSE to begin recording him or her.
7. Watch the index counter for the EDIT OUT point. When you reach it, terminate the edit by pressing PAUSE, then STOP or whatever buttons end the INSERT.

When you view the tape you will see the bride marching down the aisle, then catch a view of the organist for a moment, and then see the bride again. All this will happen to the uninterrupted tune of "Here Comes the Bride."

Editing from Another Videotape

The problem with ASSEMBLE editing is that everything must be done in sequence. You progress through your shots in chronological order unable to shoot the end scene first, then shoot all the airplane shots, then go to all the bedroom scenes. If you shoot all the similar scenes in one sitting (or lying, if there are bedroom scenes), you could save a lot of running around locating your performers, setting up lights, and so forth.

For this reason, most professional teleproducers shoot RAW FOOTAGE or as the film industry calls them RUSHES. These are recordings made (on separate tapes, usually) at different locations, at different times, sometimes by different people. These tapes are brought back to the videotape editor who assembles the best scenes together to make a final tape. One nice thing about shooting RAW FOOTAGE rather than the real thing is that you can take chances shooting scenes that might not work out in the final production. If they don't, well, just don't use them; you are not stuck with them. Also, you can shoot the same scene over and over, perhaps from different angles until you get it right. Afterwards, you can select the best of the RUSHES to incorporate into your final production.

How to do it   The mechanical process of editing from another videotape is the same as for copying a tape, only you are doing little pieces at a time rather than a whole tape. The procedure would go something like this:

1. Connect your MASTER and SLAVE VCRs for copying a videotape.
2. Play your SLAVE up to where you want the edit to begin, hit PAUSE, then press RECORD/PLAY.
3. Play your MASTER up to where the scene to be copied begins and hit PAUSE about five seconds before that point.

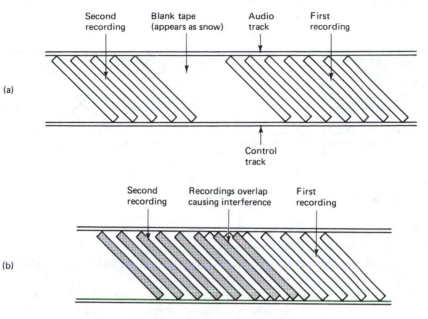

FIGURE 10-6 How a STOP EDIT is recorded on the tape

4. Take a deep breath. Then, UNPAUSE the MASTER player. Immediately position your finger over the SLAVE'S PAUSE button.

5. Two seconds before you see the desired scene come up, UNPAUSE the SLAVE.

6. Hopefully, the SLAVE VCR will kick into action just as the MASTER tape begins playing the desired scene.

7. When the scene ends, PAUSE the SLAVE.

8. If it won't take you long to set up the next scene, just leave the SLAVE in PAUSE.

9. Repeat steps 3 through 7 for each successive edit.

HOW VCRS EDIT

Nonediting VCRs

Figure 10–6a shows what happens on a tape when you perform a STOP EDIT. Because the tape doesn't rethread to exactly the same point where you left off, there may be a space of unrecorded tape between the two scenes. This will appear as snow. When they rethread themselves, some machines back up the tape causing the new recording to be laid over the tail end of the old one as shown in Figure 10–6b. Here the old and new recordings interfere with each other causing the effect shown in Figure 10–3.

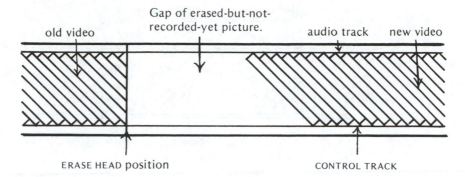

old video   Gap of erased-but-not-recorded-yet picture.   audio track   new video

ERASE HEAD position   CONTROL TRACK

FIGURE 10–7 Gap of unrecorded tape left at end of home-style INSERT edit.

When you replace a segment in the middle of a recording (INSERT edit), the end of your edit looks like Figure 10–7. While the VCR is recording, its ERASE HEAD is erasing old pictures and sound from the tape several inches upstream from the video and audio record heads as was shown back in Figure 3–25. When you stop the edit, the ERASE HEAD has erased some tape which the record head hasn't caught up to. This gap of erased tape appears as snow when played back. The snow slides off the screen as the spinning video head passes further into the old video as was shown in Figure 10–2.

Wouldn't it be nice if when you finished your INSERT edit there wasn't any gap of snow? One way to eliminate this gap would be to have the ERASE HEAD stop erasing a few seconds before the end of the edit. This way, the old video would "catch up" to the new video. There might be some overlap between the old and new video causing the color moire and squiggly lines described earlier, but even *this* is nicer than the snow. Some luxury home VCRs have an INSERT EDIT function which does exactly this. When you press the END INSERT button, the VCR turns off its ERASE HEAD, keeps on recording for a couple seconds, and then stops.

PAUSE edits diagrammed in Figure 10–8 are much neater. If the tape shifts a little while it's in PAUSE, it may leave a tiny extra gap between the video from scene 1 and the video from scene 2. This will cause a minor glitch. If the tape backs up a little during PAUSE, one or two video tracks may overlap also causing a brief glitch.

Electronic Editing VCRs

Electronic editing encompasses an assortment of VCRs which at a push of a button will do what is necessary to make a "clean" edit (unlike the edits discussed up to now). How clean is "clean"? As clean as you can afford to buy. The least expensive VCRs make slightly ragged edits; the most expensive ones make perfect edits every time. It may be useful to know a little about how a VCR edits in order to select an editor and to recognize problems with your present editor.

The object is to make a smooth, clear edit. For this, four requirements must be met:

1. The tape must be erased clean as it approaches the record head.
2. The CONTROL TRACK must be continuous and have no interruptions.
3. The switchover must occur invisibly between video pictures.
4. The sync must remain continuous without any abberations.

The first requirement (clean erasing) is performed by a FLYING ERASE HEAD. It's not a bird and not a plane; it's a super idea. Attached to the spinning video head is a tiny ERASE HEAD, just ahead of it. When the EDIT button is pressed, the FLYING ERASE HEAD starts erasing the tape directly before the spinning record head gets to it. Figure 10-9 diagrams the arrangement. Incidentally, many 8mm camcorders come with FLYING ERASE HEADS built in.

The second requirement—continuous CONTROL TRACK—must be met by all video editors. The CONTROL TRACK is a series of pulses recorded on the tape while the VCR is recording video. During playback these pulses guide the tape speed, tracking, and the timing of the video signal. Video recordings are fine when the tape is moving, but when the tape stops, the video and CONTROL TRACK signals become garbled. For this reason, editing VCRs are designed to perform the actual edit while the tape is still moving. Since the tape doesn't have to stop, start, and then pick up speed again, the timing of the CONTROL PULSES doesn't get messed up.

Professional editing video recorders will BACKSPACE the tape five seconds to get this "running start" before they perform an edit. This gives plenty of time for

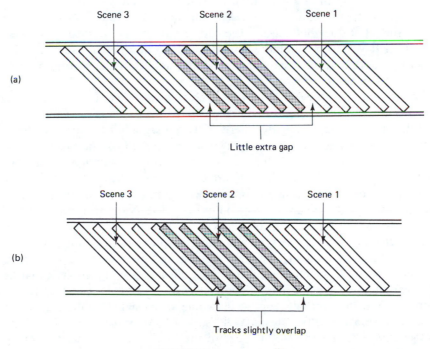

FIGURE 10-8 PAUSE edit

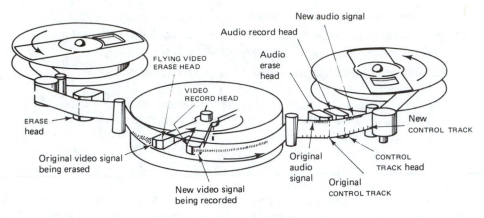

New audio signal

Audio record head

FLYING VIDEO
ERASE HEAD

Audio
erase
head

VIDEO
RECORD HEAD

New
CONTROL TRACK

ERASE
head

Original video signal
being erased

Original
audio
signal

New video signal
being recorded

CONTROL
TRACK head

Original
CONTROL TRACK

FIGURE 10-9 FLYING ERASE HEAD

the tape speed and machine to stabilize and create new CONTROL TRACK pulses right in step with the old ones.

The third requirement—switchover between pictures—separates the good editors from the excellent ones. Say you start playing a tape in preparation for an edit. When you press the EDIT button, the heads instantly start recording. What if the video heads are right in the midst of playing back a picture? That picture will be interrupted with a brand new one if you didn't happen to press the EDIT button at precisely the moment in between pictures. You get edits anywhere, right out there on the screen where you can see them. With the more elaborate VERTICAL INTERVAL EDITORS, the VCR does not execute the edit exactly at the moment you press the EDIT button. It waits a few hundredths of a second and performs the edit during the VERTICAL INTERVAL, that part of the picture just below the bottom of your TV screen where you can't see it.

Continuous sync, the fourth requirement, is the last piece to the editing puzzle. You would like to edit during the VERTICAL INTERVAL, that split second when the image is invisible to the viewer. But there are two images to be considered here: the old one on the tape and the new one you're about to record. The VERTICAL INTERVAL for one might not come at the exact same time as the VERTICAL INTERVAL for the other. So that the VCR and TV picture do not miss a beat when you edit from the existing taped rhythm to the new incoming rhythm, something must be done to match the two up. If we can get both VERTICAL INTERVALS to occur at the same time, we can edit during the invisible parts of *both* pictures. The resulting edit will look super clean as long as the sync and CONTROL PULSES flow smoothly.

To get the sync to match up, the VCR must "listen" to the new incoming video signal and try to synchronize it to the signals it is playing. A VCR that listens to an incoming signal while it is playing its own picture is called EXTERNALLY LOCKED. A VCR that doesn't react to incoming video signals while it is playing is called INTERNALLY LOCKED. When a VCR is EXTERNALLY LOCKED, a feature called CAPSTAN SERVO changes the motor speed of the VCR a little so that the tape plays faster or slower until its VERTICAL INTERVALS and CONTROL PULSES match up to the sync of the incoming video.

In short, electronic editing VCRs, to perform their magic, need

1. FLYING ERASE HEADS to clear the tape just before it's recorded.
2. BACKSPACING to allow a recording to begin while the tape is moving (to preserve a steady CONTROL TRACK rhythm).
3. VERTICAL INTERVAL EDITING to perform the edit "off screen."
4. EXTERNAL LOCK so that the VCR will synchronize the timing of the pictures it's playing with the timing of the pictures it's about to record.

In short, depending upon the kind of VCR you have, you can make perfectly clean, glitchless edits or you can make ragged, glitchy edits. You have to coordinate your editing techniques with the kind of machine you are using in order to get best results. If using the least expensive home VCRs and camcorders, you may wish to assemble your show using PAUSE edits only. If you have a deluxe VCR or camcorder with FLYING ERASE HEADS, you could either assemble your program with PAUSE edits or do INSERTS (changing parts of your program in the middle after it has already been recorded). The better VCRs also allow you to INSERT new video leaving the old sound untouched or to INSERT new audio without touching the old video. More on this in a moment as we study how to use professional editing VCRs.

USING PROFESSIONAL EDITING VCRS

If you are going to do video recording for a business, then you will probably buy or rent professional editing VCRs and editor controllers.

Professional editing VCRs generally work at the fastest tape speed (the two-hour VHS SP mode, for instance) and will often not play tapes recorded at the slower speeds. Think about this compatibility when you make those original tapes, and record them always at your VCR's fastest speed.

Another thing to remember when recording RAW FOOTAGE for later editing: Always start your camcorder or VCR about eight seconds before your scene begins. Later on, when the editor tries to BACKSPACE your tape, there will be good video on it for the editor to "lock on" to.

An Important Technical Difference between Insert and Assemble Edits

When you ASSEMBLE edit, the VCR records the picture, sound, sync, and CONTROL TRACK PULSES. The VCR listens to the incoming video and produces the CONTROL TRACK pulses in step with the incoming vertical sync pulses. The CONTROL TRACK will later help the VCR play the tape at exactly the right speed; they are like a "drumbeat" which keeps the tape heads revolving precisely over the magnetic recorded paths on the tape.

You record a new CONTROL TRACK when you record a blank tape. You create a CONTROL TRACK when you ASSEMBLE edit a tape. If you make bad ASSEMBLE edits, you will create a flawed CONTROL TRACK and your tape will play back with a glitch. If you copy a videocassette or ASSEMBLE edit parts from another videocassette which has a glitch, it will ruin the CONTROL TRACK you are recording on your VCR.

INSERT editing, on the other hand, doesn't create CONTROL TRACK pulses. These pulses have to be laid down ahead of time. You could do this, for instance, by recording a tape of *black* by capping your camera lens and recording *nothing* on the tape. When INSERT editing, the VCR only records new picture, new sound, or both, but it never touches the existing CONTROL TRACK.

For this reason, you cannot INSERT EDIT on blank tape. INSERT EDITS only make video and/or audio, and not a CONTROL TRACK. Since there is no CONTROL TRACK on a blank tape, your insert edits won't work. There is also a second reason why you cannot INSERT EDIT on a blank tape. The EDITOR CONTROLLER keeps track of where you are on the tape by counting CONTROL TRACK PULSES and turning them into the time display on your EDITOR control panel. Without these pulses, the editor can't keep track of where it is or how far it has backed up, or where it should place an edit.

If a CONTROL TRACK is laid down correctly ahead of time, it will remain good, no matter what pictures you INSERT EDIT on the tape. Bad edits and bad sync won't hurt the CONTROL TRACK (they won't made good pictures, but at least they won't hurt the CONTROL TRACK). If you discover that you've INSERT EDITED a glitch, you merely need to perform the edit over, using a more stable signal.

You are more likely to get a perfect CONTROL TRACK throughout your tape if you have recorded it from beginning to end using your best equipment. Now you can trust your CONTROL TRACK. If instead you ASSEMBLE EDIT your production, the following hungry gremlins may sneak up and bite you:

1. Your portable VCR may have a weak battery.
2. Nearby electrical interference may mess up your sync.
3. If you move your portable VCR while it is running, gyroscopic aberrations in the spinning video head will mess up your video.
4. Humidity in the field may make the insides of your portable VCR sticky.
5. You make a bad (glitchy) ASSEMBLE EDIT while editing your tape, but don't notice it until you finish editing your entire tape. Sometimes in the process of editing you get so involved in the program that you forget to keep a sharp eye on the technical quality of every edit. That bad ASSEMBLE EDIT will create a bad CONTROL TRACK.
6. You ASSEMBLE EDIT a piece from another videotape that had a minor flaw in its playback speed or an unseen glitch in its sync. The imperfect material from the other tape all gets recorded onto your edited tape along with its imperfect CONTROL TRACK pulses.

Now that you see the glitch, what can you do about it? The answer is nothing. You can't just redo that one edit on the tape. If you try to use the INSERT mode to cover the bad edit, it won't help. It will change the video but won't change the defective CONTROL TRACK. If you try to make a new ASSEMBLE EDIT over the old one, starting the edit a few frames earlier so that the bad edit is totally erased, you will have corrected the defective edit at the beginning of that scene, but now, how do you stop the edit? With the VCR in the ASSEMBLE mode, it cannot make a clean EDIT OUT. Only INSERT EDITS can both EDIT IN and EDIT OUT. In other words, you get a nice EDIT IN, but you get a ragged edit at the end of the scene. Now, *that* edit has to be corrected. The only way to fix it is to redo the next scene and so it goes to the end of your tape.

In conclusion, it is best to first create a BLACKED tape under reliable conditions and later INSERT EDIT your scenes onto it. You can still perform your edits in order as if you were ASSEMBLE EDITING. You just happen to be doing them in the INSERT MODE.

Creating a Blacked Tape

INSERT edits can only be made over existing video and CONTROL TRACK. Although you could record your edits over old "Wheel of Fortune" reruns, it is generally neater to prepare (and stockpile) a number of BLACKED tapes.

A BLACKED tape is simply a tape recorded from beginning to end (or at least a little longer than your intended editing tape will be) with a stable, glitch-free CON-

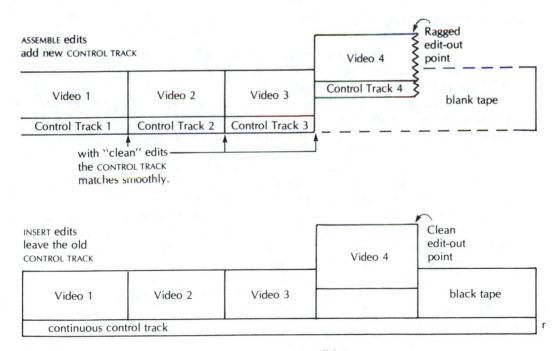

ASSEMBLE VS INSERT editing

TROL TRACK. You make such a CONTROL TRACK by feeding stable video (and sync) to your VCR, switching it to the ASSEMBLE or NORMAL mode, pressing RECORD/PLAY, and letting the machine do the rest.

Where do you get a stable video signal? At Poverty Productions, Inc. you would probably connect a camera to your VCR and let it record the image. It doesn't matter what the image is. In keeping with the concept of BLACKED master, you could cap the lens.

Overcoming the Murphy Factor while Editing

Murphy's First Law, "Anything that *can* go wrong *will* go wrong . . . and at the worst possible time" applies exquisitely to video editing. Murphy keeps a nest of gremlins behind every editing console. Here's how to Murphy-proof your VCRs when editing two tapes together:

1. Put adhesive tape (or a bandage or something) over the RECORD button of your *playback* VCR. Pushing that button by mistake could wipe out your original tape.
2. Double check your editing mode. Don't get so wrapped up in what you are doing that you forget to *make sure that the MODE SELECTOR is in the proper position*. Untold numbers of tapes have been ruined by a selector in the ASSEMBLE position when an INSERT was desired. Hours of audio tracks have been wiped out by an INSERT when a VIDEO-ONLY INSERT was called for.

Using Editor Controllers

An EDITOR CONTROLLER or AUTOMATIC BACKSPACER is an electronic device that is wired to the editing VCR and VCP and controls the two during an edit. Figure 10–10 shows how one may be connected.

Most EDITOR CONTROLLERS have digital readouts for the VCP and VCR showing exactly where you are on the tape in hours, minutes, seconds, and frames (thirtieths of a second). They create this TIME CODE by electronically counting the CONTROL TRACK PULSES on the tape as it plays.

When you load a tape into the VCP and start it playing from the beginning, you should set the EDITOR CONTROLLER's time code readout to 00:00:00:00. Do the same for the VCR. This marks the beginning of both tapes.

Using this device, you can determine that a particular scene starts at zero hours, 14 minutes, 32 seconds, and 12 frames from the beginning of the tape. These TIME CODE numbers are helpful for locating scenes or for logging events on a videotape for later editing. You could, for instance,

1. List the TIME CODE numbers of the various scenes on the tape.
2. Use those numbers to locate the first scene you wanted to edit.
3. Program the controller to perform the edit using those numbers.

Method 1:

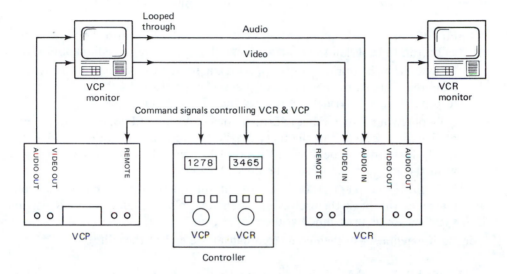

Method 2:

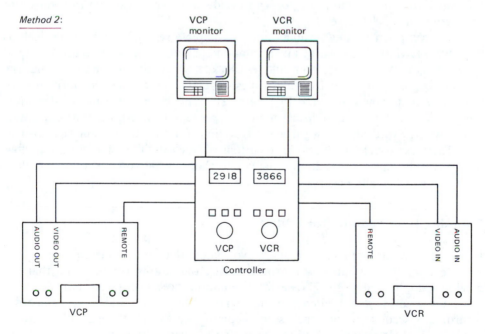

FIGURE 10-10   Connection of an EDITOR CONTROLLER

On the other hand, it is also possible to edit tapes together without paying any attention to the TIME CODE numbers. The process might go like this:

1. Find the desired edit point on the VCR "by eye." Next push the VCR's EDIT IN button to program the CONTROLLER telling it where the edit should start.

2. Browse through your RAW CAMERA FOOTAGE to find the scene you wish to take from the VCP. At the beginning of that scene, press the VCP's EDIT IN button to program the CONTROLLER to start the edit with this scene.

3. Now play your RAW CAMERA FOOTAGE on the VCP until you come to the end of that first scene. Stop the tape, maybe backing it up a little or moving it slowly forward (a process called JOGGING) to find the *exact* place where you want the edit to finish. Press the EDIT OUT button.

4. Now press the EXECUTE or PERFORM button on the CONTROLLER and both machines will back themselves up, then start playing, and the VCR will be switched to the EDIT mode at the proper time.

5. Both machines will then come to a halt at the end of the edit.

Some EDITOR CONTROLLERS allow you to rehearse an edit, once the edit points are programmed. In this case, instead of pressing EXECUTE, you press PREVIEW and the machines will go through the motions without actually performing the edit. You can see what the edit would look like by viewing a TV monitor connected to the CONTROLLER as shown in Figure 10–10, method 2. Once you have previewed how the edit looks on the monitor, you can decide whether to execute the edit or to reprogram the edit differently.

EDITOR CONTROLLERS usually have a complete set of VCR controls such as RECORD, PLAY, FAST FORWARD, REWIND, and PAUSE on them for both the VCR and VCP. Many also have a SHUTTLE SPEED CONTROL which allows you to run the tape forward or backward at twice, three times, or maybe nine times the normal speed while viewing the picture on the TV screen. The SHUTTLE CONTROL may also allow you to play the tape at half speed or slower, perhaps JOGGING the tape one frame at a time, forward or backward while searching for the exact point you wish to edit. The CONTROLLER may also have buttons for ASSEMBLE, INSERT VIDEO, INSERT AUDIO 1, and INSERT AUDIO 2, allowing you to choose what you are going to replace when the edit actually occurs.

Shooting Raw Footage for Editing

If you plan to edit your RAW FOOTAGE, you know that the editing equipment will have to BACKSPACE your RAW FOOTAGE during the editing process, and that the machines don't want to see glitches while counting CONTROL TRACK PULSES. Thus it behooves you to avoid glitches at the beginning of scenes. Start your camcorder recording 8 seconds before each scene actually begins. This "preroll" insures a smooth, glitchfree signal before the beginning of every scene.

EXAMPLE OF AN EDIT

To make the editing process more clear, let's imagine ourselves performing an edit of someone telling the history of an old house. Imagine that we went out to visit the town octogenarian and videotaped him for one-half hour describing the things that happened when he was a boy living in the town's oldest historical house. Say we also made a tape showing the exterior of the old house from different angles. Say we also read the previous section of this book and made a BLACKED master tape on which to edit.

We would take these to our editing console and place the BLACKED MASTER in the VCR and the first tape of the octogenarian in the VCP. After checking video levels, tracking, and setting our recording mode to VIDEO AND AUDIO INSERT, we are ready to go. We plan to edit the old man's story down to three minutes.

1. Let the VCR play the BLACKED tape for about 30 seconds and park the tape there. This will leave a LEADER before the program begins and also guarantees that there is room for the VCR to BACKSPACE. (It also leaves space for you to insert a quickie title later, if you want.) Press the EDIT IN button on the VCR.

2. Play the VCP until you come to the spot where the old man's story starts to get interesting. Back up the tape and play it a couple of times to be sure you have found a good place to EDIT IN. Find a pause between sentences and at that spot, press the EDIT IN button on the VCP.

3. Now play the VCP from this point until the story begins to go astray. Find a good pause in conversation and mark that spot as the EDIT OUT point on the VCP.

4. You could now PREVIEW the edit or PERFORM the edit depending upon your confidence in how you think it will look.

5. Pressing PERFORM, the VCR and VCP will BACKSPACE and perform the edit and park themselves at the end of the scene.

6. You would then play the VCP, skipping trivial and unwanted material, hunting for a few more good lines that tell the story. When you find them, start the process again by marking the EDIT IN point on the VCP.

7. As before, play the VCP until you find the man's last good sentence and mark that as the EDIT OUT point.

8. Some VCRs will do this automatically, but you can also do it manually: Find the EDIT-OUT point from the last scene *on the VCR* and mark that as the new EDIT-IN point. When in doubt, you can check or change the EDIT-IN point on the VCR by slowly running it backwards and, when you come to the tail end of the previous scene, pause the tape just a couple of frames before the end of the scene. Mark this as the new EDIT-IN point. You chose to start the new EDIT IN a couple of frames before the end of the last scene to guarantee that you didn't accidentally run past the end of the previous scene leaving a momentary flash of black before the following scene began. This tiny overlap

isn't absolutely necessary, it's just insurance and will not make a visible difference to the action on the tape.

9. As before, you can preview the upcoming edit or execute it.

10. Because we have jumped abruptly from one part of the man's story to another, his head will snap from one position to another, a phenomenon called by various names just as CAMERA MAGIC, JUMP CUT, or SNAP CUT. This kind of edit makes his story flow nicely, but the picture betrays the fact that you have been editing. We will now endeavor to hide this JUMP CUT.

11. Switch the VCR to the VIDEO ONLY INSERT mode.

12. Back the VCR up to maybe one second before the tail end of your first edit. Mark this as an EDIT-IN point.

13. Eject the VCP's cassette of the man's speech and insert the cassette showing the house he is talking about.

14. Now play that cassette looking for an excellent shot of the house, something that goes along with his story at that point. The scene should be about five seconds long.

15. When you find this good shot, mark the EDIT-IN point on the VCP.

Getting organized

TABLE 10–1   SHOT SHEET FOR LOGGING "TAKES"

SHOT SHEET   Cassette #3
Project: Dining Out   Date: 12/7/89

Take	Counter	Action	Comments
1	0–23	Leader	NG
2	24–44	Testing	NG
3	45–65	CU sandwich hits floor	Excellent
4	66–88	CU sandwich hits floor	Dark
5	89–100	CU sandwich hits floor	OK
6	101–152	MS sandwich hits floor	Fuzzy
7	153–208	Al sits at table	OK
8	209–250	Al sits at table	Glitch
•	•	•	•
•	•	•	•
•	•	•	•

16. Play the VCP looking for a good EDIT-OUT point two to five seconds later and mark that. What you are doing now is creating a CUTAWAY, where the scene keeps the same sound of the man talking (no one hears the fact that you edited out some sentences) while the viewers see a shot of the house the man is describing.

17. By previewing the edit, you can see whether the result is aesthetically pleasing. If it is, press EXECUTE and the VCRs will back themselves up and do their thing.

18. When you later view the tape, you will see the man speaking, then you'll see the house the man is talking about, and then you'll see the man again as he continues to speak, not skipping a beat.

This exercise was a very short and simple example of how to *layer* edits together. A normal program might have dozens or hundreds of these edits, some of them being audio-plus-video, some of them being CUTAWAYS, and some of them being AUDIO DUBS to fill in where there is picture and no sound.

GETTING ORGANIZED

The Oregon loggers used to say, "Take time to sharpen the saw." The advice applies to video as well. Before you start, decide how your story will unfold and determine the scenes necessary to tell the story (more on this in Chapter 11). On a piece of paper, list the shots you want to take and bring the paper with you to make sure you don't skip any necessary shots. Then go shoot your RAW CAMERA FOOTAGE.

View all your RAW FOOTAGE and log it with your VCR's tape index numbers or your editor's time code numbers as shown in Table 10–1. In this example, NG stands for "no good," CU for "close-up," and MS for "medium shot." This sheet

TABLE 10–2 EDITING SHEET OR EDITING DECISION LIST FOR ORGANIZING A SEQUENCE OF SCENES

EDITING SHEET   Cassette #27
Project: Dining Out   Date: 12/15/89

Segment	Action	Cassette	Edit In	Edit Out
1	Intro	Camera	275	301
2	Boy meets girl	5	870	880
3	Invites her to dinner	5	40	65
4	Takes her to restaurant	1	153	208
5	Sits at table	3	159	175
6	Orders jelly sandwich	2	422	435
7	Sandwich arrives	2	501	503
8	Boy spills sandwich	2	61	63
9	Sandwich hits floor	3	70	75
10	Girl leaves	1	93	94
11	Boy stunned	1		
12	End	Camera		

will make it easy to find quickly the desired "take" on the tape when you get around to editing this scene into your final production.

SHOT SHEETS are especially helpful when you record your scenes in January but don't edit them until August.

Plan your editing strategy using an EDITING SHEET such as that shown in Table 10–2. You lay out the sequence of scenes you wish to assemble, enter the counter numbers of these scenes from your SHOT SHEETS, and you are ready to edit.

Notice that the beginning and end titles can be shot "live" with a camera (as could other scenes) and be included along with taped scenes.

If your editing equipment is very simple or your tape index is inaccurate, you may decide to play the edit sequence several times rehearsing it, and then perform the edit manually using the action in the scene as a guide. If your equipment is advanced, you may be able to "edit by the numbers," selecting the scenes by their TIME CODE numbers and then having the machine execute the edits on the numbers you have selected. If you don't like how the edits are coming out, you can always pick new numbers and redo the edits.

EDITING SOUND OR PICTURE FIRST

Sometimes it is easier to put all the visual scenes together and then go back and DUB in the sound (assuming lip synchronization is not required). This method, called a VOICEOVER, works best when you find it hard to judge (or don't wish to take the time to calculate) how long each scene will be, and when you don't wish to adjust any of the visual scenes to make them fit the sound. So you first make a "silent movie" and then go back to DUB in music, narration, or nothing (leaving the original soundtrack intact). With this method, the picture is most important and the sound is a slave to the visual timing. The narrator reads, watches, pauses, reads again; and if the scene is too short for the narrator's text for the scene, the narrator's script must be abbreviated to fit the scene. During gaps in narration, light music or background sounds may be used to fill in the silence.

Sometimes it may be necessary to have lip synchronization, perhaps, for example, as a process is explained by a factory worker at his machine. This case calls for a combination of editing techniques.

1. You may wish to shoot the first sequence in "silent movie" style. It may show the titles, an exterior shot of the factory, plus a wide interior shot of the equipment as we dolly in toward the lathe. Once these scenes have been edited on the tape, we can go back and DUB IN music plus the narrator's voiceover introducing the program.

2. The next sequence shows the factory worker describing how to program the computer which runs the lathe. For this scene, we record both picture and sound together and edit them both into our finished tape.

3. As the lathe goes to work, we zoom in, hearing its "live" sound in the background. As the next scene is edited into the program, we can fade out the background sound and fade up the narrator's voice as he/she describes the dangers of getting one's shirt caught in the spinning lathe.

   Thus the scenes went: "silent movie" with DUBBED IN narrator, followed by live sound, followed by combination live background mixed with DUBBED narration.

One of the great strengths of AUDIO DUBBING is its ability to tie scenes together. A montage of unrelated pictures all become related by a single strain of music, sound effect, or conversation.

Editing scenes with divergent sound levels can be smoothed with an OVERDUB. Say you shoot a birthday party. The long shot of the whole gang has a lot of kids screaming in the background. The close-up of the cake's candles being blown out is fairly quiet. The close-ups of someone eating cake has many voices in the background. The visual scenes here are fine, but the disparate sound levels are jarring. To smooth this out, these shots should have the same continuous sound in the background.

This sound could come from the VCR's original soundtrack during part of the party (as long as the VCR ran continuously long enough to get an adequate stretch of sound—this is called a SOUND BITE) or it could have been made by a separate audiocassette recorder. Except where important words are spoken and must be heard synchronously with the lips speaking them (LIP SYNC) you simply DUB your prerecorded background sound onto your edited tape to create a smooth din of authentic party noise. No one may ever notice that the cacophony of sound doesn't exactly match the bedlam of visual activity.

Many of the TV ads that you see have had their audio DUBBED. Sometimes it is because the best-looking models don't have the best voices or because better sound control is available with someone standing exactly one foot in front of a mike in a sound studio rather than moving around an echoey bathroom (sounds of a running shower can be added later). Although you would have difficulty performing an exact LIP SYNC like the pros, you can often use these techniques in many scenes where a close, well-aimed mike is impossible. Redoing the audio later permits you to remove unwanted sound effects (such as jet planes in an old time Western or the roar of electric fans in your "windy" scene). In the studio, you get only the sounds you want and while you are at it, perhaps you can *add* a few sounds of your own for authenticity (clippity clop in your Western, thunder and gale winds in your storm scene).

After all this buildup, it is only fair to mention that editing audio on a VCR is rather cumbersome. *Depending on your machine,* the beginning of a DUB may have the new sound recorded on top of the old (and not-yet-erased) sound for a moment. The end of the DUB may be followed by a few moments of silence as the erased-but-not-yet-recorded tape comes around. For this reason, avoid complicated DUBBING. Never try to delete just a word or two. Try to start and finish the AUDIO DUB during pauses in conversation. Experiment to see what your machine will do.

Don't forget, AUDIO DUBS like INSERT EDITS, *replace* material. You don't add or subtract it. The total program always remains the same length. Also, with a true AUDIO DUB, you lose the old sound as you record the new sound. Only if you are copying from one tape to another or recording your new sound on one channel while leaving the old sound on the other channel can you preserve your original sound in case you've made a mistake.

There are times when the soundtrack carries the main theme of your tape. Here, the visuals are enslaved by the timing of the audio. Such is the case when you have a prerecorded song and you wish to have the visuals coincide with the melody or change to the beat of the music. You can't change the music to fit the visuals; rather the visuals must be stretched or condensed to fit the song.

The first step is to lay down the soundtrack while recording "black." Next, you make VIDEO INSERT ONLY edits for all the visuals. Here is an example.

Using a single camera, you record a dance number from beginning to end, taking care to feed your VCR good sound from whatever music source is used. Next, you arrange for the dancers to repeat portions of the dance for you. Arrange your tape machine so that it will play back the music which it recorded earlier, for the performers to dance to. Change your camera angle to catch a particular move. Back up the tape a half-minute or so, play it, and follow the action with your new camera angle. Have an assistant hit the VIDEO INSERT button on the VCR to cut to a close-up of the desired move. End the insert when the move is over. When the tape is viewed, it will look as though two cameras were used—one for long shots and the other for the close-ups. This process can be repeated several times for further close-ups until the dancers get tired of repeating the performance and drill a pirouette into the top of your VCR.

A similar technique is useful for music videos. The song may be recorded in a sound studio and copied onto the soundtrack of a BLACKED tape. The musicians are then gathered in the TV studio under proper lighting with fog props and video effects at hand. Listening to their soundtrack play from your tape, they LIP SYNC and perform to the music they hear. It is even possible to take the performance outdoors, into the street, or underwater, just as long as the performers can hear the sound on your tape and act in rhythm with it.

Once you get used to editing both ways (video first, sound later or sound first, video later), you'll discover at your disposal the power to have almost anything come out the way you want. Your flexibility is almost limitless.

For another example, a reporter could memorize the first and last paragraphs of her story and read the rest. The entire report is shot at the scene with the reporter holding a microphone and speaking to the camera. With action buzzing in the background, everything looks candid and unscripted. All the places where the reporter reads from her notes get replaced with VIDEO INSERT edits of the action, close-ups, and so on. The same voice carries through from beginning to end and since the viewer never saw the reporter refer to her notes, it appears that this very gifted reporter was able to give the entire report candidly and directly to you, the viewer.

Another example of using a combination of editing methods is employed in places where you are unable to shoot everything you want at a particular time. Say you are trying to show how preschoolers in a day care center deal with some educational toys. With little trouble, you shoot the kids playing in the room, but every time you get in range of the close-up action, the little buggers stop what they are doing and look up at you. So you try sneaking up on them and you happen to catch a few absorbed in their play. But in the few moments before you're noticed, you can't get focused. The lighting is poor for close-ups; the kids move the toys around so fast that you can't get a tight close-up on important details. Solution to the problem:

1. Assemble with sound as many of the various medium and long shots as possible of the children playing with the toys.

2. Later, either at the TV studio or at the day care center, after the children have gone home, you set up the toys again. This time you light the toys perfectly. Choose your shots carefully. This time you can zoom in tightly on every detail. Also, you hire one of the youngsters to lend his or her hands to move or manipulate something in the picture. These carefully prepared scenes all get included as VIDEO INSERT ONLY sequences scattered amongst the medium and long shots recorded in step 1. (As a good documentarian, I hope that you will create INSERTS which represent what really happened in the day care center.)

3. Next, add narration and explanation by playing the first audio channel into a mixer and combining that sound with a narrator and music, and recording the result onto the second audio channel. The original background sounds of the children can play at full volume except where brief explanations are needed. At those times, the background is reduced and the narrator speaks. Sequences (recorded in step 1) of day care center personnel or children showing and explaining something would certainly have the original audio boosted and the narrator silent. In the end, one may slowly fade from the day care center sounds to music, and end the tape with the end of a children's song.

4. Now that you know all the people who participated in making the tape, you prepare the CREDITS and at the end of the tape, edit them in via VIDEO INSERT ONLY.

5. By this time, somebody has thought of a title so you rewind to the beginning of the tape and VIDEO INSERT ONLY the title.

The end result is a fairly professional-looking tape with varied shots and varied sound. Everything looks natural, although plenty of it is contrived with painstaking care. That's the object. Every scene is thoughtfully edited for maximum information and maximum impact.

The viewers should be so hypnotized by the content that they are totally unaware of any production techniques and totally unaware of your effort behind those techniques. Like the perfect thief and the perfect spy, you are only successful if no one realizes what you did.

TRANSITIONS

Transitions are the method we use to get from this shot to that shot. Sometimes you can't get there from here and need inbetween shots to smooth the way.

When a shot changes, there should be a reason for the change, such as

1. A look at something new.
2. A look at the interviewer.
3. A look at the subject being talked about.
4. A different camera angle of the person being interviewed.
5. A closer or farther shot of the talent.

By showing something from a different perspective from shot to shot, you provide the viewer with a reason for the change in scene, making the edit less intrusive. You also make your program more enjoyable to watch. In short, *change the kind of shot when you change shots.*

When this isn't feasible, try using CUTAWAYS or COVER SHOTS to hide the JUMP CUTS you get when you edit a speech or activity. The COVER SHOT might be a wide view of the talent speaking, one where you cannot see their lips moving or maybe a shot of the audience, an interviewer, or an object being discussed.

Watch a newscast and notice how the camera jumps from the reporter to the things he or she is talking about. Observe how presidential press conferences are interspersed with shots of the reporters and photographers. Those folks aren't trying to show you their pretty lights and cameras; they're covering up their edits. The press club shots, audience shots, and long shots are all COVER SHOTS or CUTAWAYS and are included as VIDEO INSERTS.

Unless you are switching scenes from night to day where scene brightness is

DON'T   DO

JUMP CUT between long shots and
close-ups without changing angle.
With a cut, the viewer expects a
substantial change in visual
information but doesn't get it.

Change angle about 30° when cutting.
Adds variety and smooths transition.
Builds fuller perception of subject.

To avoid JUMP CUTS, change camera angle and closeness

meant to change, keep the light levels in your pictures the same. Illuminate scenes
to an equal brightness so that the edit doesn't call attention to itself.

Here are some tricks to get you from shot to shot.

Walk-Past

Following people around as they walk from place to place is always hard to con-
dense. One useful trick is to allow the performers to stride toward and past the
camera (and out of the picture) and then to edit to another scene of them coming
into view from alongside the camera. Also, performers may be allowed to turn cor-

DON'T   DO

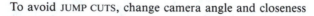

Change angle without changing shot size. Twists performer without apparent purpose.

Change shot size as you change angle to add variety and interest.

To avoid JUMP CUTS, change camera angle and closeness

ners or pass through doors, leaving the camera viewing an empty set. The next edit begins with another empty set with the performers entering a moment after the edit.

Condensing a long distance drive into a few seconds is possible by having the vehicle start its journey in one location and drive "into" or "over" the viewer. EDIT OUT (if you survive). The next edit starts with the vehicle going away from (or out from over) the viewer into the new location.

Blank Surface

Here, the angry wife exits a room slamming the door in the viewer's face, leaving the blank surface of the door filling the screen. EDIT OUT at this point and start the next sequence on another blank surface, perhaps another door which later opens.

To travel from one place to another, one can tilt up past the tree tops into the blue sky and EDIT OUT. Later, starting with the blue sky, one can tilt down past the tops of city buildings to a new scene.

Swish Pan

To show a move from one location to another (as if to say, "Meanwhile, across town . . . "), pan the camera rapidly to a blur. EDIT OUT during this pan. EDIT IN the next scene starting with a fast pan that stops on the next subject that is to be viewed. The result looks like a hectic pan from one scene directly into another.

Defocus-focus-hocus-pocus

One method of making a CUT look smoother while adding variety to your edits is to defocus at the end of a scene, make your edit at another defocused shot, and then have the next shot refocus. As an example of what this could look like, imagine a close-up of a guitar player's hand becoming fuzzy and then magically refocusing into a singer's face.

Two things to keep in mind when you apply this method are: First, it is far easier to get a close-up way out of focus than it is to get a medium or long shot out of focus. If you want to defocus easily, direct your attention to things you can get close-ups of. Second, use this method sparingly or else the method won't add variety any more.

Leading the Action

You are recording a child's birthday party with the usual bedlam. As you tape the proceedings, one child suddenly looks "stage right" and in a few moments all eyes are looking to the right. Now is the time to cut to Mom carrying the blazing birthday cake into the room. The children's looks made a perfect lead-in to your next shot. The viewer *expected* to see a new shot.

Seated performers shuffle in preparation to stand. There is your excuse to cut to a long shot of them getting up and strolling off.

Somebody is holding a gem up to his eye. It's time for a close-up of the gem.

The runner lifts her hips in preparation for the gun. It's time for a long shot of the take-off.

The switch from a medium shot to a long shot of a performer indicates that the preformer is about to move or be joined by someone. Cutting to a close-up of the face readies the audience to catch the expression. A gesture will be expected if you now switch to a medium shot. And a shot of the door prepares the viewers for an entry.

In each case just mentioned, the action prepares the viewer for a shot change. The transition from one shot to another becomes natural and comfortable to view. Making any of these shot changes without a specific purpose will not add variety to your show; it will only confuse your viewers. Therefore, change shots for a purpose, not for idle variety. By building such transitions into your editing strategy, your scenes will introduce each other and flow together.

180° Rule

You almost never shoot any subject from opposite sides. The opposing shots can easily confuse the audience because what was moving left in one shot is suddenly moving right in the other.

This mistake is very easy to do when you are shooting scenes hours, days, or weeks apart. If you forget how the flow of the action was moving, you have a 50-50 chance of starting your next scene with the flow going in the wrong direction. If you shot a patient in a hospital bed from one side this week and next week shot some more of the person from the opposite side, you'll be unpleasantly surprised when you try to edit these scenes together. To avoid these problems, take notes and draw pictures showing your camera angles and setups. This will assure smooth continuity from scene to scene. And now, more on continuity:

Continuity

Al sits down at the table, picks up his knife and fork and begins to cut his asparagus. "Cut," you call out and he feverishly speeds up his sawing until he realizes that the scene is over. You continue the scene with the camera in another position for a close-up of his plate. "Okay, roll," you call out, and when Al realizes you're not calling for his buns, he again picks up his fork and dips into his mashed potatoes. Somebody is in for a surprise when editing time comes; somebody who didn't take notes or didn't examine the tail end of the preceding scene to assure matched shots. How many viewers will you entertain with this little slip-up?

One way to call the least attention to the exact position of something is to change shots while it is moving. *Cutting on the action* (as it is called) also makes the movement part of *both* shots, fusing the continuity between them.

For example, someone is about to walk out through the door. You shoot the scene first from the inside hitting PAUSE *as the door begins to open.* Have the talent memorize which hand was on the knob and which foot was forward. Now run outside, compose your door shot, and have the talent repeat the process of opening the door, hands and feet equivalently placed. UNPAUSE as the door opens.

If recording RAW FOOTAGE for later editing, the process is similar. Instead of PAUSING, let the talent complete the exit. Have the talent repeat the process while you shoot it again from the outside angle. Start your tape even before your talent begins to approach the door. During editing, you will now be able to carefully control exactly where you switch from one scene to the next (before the door opens, as it opens, or as the person passed through). As long as the action is matched in both "takes," you should have a number of choices of where to make the switch from the indoor view to the outdoor.

Pacing

Just as camera angles can create a mood, so can the way you edit a program to-gether. Action and excitement call for quick, short edits usually showing close-ups or motion. To heighten the excitement further, you can speed the tempo of edits to a staccato of brief scenes, some of which are on the screen hardly long enough to be comprehended. Study the action scenes from *Jaws, Psycho,* and *Star Wars* and you'll see the shots changing at a frenzied pace.

Calm, relaxing love scenes, travelogues, suspense, and drama are edited into longer, more leisurely scenes. Often the change from one tranquil scene to another may be a dissolve rather than an abrupt cut.

The beauty of editing is that it leaves an unconscious message. The viewers think that they are only seeing what you are showing them. They don't realize that they are also seeing *how* you are showing them. As your program progresses, you can bring your audience to the edge of their seats and then relax them back down just by varying the pace of your edits. Incidentally, it's good not to maintain the same pace for too long. A sustained slow pace may put your audience to sleep, yet sustained fast pace may jangle their nerves, leaving them desensitized. The technique here is to grab the audience to get their attention, shake them a few times, and then ease them back into their seats and let them breathe.

WHEN YOU'RE FINISHED EDITING

It's 4 a.m. Your masterpiece is finished. Amid a heap of candy wrappers and coffee cups you stand up for the first time in 12 hours. It's time to call it a night, maybe have a drink, or maybe a nervous breakdown, right?

Oh, no, CONTROL TRACK breath!

Have you labeled your EDITED MASTER so some joker doesn't come around tomorrow morning and record a Bugs Bunny cartoon over your precious program? The world is filled with doodleheads who think that any program which isn't theirs is expendable. Label that tape! Put it in a safe place from doodleheads.

Next, copy your EDITED MASTER *now,* using the editing VCR to do the *playing* and some other VCR to make the copy. This guarantees that one perfect playback of your tape will occur before something happens to "mother," the VCR who can play your tape best. Besides, after all those hours, could you sleep knowing that there is only *one copy* of your masterpiece in existence? A second copy kept in another place is excellent insurance.

11

Planning and production techniques

The French Foreign Legion had a saying, "When in doubt, gallop." Successful TV productions, however, are 90% planning and 10% galloping, although it is the galloping that gets all the glamour. The things a director does before and after the production most likely will determine the quality of the show.

You may find it constructive to involve your talent (your family or other participants in your show) in your planning stages. Their advice will improve your show while giving them a feeling of personal contribution, adding a sense of commitment to the program. This kind of sharing was instrumental in making *M*A*S*H* such a hit for ten years.

PLANNING

1. Don't start writing until you have a concrete idea of what you want to communicate. One way to pin down a show's illusive purpose is to require yourself to *write in one or two sentences what the program is supposed to achieve*. This focuses your energy on a main purpose—an anchor that will keep you from rambling or getting lost in detail.

2. *Keep the plan simple.* Use the KISS method which stands for "Keep It Simple, Stupid". How many of your neighbors would like to watch a two-hour recording of a party you had three years ago? The magic of videotape is its ability to compress time, focusing on the high points and discarding the chaff. A three-hour-long wedding and reception doesn't deserve a three-hour program, or even two, one, or one-half. Try six minutes. A good six minutes will hold your audience, will stand repeated showings, and will surprise you at how well it will cover the entire event.

3. *Choose a format* or a combination of formats for your show. If you draw a blank trying to imagine where to start, Table 11–1 lists some possibilities.

4. *Be visual.* Words, words, words—is this television? Think pictures. Close your eyes. Imagine telling your story *without a single word.* Sure, it's not easy, but try anyway. Close your eyes. (You're still reading!) What do you see? Can you visualize the story unfolding? The script that you are *now* creating is the difference between radio and television. Consider this: The movies *Alien, Close Encounters of the Third Kind,* and *2001: A Space Odyssey* ended in long stretches without words. There were plenty of script pages, plenty of shots and planning, and finally a feast for the eyes, ears, and imagination—but no words.

5. *Grab the audience.* This doesn't apply just to *Mission Impossible* scripts. All televison programs need the audience's attention to succeed. Show them some action, drama, beauty, humor, or tease them with some mystery.

SCRIPTING

First you learn how to write. Then you learn how to write between the lines; that's poetry. Scriptwriting gives you many more lines to write between. There's the narration or spoken channel with its statements and nuances. There's the audio channel with its mood creating musical track or environment establishing sound effects. There's the visual channel displaying not only the obvious, but implying further messages through camera angle and editing. When you write a serious script, you want to think in *all* these dimensions at once, weaving the sound, the picture, the

TABLE 11–1 SEVERAL TV SHOW FORMATS

Format	Uses
Show and tell	Straightforward presentation of facts. You explain an activity as you show it.
Spokesperson	A recognized authority adds credibility to your message.
Interview with man-on-the-street, victim, or groupie, etc.	Viewers identify with J.Q. Citizen. Adds color to facts and statistics by introducing a human element or drama.
Skits	Visually more exciting. Acted-out situations leave a more memorable impression than a simple declaration of facts.
Animation	Costly but cuts out extraneous visual material and is more entertaining.
Charts and graphics	Simplifies complex ideas. More memorable.

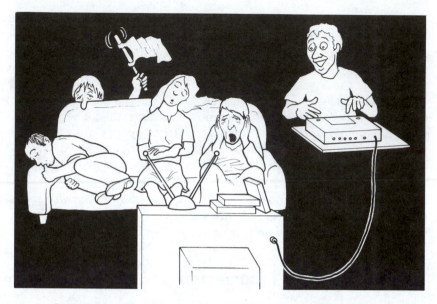

Grab the audience, be visual, and KISS (Keep It Simple, Stupid!)

words, the lighting, and the camera angles and transitions all into one cohesive program.

Mechanics of Scripting

Professional television scripts generally divide the page down the middle, placing the dialogue or narration on the right side of the page and the camera cues, shot angles, and audio information on the left side of the page.

Another technique—more popular today now that people use word processors (which don't handle columns very easily)—is to put all the camera moves and dialogue in the same column. In the margin, the director might list the shot angles or even draw a picture showing where props or people may move (Figure 11–1).

Fully scripted shows assist in planning shots—a necessity during complex productions. The director can see everything that will happen and has few surprises to contend with. On the other hand, a detailed script burdens the director with many things to keep track of during the whirlwind of performance. More appropriate for the home TV producer (and more in keeping with the KISS strategy) is the RUN-DOWN SHEET.

A RUNDOWN SHEET is the most minimal script. It is a list of things scheduled to happen during the production and the order in which they will occur. For example, the RUNDOWN may say (where CU means close-up, MS means medium shot)

1. Music, title graphic.
2. CU of Dad munching cookie. Pan to LS of Mom in kitchen. Mom describes how to make "Forgotten Cookies."

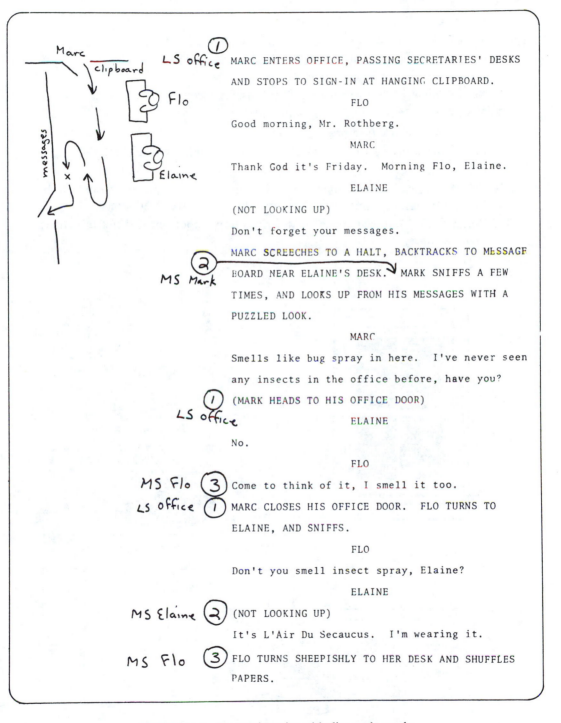

MARC ENTERS OFFICE, PASSING SECRETARIES' DESKS
AND STOPS TO SIGN-IN AT HANGING CLIPBOARD.

                    FLO

Good morning, Mr. Rothberg.

                    MARC

Thank God it's Friday. Morning Flo, Elaine.

                    ELAINE

(NOT LOOKING UP)

Don't forget your messages.

MARC SCREECHES TO A HALT, BACKTRACKS TO MESSAGE
BOARD NEAR ELAINE'S DESK. MARK SNIFFS A FEW
TIMES, AND LOOKS UP FROM HIS MESSAGES WITH A
PUZZLED LOOK.

                    MARC

Smells like bug spray in here. I've never seen
any insects in the office before, have you?

(MARK HEADS TO HIS OFFICE DOOR)

                    ELAINE

No.

                    FLO

Come to think of it, I smell it too.

MARC CLOSES HIS OFFICE DOOR. FLO TURNS TO
ELAINE, AND SNIFFS.

                    FLO

Don't you smell insect spray, Elaine?

                    ELAINE

(NOT LOOKING UP)

It's L'Air Du Secaucus. I'm wearing it.

FLO TURNS SHEEPISHLY TO HER DESK AND SHUFFLES
PAPERS.

FIGURE 11-1 Dramatic script with director's marks

3. CU of ingredients while Mom lists.
4. MS of Mom mixing ingredients.
5. CU of stove thermostat as Mom preheats oven to 350°.
6. MS of Mom dabbing mixture onto cookie sheet.
7. MS of stove. Mom turns oven off and inserts sheets of cookies.
8. CU of clock face. Mom narrates instructions. DEFOCUS.
9. REFOCUS on clock face next morning.
10. MS of Mom taking finished batch from cool oven. She displays.
11. CU of cookies.
12. MS of Dad lying on the floor very still, half of a cookie sticking from mouth. Mom approaches, removes cookie, and slips sheet over Dad's face.
13. Zoom in on Mom grinning. She describes how important it is not to eat too many at once.

Murphy's 78th Law: No script is finished until it's 2:30 AM

TABLE 11-2

Regular Prose	TV Style
1 Uses complete sentences.	1 Uses incomplete sentences, phrases, and may resemble captions.
2 Is concentrated, compact, and compressed.	2 Is repetitive and more wordy.
3 Uses formal arguments and deductive reasoning, sometimes requiring mental consideration of an abstract thought.	3 Is descriptive. Announces, proclaims, declares.
4 Uses logical transitions between sentences, like thus, because, therefore.	4 Uses adverbial transitions such as here, now, then.
5 Presents a logical argument to make a point. Develops a thesis. Ideas are derived through reasoning, surmised.	5 Illustrates the point or narrates a process.
6 Explains verbally.	6 Directs attention.
7 Tends to participal modification such as: "the grid lights" rather than "the lights in the grid."	7 Tends to prepositional modification such as: "on the dimmer panel" or "at the beginning of the recording."
8 Uses long complex sentences.	8 Uses short simple sentences.
9 Uses variable sentence construction.	9 Uses declarative sentences—subject to verb to object.
10 Uses formal vocabulary and infrequently used words.	10 Uses the common, frequently heard words found in everyday speech.
11 Uses synonymns. Says something only once figuring the reader can always come back to review the point.	11 Avoids synonymns. Tends to redundantly repeat the same thing over and over again, tautologously duplicating the . . . (you get the idea).

14. Graphic listing recipe. Music fades in.
15. "End" graphic. Music fades out. Graphic fades out.

Since Mom isn't renown for her acting ability, or her willingness to memorize lines, often the RUNDOWN is as close to a script as you will get.

Writing for TV

TV language is a lot different from printed language. Table 11–2 lists some of these differences. Here is an example of printed prose:

Place the camera on the tripod head aligning the camera mounting hole with the tripod's fastener bolt, and finger-tighten the bolt.

Here's how the prose might be matched to the video:

Have the cameraman hold the camera over the tripod. A helper positions the tripod underneath. The helper aligns the fastener bolt with the hole in the base of the camera.

When the holes are properly aligned, the helper threads the bolt into the base of the camera. Here the helper tightens the bolt until it is finger tight. The camera is now mounted to the tripod.

Notice how redundant the TV prose is compared with printed prose? Sentences are kept down to one single thought each. Also, cues to direct the viewer's attention assure that important visual elements are not missed. The narration in this example may look wordy, but it isn't if you consider that actions usually proceed slower than words. What sometimes takes one moment to describe, takes three moments to show. Thus the words have to be spread out to coincide with the action.

STORYBOARDS

A STORYBOARD is a series of sketches depicting the main pictorial elements of a scene. Figure 11–2 shows an example. Narration, if scripted, usually accompanies each picture. The result is quite similar to a comic strip only the words are outside the picture.

STORYBOARDS become especially worthwhile when

1. It is difficult to describe a scene with only words.
2. Others will have to carry out your plan. The STORYBOARD clearly shows what you want your talent to do and your audience to see.

If you think only sissies use STORYBOARDS, that they are amateur and time consuming, consider this: Alfred Hitchcock drew his own STORYBOARDS—shot by shot, for every one of his movies.

CUE CARDS

Irreverently aliased "idiot cards" (but don't call them that in front of your talent), these two-foot by three-foot posters covered with felt pen printing are the backbone of educational and home TV prompting. Number the cards to keep them in order. (You can imagine what happens to your show when they are presented out of order.) The CUE CARD HOLDER (catchy job title) holds the cards near the camera's lens and to the side so that he or she can read along with the talent and know when to change cards (Figure 11–3). Since the cards are not *in front of* the camera lens, the talent will have that familiar off-center stare during close-ups, so try to use medium shots.

FIGURE 11-2   Regular prose versus television prose

FIGURE 11-3 CUE card, held to the side, near camera lens

PUPPETS

The fantastic thing about puppets is that they can look straight into the camera and jabber away while their operators move their hands and read a script (or move their hands to prerecorded dialogue). This method is so deceptive and entertaining, there's no excuse for why it isn't used more. Granted you have to buy or make a good puppet (or puppets), find operators who can bring personality to the inanimate characters, and create an excuse for having puppets carry the show, but in cases where a lot of speech has to be learned, puppets are unbeatable for saving hours of memorizing, for providing pseudo eye contact, and for plenty of apparent spontaneity.

VIDEOTAPING IN THE WINTER

Portable video equipment, if it could talk, would beg to stay inside where it's dry and warm, but ice skating, skiing, snowball fights, snowmobiling, and traffic snarling blizzards occur outdoors (you needed this book to tell you that). What problems will you and your equipment face in the cold?

Shortened Battery Life

Above all others, this may be your biggest problem. Up to 50% of your battery's life is lost when the temperature reaches freezing. Expect your one-hour battery to last about 30 minutes. This goes for NICADS as well as GEL CELLS.

To avoid this problem, keep the battery warm, keeping it in your pocket or wrapped in a blanket until you're ready to use it, *then* chuck it into the machine.

You may even keep the whole VCR (and thus the battery) warm with a blanket while it operates. By all means, don't set the recorder down on the ice or frozen ground; this will cool it and its battery very quickly.

Try reducing power demands on the battery. Don't stand around in PAUSE or STANDBY any length of time. Either shoot, or kill the power. Remove the plug-in RF GENERATOR if it is not being used; save a watt.

Bring two batteries for more shooting time. Keep the second battery warm until used.

Condensation

Ever notice how moist the outside of a glass of iced tea becomes on a humid day? VCRs and cameras suffer the same problem. Whenever they are cooler than their environment, dew collects on them. This isn't such a big problem when you move outdoors to shoot in the cold, but when you come back in with frigid gear, it starts collecting humidity from its warm surroundings. The dampness is devastating to the electronics, makes the tape stick (instead of slide) inside the VCR, and will most likely trip the DEW SENSOR, a safety device in the VCR which turns it off (wisely) when there's excessive condensation.

When bringing cold equipment inside, immediately cover it with a plastic bag and let it warm up for an hour or more. The bag will seal out the humidity-laden air so that water can't collect on the goodies. When the equipment reaches ambient temperature, it's ready for use. Take it out of the bag first.

Puppets

Videotaping in the winter.

If your machine becomes damp (its DEW LIGHT comes on), one way to hasten the drying out process would be to open the cassette tray (removing the cassette) and blow warm (not hot) air from a hair dryer into the VCR. In a few minutes, the machine should be defrosted. Let the inside temperature restabilize for a couple more minutes before chucking in your cassette.

Don't play a cold tape in a warm machine and vice versa. The tape will act "sticky" if it is not the same temperature as the machine.

None of this applies to batteries. It is perfectly fine to use warm batteries in a cold VCR.

Extreme Cold

If it gets *really* cold (below −40°F), don't use your VCR. Its circuits could become damaged.

Go out in a blizzard, and your lens might ice up.

Slightly damp skin will freeze to very cold metal. If it is really cold, wear gloves.

Glare

Snow and ice reflect a lot of sunlight. Shoot at a high f-stop or attach a neutral density filter to your lens. Use a polarizing filter to reduce snow and ice surface reflections. Keep the sun to your back lest your subjects become backlit so strongly that they look like silhouettes.

Video equipment (except batteries) works quite well when cold. It works poorly when it is changing temperature. Your camera may give poor color. Your tape may stick. Your lens may fail to zoom smoothly.

VIDEOTAPING AT THE BEACH

Video is an action medium and what better place for action than at the beach. The beach, with its games, kids, and bathing beauties, can be a recording gold mine— if you know how to insulate your equipment from the harsh environment. Here are your enemies and how to avoid them.

Salt Air

Ocean beaches are bathed in an invisible spray of salt air. The salt corrodes the switches, gums up VCR mechanisms, and clouds lenses.

Wrap your equipment in plastic bags and tie them closed. White or clear plastic is better than black. Black will get hot in the sun. Since your wrapped equipment can't "breathe" and cool itself on hot days, keep it in the shade between shots. Wrap the camera so the lens sticks out (it has to "see") and make a little hole and tape it tight to your viewfinder opening so that you can "see," too. Later, you can wipe the salt spray off the lens and viewfinder glass with a wet swab. Use *fresh* water for this. This is a perfect example of where a UV filter or clear glass filter can protect your camera lens.

Dampness

Strangely, your greatest danger isn't a tidal wave or your boat capsizing. It's the "dry land" danger of dripping swim suits, kids with water buckets, and half-empty drinks spilling into your gear.

Next in line comes the sea dampness that permeates your equipment and collects. Then comes the total dunking—a total disaster at best.

As before, wrap everything while shooting. Store your gear in waterproof cases. A waterproof ice chest makes a fine temporary home for your little treasure (and it may even float in a capsize). Suitcases or other containers will work too. Avoid cardboard; it get soggy when wet. Pack towels or whatever around the equipment to cushion it during travel. Don't, however, bring the equipment home wrapped in *sandy* beach towels.

For long-term storage in damp environments, buy some packets of SILICA GEL from your photo store and pack them in with your equipment. *It* will absorb the humidity rather than your machinery. When the packets get damp, simply bake them on low heat in the oven to dry them out (if they are cloth covered, wrap them in perforated tin foil to keep the cloth sacks from scorching).

Sand

You know how it feels in your bathing suit, and you know how it tracks into your car, into your home, and somehow into your bed, and magically into your breakfast cereal the next day. Similarly, that abrasive, destructive grit will find its way into your machinery unless you wrap it and store it tightly. Also keep your cables off the ground—they'll transfer sand to your storage box.

Heat

Store everything out of the sun. Heat damages tape and makes VCRs "sticky" inside.

Above all, don't move your equipment quickly from a cool air-conditioned environment to a sun-baked beach. (Where have you heard this before?) It will collect water like a cold drink can and the salty condensate will eat battery contacts, switches, everything. If you are changing from cold to hot places, put the equipment in plastic (keeping out the moisture) and let it "warm up" to outside temperatures.

After the Damage Is Done

Even after wrapping the equipment, you may come home and find sand or salt water film on your equipment. Here's what to do:

1. With a fresh water-moist sponge, wipe down your VCR and camera casings.
2. Decake dried salt with undiluted alcohol on a soft, lint-free cloth. Avoid scented cleaners; they leave a film.
3. Take off any removable covers and open any trap doors or compartments on your VCR and camera, and, using an alcohol or fresh water dipped swab, clean the seals, gaskets, and edges of the covers.
4. Clean around switches and movable parts.
5. If dampness gets into your camera lens, fungus will grow causing a fine, spidery, light-colored build-up on the glass. You can minimize the likelihood of this by "drying out" the lens in a warm dry place (such as under a lamp) after shooting. Otherwise, if you notice the fungus is growing as you hold the lens up to the light, bring it to a camera store for cleaning. If the fungus builds up too much, the camera store may be unable to remove it.

Videotaping at the beach.

6. If your boat capsizes and really "deep sixes" your gear in salt water,
   a. Turn it off.
   b. Remove the battery *immediately*.
   c. Swim—don't paddle—to your nearest bucket of fresh water and dunk it. Slosh it around to get out all the salt—immediately. Repeat the rinse five more times, each time using a new batch of fresh water.
   d. Take it in for service or if you're handy, open it up and dry it out in a warm place. Blow a fan on it for a day or use a blow dryer (set to warm) and thoroughly go over every millimeter of the machine. A vacuum cleaner might also help suck water out of crevices, or in a pinch could be set to "blow" to create a steady whirlwind inside the mechanism. Still it will be wet *somewhere*. Check carefully for moisture. Don't try to use it until you're absolutely sure it's dry. With luck, it may work. Then again your drowned machine may still need resuscitation by an expert.
7. If your equipment drowns in *fresh* water, do the same as above, omitting step c.

SHOOTING ON LOCATION

Location shooting brings with it all the pleasures of camping out. You must remember to bring everything imaginable, or you'll end up with coffee but no coffee pot, a flashlight but no batteries, and perfume instead of insect repellent.

Experienced truckers check their brakes *before* starting down a mountain. There is no preparation for the future like the present well done. If you ever expect to need your equipment in a hurry, take the time to pack it ready to go. Store things

"The Distant Shoot"

together, ready to carry away in one box. Charge the batteries so they will be ready for your next mission. Repair loose or broken parts right away rather than "learning to live with them."

Before packing your equipment for a journey of any importance, take this added precaution: *Connect all equipment together and make a one-minute sample tape. Next, play the tape to make sure everything works.* This is perhaps the most improtant step prior to going "on location." This superfluous-sounding routine pays off in the long run! Most of the time, this testing procedure reveals no problems. About 20% of the time it will. It's better to face your gremlins at the outset rather than getting bit by them on location.

What to take with you depends upon what you will be doing. The watch words, nevertheless, are the same: *Be prepared.* For shooting about two hours of tape in the next town, one might bring the items listed in Table 11–3.

One item mentioned in the list is a RELEASE FORM. If you plan to sell or distribute your tapes, you will generally need permission from the participants to use their pictures in your production. Figure 11–4 shows a sample model release form used by Prentice Hall.

TRAVELING HINTS

Unless you like hauling a half a ton of stuff up and down corridors and stairs, try to get a ground-floor motel room with a parking lot right outside your door.

To avoid subjecting your equipment to extremes of hot and cold, don't store it outside in a car. Besides, it may get stolen, especially if it's in a rented car or station wagon.

Prentice-Hall, Inc.
Englewood Cliffs, N.J. 07632

Telex No. 13-5423

MODEL RELEASE

I hereby give Prentice-Hall, Inc. the absolute right and permission to copyright and/or publish, or use photographic portraits or pictures of me, or in which I may be included in whole or in part, or composite or distorted in character or form, in conjunction with my own or a fictitious name, or reproductions thereof in color or otherwise, for art, advertising, trade or any other lawful purpose whatsoever.

I hereby waive any right that I may have to inspect and/or approve the finished product or the advertising copy that may be used in connection therewith, or the use to which it may be applied.

I hereby release, discharge, and agree to save Prentice-Hall, Inc. from any liability by virtue of any blurring, distortion, alteration, optical illusion, or use in composite form, whether intentional or otherwise, that may occur or be produced in the taking of said pictures, or in any processing tending towards the completion of the finished product.

DATE_____   MODEL _____

                          ADDRESS _____

                          PARENT OR
WITNESS _____   GUARDIAN _____
                          (Required only if model is
                          a minor)

FIGURE 11-4   Prentice Hall model release form

Anything that can crunch suitcases into tiny bits can misalign a VCR. So pack everything with plenty of foam. Excellent, sturdy, foam-cushioned carry cases are available for video equipment.

Try to book your nonstop flights so that the baggage crunchers don't juggle your bags twice.

Smaller, delicate things like camcorders might best be carried on board with you for safekeeping.

Customs Registration

Leaving the U.S. with your foreign-made VCR is easy. Getting it back into the U.S. without paying about 5½% duty on it is difficult. A receipted U.S. bill of sale showing serial numbers may act as proof that you bought the gear in the United States. Better yet, fill out a ''Certificate of Registration for Personal Effects Taken Abroad'' with U.S. Customs *before* you go, listing make, model, and serial numbers of all the foreign-made possessions you're taking abroad.

TABLE 11–3 WHAT TO BRING ON LOCATION

Items to Bring	Bring These as a Backup in Case Something Fails on Location
1 VCR and camera or camcorder, cassette, and carrying case.	1 additional VCR/camera/lens ensemble if the shooting is very important. Shoot with both machines simultaneously. This way, if the camera operator goofs up or the heads clog on one VCR during a shoot, the other will still catch the scene. Bring a complete set of accessories (batteries, tripod, tape) for the second machine. If the scenes aren't rare enough to require two-camera coverage but you're traveling a long way at some expense to do the shooting, bring a second camcorder anyway and store it on the site. If the first machine fails, you'll have a backup with which to keep shooting.
1 3-hour battery (or more for long shoots).	1 AC power supply, in case the first battery dies prematurely or the shooting runs longer than expected.
6 ½-hour cassettes of tape in boxes.	4 extra ½-hour cassettes in boxes. It doesn't cost anything to return with unused tape, but it is inexcusable to run out during a production. Having extra cassettes also makes it easier to categorize your shots during editing.
1 roll of masking tape and a *good* felt pen to label the tape boxes. Keeping track (and not accidentally erasing) of what you have is just as important as shooting it. The adhesive tape is also handy in unpredictable ways.	
1 portable tripod.	
1 lavalier and 1 shotgun microphone with 25 feet of mike cable and an appropriate plug for the VCR.	1 extra length of mike cable in case the first conks out or you need an extension.
1 pair of headphones with the proper plug for the VCR. The headphones will permit an accurate monitoring of audio during taping.	

1 12-foot headphone extension cord if the shotgun mike is to be aimed by a sound person who needs to hear what's being recorded.

2 portable lamps with tripods and barn doors.

3 heavy-duty, grounded, multiple outlet extension cords. Two are for the lights; the third is for the VCR if AC is used. The multiple outlets make it possible to power other accessories near the VCR (a TV monitor, a mixer, a lamp, or a battery charger).

1 TV receiver. This allows you to play back, with sound, the raw footage on site for you and others to evaluate.

1 flashlight to help you find switches and sockets and to label the tape.

1 set of close-up lens attachments, if appropriate.

3 grounded AC plug adapters to allow you to use your 3-prong AC plugs with wall sockets having only two holes.

1 head-cleaning kit.

1 audio kit, *if needed*. Kit includes a mixer, mixer batteries, mikes and cables, a cable going to the VCR with the proper plug, assorted audio adapters, audio cables, and an attenuator (in case you must record from someone's loudspeaker system).

1 pad and pencil to take notes.

1 copy of the script.

20 model release forms, if working professionally.

1 enormous two-handled box to carry it all in.

1 spare earphone (the tiny one that fits in the VCR carrying case).

2 spare bulbs for the lamps.

2 extra extension cords. In case the first ones don't reach, these can be connected in series.

RF cable with a 75-300 Ω adapter, in case you need to use someone else's TV set to view footage.

1 extra copy of the script.

Hernia insurance.

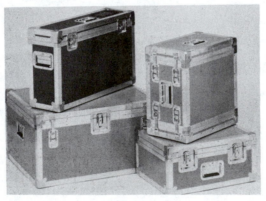

Sturdy cases for carrying portable TV equipment

MUSIC VIDEO

Unless you've just arrived from Mars, you have probably seen MTV (Music Television) and know what music video is all about. The professional stuff is shot at great expense usually on film under very controlled conditions. You may however have an opportunity to make a low budget music video for a shaggy friend. Here are a few strategies.

1. Simply recording the musicians performing their song in a room and using a few camera angles, special effects, and lighting tricks is not likely to be stimulating enough. The music video fans expect more. You may have to go on location, perhaps one suggested by the song. The Amazon may be farther than your budget will take you, but a railroad station, a garbage dump, a supermarket, or baseball field may do just fine.

2. After establishing the group in a long shot, move to tight close-ups for most of the show to keep the energy high.

3. Use low camera angles to accentuate the presence of the performers.

4. It is hard to get good sound when producing in the field. It may be best for your band to perform the song in its entirety under controlled conditions with good microphones, proper acoustics, echo, and other enhancements. Next, you travel to your locations and play that music *to* the performers while they lip-sync to it. Essentially, you are shooting video without audio. All the pictures are later edited together to match the original soundtrack.

One technique that makes the process a little easier is to have the performers record the music carefully while you make a "blacked" videotape (lens cap over the camera). Next, you make VIDEO-ONLY INSERTS to go along with the music. You might do this by taking the tape machine out to the field and playing its prerecorded sound track through a loudspeaker system. After a few rehearsals, you press the VIDEO INSERT ONLY button on the VCR to begin recording this part of the performance. Hit the button which ends the INSERT when this scene is completed. When done, you will have inserted video scenes in sync with the sound all on the same tape. You don't even have to shoot the scenes in sequence; you can checkerboard them.

One problem with the preceding technique is that hi-fi sound is part of the picture. If you wish to record your sound first and your pictures later, your sound will end up coming from your low fidelity linear audio tracks. Nevertheless, this method is easy and only requires one VCR.

If you *must* preserve your hi fi sound quality, and have 3 VCRs (2 must be hi fi), here's how:

1. In an audio studio, make a good music recording, feeding the audio signal to 2 VCRs simultaneously (one must be hi fi).

2. Put the hi fi tape away. Using the *other* tape, put together the video show using INSERT edits where the performers gyrate to the prerecorded music on the tape. When done,

3. Set up the 3 VCRs so that the tape with INSERT video edits, feeds video to a hi-fi VCR. Simultaneously, another hi fi VCR plays your original hi fi sound tape into the audio inputs of your hi fi VCR.

4. Painstakingly synchronize the audio and video tapes, then record the results: hi fi sound plus pictures.

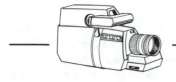

12

Other TV production gadgets

"Old boys have their playthings as well as young ones: The difference is only in the price"—Benjamin Franklin.

"Buying your camcorder may be the least expensive part of your hobby"—Peter Utz

The video stores will be more than happy to sell you accessories. If you yearn to invest in your video addiction, try reading some of the home video magazines like *Video, Video Review,* and *Videomaker.* The more you read, the more you'll want. This chapter tells you about some of the goodies that you can buy and what they do.

SIGNAL IMPROVING EQUIPMENT

Processing Amplifier or Stabilizer

A PROCESSING AMPLIFIER, PROC AMP, or STABILIZER, as it is usually called, can improve your video signal in a number of ways. It can make the picture more stable, remove jitter, increase contrast, thwart some anti-piracy (COPYGUARD) signals, and reduce FLAGWAVING.

There are some problems a PROC AMP cannot fix. It can't reproduce a picture that is not there. Feed it a snowy or grainy picture and out will come a snowy or grainy picture. Feed it sync abnormalities such as PAUSE edits, and the picture com-

Buying your camcorder is the least expensive part of your hobby

Assorted optional video equipment available from Showtime Video Ventures. (Courtesy of Showtime Video Ventures)

ing out will hiccup a couple times. It may re-create stable sync *between* the edits, but it will not fix the glitches *during* the edits.

If you copy a lot of tapes or need to adjust the color or brightness of the picture on your tapes, then a PROC AMP is for you.

To stabilize a picture you are recording, the PROC AMP is connected between your source (camera or VCP) and your VCR as shown in Figure 12–1. It can also be connected between your videocassette player and a TV monitor to stabilize a picture being viewed.

A PROC AMP works only with video signals, not with RF. You'll have to convert your original signal from RF to video and your output from video back to RF if that's what your sources and your TV set use.

The simplest PROC AMPS are called STABILIZERS and only have an on/off switch. More advanced PROC AMPS have knobs to adjust the following:

- *Gain*—Picture contrast.
- *Setup*—Picture brightness.
- *Chroma gain*—The amount of color in your picture.
- *Hue or burst phase*—Adjusts all the colors at once.

These controls allow you to correct some of the errors made in recording your original tapes, or could be used to create special effects such as green faces and orange grass. Meanwhile, the machine is inserting brand new, clean sync on your video signal, making your picture more stable. This is sometimes helpful when you are trying to copy an nth generation tape which just barely plays, or correcting a signal which wasn't perfect to start with, such as the signal from a misadjusted camera, a malfunctioning VCR, or a signal from a computer which has slightly weird sync.

PROC AMPS cost from $90 to $500 (ouch!). The cheapest ones just stabilize your picture and defeat the more common types of anti-piracy signals. More expensive models not only stabilize your picture but include some of the aforementioned bells and whistles.

Video Enhancer or Detailer

A VIDEO ENHANCER or DETAILER does just that; it enhances or crispens the TV picture. It cannot create sharpness out of a fuzzy or grainy picture. It can make the picture *look* sharper by accenting the edges of the picture giving it more "punch." Figure 12–2 shows images before and after enhancement.

ENHANCERS are helpful in reclaiming some of the sharpness lost in the copying process, can help boost the apparent sharpness of a camera's image before it gets recorded, and can "sharpen" a video signal before it goes into a video projector. But ENHANCERS, while amplifying the apparent detail of the picture, also highlight video "noise" and other aberrations of the picture. They enhance the chaff along

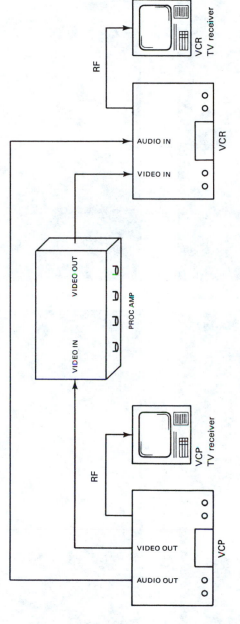

FIGURE 12-1 PROC AMP connection

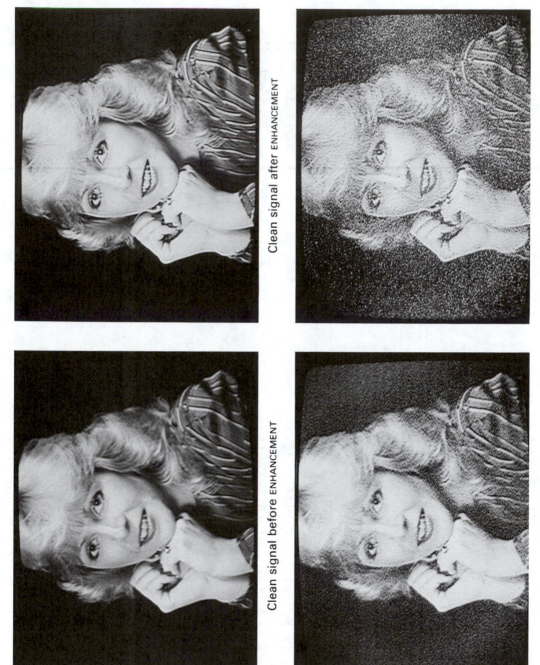

Clean signal after ENHANCEMENT

Grainy signal after ENHANCEMENT

Clean signal before ENHANCEMENT

Grainy signal before ENHANCEMENT

FIGURE 12-2 IMAGE ENHANCEMENT

with the wheat. Consequently, clean pictures can be enhanced to look sharper, but noisy, grainy, or snowy pictures will only look more noisy, grainy, or snowy.

Fuzzy pictures will tend to smear and overenhanced pictures will display noticeable edging along all vertical lines, giving a cartoon-like effect.

ENHANCERS cost about $150 to $250. The expensive ones, with more knobs, allow you to improve the picture while only slightly increasing the noise.

You set up ENHANCERS as shown in Figure 12–3. Notice how they work with *video* signals only. That's fine between VCRs and most video projectors, but if you are just trying to crispen your VCR's playback into your regular TV, you'll have to use a separate RF MODULATOR to convert the video and audio into channel 3 for

For copying a tape:

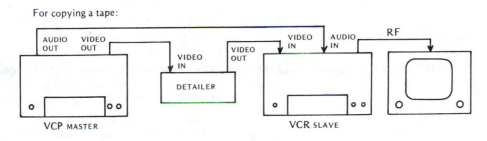

Note: Some DETAILERS have several outputs for video monitoring or for copying onto several SLAVE VCRs at once.

For projection TV:

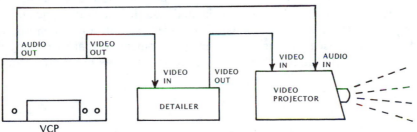

For regular TV set:

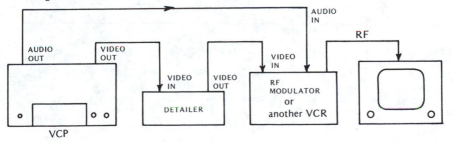

FIGURE 12–3 ENHANCER connection

your TV. Similarly, if you wish to "crispen" a TV broadcast before recording it, you'll have to DEMODULATE the antenna (or cable) signal into video and audio before the ENHANCER can work its magic on the video.

Some manufacturers combine a PROC AMP and IMAGE ENHANCER into one box, allowing you to adjust the color and brightness of your picture while stabilizing and crispening it.

Time Base Corrector

A TIME BASE CORRECTOR (or TBC, as it is called) removes jitter from TV pictures (which usually occurs when tapes are played back), corrects color and sync timing errors, and in some cases can store an entire TV picture in its memory (called a FRAME STORE). If you took a picture of a round dinner plate and played it back only to find a jiggly pie-crusty edge, your plate would be suffering a TIME BASE ERROR.

TBCs are quite expensive ($2,000 and up) and are seldom used by home video producers. Fortunately, they are seldom needed. The pie-crusty problem is seldom severe enough to bother anybody. The rest of what a TBC does cannot be seen by the eye. It corrects picture and sync problems which, although they aren't visible on your home TV screen, would cause a problem if the signal were broadcast to thousands of homes. This is why TV stations employ TBCs when playing back their videotapes.

The FCC (Federal Communications Commission) requires that broadcast TV signals be extremely stable. The stability they are talking about does not appear on the TV screen (unless the problem gets really bad), but it affects the sync pulse, just off the edge of your screen. TBCs make this unseen part of your picture perfect.

TBCs are also used to synchronize video equipment so that their images can be mixed together. If, for instance, you wanted to edit together a tape from two

ENHANCER/PROC AMP combo (Courtesy of Quality/Universal)

FIGURE 12–4　RF PATCH BAY (Courtesy of Philmore Manufacturing Co.)

other tapes and wanted to dissolve from VCR1's picture to VCR2's picture while recording the result on VCR3, you would need a TBC for VCR1 and VCR2 to synchronize their pictures and make their sync pulses absolutely perfect. Once this was done, the two signals could be passed through a FADER, SPECIAL EFFECTS GEN- ERATOR, or fancy TV production switcher with the result sent to your VCR.

SIGNAL DISTRIBUTION EQUIPMENT

When you ran one antenna wire to one VCR and sent its signal to one TV, you had no problem. There was enough signal for everybody and just a few wires. So you buy two extra TVs, a camera, a projection TV, an extra VCR for copying, and add to that your home computer, a videodisc machine, and a video STABILIZER. Your antenna signal is split in a zillion ways, your video signal is connected like an octo- pus, and the ball of wires behind your machines needs a Portuguese fisherman to untangle it. Every time you connect something to something else, you have to climb behind the equipment with the flashlight in one hand and a wiring diagram in the other and begin routing the signals to the right places, hoping that you labeled the cables correctly. Cheer up, pal—for every cabling problem, there is an expensive accessory to solve it.

Patch Bay

A PATCH BAY or PATCH PANEL, much like the telephone operator's switchboard, can route TV signals between devices. Without a PATCH BAY, you would have to reach behind the equipment to get to the cables if a change in wiring were desired. Some of the cable connectors wouldn't mate and would require adapters.

The PATCH BAY solves this problem by displaying all the inputs and outputs in the open where they are easy to reach. The connections are all standardized and the sockets can be arranged and labeled in an organized way.

Figure 12–4 shows an example of an RF PATCH BAY. All of your sources' RF OUTPUTS would be connected to sockets in the back of the PATCH BAY which are wired to the labeled sockets in the front. Similarly, all your TV and VCR RF INPUTS would be connected into the bay and would be wired to the front spiggots. Now you can send your computer game's signal to one TV by connecting those two sockets together with a PATCH CORD, a short antenna cable that plugs into the BAY. At the same time, you can send your cable TV signal to your VCR to make a recording; just connect those two sockets with another PATCH CORD.

Some PATCH BAYS are designed for VIDEO only (you need a separate BAY for audio). These are handy when you are sending video from one VCR through a STABILIZER and then into anther VCR or whatnot.

PATCH BAYS cost about $75, professional models $1000.

Routing Switcher

Just as the phone company replaced its spaghetti wired switchboards with buttons, so can you. The ROUTING SWITCHER is a PATCH BAY that uses buttons instead of wires. You connect all your sources to the rear of the switcher and from then on, simply push buttons to route a source to a particular destination.

A three-input, two-output RF router, for instance, would allow you to connect any of three sources (say videodisc, cable TV, and VCR RF output) to any of two destinations (say, a TV set and a VCR's ANTENNA INPUT). Thus, you could be recording a show off the cable (CABLE OUT to VCR IN) while watching a videodisc on the TV set (DISC OUT to TV IN). To check your recording, you could go to the switcher's TV group of buttons and push the one marked VCR to route the VCR's output to your TV.

ROUTING SWITCHERS cost $60 to $200. Not-so-good ones may have poor ISOLATION allowing the signals to interfere with each other. ROUTING SWITCHERS (and PATCH BAYS, too) with this problem may exhibit wavy lines which look a lot like

Captioned TV adapter enables a standard TV to receive subtitles on certain programs

FIGURE 12–5   SPECIAL EFFECTS generator

Figure 10–3 or graininess like one of the pictures in Figure 12–2. If you encounter this problem, bring your SWITCHER back to your dealer and get another type with more ISOLATION.

CAPTIONING EQUIPMENT

Deaf and hard-of-hearing folks like to watch TV, too. Up until recently they had to read lips and concentrate like crazy to make up for the sound message they weren't getting. In recent years, programs of national importance have been televised with a CORNER INSERT of someone translating the speech into international sign language.

Another method for getting the message on the screen is to use CLOSED CAPTIONS. These captions are not seen by normal viewers. They are invisibly coded into the TV picture using a computer language. By employing a special decoder connected to your TV (or a special TV with this built in), this signal is decoded and displayed on your TV as a visible caption. Thus only those people with the device can view the captions in CLOSED CAPTIONED programs. More and more programming, specials, series, even some commercials are becoming regularly encoded with the CLOSED CAPTIONED signals. You can get more information on this subject from the National Captioning Institute, Falls Church, VA. If you ever wanted to give a "gift that keeps on giving" to a close friend who is deaf, perhaps this would be it.

SPECIAL EFFECTS GENERATORS

Figure 12–5 shows a SPECIAL EFFECTS GENERATOR capable of producing colors, wipes, keys, and other fancy effects. These devices generally connect between your camera and your VCR or between one VCR and another. They spice up your picture by creating colored backgrounds or by allowing you to frame parts of your TV picture with a colored border.

FIGURE 12–6 TBC, switcher, and SPECIAL EFFECTS generator all rolled into one (Photo courtesy of Alta)

The more advanced models, with the help of professional TV cameras which have external sync inputs or genlock inputs, can mix the pictures from these cameras together, sending them to your VCR.

For about $6,000 you can buy a device that rolls all of these features into one giant enchilada. The Alta Pyxis-E (Figure 12–6), for instance, contains two time base correctors, a special effects generator capable of wipes, dissolves, and push-on/push-off effects as well as an audio mixer. With it you could take two common (not professional) cameras, two common VCRs, or a combination of cameras and VCRs, and mix their signals together with a push of a button. The resulting picture would be time base corrected and processed with perfect sync, and with color and video level any way you wanted it. The machine will also mix the sound from two sources. The device is good for performing professional-looking effects between two tapes or two cameras. It's the perfect gizmo for Yuppie Heaven.

Panasonic has recently introduced its MX-10 mixer which, for a mere $3,000, will allow you to mix (fade, wipe, freeze frame, posterize) the images of two consumer VCRs *without two TBC*s (seemingly breaking the aforementioned laws of synchronization). Your resulting picture *may* be slightly jittery (it's not time base corrected in any way) but indeed your two VCR signals are mixed.

13

Video maintenance

An ounce of prevention is worth a pound of aspirin. Today's video equipment, though very complex and expensive to fix, rarely breaks down if properly maintained. You can save a lot of repairs by caring for your video equipment. I don't mean romantically, I mean like someone who just bought a $1,000 piece of artwork. You would probably grace it with a dust cover when it wasn't in use, right? You probably won't set drinks or pizza slices on it either. Although this may seem a bit extreme, you might even forbid smoking in the same room. Smoke film builds up on VCR innards and glass lenses just as it does on windows and curtains.

VCRs and other video gear generally don't like the following things and will find frequent excuses to visit the repair shop to avoid them:

1. *Dust:* chalk dust, plaster, cement, sawdust from renovations, beach sand.
2. *Dampness:* rain, sprays (including beach salt sprays), dripping bathing suits, spilled drinks, damp basement storage, being used in a warm room when a machine is cold (water vapor condenses inside).
3. *Shock:* rough handling during transportation (often due to inadequate padding), falling over after being balanced on something.
4. *Heat:* radiator tops in the winter, car trunks in the summer, operation without ventilation (sitting on a deep pile carpet, for instance).

Video maintenance.

REPAIR SERVICES

The smaller your video operation, the more likely it is that you will be the person maintaining the equipment and the more likely it is you will have to send it to someone else for real repair. Some schools and small video users buy MAINTENANCE CONTRACTS, agreements made with an outside repair facility guaranteeing the upkeep of your equipment for a fixed yearly cost plus parts. Some MAINTENANCE CONTRACTS even include a yearly "tune-up"—a very minimal preventive maintenance schedule.

Individuals who buy home video equipment are often pressured by the store salespeople to purchase a MAINTENANCE AGREEMENT which lasts for about two years. Such an agreement for a single VHS VCR might cost $125. These are generally bad deals because

1. If something is likely to go wrong with the VCR, it will happen within the first five days after you take it out of the box. Therefore, it is wise to use the heck out of the equipment for the first five days to spot such potential problems.

Most dealers will take their equipment back within the first five days and will replace it with another, assuming you kept the box and packing and didn't damage anything.

2. The manufacturer's warranty lasts for 90 days to a year, so this time is already covered without the help of the SERVICE CONTRACT.

3. VCRs generally don't break down during their first two years of use.

CLEANING VIDEO HEADS AND TAPE PATH

This is the most common video maintenance you are likely to do.

When to Clean

If you play a tape that you know is good and you get a very grainy or totally snowy picture (as in Figure 13–1), but the sound remains okay, then you've most likely got dirty video heads. This problem may come on gradually or all of a sudden.

Be absolutely sure that the tape you are testing your VCR on is indeed good (imagine scrubbing the heads for hours only to find out that the tape was bad). What can you do to *really* be sure your sample tape is perfect? One solution is to record one good videocassette under the most perfect conditions and save that cassette as your TEST TAPE. Always keep your TEST TAPE handy, even when shooting on location, to test out your VCR.

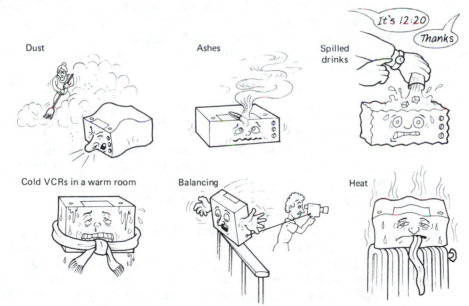

VCRs and other video equipment abhor . . .

FIGURE 13–1 Sound okay but picture grainy or snowy

If you've just cleaned the heads and the problem still persists, clean the heads again. Unlike the overalls in detergent commercials, the heads sometimes require several scrubbings.

If you run the VCR near the sea, near acid or alkali gases, or in a dusty or dirty environment, expect to clean the heads once per hour or so. The same is true if you use flaky, wrinkled, or old tape.

If you perform a lot of pausing and editing, the heads get dirty quicker. Under heavy use, clean the heads once a day.

If the VCR is used in a clean, climate-controlled room, it can probably go for months without cleaning. Closing the cover over the VCR between uses also lengthens the interval between cleanings.

When shooting on location, make frequent test recordings and always carry head cleaner with you.

If you make a test *recording* and play it back and find the picture is snowy, you've probably got dirty heads.

If numerous serious head cleanings have not solved your snowy picture problems, it may be that your heads are worn out. Video heads generally last 1,500 to 2,500 hours. After that, as the heads wear, your picture becomes grainy. You lose sharpness. Colors smear, especially the saturated reds. Dropouts seem more prevalent. In the bitter end, you finally get snow.

Although head wear is gradual, sometimes heads can be suddenly damaged by snagging on a wrinkled videotape, splices, or by riding over a few grains of sand.

A dirty tape path can also cause picture problems. If you play a tape that you know is good, and the picture is unstable, tracks poorly, FLAGWAVES uncontrollably, or if the VCR motor speed wanders (you can hear the speed changing), it may be due to a dirty CONTROL TRACK HEAD. As one of the components in the tape path, the CONTROL HEAD guides the speed of the motor and keeps the picture stable. The problem could also be the fault of a dirty CAPSTAN. If oily, the CAPSTAN may slip and fail to keep the tape moving at the smooth constant pace that is necessary for a stable picture. Sometimes the instability problems can be caused by a lumpy or dirty PINCH ROLLER. It, too, can upset the constant speed of the tape as it passes through the machine.

If the tape squeaks or sticks as it passes through the VCR, clean the tape path. (This problem may also be caused by a cold VCR or a cold videotape. In this case, let them warm up to room temperature before you use them.)

What to Use

If you've been reading the previous chapters, you know not to use Head & Shoulders and a scrub brush to clean video heads. Essentially, you have four choices for cleaning the heads and the tape path:

1. Use a nonabrasive head cleaning cassette.
2. Use an abrasive head cleaning cassette.
3. Open the VCR and manually clean the heads and tape path with a swab and solvent.
4. Send the machine out for cleaning.

Number 1 above is the easiest, least harmful, but ineffective against really tough dirt. Number 2 is easy, works pretty well, but wears down your heads. Use this method sparingly. Number 3 is best—*if* you are handy with a screwdriver (or a vodka collins) and a swab. It's thorough and effective against sticky dirt. Number 4 is expensive, unnecessary, but wise *if* you are having your machine periodically cleaned, adjusted, and lubricated while it's on the shop's operating table.

Bring a head cleaning cassette with you when shooting on location. If your video heads clog, you can fix them in a few seconds by chucking in a head cleaning cassette. Otherwise, you might get stuck trying to disassemble your portable VCR to the sound of jungle drums or the sway of a sail boat in a storm.

Let's study each cleaning technique in detail.

Nonabrasive head cleaning cassette   These look like regular videocassettes but contain a cleaning fabric instead of normal recording tape. Some brands you simply slip into the cassette compartment and then press PLAY. Hit STOP after about 15 to 30 seconds and you are done. Do not rewind. EJECT and the cassette is ready to use again. Other brands require you to wet the fabric with some head cleaning fluid before you insert the cassette and play it.

Nonabrasive cassettes give a very gentle cleaning. This is both good and bad. They are gentle on your video heads, not sanding them down like the abrasive cleaners do. However, they are not very effective against stubborn dirt or head clogs. For this reason, it's good to use them often enough to avoid any major buildup. About once every 500 hours should do it. It is also advisable to clean the heads before storing your machine for several months. Just as tomato sauce and grape juice have a way of staining your white dinner jacket if not attended to immediately, video dirt has a tendency to "harden" with time, making it more difficult to remove after it has "set."

Some brands of cleaning cassettes should be used only once, while others are used to the end, rewound and used over. Naturally, the more they are used, the dirtier the fabric becomes, and the less cleansing occurs. Conceivably, the dirt could even come off the fabric and *add* dirt to your heads and tape path.

Head cleaning cassettes cost $15 to $25.

Abrasive cleaning cassette   Abrasive cassettes are usually made of unfinished videotape—tape which is not polished smooth. The tape acts like very fine sandpaper which cleans the heads while renewing their surface. While buffing the surface, the abrasive is also wearing down the video heads, so use this cleaning method only when actually necessary and apply the treatment only briefly. You might use the abrasive cleaner only once for every 500 hours of playing time and run the cleaner through the recorder for only about five seconds for each application.

The abrasive cleaners are quite effective cleaning out stubborn head clogs that the nonabrasives can't get. The use of abrasive cleaners is somewhat contested among the experts, however, and their overuse or misuse could be hazardous to your video head's health.

Some brands of abrasive head cleaning cassettes have a message tape recorded on the cleaning cassette which may say, "When you can read this message, your heads are clean. Stop the recorder now."

Swabs and solvent   You can use cotton swabs, but they tend to leave cotton fibers behind. It is better to use chamois-covered sticks, or foam swabs. If you are creative, you could buy a single sheet of chamois from an auto parts store, cut it up into little squares and glue the squares to tongue depressors and have a lifetime supply for very few dollars, or you can buy a head cleaning kit with several chamois swabs in it.

You can buy VCR cleaning fluid, or use ethylene dichloride, or liquid freon, or ethyl alcohol. Ethyl alcohol is commonly available at drug stores. Its toxic brother methenol or denatured alcohol is sold in paint stores.

Don't use rubbing alcohol. It has water and oil mixed in it.

Don't use water or soap and water to clean heads. You'd be risking residue and rust.

There are some professional spray can solvents on the market for cleaning heads. Do not just blast the dirt away with a squirt from the can. The spray is icy cold and can shatter warm heads. Instead, spray a swab and use *it* to scrub the heads.

If you're shooting on location with actors costing $100 per hour, and the only VCR within a hundred miles has a clogged head, and you don't have head cleaner, it's time to take a chance. Open the machine, stick your teeshirt over your finger, spit on the end, and wipe the heads. Inelegant, but effective.

Manually Cleaning Heads and Tape Path

One problem with head cleaning cassettes (besides their expense) is that they aren't thorough. They don't remove stubborn dirt very effectively and they can't clean places other than their route along the tape path. You can do a better job by hand.

You can also void your warranty with some companies if you disassemble your machine to clean the heads. You'll need a philips head or better yet, a cross-point screwdriver for removing the screws which hold down the VCR's cover. If you don't have such a screwdriver, go out and buy one, the right size, and of good quality so it stays sharp and doesn't grind down your screw heads.

To clean the video heads, follow the manufacturer's instructions, if you have them. Otherwise, follow these general procedures:

1. Turn off the power to the VCR. Remove the tape, at least from the area where you will be working. You don't want the solvents dripping on the tape. Place the machine on a clean uncluttered work table. Assemble your tools so they are handy. If your machine has been in use, let it cool down for a half-hour before you commence work. Wash your hands thoroughly and dry them. Extinguish any cigarettes as many head cleaning fluids are flammable. Also, ashes dropping into your machine aren't helping you clean it. Besides, smoking is bad for *your* innards too.

2. Following the manufacturer's maintenance instructions, loosen and remove the screws holding down the VCR's lid. Use your philips head screwdriver for this. On some machines it is necessary to remove a knob or two or to pop the cassette lid up before you can remove the machine's top.

3. Locate the HEAD DRUM, a round silver cylinder near the center of the VCR. It will have two small black indentations on the side of it, 180° apart. These are the famed video heads. Some machines have four video heads 90° apart on the drum. On most machines, the head and drum are attached and rotate together. To bring a head around to where you can see it, simply rotate the drum with your hand. Try not to leave fingerprints on the shiny curved outside surface of the drum.

   On other machines, the drum may be stationary with the head spinning inside it, peeking out through a gap in the drum. To bring the head into view, locate the VCR's motor and rotate the motor fan shroud. This will move the heads. You'll see them appear somewhere along the gap in the head drum.

4. Moisten a swab with cleaning fluid. If using freon, cap your bottle immediately as the stuff evaporates like crazy. (If you have a choice, avoid freon altogether as it damages the atmosphere).

5. Wipe the swab *horizontally* back and forth across a video head while holding the head drum stationary with the other hand or by immobilizing the opposite head with your fingertip (covered with a cloth to avoid fingerprints).

   The solvent dries quickly so check your swab from time to time. Be gentle but not too timid. Don't scrub—the heads are delicate; don't tickle them

Cleaning the tape path and video head drum

Camcorder head drum

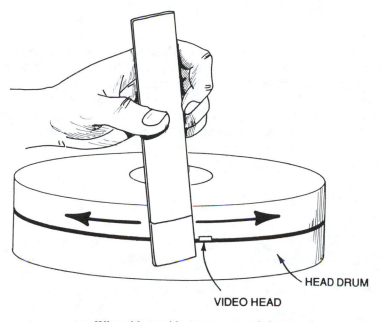

HEAD DRUM
VIDEO HEAD

Wipe side-to-side, never up-and-down

with a feather touch either, the heads aren't that delicate. About 10 swipes should do the trick, then move on to the opposite head. If there are four heads, do all of them.

Do not, under any circumstances, rub up and down against the heads. They are flimsy in the up-and-down direction and will definitely break. Wipe *only* in the direction the tape moves, *horizontally.*

Camcorders are usually so crammed with parts that you may be unable to disassemble them for cleaning. Here's a trick which works in many cases: Pop open the cassette lid and peek inside the VCR's mouth. Way inside you may recognize the HEAD DRUM. With a long swab and stretched fingers you may be able to clean the video heads from the outside. Remember, wipe *sideways.* Incidentally, some portable VCRs have cassette lids which are easy to remove, gaining you easy access to their innards.

Tape path   Since you've gone to the trouble of opening your machine, you might as well clean the tape path while you are working on the heads.

You can use the same swabs and head cleaner to clean the tape path that you used to clean the heads, but the swabs will get dirty very quickly. The video heads have to be super clean so bathe them first with a fresh swab. The used swab is still clean enough to wipe down the rest of the tape path.

Some cleaning fluids (like ethylene dichloride) shouldn't be used on the rubber PINCH ROLLER in the tape path; the chemical tends to dissolve the rubber. Alcohol, when used lightly, won't hurt the rubber parts.

It is sometimes difficult to determine where the tape path is, there being so many pins and rollers in the machine. It could be instructive to plug in the VCR (definitely keeping your paws out of the machine now), and using an unimportant videocassette, switch the VCR's power ON and turn it to PLAY. Watch how the tape threads through the machine. Memorize the tape path. Note the important parts like the ERASE HEAD, AUDIO and CONTROL HEAD, TAPE GUIDES, CAPSTAN, and PINCH ROLLER. Next, STOP and EJECT the cassette, turn off the VCR's power, unplug the VCR, and proceed with the cleaning (unless you are hopelessly mesmerized by watching the whirring machine do its stuff).

Clean the tape path in this order:

1. AUDIO and CONTROL HEAD.
2. CAPSTAN.
3. TAPE GUIDES.
4. ERASE HEAD.
5. PINCH ROLLER.
6. Anything else that seems to have accumulated dust or powder.

Figure 13–2 shows a simplified diagram of a VHS and a VHS-C threading pattern. Note the positions of the CAPSTAN, a vertical shiny rod, and the PINCH ROLLER, a black rubber-coated wheel. They are important to the smooth motion of tape through your machine.

When finished with the head and path cleaning, let everything dry before re-threading a tape into the machine.

If a snowy picture was what drove you to cleaning the heads and tape path, then before putting everything back together, you may want to check out your work to see if you did indeed unclog the video heads. I must warn you, however, that your "open" machine poses a shock hazard. Don't do this if you are inept at things electrical. Connect up your machine, turn it on, insert a tape, and play it. A clean picture means clean head and tape path. Snow and instability mean

1. Maybe the tape is bad or blank.
2. Maybe you weren't thorough enough. Remove the tape and do the whole procedure over. A piece of dirt the size of a particle of smoke is all it takes to clog a video head.

DEMAGNETIZING VIDEO AND AUDIO HEADS

Audiophiles periodically demagnetize the heads on their audio equipment. They use a HEAD DEMAGNETIZER, an electric device about the size of a cucumber. This practice, although beneficial for audio equipment, is of no measurable value to video equipment. Video heads don't need demagnetizing, so don't bother with it.

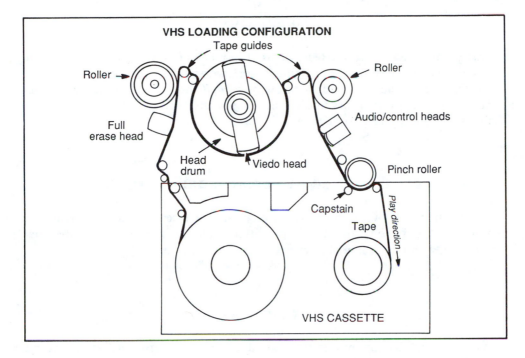

VHS LOADING CONFIGURATION

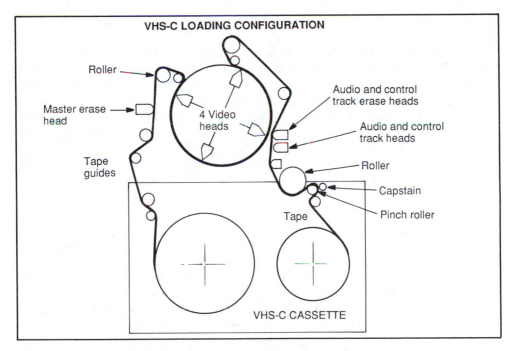

VHS-C LOADING CONFIGURATION

FIGURE 13-2 VHS and VHS-C tape threading patterns

LUBRICATION

Lubrication is best left to the technicians. Too much oil hanging around your machine will collect dust and dirt making it work worse rather than better.

One place where you might throw *one small* drop of oil is the *base* of the CAPSTAN where it disappears into the housing of the VCR. *Do not* put oil on any shiny surface that touches the tape.

CLEANING VCR AND CAMCORDER CABINETS

Most cabinets have wood grain, vinyl, or plastic surfaces. Clean them with soap and water. Avoid strong solvents like paint thinner, acetone, or benzene as they may dissolve the plastics or mar the veneer.

TAPE CARE

Chapter 3 went on about how to store tape and to protect it from accidental erasure. But what do you do halfway through your favorite recording of *The Galloping Gourmet* when the VCR decides to eat some tape for lunch? Here's how to prepare the leftovers.

Folded or wrinkled tape can be flattened out and played if it doesn't look too rough. The image will have lines of snow running through it (as in Figure 3–37) until the bad tape has passed. Using such tape runs the substantial danger of abrading the spinning video heads and perhaps nicking them. Badly stretched, torn, ragged, or ground-up tape runs a *very high* risk of head damage and should always be avoided. The image would be unrecognizable when played anyway. What if part of the tape is physically destroyed and this is your only copy?

The damaged part will never be reclaimed. To make the remainder playable, the bad part has to be cut out and the two good ends SPLICED together.

Splicing a Broken Tape

Even well-made splices have a bump to them and the adhesive can eventually bleed out, contaminating the cassette. Worse yet, the splice itself may snag on a video head and chip it. It is advisable to fix your tape, copy it right away, and thereafter play only your copy. Unfortunately this leaves you playing a second generation tape.

Another option may be possible in those frequent cases where the tape breaks near its beginning or end. Here you can cut off the bad tape and attach the new end to the appropriate hub. You lose a little of the beginning or end of your show (often a less important part) and get to keep your original tape without having a nasty splice go through your VCR.

In the preceding case, if a tape breaks and you don't care about the recording, you can always throw away the shortest half of the tape, reattach the longer half to the other hub, and create a shorter length cassette from the remaining tape. Be sure to label it so the odd-ball length doesn't surprise you later.

Simple reconnection outside the cassette   The simplest and commonest repairs involve reattaching a tape to its leader or cutting out damaged tape segments and reconnecting the ends together. Often both are protruding from the cassette so you don't have to open the shell to find the ends. Here's how the repair is done:

1. Make a clean work space. A sheet of paper works nicely. Across the bottom of the paper mark a straight line.
2. Wash your hands thoroughly and dry them.
3. Open the trapdoor (process described in Figure 13–3) and prop it open with a stiff piece of cardboard. This is so it doesn't snap shut crunching your tape.

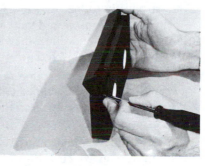

Press lever at bottom of right side of BETA cassette to release trap door. Reels are free to turn when trap door is open.

Press lever at bottom left side of VHS cassette to release trap door.

To rotate tape reels (advancing or rewinding tape manually), press button in bottom center of VHS cassette to unlock reels.

FIGURE 13–3 Opening the trap door on a videocassette

On beta VCRs, this also releases the tape hubs so that you can withdraw more tape from the cassette. On VHS cassettes, however, you free the hubs by inserting the tip of a narrow screwdriver into a hole in the center of the cassette's underside. Be gentle.

4. The outside surface of the tape (shiny side) has contact with the video heads. You don't want any bumps or splicing tape there. Lay your tape down on your paper *inside surface* (dull side) *up*. Using that straight line you drew earlier, line up the edges of the two good tape ends even with that line. Butt them exactly together. Lay coins on the tape to hold it flat and stationary as you position it.

5. Using aluminum-backed self-adhesive mylar tape, apply the splicing tape across the juncture anchoring the excess to the paper. Press firmly. Don't try to use the splicing tape lengthwise. It's nearly impossible to line up.

   If you plan to recopy the tape immediately then throw away the original, you can cheat a little and use transparent tape or some other strong, thin, pliable tape. Masking tape, most cellophane, and wrapping tape won't do; they are likely to bleed "goo" into the splice or come loose.

   Note beta owners: Don't use aluminized tape. Many beta VCRs sense the shiny splice and think they are at the shiny leader at the end of the tape and will switch themselves to stop mid-tape.

6. Trim off the excess SPLICING TAPE with a razor blade or x-acto knife making a very slightly cresent shaped cut as you trim. This will make the spliced portion just a hair narrower than the rest of the videotape so it won't rub against the cassette walls.

7. Wind the tape back into the cassette, unprop the cassette door, and you are back in business. Figure 13–4 diagrams the process.

For those who expect to do frequent splicing, there are kits consisting of a SPLICING BLOCK which will line up your tape and guide your razor blade, and a set of gummed tape splices.

Opening the cassette   As many sea creatures do when disturbed, the tape sometimes retreats into the safety of its shell. Getting it out is a project. You have to take the cassette apart. Do this job right and you'll only have to deal with two or three parts and some screws. Do it wrong and all thirty-six internal components will spring out at you plus umpteen-hundred odd feet of recording tape in a nice neat ball. If you are the kind of person who took clocks apart as a kid—and put them back together so they'd work—then you've developed the kind of skills necessary for "open-cassette surgery."

1. Start with a clean surface and clean hands.

2. If the cassette has a spine label, slit it down the middle along the seam between the two halves on the cassette (the cassette can't hinge open; it must be completely separated into two parts).

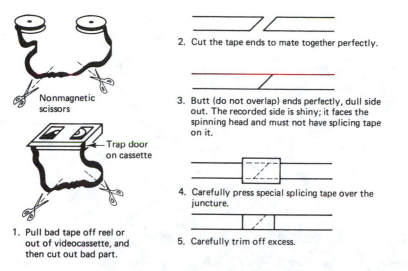

FIGURE 13-4 Splicing a video tape

3. Place the cassette upside down and remove the four to six screws holding the halves together. Use a proper sized, good quality philips head screwdriver. Keep track of which screws came from which holes so you can put them back in exactly the same places. VHS cassettes usually have two long screws in the front edge and three short ones in the back.

4. With the screws removed, carefully pick up the cassette sandwich and turn it right side up. If you are the clutzy type, you may wish to scotch tape the halves together before you turn the cassette over, because if you let the halves separate at this crucial point, you'll be vacuuming parts out of the carpet for weeks.

5. Lift the top half away from the bottom. You first may have to release the trap door manually (Figure 13–3) before the halves will separate.

6. Find the loose tape ends and rethread them through their guides and hold-back pads until they emerge outside the cassette in the proper fashion. See Figure 13–5. For betas the tape threads between the hold-back pad and guides on each side of the cassette. For VHS, there is only one hold-back pad situated on the left side. On the right side, thread the tape between the metal tape guide and the plastic one just behind it.

7. Once you've gotten the tape ends out (don't try to take the roll of tape out unless you have a degree in neurosurgery), reassemble the cassette halves. The trap door may have to be part-way open for the halves to mesh. You may wish to reinstall the screws (before you forget to or before you bump this little land mine) or if you are the type who is likely to lose the tape ends back into the cassette while working on them, just scotch tape the halves together for now.

8. Splice the tape as described earlier, then flip the cassette over and reinstall the screws into their proper holes.

Don't try to take the roll of tape out of the cassette

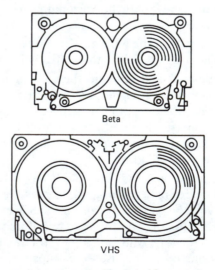

Beta

VHS

FIGURE 13-5   Inside the videocassette

Sometimes the tape or leader doesn't break but pulls free of the reel hub inside the cassette. You can recognize this situation by noting that the free end of the tape still has a leader attached to it. When you open up the cassette you'll probably see a little clamp floating loose in there somewhere. That clamp was supposed to secure the tape to the hub. This is easy to fix:

1. Remove the empty reel from the lower shell. You can release the reel lock by gently pressing a spring in there.
2. From the full reel, draw off just enough tape to work with.
3. Attach the leader to the center of the hub and press the plastic clamp back into its socket. Be careful when applying pressure so as not to bend or break the reel flanges.
4. Rethread the tape through the guides, reinstall the reel, and close the patient.
   When done, try out the cassette. If your VCR ejects it, maybe the tape is loose inside. Try winding or rewinding it for a few moments to tighten the tape. If it still ejects, maybe you've threaded the tape wrong inside the cassette.

Handling wrinkles When you get wrinkled, you can get a face-lift. When your tape gets wrinkled, you have two choices:

1. Cutting out the bad part (a technique that doesn't work so well on people wrinkles).
2. Ironing the tape if it is not wrinkled too badly (this technique is not recommended for people wrinkles, either).

The ironing process takes some skill and should not be tried for the first time on your most important piece of tape. Here's the process:

1. Clean the tape of dust and tape fragments.
2. Preheat a household iron to 190°F (this is often the permanent press setting). Make sure that there is no water in the iron and that you don't accidentally leave it in the steam setting.
3. Sandwich the tape between two sheets of clean white typing paper.
4. Place the sandwich on a hard, smooth, flat surface.
5. Apply the iron with light to moderate pressure for 8 to 12 seconds.

Even if you manage to eliminate the wrinkles in the tape, chances are that some of the oxide will have still flaked off the plastic tape at the places where the tape was creased. These empty spots will show up as dropouts when you play the tape. With VHS tapes, an automatic light sensor in the VCR may "see through"

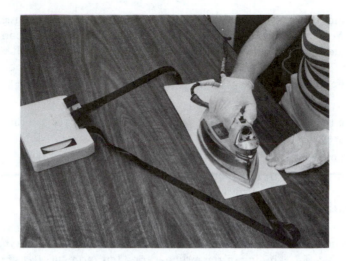

Ironing videotape

some of these holes and shut down the machine. To solve this problem, use a black felt marker to "paint out" the pinholes on the back side of the tape.

While we're on the subject, if you discover one cassette tape in your collection which seems to stop itself at the same spot always, suspect a pinhole or scratch on the tape to be the blame. When the VCR's sensing light can shine *through* the tape, the VCR coughs it up. (On betas, shiny splicing tape has the same effect.) The solution is to black over the holes with a black permanent felt pen.

CLEANING LENSES

Generally, dust the lens with a new, clean, artist's paint brush or a photographer's camel's hair dusting brush (Figure 13-6). The professional dusting brush even has bellows for blowing lint off the lens. To remove fingerprints, fog the lens with your breath and use lens tissue. For stubborn fingerprints, use a soft cloth over your finger dampened with a mild nonabrasive soap and water. Windex—sprayed on the cloth, not directly on the lens—works pretty well. Clean in a circular motion. Wipe off the soap. Wipe the lens dry. Some manufacturers advise against using eyeglasss lens tissue to clean camera lenses because it may scratch the lens or the delicate blue or amber coating on the lens.

Many photographers protect their lenses by screwing a clear glass lens filter onto their lens. Thus, salt spray, blowing sand, fingerprints, and mud end up on the lens attachment rather than on the lens itself. The attachment is easier to clean, and if damaged, is cheap to replace. Some photographers use UV (ultra violet) filters or SKYLIGHT filters in place of a clear glass filter. These two filters don't hurt the picture any, and may even help it while protecting your lens.

BATTERY CARE

The rechargeable batteries used with portable VCRs come with instructions for their care and recharging.

The two popular types of batteries used in portable video equipment are GEL CELLS and NICADS. If using both types of batteries, be sure to charge each on its *own* charger. A GEL CELL charger should not charge a NICAD battery and vice versa.

Gel Cells

GEL CELLS use the same technology that starts your car in the morning; lead and acid interact to push electrons out one of the two poles on the battery. By pushing the electrons back into the same pole, you recharge the battery. Unlike your car battery which has acid which can spill, the GEL CELL contains a gelatinous electrolyte which is sealed in for safe operation in any position. For safety's sake, keep GEL CELLS upright when charging.

GEL CELLS cost one-half what NICADS cost and are very reliable. Many are one-piece units which simply insert into your portable VCR through a trap door and will run your machine for up to an hour (depending on how much juice your camera uses).

GEL CELLS have an excellent shelf life—once charged, they retain 80% of their charge for nearly a year if unused, and much longer if kept in the cold. GEL CELLS operate over a wide temperature range, but give less power the colder they are. GEL CELLS should last three to five years or about 200 discharge cycles before they die. As they reach the end of their life, they lose some of their oomph and can power your VCR for only 45 minutes or less. After using a GEL CELL, charge it back up as soon as you can or the insides will start to crystallize, shortening the battery's life.

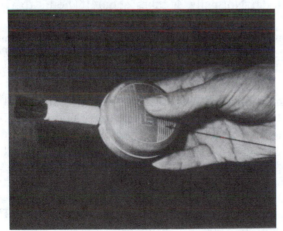

Handle is bellows that blows air when squeezed.

FIGURE 13-6 Camel's hair dusting brush

A discharged GEL CELL will take up to eight hours for an 80% recharge or 16 hours for a total recharge. A brand new uncharged GEL CELL may take 24 hours to charge and a 100% discharged GEL CELL may take 32 hours to totally recharge.

GEL CELLS don't pack the power of NICADS and are bulkier and heavier. If you run your portable VCR on AC most of the time and on batteries for about an hour once in a while, a GEL CELL is probably the best buy for the money. If you are into heavy-duty battery use, then NICADS may be your answer.

Nicads

NICADS are made with nickel and cadmium, hence their name. They cost about twice as much as GEL CELLS but hold about three times the usable power for the same weight and size package. Notice that I said *usable*. As a NICAD expends its energy, its voltage remains fairly constant up there at a level where the VCR can use it. Thus the NICAD can empty nearly completely before it poops out. GEL CELLS, on the other hand, lose voltage gradually. When your VCR senses that your battery voltage has dropped about 10%, the VCR turns itself off, essentially rejecting the battery even though it has life left. Thus, not all of a GEL CELL's power can be used by a VCR.

Although one-hour NICAD packs can be bought which can slip into your VCR, three-hour external models are also available.

The NICAD packs can be charged 500 to 1,000 times, but their lifetime would be better measured in years (three years, typically) rather than discharges.

NICADS can operate over a wide temperature range but don't lose as much of their oomph when the temperature drops as do GEL CELLS. They can operate in any position and do not leak.

NICADS can be "fast charged" in two to three hours using a special charger which senses whether it is overheating the cells in the process. Overheating could cause the batteries to explode. Normally, it takes about 16 hours to recharge a NICAD.

Unlike GEL CELLS, NICADS put out approximately the same voltage until they are nearly out of juice. Then the voltage drops precipitously. In one respect this is good; machinery and circuits will run as well from the battery's fortieth minute as they did from its fourth minute. In another respect, this is bad because a simple meter won't tell you how much charge is left in the battery; it will read full strength for maybe 55 minutes and drop on the next as the battery poops out. Since the meter doesn't signal the impending power failure, you have very little advanced warning that your shooting is about to screech to a halt. To protect against this unwelcome surprise, many video producers carry several battery packs into the field. You know your shoot is three-quarters over when three of your four batteries are used up.

Although NICADS charge quickly, their shelf life isn't too great. They lose about 1% of their charge per day while just sitting—more if they are sitting in the heat. To keep them ready for action, charge them once per month even if unused.

Some users "trickle charge" their NICADS to keep them 100% charged all the time. This process requires only a tiny charger which pumps a small amount of current (a trickle) into the battery every day to make up for the NICAD's 1% daily loss.

NICADS like exercise. Give them a deep discharge occasionally to keep them fit.

CABLE CARE

1. *Do* keep a couple of spares around. By substituting a spare you can determine if the cable has failed or some other component. Also, the inevitable cable failure is less devastating if you can substitute a good one and get back to business immediately, replacing the broken one at your leisure.
2. *Do* buy heavy-duty name brand cables and connectors like Amphenol or Switchcraft; they'll last longer.
3. *Do* keep your connectors off the floor. They can get dirty and flattened underfoot.
4. *Do* clean the contacts on a plug with emery or fine sandpaper, or even a pencil eraser when it appears that corrosion is causing you to have an intermittent, weak, or "crackly" connection.
5. *Don't* try to force a plug into a socket if it doesn't want to fit. It will break.
6. *Don't* try to use a plug with a pin missing. It won't work unless all the pins make connection.
7. *Don't* coil cables tightly. *Do* coil them in 15-inch loops to avoid strain.
8. *Don't* let your pets chew on the cords—especially the power cord. Fido might be in for a shock. Chewed video and audio cables don't work so hot either.
9. *Don't* pull a cable out by its cord. Always pull it by the plug. The wires are frail; the plug is strong.

LIGHTNING PROTECTION

Countless VCRs are damaged by nearby lightning strikes sending a surge of electricity into your antenna wires, cable TV wires, or AC wires. If you come home some day after a rip-snortin' thunderstorm and find that your VCR won't turn on, its power supply may be cooked. This can happen whether your VCR was turned off or left on during the storm. The repair costs about $50 to $100. If the lightning came in on the antenna or TV cable line, then it may have zapped your tuner. Your VCR will *play* tapes all right, but it won't tune in any channels. This repair generally costs around $150.

The absolute solution to the lightning problem is to unplug your VCR from the wall outlet and from its antenna or cable hookup. Then nothing can hurt it save a direct lightning strike going straight through the middle of your house (somewhat rare). Unfortunately, disconnecting your VCR from the wall outlet will often discombobulate your timer and you will have to reset the clock next time you use the VCR.

Less safe, but better than nothing, is a LIGHTNING ARRESTOR placed on the circuit breaker box in your home. This fist-sized attachment will absorb many "spikes" of electricity that come down the electric line when lightning strikes the wires near your home. The device costs about $50 to $100 to install and will protect *all* the appliances in the house against most surges.

SURGE PROTECTORS, built usually for computers, are small electric boxes which plug into the wall, and you plug your computer, VCR, or whatever into the box. These also hold back "spikes" of electricity but are not 100% effective. A really big spike from a nearby lightning strike will still go through them.

Home TV antennas generally have their wires grounded using a special device called a LIGHTNING ARRESTOR which connects to the antenna wire and goes to a

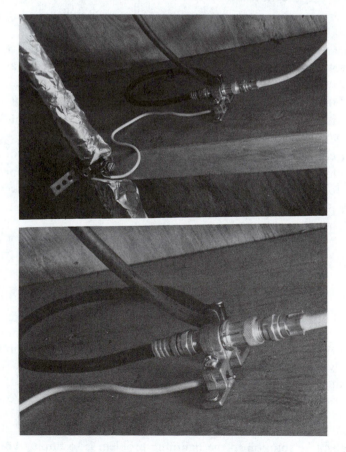

FIGURE 13-7 Cable TV grounding

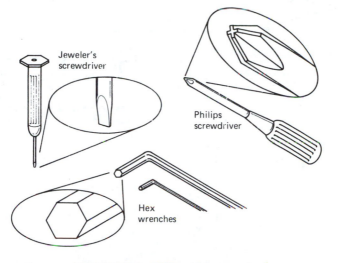

FIGURE 13-8 VCR and camera tools

post driven into the ground outside your house. Supposedly, lightning will strike your antenna and will travel down this wire and straight into the ground. The antenna LIGHTNING ARRESTOR may keep your house from catching fire but probably will not save your TV or VCR from some of the "surge" which doesn't go straight to the ground.

Cable TV hookups usually employ a grounding connection that ties to a cold water pipe (Figure 13-7). This generally protects your VCR and TV from being zapped when lightning strikes the cable company's wires. Again the process is not foolproof; a nearby lightning strike can still make a surge big enough to singe your circuits.

GENERAL CARE

Invest in some tiny jeweler's screwdrivers, a *good quality* little philips head screwdriver, and some small metric hex wrenches. No, a philips screwdriver is not a vodka and milk of magnesia cocktail, nor is a hex wrench used by a witch. These are specialized tools (diagrammed in Figure 13-8) to keep knobs, screws, bolts, catches, latches, do-dads, and thing-a-ma-hoosies tight. Once the bolts fall out, finding replacement latches and new bolts is next to impossible. This is one situation where an ounce of prevention definitely saves you a pound of hard work—it is so easy to tighten loose screws and so hard to replace lost ones.

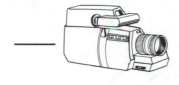

14

Selling your productions

When you're particularly proud of the tape you've just made, the thought probably passes through your mind, "I bet I could sell this." Or maybe you've just laid out five grand upgrading your video equipment and are now wondering how to earn some of those expenses back. Or, maybe you've watched one TV show too many and have decided, "Anybody can do better than that." Whatever your motive, you are on the edge of a whole new dimension of videomaking—selling your wares.

Surprisingly, videotapes are more easily made than sold. Buying equipment and producing a show before having an established market for your programs puts the cart a mile before the horse. It is wise to spend some time thinking out marketing strategy before spending big bucks on equipment and production.

AUDIENCE

If you plan to sell your TV productions to the broadcast or commercial markets, you'll have to use the best of everything. This audience expects pizzazz and glitter and will not tolerate grainy pictures, poor acting, muddy sound, or wobbly camera angles. You will have to produce in a sound controlled environment (perhaps a studio) with proper color-corrected lighting, using expensive TV cameras, recording and editing the results on one-inch or similar tape. VHS or beta mastering is absolutely out of the question. You *might* get by mastering on 3/4 U or Super VHS and editing on one-inch, but this lowers your picture quality to the bare minimum right at the start. Some producers, however, shoot in the field using 3/4 U or S-VHS because the equipment is portable, and is rentable at a reasonable price (an important factor when you spend a lot of hours producing raw footage). If you *must* master on 3/4 U, try to use a 3/4 U-SP (superior performance) VCR. The picture quality is better.

If you are thinking of selling your wares to PBS, MTV, HBO, or National Geographic, then give up *any* notion you have of mastering on VHS, beta, or 8mm. The quality just won't cut it. Go out and rent an $8,000 TV camera, a $10,000 VCR, and maybe professional lights, microphones, and tripod to start the job right. Then edit the works at a postproduction house.

There is another audience that is less discriminating. Local cable TV, local business and industry, some nonbroadcast educational distributors, distributors of home video "how to" videotapes, and some educational UHF broadcast stations will accept productions mastered on 3/4 U and edited on 3/4 U. These viewers know that they are not watching network television. This audience won't laugh at semiprofessional acting, and will forgive slightly grainy pictures shot in slightly echoey rooms. Here 3/4 U (or better, 3/4 U-SP, or S-VHS) is the minimum mastering medium if you want your pictures to survive the edit experience.

The editing process usually requires that you shoot the raw footage, then edit it onto another tape (now second generation), and then copy the edited master for distribution (now third generation). VHS and beta when shot at their fastest speed may look okay as masters but don't copy very well. Even 3/4 U deteriorates a bit by the time it reaches the third generation.

FIND A NICHE

If you can produce a tape that no one has ever produced before, that appeals to an audience large enough to sell your program to, yet small enough not to interest the big commercial guys, then you've found a niche. Say you have unusual access to a police dog training academy and wish to make a tape on how to train police pooches. Say you've also poked through some tape catalogues and discovered that there are no tapes already available on this subject. Say you did some further research and discovered 140 mini academies for training police dogs elsewhere in the nation. This all adds up to a reasonable argument for producing your police dog academy tape.

With a captive audience of potential buyers sharing an intrinsic interest in your "rare" tape, you have a good chance of selling it to them even if you didn't spend $20,000 producing it. This otherwise discriminating audience has become a less discriminating audience because your show has a special meaning to them.

Incidentally, tapes made for classroom instruction should run about 20 minutes in length. That's the attention span of most students and it fits comfortably into most class schedules. "How-to" programs for home viewers should run longer; this audience tends to expect a lot of content for their money.

BUDGET

Whatever you spend on a project, you want to make it back plus a few sheckles more. You estimate your income by projecting the number of copies you will sell times the price per copy. How many copies you will sell is anybody's guess, but sometimes you can establish a fairly concrete minimum number by locating a list of people and organizations who are very likely to buy your product. If there are 140 police dog academies nationwide, it may be reasonable to expect to sell your tape to maybe a quarter of them. If you price your tape at $150 (a common figure for 20-minute instructional programs), then you know you can spend $5,250 on production and advertising to break even. If your program, however, is of interest to the general public, you will have to charge less (perhaps $60 per tape) to stay competitive. Institutions are generally willing to pay more for a program than home consumers are.

BUYING VERSUS RENTING EQUIPMENT

Renting video equipment is expensive. Buying it is often more expensive. You have to amortize the cost of your equipment over all the days of its use and all the productions you make. Video equipment is a lot like race horses. It eats while you sleep.

Will the equipment you buy pay for itself?

Every day you *don't* produce with your equipment, it costs you money. So before buying an expensive video outfit, make some conservative calculations on how many times you expect to use it over its useful life (perhaps three to five years). Now compare that number with what it would cost to rent the equipment over the same period of time.

Additional factors to consider when making your decision are

1. When you rent equipment, it is generally less than one year old, not three to five as yours would become.
2. Rented equipment is usually maintained on spec by professional technicians. Who will be maintaining your equipment?
3. You can generally rent better equipment than you can afford to buy. Where you might buy a $1,200 "good enough" camera, you would most likely rent a $5,000 professional grade camera.

Until you have a track record of successful program sales, it's usually better to rent than to buy video equipment. In fact, the Utz Law of Video Purchases goes like this: *If you can't make a profit producing video with rented equipment, you won't make a profit producing with purchased equipment.*

DISTRIBUTION

You can advertise your wares in the classified sections of various magazines like *Video Review, Video, Videomaker, Popular Science,* or even *Popular Photography,* wherever you think your market lies. Another possibility is to sell your tape to catalogues which will distribute your programs along with many others.

Video Schoolhouse, out of Monterey, California, is one of the largest video catalogues listing over 5,000 titles from 400 producers. This 136-page catalog is sent to both home video stores and home consumers who request it. Independent producers can enter a nonexclusive contract with Video Schoolhouse receiving about 50% of the tape's retail price minus duplication costs (about $6 per cassette) for each copy.

Co-op advertising catalogues such as SMW Video of Davis, California, go about the process in a different way. You buy space in the catalog for $200 to $6,000 (depending on whether you simply want to list a tape's title and description or to place a full-page color ad). The catalogue is then mailed to about one million prospects.

Bookstores are becoming more and more inclined to sell videocassettes. One company that specializes in marketing independently produced videotapes to bookstores is Paperback Video of Novato, California. Your arrangement with Paperback Video would be much like the contract between an author and a publisher. The publisher handles making the duplicates (using high quality equipment) and packaging your tape with an attractive cover. Your tape will probably sell for about $40 with a royalty of about $5 to you per copy. Table 14–1 lists some videotape distributors who serve independent video makers.

Cutting the Deal

The distribution deal that you make may last for years and involve thousands of dollars. Take care not to sign with the first distributor that comes along, but to get as many offers as you can from reputable distributors. If several distributors think that your video will make money for them, this will give you the confidence to bid one against another for the best offer.

Consider the distributor's ability to promote and sell your tape. Take careful notes or make a grid, listing the distributor's names down one side of a sheet of paper and the royalties and other important factors across the top. Some important aspects to consider are

1. What percentage of gross income will you receive? (Don't measure anything by net income because that number is too easily manipulated. Also beware that a smaller percentage royalty will encourage the distributor to promote your work more, generating a higher volume of sales.)
2. What are the purchase and rental prices?
3. How many rental copies of your tape will the distributor keep on hand?
4. Does the distributor already have tapes similar to yours? How many per year are sold/rented?
5. To whom will the distributor market your tape?
6. When is the distributor's next catalogue coming out? Will your tape be in it?

TABLE 14–1   VIDEOTAPE DISTRIBUTORS WHO MAY MARKET YOUR WORK

ABC Video Enterprises
2040 Avenue of the Stars
Los Angeles, CA 90067
    Sports, cultural, children, science, entertainment, how-to

Active Home Video
211 S. Beverly Drive
Suite 100
Beverly Hills, CA 90212
    Sports, features, how-to

American Home Video Library
1500 Broadway, Suite 1807
New York, NY 10136
    Travel, health, children, how-to

American Video Tape/Electric Video
1116 Edgewater Avenue
Ridgefield, NJ 07657
    Features, documentaries, children

Astralvision Communications
8949 Sunset Blvd.
Los Angeles, CA 90096
    Video art, music concerts

Bookshelf Video
301-BW Dyer Road
Santa Ana, CA 92707
    Sports, cultural, entertainment, how-to

Castelli-Sonnabend Gallery
420 West Broadway
New York, NY 10012
    Art, experimental

Children's Video Library
1011 High Ridge Road
Box 4000
Stamford, CT 06907
    Children

TABLE 14–1 (CONTINUED)

Chronical Video Cassettes
9000 Sunset Blvd., Suite 415
Los Angeles, CA 90069
  Sports, arts, children, educational, music, entertainment, how-to

Corinth Video
410 East 62nd Street
New York, NY 10021
  Educational, entertainment, features, documentaries

Electronic Arts Intermix
10 Waverly Place
New York, NY 10003
  Video art, documentaries

Karl/Lorimar Home Video
17942 Cowan Avenue
Ervine, CA 92714
  Children, sports, documentaries, exercise, how-to

Kultur
1340 Ocean Avenue
Sea Bright, NJ 07760
  Cultural

Media Home Entertainment
5730 Buckingham Parkway
Culver City, CA 90230
  Features

Monterey Home Video
7920 Alabama Avenue
Canoga Park, CA 91304
  Music, health

New Age Video Inc.
Box 669 Old Chelsea Station
New York, NY 10113
  Dance, educational, music

New Day Films
7 Harvard Square
Brookline, MA 02146
  Aging, alternative health care, women, social programs, labor history

Nightingale-Conant Corp.
3730 West Devon Avenue
Chicago, Illinois 60659
  Self-help, motivational, how-to

Pacific Arts Video Records
26382 Carmel Rancho Lane
Carmel, CA 93923
  Concerts, video art, music videos, comedies

Paperback Video Inc.
448 Ignacio Blvd.
Number 254
Novato, CA 94947
  How-to

Phoenix Films/BFA Educational Media
468 Park Avenue, South
New York, NY 10016
  Arts, cultural, educational, entertainment

Pyramid Film and Video
Box 1048
Santa Monica, CA 90406
  Health, children, business, experimental

SMW Video
803 Russell Blvd. #2
Davis, CA 95616
  Coop listings in *The Video Tape Catalog*, circulation of 1 million.

Vestron Video
1011 High Ridge Road
Box 4000
Stamford, CT 06907
  Exercise, sports, travel, cultural, how-to

Vidamerica
235 East 55th Street
New York, NY 10022
  Children, sports, health, how-to

Video Associates
5419 Sunset Blvd.
Hollywood, CA 90027
  Features, children, how-to

Video Gems
731 North LaBrea Avenue
Los Angeles, CA 90038
  Documentaries, health, sports, children, how-to

Video Schoolhouse
2611 Garden Road
Monterey, CA 93940
  Crafts, skills, how-to

Wishing Well Distributing
Box 529
Graton, CA 95444
  Holistic health, health food

Taping for the news

TAPING FOR THE NEWS

If you keep your equipment charged up and ready, you never know when you might be lucky enough to witness some terrible disaster and get it on tape, blood, guts, and all. Now that you have this fancy footage, where do you go to convert it into dollars and fame? How do you shoot it so that news broadcasters can use it? How much should you ask for your "priceless footage"? There are no hard and fast rules to follow, but here are some guidelines.

Shooting for News

1. Use a new videocassette and record at the fastest speed.
2. Let your shots run at least 30 seconds. Don't try to "edit in the camera."
3. Include the natural sounds of the event. Don't talk when you are shooting or your voice will become part of the background.
4. Include a wide angle establishing shot and later go in for close-ups on the action. Also include faces; they help tell the story.
5. Pans and zooms should be very slow.

6. If you are really getting into it, then include some interviews. Ask your questions from behind the camera and get people to tell what happened. Try to position them in front of the turmoil of the event taking place.

7. Don't spend too much time on the event. Once you have the essential footage, start working immediately on getting your tape into the news pipeline.

Whom to Call

Call the news desks at your local TV stations starting with the network affiliates. Events with the impact of a department store opening will only interest the smallest and most local of stations. Bigger events like apartment fires would probably whet the nearest big city stations. Tornados, train wrecks, floods, and shootouts are juicy enough to attract the networks, usually via their affiliate stations. Table 14–2 lists the network news bureaus and their phone numbers in some major cities.

You may not have to make a phone call at all. If the TV crews arrive after you've shot the good stuff, leave your name and number with a reporter from a local station, or better yet, wait and see what station doesn't show up; they may be more desperate for your tape.

Time is of the essence and is always working against you. Your tape may have to be driven for several hours and then take a chopper ride for another hour and be jet planed halfway across the country, eating up four to six hours on its way to the newsroom. On the other hand, local affiliates may be able to play your tape and beam the signal back to the New York office for replay to the nation. Whatever the case, news time is over at 6:30 pm in New York and after that, your tape loses value fast.

TABLE 14-2   NETWORK NEWS BUREAUS

Atlanta			Denver			San Francisco		
NBC	404-434-7000		CBS	303-720-3425		CBS	415-362-0051	
CBS	404-321-4321		Los Angeles			Washington		
CNN	404-827-1500		ABC	213-557-4517		ABC	202-887-7777	
NBC	404-881-0154		CBS	213-852-2202		CBS	202-457-4444	
Boston			CNN	213-469-5533		CNN	202-342-7900	
CBS	617-720-3425		NBC	213-840-4133		NBC	202-885-4200	
Chicago			Miami					
ABC	312-750-7777		ABC	305-448-9036				
CBS	312-337-1341		CBS	305-545-5000				
CNN	312-661-1100		CNN	305-947-9016				
NBC	312-861-5400		NBC	305-868-1501				
Dallas			New York					
ABC	214-641-7777		ABC	212-887-7777				
CBS	214-742-4743		CBS	212-975-4114				
CNN	214-747-1440		CNN	212-839-6000				
NBC	214-998-1300		NBC	212-664-4444				

CNN also has a nationwide news number: 1-800-544-NEWS.

How Much to Ask

Price is determined by the marketplace, the rarity of the event, the quality of the recording, and the significance and dramatic impact of the footage. Exclusivity also affects the price. As important as it is for NBC to have your sinking ferryboat shots, it is equally important that the other networks *not* have the shots. Yet, sometimes it is better to keep your tape nonexclusive so that you may sell the program several times over.

CNN and unaffiliated local stations generally pay about $150 per event. Bigger, juicier stories go for more. Really good shots could run from $2,000 to $10,000, but only the major networks will pay this much.

One way to learn the value of your footage is to offer it to all the networks and see how the bidding goes. A couple thousand dollars is routine payment for material used on network evening news shows.

The worst thing you could do is hand your tape to your local TV station and get nothing in writing. If the event is really juicy, your program may end up on network TV, but no one will admit that they agreed to pay you. Get an agreement in writing with someone in authority such as the News Director. Have in writing the amount to be paid to you and whether that amount is for local or network showing. You should be able to get an additional amount for network showing. Unless you are offering an *exclusive* to the station, keep your hands on your tape. Let the station make a copy of it and give it back to you to peddle elsewhere. Besides, the legal paperwork is often filled in at the bureau headquarters so you might as well drive the tape there yourself.

Sometimes you record an event on a specialized recorder that the station or network might not have, such as a foreign PAL or SECAM videocassette recorder or an 8mm deck. Here you may find yourself bringing your recorder along with you so that the station can quickly make a copy from your format to theirs.

To many videographers a network screen credit is as valuable as dollars. Ask to have your name listed when your tape is used, or have your name listed in the credits at the end of the show.

LOCAL CABLE ACCESS

For some, making a buck isn't a big motivation; having their work shown to others is. Local cable TV access is one way to get your videos into the homes of others. Be aware that not many people tune in to local cable access channels and even though your cable TV company may serve 100,000 customers, only two or three of those customers may be watching this "no frills" channel at a time. In short, playing a tape doesn't get people to watch it. *Marketing* the tape through newspaper ads or direct mail may increase your viewership.

The cable stations aren't likely to pay you anything for your show, but if it's a public access channel, they are not likely to charge you for playing your tape either.

Accessing Public Access

In 1984, the Congress passed the Cable Communications Policy Act giving local governments the authority to require public access channels as part of franchise agreements and giving the FCC the muscle to enforce the local provisions. Previously the FCC had created its own rules regarding cable, but these were overturned in the courts. In short, it's the *cable franchise agreement* with the local towns and cities which provides cable access channels, not some special law applying statewide or nationwide.

Sometimes it is difficult to get cable companies to play your stuff. To access the cable access channel you may have to prod a bit:

1. Study your local cable system and figure out which channel is the public access channel.
2. Call the executive offices of your local cable system (not the billing department; not the national headquarters) and speak to the Director of Programming or General Manager, asking for public access time. Find out what format videocassettes the cable company allows; you may need to dub a copy of your tape over to their format.
3. If the company offers no provisions for public access, ask about leased access whereby you could pay perhaps $100 per hour to show your program.
4. If the cable company seems totally unwilling to play your tape, here are some tactics perhaps to change their ways:
   a. Offer to volunteer to help the company with local productions such as cablecasting city council meetings. By rubbing elbows with the local power-brokers, you may be able to get your *own* shows on the cable later.
   b. Check with City Hall to view a copy of the local television franchise agreement and look for provisions relating to public access, community programming, leased access, local programming, and educational access. You may find some sweet-sounding promises in the franchise agreement that you can convert into leverage with the company. If you don't, you may have to wait until the franchise is up for renewal.
   c. Go to the library and request a copy of Public Law 98-549, the Cable Communications Policy Act of 1984. Cite Sections 611 and 612 to the cable company management. If that doesn't work, call your congressman or senator and cite the statutes to them for enforcement.
   d. Call the National Federation of Local Cable Programmers (202-544-7272) and ask for help for pursuing public access. You also might call the FCC

(202-632-7000) if you think your local cable company is in violation of its franchise agreement and the Cable Act.

Most cable operators would like to appear community minded and will try to cooperate with you. If nothing else, they would like to avoid a big stink, and one way to make you go away is to let you play your tape.

Some cable operators, on the other hand, encourage participation in local access. They even provide small studios and will train you in how to use their equipment to produce your own shows. You may even be able to build a profitable and mutually beneficial relationship with your cable company.

CABLE PROGRAMMING DIRECTORIES

The National Federation of Local Cable Programmers in association with *Broadcasting Magazine* publish the *Cable Programming Resource Directory* which lists more than 1,100 locations where local-originator access programming is produced. The directory includes information on management and facilities, gives tips on programming success factors, and features international cable programming sources. You can order the catalogue through the NFLCP's national office at 906 Pennsylvania Avenue, SE, Washington, DC 20003.

The Foundation for Community Service Cable Televison provides a tape exchange program for underutilized local cable channels while helping independent video makers reach a wider, more diverse audience. Your tapes must be noncommercial and copyright cleared to be listed in the FCSCT computer database. Although the organization is not a distribution service, the information they offer to cable

TABLE 14–3 FILM AND VIDEO ORGANIZATIONS
AND CLUBS

Boston Film and Video Foundation
1126 Boylston Street
Boston, MA 02115
(617-536-1540)

Association for Independent Video and Film Makers
625 Broadway (9th Floor)
New York, NY
(212-473-3400)

Center for New Television
11 East Hubbard Street (5th Floor)
Chicago, IL 60611
(312-565-1787)

Image Film/Video Center
972 Peachtree Street (Suite 213)
Atlanta, GA 30309
(404-352-4225)

companies may result in your tape finding uses elsewhere in the country. For information, contact the FCSCT at 5010 Geary Blvd., Suite 3, San Francisco, CA 94118.

CLUBS, ASSOCIATIONS, ORGANIZATIONS

A comprehensive resource guide for independent producers and video artists listing various associations and organizations involved in videotaping and filmmaking around the country is available for $4 through the Bay Area Video Coalition (BAVC) at 1111 17th Street, San Francisco, CA 94107 (415-861-3282). Some other notable organizations are listed in Table 14–3.

You can also check the bulletin boards and classified sections of various video magazines such as *Video, Video Review,* and *Videomaker.*

TABLE 14–4 HOME VIDEO FESTIVALS

American Independent Feature Market
21 West 86th Street
New York, NY 10023
(212-496-0909)
  All categories.
  Formats: 3/4U, film

Athens Video Festival
P.O. Box 388
Athens, OH 45701
(614-594-6888)

Birmingham International Educational Film Festival
Alabama Power Company
P.O. Box 2641
Birmingham, AL 35291
(205-250-1000)
  Programs showing that educational media can be entertaining. Students, independents, and commercial producers invited.
  Formats: beta, VHS, 3/4U
  Deadline: early January

The Chicago International Film Festival
415 North Dearborn Street
Chicago, IL 60610
(312-644-3400)
  United foreign and domestic films with critics, distributors, and exhibitors via award ceremonies.
    Selected productions are screened at the Center for New Television.
  Formats: VHS, 3/4U
  Deadline: Mid September

Global Village Documentary Festival
454 Broome Street
New York, NY 10013
(212-966-7526)
  Independent documentaries. Cash awards and broadcast via festival programming.
  Format: 3/4U
  Deadline: Mid November

Hometown USA Video Festival
National Federation of Local Cable Programmers
906 Pennsylvania Avenue, SE
Washington, D.C. 20003
(202-544-7272)
  Community cablecast programming. Awards at NFLCP's annual convention and nationwide cable broadcasting.
  Formats: beta, VHS, 3/4U
  Deadline: Mid March

Independent Videomakers Exclusively
  Cash and equipment prizes
  Cablecast and festival roadshow exposure
  Formats: VHS, 3/4U
  Deadline: Mid February

International Amateur Film Festival
MOAS
P.O. Box 17746
Rochester, NY 14617
(716-342-0691)
  Sponsored by Movies on a Shoestring, Inc.
  $7 entry fee.
  Formats: 8mm, beta, VHS, 3/4U, Super 8, 16mm

TABLE 14–4 (CONTINUED)

National Video Festival Student Competition
The American Film Institute
P.O. Box 27999
2021 North Western Avenue
Los Angeles, CA 90027
(213-856-7745)
> Recognizes work of young videomakers and their instructional programs. Equipment prizes and exhibition at the AFI National Video Festival. Entry fee is $7.
> Format: 3/4U
> Deadline: Early May

Poetry Film Festival
Fort Mason Cultural Center
San Francisco, CA 94123
(415-621-3073)
> Poetry, films/videos with verbal poetic statement in narrated or captioned form.
> Formats: 3/4U, beta, VHS

Stroh's Southern Images Film and Video Fest
Red River Arts Festival
101 Milim
Shreveport, LA 71101
(318-424-4000)
> Drama, documentary, animation, experimental.
> Formats: 3/4U, film

Thomas A. Edison—Black Maria Film/Video Festival
Essex/Hudson Film Center (East Orange Public Library)
21 S. Arlington Avenue
East Orange, NJ 07018
(201-736-8575)
> All categories.
> Formats: 3/4U, 16mm

Tokyo Video Festival
JVC Company of America
41 Slater Drive
Elmwood Park, NJ 07407
(201-794-3900)
> Variety of categories and professional levels. Equipment and cash awards and trips to Japan. No entry fee.
> Formats: beta, VHS
> Deadline: Early September

US Film Festival
Sundance Institute
19 Exchange Street
Salt Lake City, UT 84111
(801-521-9330)
> Dramatic features, documentaries.
> Formats: 3/4U, film

USA Film Festival
Short Film/Video Competition
P.O. Box 58789
Dallas, TX 75258
(214-760-8575)
> Recognizes excellence in creative and imaginative use of short film and videos. Both professional and nonprofessional entries accepted.
> Formats: beta, VHS, 3/4U
> Deadline: Mid February

Video/New Media Competition
94 Scarsdale Road
Don Mills, Ontario, Canada M3B 2R7
(416-446-6996)
> Symposia, workshops, and seminars are held in conjunction with this high tech festival.
> Formats: beta, VHS, 3/4U
> Deadline: Mid September

Video Shorts
P.O. Box 20069
Broadway Station
Seattle, WA 98102
(206-322-9010)
> All entries must be shorter than five minutes. Cash prizes and broadcast. Entry fees, $10.
> Formats: beta, VHS
> Deadline: Mid September

Visions of US, 1/2" Video Competition
P.O. Box 200
Hollywood, CA 90078
(213-856-7745)
> Sponsored by Sony and administered by the American Film Institute, this is the only national festival dedicated only to tapes originated on 1/2" systems. Equipment prizes, exhibition, and broadcast. No entry fee.
> Formats: beta, VHS, 8mm video
> Deadline: Early October

COMPETITIONS AND FESTIVALS

One way to get your work seen by professionals and perhaps establish yourself as a skilled video craftsperson is to enter a few festivals or competitions. You will end up paying entry fee expenses, dubbing expenses, mailing expenses, and may have a few long distance phone calls to show for your effort, but the accolades of a winning show may be worth it. You may even win a few prizes and your work might be exhibited or broadcast to a wider, more discriminating audience than you would have been able to reach yourself. You may even make the kind of contacts needed to finance your next project. Table 14–4 lists some home video festivals. Table 14–5 lists professional and industrial video competitions. Although the professionals have more money to spend on their shows, creativity and good workmanship are mightier than special effects and impeccably sharp pictures.

It can be very gratifying to see your work exhibited or offered for sale. It is tacit recognition that your work is worthy and valuable to someone. Selling your work, however, is not a high profit business for most. There are a lot of *excellent* videomakers out there making only a few thousand dollars per year in this trade— truly a labor of love. But just think, it used to be storytellers and bards who carried cultures and entertainment from land to land. Then came the prose and poetry of the printed word, widely disseminated by the Gutenberg and offset presses. Now we are in the age of the electron with our magnetic messages stored on a flimsy ribbon of videotape. We are now the poets. We carry the culture from land to land, entertaining and educating as we go.

As master of your new medium, consider the influence you wield next to your cheek. The tiny camcorder has the power to teach, the power to inspire, the power to give happiness, as well as the power to explore the deepest thoughts. It also has the power to bore people silly. What kind of a videomaker will you be?

TABLE 14–5   INDUSTRIAL VIDEO FESTIVALS

American Film and Video Festival
Educational Film Library Association
45 John Street
New York, NY 10038
(212-227-5599)
    Format: 3/4U, 16mm
    Deadline: January 15th

Asian American International Video Festival
32 East Broadway
New York, NY 10002
(212-925-8685)
    Format: 3/4U

Atlanta Film and Video Festival
Image Film and Video Center
75 Bennett Street, Suite M-1
Atlanta, GA 30309
(404-352-4225)
    Fee, $25.

    Format: beta, VHS, 3/4U, 16mm, super 8 movie
    Deadline: Mid February

Cindy Competition
Association of Visual Communicators
900 Palm Avenue, Suite B
South Pasadena, CA 91030
(818-441-2274)
    Many categories.
    Format: 3/4U, 16mm, filmstrip, slides, audio production
    Deadline: June

CINE
Council of International Non-Theatrical Events
201 16th Street, NW
Washington, DC 20036
(202-785-1136)
    Many categories.
    Format: 3/4U, 16mm
    Deadline: February 1st, August 1st.

Gold Quill Awards
International Association of Business
Communicators
870 Market Street, Suite 940
San Francisco, CA 94102
(415-433-3400)
  Fee, $80
  Format: VHS, beta, film, slides
  Deadline: January

ITVA Video Festival
International Television Association
6311 North O'Connor Road
LB-51
Irving, TX 75039
(214-869-1112)
  Format: 3/4U
  Deadline: November-December

International Film and TV Festival of New
York
5 West 37th Street
New York, NY 10018
(914-238-4481)
  Format: 3/4U, 16mm, 35mm
  Deadline: June and September

JVC Pro Awards
JVC Company of America
Pro Video Communications Division
41 Slater Drive
Elmwood Park, NJ 07407
(800-255-6038)
  Communications training, promotion,
  merchandizing, local cable production.
  $25 student entry, $50 pro entry.

Formats: VHS, 3/4U
  Deadline: First week of January

Monitor Awards
International Teleproduction Society
990 Avenue of the Americas
Suite 21E
New York, NY 10018
(212-629-3266)
  Format: video
  Deadline: January 31st

National Educational Film and Video Festival
314 East 10th Street
Oakland, CA 94606
(415-465-6878)
  Format: VHS, 3/4U, 16mm
  Deadline: December 1st

National Media Awards
Retirement Research Foundation
CNTV
11 East Hubbard, 5th Floor
Chicago, IL 60611
(312-565-1787)
  Issues on aging. No entry fee.
  Format: Video, film
  Deadline: Beginning of February

Telly Awards
4100 Executive Park Drive
Cincinnati, OH 41230
(606-329-0077)
  $25 entry fee.
  Format: 3/4U
  Deadline: December

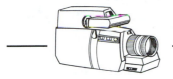

Periodicals, books, tapes

PERIODICALS

I strongly recommend that anybody entering the TV field subscribe to at least two monthly video journals. The industrial ones are free to professionals in the field.

*AV VIDEO
Montage Publishing
25550 Hawthorne Blvd., Suite 314
Torrance, CA 90505
(Industrial, AV and video production
and equipment)

**EDUCATIONAL AND
INDUSTRIAL TELEVISION
(E&ITV)**
Broadband Information Services, Inc.
295 Madison Avenue
New York, NY 10017
(Industrial and professional TV
techniques and equipment)

*Especially recommended

INDUSTRIAL PHOTOGRAPHY
475 Park Avenue South
New York, NY 10016
(Industrial video and photography)

ON LOCATION
6777 Hollywood Blvd., Suite 606
Hollywood, CA 90028
(Commercial film and video
production)

*VIDEO
Reese Publishing Company
Box 56293
Boulder, CO 80322-6293
(General home video info, products)

VIDEO TIMES

MPCS Video Center Building
514 West 57th St.
New York, NY 10019
(Industrial and commercial video)

VIDEO PRO

350 East 81st Street
New York, NY 10028
(Commercial video)

*VIDEO REVIEW

Viare Publishing Corp.
Box 57751
Boulder, CO 80322–7751
(General info on home video
   techniques, products, reviews)

*VIDEO SYSTEMS

9221 Quivera Road
Overland Park, KS 66212
(Industrial TV techniques and
   equipment)

VIDEOGRAPHY

United Business Publication
475 Park Avenue South
New York NY 10016
(Industrial video equipment and
   techniques)

*VIDEOMAKER

Box 3727
Escondido, CA 92025
(Home video production for
   semiprofessionals)

TAPES

ELECTRONIC EDITING

Smith Mattingly
2560 Huntington Avenue
Suite 303
Alexandria, VA 22303
(Demonstrates setup and operation of
   editing system, 30 min.)

**FAMOUS PHOTOGRAPHER
   SERIES—David Chan**

Sherwood Video
Box 14212
Chicago, IL 60614
(Series of 1-hour videocassettes by
   Playboy photographer David Chan
   on shooting nudes, fashion, nature,
   sports)

GETTING IT ON VIDEO

Knowledge Industry Publications,
   Inc.
701 Westchester Avenue
White Plains, NY 10604
(Two 45-minute tapes instructing use
   of VCRs, cameras, etc.)

**HOME VIDEO PRODUCTION:
   HOW TO DO IT**

Smith Mattingly
2560 Huntington Avenue
Suite 303
Alexandria, VA 22303
(45-minute instructional tape on video
   techniques)

IMERO FIORENTINO ASSOCIATES EDUCATIONAL DIVISION

44 West 63rd Street
New York, NY 10023
(Four videocassettes teach
nonbroadcast lighting and staging
techniques, news set lighting, basic
makeup techniques)

INSTRUCTIONAL PROGRAM FOR VIDEOGRAPHERS

Cinema Collector's Society
7225 Woodland Drive
Indianapolis, IN 46278
(Five videocassettes teaching: Basic
home video, lighting, sound, how
to shoot weddings, how to shoot
sports)

INTRODUCTION TO WAVEFORM MONITORS

Columbia Circle
Box 896
Merrimack, NH 03054
(Videocassette on how to read
waveform displays)

KNOWLEDGE INDUSTRY PUBLICATIONS

701 Westchester Avenue
White Plains, NY 10604
(12 videotapes teaching professional
camera techniques, video
maintenance, lighting, sound,
production, directing
nonprofessional talent, writing, sets
and locations, graphics, editing and
special effects, troubleshooting)

ON-LOCATION LIGHTING

Knowledge Industry Publications,
Inc.
701 Westchester Avenue
White Plains, NY 10604
(Fundamentals of remote lighting)

*SIGHT AND SOUND VIDEO TRAINING SERIES

3 M Company
Building 223-5N
St. Paul, MN 55101
(10 20-minute tapes instructing VCR
and camera use)

BOOKS

—*Home Video Marketplace.* (Directory of major buyers and sellers of videocassettes for home market.) Knowledge Industry Publications, 1985. 184 pp.

ALLMAN, PAUL, *Exploring Careers in Video.* Rosen, 1984.

ALTEN, STANLEY R., *Audio in Media.* Wardsworth Pub., 1981. 428 pp.

ANDERSON, GARY H., *Video Editing and Postproduction: A Proessional Guide* (Video Bookshelf Series). Knowledge Industry Publications, 1984. 165 pp.

AYERS, R., *Graphics for Television.* Prentice Hall, 1984. 150 pp.

BLUM, RICHARD, *Television Writing.* Focal Press, 1984. 192 pp.

BROWN, STEVEN E., *The Video Tape Postproduction Primer.* Wilton Place, 1984. 261 pp.

CARLSON, SYLVIA and VERNE, *Professional Cameraman's Handbook.* Focal, 1980. 575 pp.

CARLSON, SYLVIA and VERNE, *Professional Lighting Handbook.* Focal, 1985. 224 pp.

CARTWRIGHT, STEVE, *Developing Video Training Programs.* Knowledge Industry Publications, 1985. 165 pp.

COSTELLO, MARJORIE et al., *Breaking into Video* (guide to job and business opportunities in home broadcast cable and corporate video facilities). Simon and Schuster, 1985. 160 pp.

DANIELS, BILL, *Illustrated Trade References: Video* (complete descriptions, photos, specifications, and pricing information on industrial and professional video equipment). Knowledge Industry Publications, 1986.

DEL PAZZO, BOB, ed., *Television Contacts.* Larimi Comm., 1984.

FULLER, B. et al., *Single Camera Video Production.* Prentice Hall, 1982. 241 pp.

GRANDE, CHARLES, JR., ed., *American Film Institute Guide to College Courses in Film and Television.* Peterson's Guides, 1980. 334 pp.

JACOBS, BOB, *How to Be an Independent Video Producer.* Knowledge Industry Publications, 1986. 197 pp.

KAPLAN, DON, *More Video in the Classroom, New Strategies for Creative Television.* Knowledge Industry Publications, 1985. 165 pp.

LAZER, ELLEN, ed., *Guide to Home Video Marketing* (marketing home videos). Knowledge Industry Publications, 1986. 160 pp.

LETOURNEAU, TOM, *Lighting Techniques for Video Production.* Knowledge Industry Publications, 1985. 175 pp.

LYLE, JIM et al., *Guide to Videotape Publishing* (how to distribute and market your videos). Knowledge Industry Publications, 1985. 174 pp.

MATRAZZO, DONNA, *The Corporate Scripting Book.* Communicom, 1985. 210pp.

MILLERSON, GERALD, *Techniques of Television Production* (Library of Communication Techniques—studio director techniques). Focal Press, 1979. 448 pp.

RAY, JO A., *Careers with a Television Station* (early careers books). Lerner Publications. 36 pp.

ROOT, WELLS, *Writing the Script: A Practical Guide for Films and Television.* Holt, Reinhart, and Winston. 252 pp.

SWAIN, DWIGHT, *Scripting for Video and TV Media.* Focal, 1981. 256 pp.

UTZ, PETER, *Complete Home Video Book* (home video equipment and techniques, antennas, cable). Prentice Hall, 1983. 562 pp.

UTZ, PETER, *Do-It-Yourself Video: A Beginner's Guide* (brief home video manual). Prentice Hall, 1984. 300 pp.

UTZ PETER, *Recording Great Audio* (beginner's guide to audio production, equipment, and techniques using amateur equipment). Quantum Publishing for Radio Shack, 1989. 250 pp.

UTZ, PETER, *Today's Video.* (comprehensive textbook of home, industrial, and professional video equipment and techniques). Prentice Hall, 1987. 606 pp.

UTZ, PETER, *Video User's Handbook* (industrial video equipment, setup, and techniques). Prentice Hall, 1989. 500 pp.

VAN DEUSEN, RICHARD E., *Practical AV/Video Budgeting.* Knowledge Industry Publications, 1984. 168 pp.

WURTZEL, ALLAN, AND ACKER, STEVEN *Television Production* 3rd Edition (studio production textbook). McGraw-Hill, 1989. 661 pp.

ZETTL, HERBERT, *Television Production Handbook* (studio production techniques). Wordsworth, 1988. 614 pp.

Index